THE
DUTCH
METROPOLIS

THE DUTCH METROPOLIS

Maurits de Hoog

DESIGNING QUALITY INTERACTION ENVIRONMENTS

THOTH Publishers Bussum

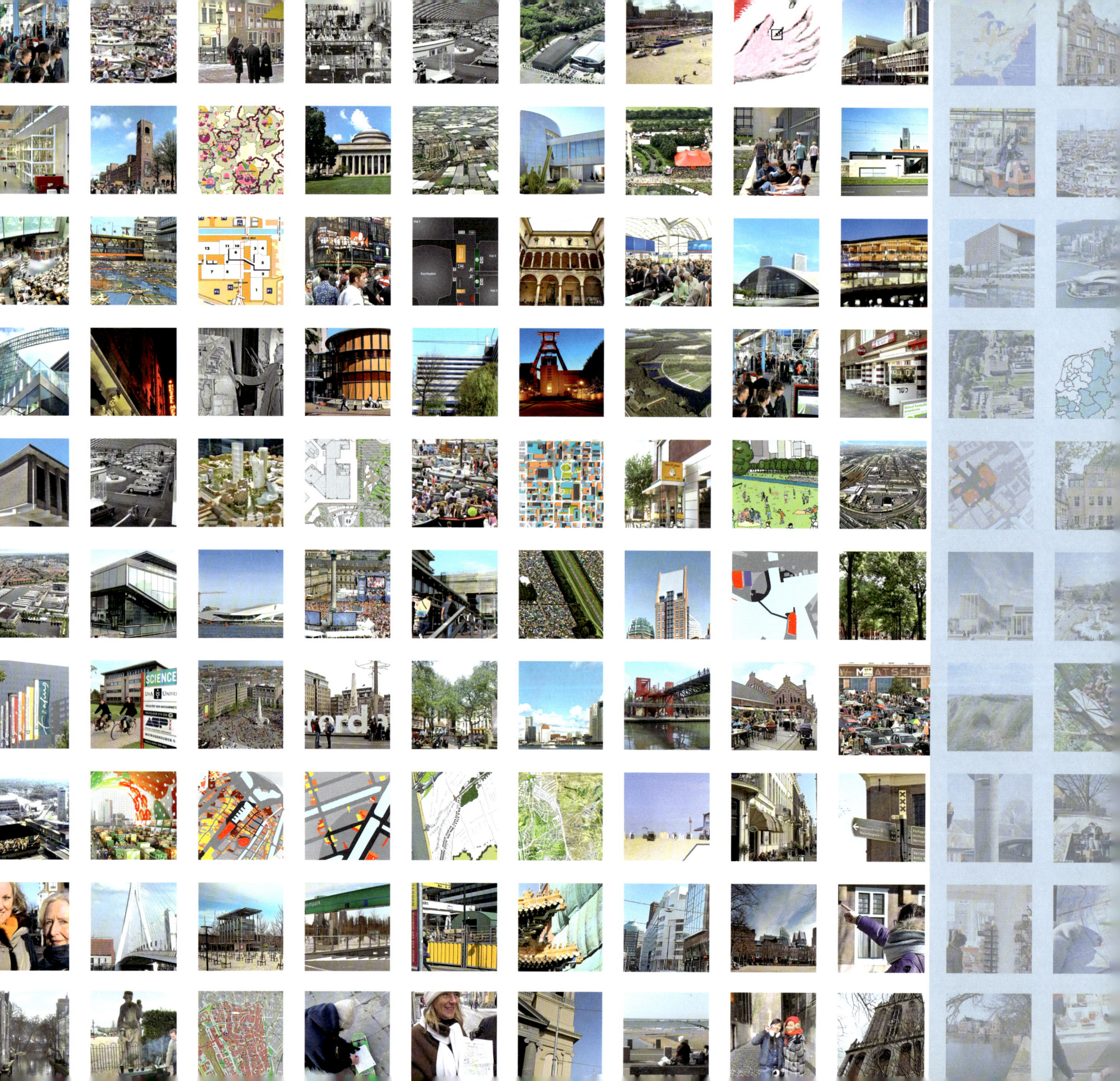

Contents

Introduction

At the presentation of the first results of the new Amsterdam Metropolitan Area collaboration in the autumn of 2007, Maarten van Poelgeest termed the city a 'metropolis in stocking feet'. Without that being its conscious aim, over a couple of decades Amsterdam had unmistakably taken on a metropolitan character. You could see and hear that on the streets, at Schiphol, in the RAI and at the universities, and we understood that from the way in which others talked about the city and its region.

The shaping of metropolises has never really been part of the Dutch design and planning tradition, nor has The Netherlands stood out in research in this field. What, really, is a metropolis, and how can one actively work on the spatial development of one?

Therefore it was a wonderful opportunity when in 2008, as professor of practice at the TU Delft, I was given a chance to spend a couple of days a week for four years, further exploring this theme. At that moment my colleague Rudy Uytenhaak was at work rounding off the final details on the study *Steden vol ruimte, kwaliteiten van dichtheid*. That was a good example of a concrete project and a concrete product. Moreover, by working together with organizations engaged in practice, the formulation of the question could be sharpened up, and a coalition would be created that could take the results further after the completion of the study.

From the very beginning the City of Amsterdam and the Deltametropolis Association played an important role in the project. From a position in the background, Eric van der Kooij and Paul Gerretsen provided input and focus. Moreover, Amsterdam provided research capacity for the four years. The Deltametropolis Association started a lecture and discussion series The International Perspectives. In March, 2012, this successful series was closed with a publication and working conference.

However, I had only been at work in Delft for a week when the Architecture Department's building burned. The resulting diaspora across the campus

was followed a couple of months later by a wave of budget cuts, and then the real estate crisis. It rapidly became obvious that the character of the practice of design and planning in The Netherlands would be altered totally. At the same time, that offered all sorts of new opportunities. We no longer could look to banks for our salvation, but city tourism remained every bit as popular as it had been. There would be no more large investments in museums and auditoriums for the foreseeable future, but there were plenty of other buildings in the pipeline. What would be the situation with the public space around them, and the tourist circuits? And investment in the Dutch knowledge infrastructure actually increased, and Delft, as the result of the fire, was faced with acute questions.

In terms of its content, the most important step in the research was to uncouple the concept of a metropolis from the size of a city or region, but instead define it with regard to specific activities and places. Initially we defined these areas as metropolitan cores. In discussions with Jos Gadet and Koos van Zaanen of the Department of Physical Planning in Amsterdam we came up with the concept of interaction environments. These are places for encounters and exchanges among people, of goods, information and capital. Interaction environments come in all shapes and sizes, and they have diverse ranges. Some are local in importance, others are significant far across national borders. The research question now became how these metropolitan interaction environments could be taken a step further.

To find answers for this, we worked with designers and researchers in the cities of Rotterdam, The Hague and Utrecht, as well as Amsterdam. In 2009 we worked collectively at the TU on perspectives for the Olympic Games in The Netherlands. Once again, insights and data files were shared in 2010, for the study of cultural clusters in the large cities. The results were discussed intensively during a workshop accompanying the lecture given by Bernd

Fesel as part of The International Perspectives. The Departments of Real Estate at the University of Amsterdam and the TU Delft were also partners. Special thanks must go to the RAI. Hans Bakker and Michael Batelaan took us along on an exploration of the trends in the convention world. The Ministry of Infrastructure and the Environment commissioned Ester Heiman of Stipo to investigate the use and experience of a number of metropolitan interaction environments. The first results were ready just in time to be included in this publication.

Rick Vermeulen and Miriam Verrijdt of the Department of Physical Planning in Amsterdam buoyed up to the project throughout its duration. Verena Balz brought in the material from her dissertation and from the *Atlas ABC*. Daan Zandbelt, Monique Arkenstein and Alexandra den Heijer worked on the new Campus Vision for the TU Delft, and carried their knowledge of campus development in other places with them. All sorts of research tasks were performed by Eric Claassen, Nick Esveld and Ruth Strootman. Anje Koop made the drawings of the clusters in the largest cities. Dena Kasraian and Flavia Curvelo Magdaniel were part of the research team for the University Library of the University of Amsterdam. Dorrith Dijkzeul, Laurens Versluis and Maike Warmerdam completed their graduate studies under my supervision, and laid the foundations for the Coastal Quality Studio, which was the first spin-off from the project.

The production of this book was a test of strength. The staff at THOTH Publishers and designer Ronald Boiten piloted me smoothly through it. The beautiful result has been made possible by financial contributions from The Netherlands Architecture Fund, the Cities of Amsterdam and The Hague, and the Department of Architecture of the TU Delft.

I dedicate this book to the latest generation of urban planners.

← **Lowlands Festival site, Biddinghuizen 2011**
Aerial photography: Jan Tuijp

Keys to the metropolitan programme

For many years the images in Fritz Lang's 1927 film *Metropolis* made the very concept of the metropolis a terrifying and unattractive prospect for Dutch planning practice. The first time that the idea of a metropolis was approached positively was when the Deltametropolis Association was founded in 1998 by the councilmen of the four largest Dutch cities; they acknowledged that the Randstad had in fact already developed into a metropolis, and in that case one had better deal with what that implied. After decades of focusing on urban renewal and regional access, strengthening the international position of the Randstad became a policy initiative.

But what makes a big city a metropolis? Since World War II the spatial policies of the national government had concentrated on the development of the urban regions around the twenty largest cities in The Netherlands. The consistent planning of supra-local urban networks in a north-west European context was of only secondary interest. Urban concentration or diffusion, and concepts like Randstad, North and South Wings, the Central Dutch Urban Ring and Delta Metropolis Cities each took their turn at striving for precedence.

This chapter will argue for strengthening the international position of the Dutch metropolis, not through population concentration, but through improving the quality of its interaction environments. High quality facilities for meeting and exchange, with international allure, are the vital core of any contemporary metropolis, and an important new focus for spatial planning and interventions. In this chapter the terms and concepts that are involved in this are introduced and placed in an historical and scientific perspective.

Times Square, New York

National spatial policy

In his 1991 dissertation *Conceptvorming in de ruimtelijke planning*, Wil Zonneveld reviewed the spatial planning concepts which had been employed in Dutch planning at a supra-local level since the 1920s, and what patterns and processes are to be seen in them.[1] The years from 1920 to 1949 were a period of *regulated urbanization*, in which a centralized urban form was the guiding principle. Rather than allowing decentralization within the urban region – the feared suburbanization – the choice was made to have decentralization within the cities, with the construction of garden towns and garden cities. Furthermore, there were massive new port complexes and industrial areas created in conjunction with the cities. The rapidly growing cities expanded vastly in area to accommodate this.

In the years 1949-1958 the central concept was *increase in scale*. Further urbanization created city-groups and conurbations. The Westen des Lands working group argued for articulating the city-groups by creating buffer zones between the cities. The city-groups formed two conurbations which together were roughly horseshoe shaped. The quality of this Randstad would be guaranteed by leaving open a Green Heart, and having urbanization take place on the outside of the horseshoe, by the draining of the IJsselmeer polders, among other interventions. Harbours and connections with the hinterland were expanded, including the Amsterdam-Rhine Canal, opened in 1952.

Spurred by continued rapid growth, during the next period, 1958-1972, concepts were worked out for a total *reconstruction of the country*: demolition and redevelopment of city centres, land consolidation in rural areas, the damming of the estuaries in the Zeeland delta, large-scale development of seaports and air-ports, straightening and deepening rivers, a complete natural gas supply network, the growth of the cities into urban regions, and – last but not least – distributing the urbanization across the country by developing urban regions outside the Randstad, in the north, east and south of The Netherlands. A network of motorways would connect the urban regions and connect with comparable networks in north-western Europe. Schiphol received a new terminal complex and a modern set of tangential runways.

In 1973 the global oil crisis ushered in a period of uncertainty and debate about the *quality of life*. Following on from this, after 1976 spatial policy focused strongly on the preservation of the cities and countryside. With the slogan of the *compact city*, urban renewal replaced clearance and redevelopment. At the same time, the ramified system of new towns and urban regions at greater distances from the Randstad was cut back, along with the regulations which had been designed to stimulate its growth. Several cities – Amersfoort, Zwolle – were designated for supplementary growth. Construction of new motorways was curtailed or delayed. With the construction of the Schiphol line and the Flevo line, the airport and new growth cores in Flevoland were integrated into the rail network.

From the late 1980s the *competitiveness of the Dutch economy* became the predominate theme, and there were signs of a new élan. The urban areas in the Randstad and the 'mainports' of Schiphol and the Rotterdam harbour were seen as the motor that would drive the economy, but with the concept of the Central Dutch Urban Ring also resurrected the idea of the two conurbations or 'wings'. The concepts of green buffers and the Green Heart were differentiated and expanded into the Primary Ecological Structure, a system of natural areas and connecting zones that embraced the whole of The Netherlands. The High Speed Rail Line was to connect the cities with other European metropolises. A new freight rail line through the Betuwe connected Rotterdam with Germany.

Zonneveld noted that the break around 1988, with the government's *Vierde Nota Ruimtelijke Ordening* (Fourth Memorandum on Physical Planning) was sharp. Between 1988 and 1991, when his dissertation appeared, countless new terms and concepts were introduced and discussed. This foreshadowed the lively discussions between 1990 and 2010 about the most desirable forms of urbanization.

The Delta Metropolis

The *Vierde Nota Extra* (Vinex) appeared in 1991. This memorandum concentrated on the housing situation. All across the country new locations in and near cities were designated for a million new homes. In part in response to this policy, the Metropolitan Debate, initiated by Dirk Frieling, was started in 1996; the founding of the Deltametropolis Association followed in 1998. The councilmen of the four large cities in the Randstad played an important role in this. The Association formulated its aim as 'given the existence of the European Union, to develop the metropolis in the West Netherlands, now already extant in rudimentary form. The existing characteristics of this metropolis, to be further strengthened, are 1) a configuration of well connected, vital cities around a green heart, rich in water; 2) a great wealth of widely differentiated economic activities, and 3) significant cultural and historical resources. In view of its location in the delta of the Rhine and Maas, this metropolis will be called the Delta Metropolis.'

The lobbying on the part of the cities was strong, and the ideas for the development of the Delta Metropolis were worked out in the *Vijfde Nota Ruimtelijke Ordening* (Fifth Memorandum on Physical Planning), a draft of which appeared in 2001. This memorandum however never reached a final form. In 2004 the new Cabinet presented the *Nota Ruimte* (Spatial Memorandum). Although billions were earmarked for housing and infrastructure, the possibility of meaningfully altering social conditions through these expenditures was questioned, and the national government retreated, shifting the emphasis to creating room for private parties to operate. One part of this was the considerable attention to developing the 'greenports' around the agricultural complexes of Aalsmeer, the Westland and Venlo. Schiphol and the Rotterdam harbour were also designated for further growth.

The Netherlands remained politically turbulent. The next new Cabinet presented the *Structural Vision for the Randstad 2040* in 2008. This vision built on the advice of the Commission for Strengthening the

Concepts for supra-local urban networks

Randstad from 2007, in which the competitiveness of the Randstad once again was an important theme. The *Structural Vision* however suggested that within the Randstad the North Wing, comprised of the Amsterdam and Utrecht regions, and the South Wing, with the Rotterdam and Hague regions, formed two coherent complexes. No pronouncement was made on the question of the level of scale at which planning should take place. Should it be for the Randstad as a whole, or for the Wings, or for the regions? It was however noted that in the A2 motorway corridor, from Amsterdam to the south, Den Bosch and Eindhoven have become important poles for economic growth. The Randstad was no longer the dominant economic motor for the country.

The following Cabinet drew up its *Structural Vision on Infrastructure and Space* in record time, bringing it out in 2011. The policy fields of Transport and Communications and Physical Planning, traditionally separate, were integrated. The role of the central government was further scaled back. The term metropolis is only mentioned in the context of the 'metropolitan strength of Amsterdam'. In addition to the Amsterdam region, the combined region of Rotterdam/The Hague and the Eindhoven region are designated as 'top regions'. Remarkably enough, at the same time the proposal was introduced to create a Randstad province. This suggestion was not to be blessed with longevity, though; it was withdrawn in 2012.

Although the concepts of *randstad*, metropolis and top-region have surfaced in many forms over the years, it would seem that the planners and policy makers are still in doubt about the actual nature of a metropolitan development in The Netherlands, and people tend to quickly lose themselves in questions of the administrative organization.[2] What is a metropolis, really?

Traditionally a metropolis has been defined in terms of population concentration. This is the case, for example, for the theories around Functional Urban Regions (FUR, sometimes also called Functional Urban Areas or Larger Urban Zones). A FUR is defined on the basis of daily home/work relations. It is an urban area in which economic activities are concentrated in a core area, and a certain percentage of the working population from adjoining urban areas are employed in this economic core area. If a FUR has more than a million residents, it can be regarded as a metropolis.[3]

FURs can be concentrated urban systems with one core area, but can also have multiple cores; examples of the latter are the Randstad in The Netherlands, and the Ruhr region and the Rhine-Main region around Frankfurt, in Germany. Peter Hall, one of the principle exponents of the FUR concept, is a fan of the Randstad. In his 1966 book *The World Cities*, he championed multiple-cored urban systems and proposed the Randstad as a model for other regions.[4] Because of the dispersion there is no concentration of people and activities. Amenities and landscape are always close at hand. In his view, the quality of everyday life in an urban system with multiple cores is therefore much greater.

In The Netherlands the urban regions around the large cities fulfil the FUR criteria, but so does the Randstad as a whole. If you apply the theory strictly, then today Arnhem and Nijmegen also belong to the urban system of the Randstad, and one can in fact speak of a 'greater Randstad', as Merijn van der Werff, et al., term this region.[5] In that case, one has the area that was previously termed the Central Dutch Urban Ring.

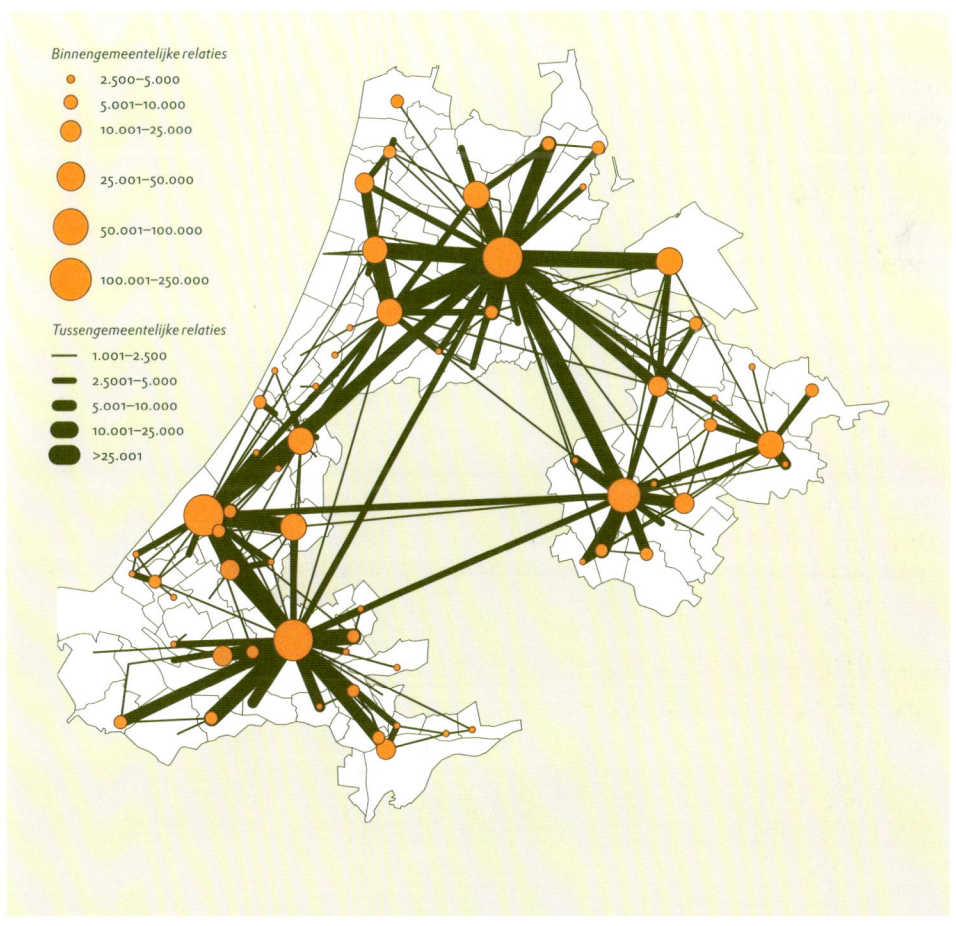

Home-work commuting in the Randstad
Ruimtelijk Planbureau 2006

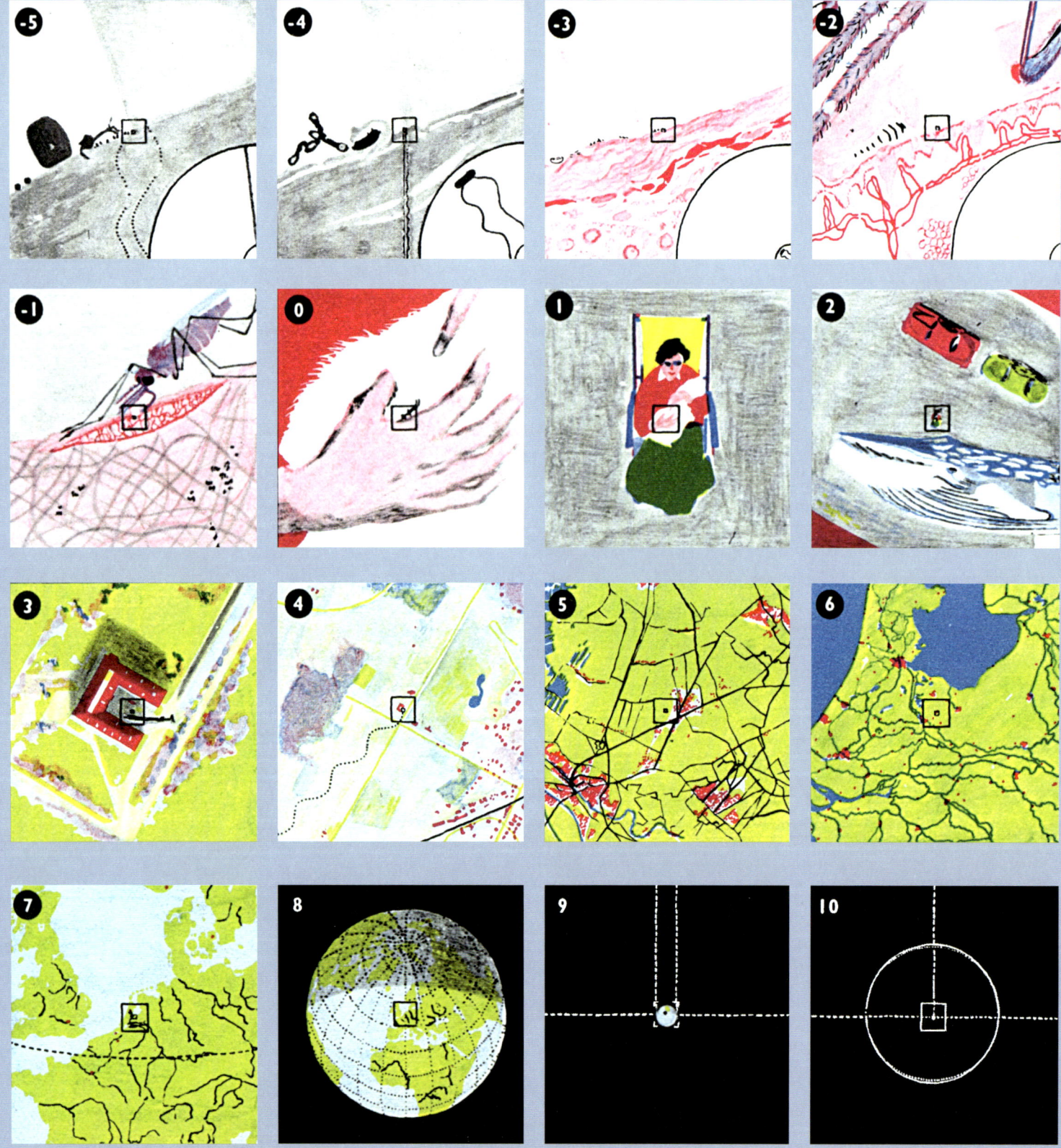

In the FUR concept, enhancing internal coherence by solving the problem of traffic jams and improving public transit will make the most important contribution to the further development of the 'metropolis'. In any case, more people could more easily reach the economic core areas of the Randstad.

In a controversial 2006 publication from what was then the Office of Physical Planning, *Vele steden maken nog geen Randstad* (Lots of cities still don't make a Randstad), Jan Ritsema van Eck and others argued that the Randstad did not function as a coherent network city.[6] The degree of specialization of the separate urban regions had, on the contrary, decreased. Nor could one say there was complementarity, let alone thorough integration. The research that Bart Lambregts et al. did in that same year, into the reasons business services firms had for locating within the Randstad confirmed this analysis. It clearly emerged that the core areas of the four urban regions was the obvious basis for serving clients in the Randstad. A firm in Amsterdam served the urban area around it, and that was true for each of the other larger cities too. Distances and travel time seem to be definitive within the Randstad, and a touchy question: some businesses in Amsterdam opened branches in Alkmaar and Amersfoort in order to be better able to serve clients on the 'periphery' of the urban region.[7]

The criteria that are employed in the theories around Functional Urban Regions for defining a coherent region, that is to say, a metropolis, thus are not very distinctive.

Powers of Ten and the Daily Urban System

The work by Taeke de Jong offers a way to get a grip on this. In his dissertation *Milieudifferentatie* he distinguishes a series of scales, somewhat related to Kees Boeke's *Tiendensprong*, and the better known *Powers of Ten* by Charles and Ray Eames that was based on it.[8] But where Boeke always makes a jump of ten in the radius (1-10-100-1000-10,000), for De Jong the series is logarithmic. Then there is a jump of ten in the surface of a region: at each level of scale a spatial entity can be subdivided into ten spatial units at a lower level of scale. The series that this creates can thus be closely related to the terms that we use for urban units, from city blocks to regions. The number of residents in these units also appears to often increase tenfold. The figures must not, however, be imposed as a norm. At each level of scale there are also compact and diffuse examples, both in terms of area and population. That is precisely what makes the urban landscape interesting. Nonetheless, the series makes it possible to sharply define what is specific in a particular region (or in a plan). De Jong illustrated the series with the example of Amsterdam, and described what design variables are related to each level of scale. Here the dominant means of transport, and the time that it takes to cover a certain distance, play an important role. This aspect of time is of great importance for the actual size of Functional Urban Regions. For many Dutch three-quarters of an hour is the maximum desirable travel time from home to work. In 2007 their average travel time was 28 minutes. In and around Amsterdam one can cover the region, including Almere and Haarlem, in that time From Dam Square to the Weerwater Square in Almere, and from Dam Square to the Grote Markt in Haarlem, it is 30 minutes by car and 45 minutes by public transit, respectively. In Dutch proportions, the urban region with a radius of 30 kilometres is therefore also the basis for daily home/work relations, often termed the Daily Urban System (DUS).

Now, it is important that cities like Alkmaar, Hoorn, Leiden, Lelystad, Amersfoort and Utrecht lie outside this 30-kilometre region, at 35 to 40 kilometres distance, and 40 minutes travel time by auto. Utrecht's Uithof Science District is therefore not a part of the Daily Urban System of Amsterdam.

Rotterdam and The Hague lie still farther away from Amsterdam, 50 and 60 kilometres as the crow flies. From the Dam to Grote Marktstraat in The Hague is 50 minutes by car and 70 by public transit; to the Westblaak in Rotterdam it is 60 and 70 minutes respectively, despite the High Speed train line. Only a limited group of people will travel such distances daily.

Furthermore, one of the striking characteristics of the urban regions around the four large cities is their relatively low density. The ten kilometre agglomeration around Amsterdam has slightly more than one million residents, which fits into the 'average' category in De Jong's series, and is thus reasonably densely built up, but the 30 kilometre region has a population of not much over 2.2 million, although it includes Almere, the Gooi and Kennemerland. Even if you count in the cities which lie within 30 to 40 kilometres – Leiden, Alkmaar, Hoorn, Lelystad, Amersfoort and Utrecht – the number of residents is low: 3.5 million. Thus the urban region around Amsterdam is relatively thinly populated and fairly diffuse. The same is true for the other regions in the Randstad.

Scale series
Taeke de Jong 1988

Legend-unit	Radius km		Surface	Population
Neighbourhood	0.3	(0.1-1)	0.3	1.000
District	1	(0.3-3)	3	10.000
City	3	(1-10)	30	100.000
Agglomeration	10	(3-30)	300	1.000.000
Region/Urban region	30	(10-100)	3.000	10.000.000
Country/Mega-region	100	(30-300)	30.000	
River catchment basin	300	(100-1.000)	300.000	

← The Powers of Ten
We in the universe - a universe in us, Kees Boeke, 1957

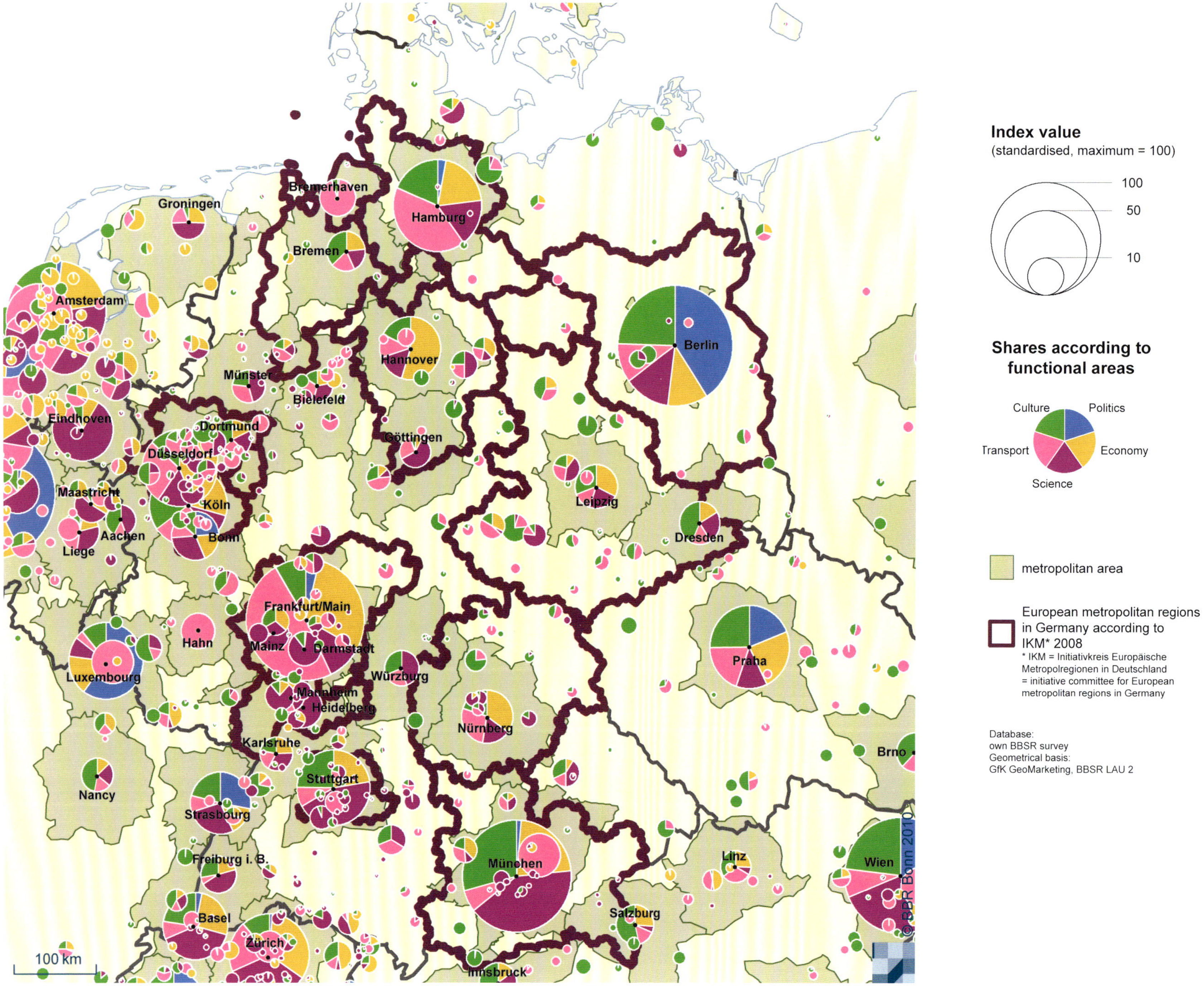

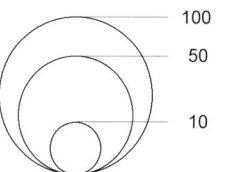

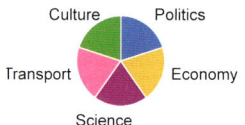

Groningen
Bremerhaven
Hamburg
Bremen
Amsterdam
Hannover
Berlin
Münster
Bielefeld
Eindhoven
Dortmund
Göttingen
Düsseldorf
Maastricht
Köln
Leipzig
Aachen
Bonn
Liege
Dresden
Frankfurt/Main
Hahn
Mainz
Darmstadt
Praha
Luxembourg
Würzburg
Mannheim
Heidelberg
Nürnberg
Karlsruhe
Brno
Stuttgart
Nancy
Strasbourg
Freiburg i. B.
München
Linz
Wien
Basel
Salzburg
Zürich
100 km
Innsbruck
© BBR Bonn 2010
Index value
(standardised, maximum = 100)
100
50
10
Shares according to functional areas
Culture
Politics
Transport
Economy
Science
metropolitan area
European metropolitan regions in Germany according to IKM* 2008
* IKM = Initiativkreis Europäische Metropolregionen in Deutschland = initiative committee for European metropolitan regions in Germany
Database:
own BBSR survey
Geometrical basis:
GfK GeoMarketing, BBSR LAU 2

Metropolitan regions in Germany
BBSR 2010

Metropolitan region

For some years now the term Metropolitan Region (*metropoolregio*) has been used in The Netherlands. The Amsterdam Metropolitan Region Area (MRA) is a consultative administrative body in which, since 2007, municipalities within a 30 kilometre radius around Amsterdam participate (thus including Almere, the Gooi and Kennemerland). Since early 2012 the Metropolitan Region Rotterdam-The Hague has represented the two urban regions and a similar 30 kilometre radius around them, with, like the MRA, about 2.2 million residents.

The term Metropolitan Region comes from Germany. There it is used for urban systems that are of importance at a European scale. In the 1990s eleven such systems were designated as *Metropolregionen*. From that point, the Ruhr regions and the urban regions of Cologne and Düsseldorf formed the Rhine-Ruhr Metropolitan Region. This covers a large part of the state of North Rhine-Westphalia. Of the eleven German metropolitan regions, Rhine-Ruhr is one of the smallest in terms of area, but it has the largest number of residents: 11.7 million on about 7000 km² (2008). That area is nearly equivalent with a radius of 50 kilometres. Here the term metropolis does not refer to the size of the region's population,

their economic power, or to home/work distances, but to the significance of *metropolitan functions*. What characterizes a metropolitan region is its strong 'decision-making, innovative and gateway functions'.[9] At their designation in 1995, a strong 'symbolic function' also played a role. It is expressly stated that these are functions which transcend the level of the Daily Urban System. Metropolitan functions have a different rhythm of use, and a different scope. This is an important step with respect to the FUR approach, and extremely relevant for the Randstad.

Every year the Bundesinstitut für Bau-, Stadt- und Raumforschung (BBSR) publishes a monitor with comparisons of the German metropolitan regions.[10] Recently comparisons with all other European metropolitan regions have been included.[11] These comparative studies look carefully at metropolitan functions and indicators. It is not the total population, but the extent and significance of the metropolitan functions that determines how strong a metropolitan region is. The radius of 50 kilometres is regarded as normative for such regions. Thus for The Netherlands, the comparison is not based on Amsterdam, Rotterdam, The Hague and Utrecht individually, but on the Randstad as a whole.

In the comparative study five *Metropolfunktions- bereiche* are distinguished: political, economic, academic-scientific, transportation and culture (see the illustration on page 18). Indicators for the academic-scientific field are, for example, the number of top 500 universities and the number of international scientific institutions, journals and patents. Among the indicators for transport is the tonnage of goods transshipped in sea ports and airports.

Depending on the spread of metropolitan functions over the five fields, there are additionally three types of metropolitan regions distinguished, with strong, moderate or limited differentiation.

The relative ranking of the metropolitan regions investigated is expressed in an index. London has the most metropolitan functions. With respect to London (=100), Paris scores 97.9, Rhine-Ruhr 51.1, Rhine-Main 41.2, Berlin 38.7 and Munich 32.9. In this index the Randstad scores 74.5, thus standing ahead of Brussels (66.8), Moscow (47.2), Vienna (45.1), Rome (40.8) and Madrid (34.6). Moreover, the Randstad is a Type 1 metropolitan region, with strong differentiation.

The German research offers a usable point of departure for defining what a metropolis is. It places the emphasis on the function of urban regions in a non-daily rhythm, and in an international framework.

Megaregions

Recent theories have studied still larger urban systems. In 2006 Peter Hall introduced the concept of the megacity region.[12] In the United States the terms megapolitan area and megaregion are being used.[13] In recent years the term megaregion has become the most common in the literature.

A systematic basis for the concept of the megaregion has been provided by the Regional Plan Association and Penn State University in Philadelphia, linked by the person of Bob Yaro.[14] A familiar

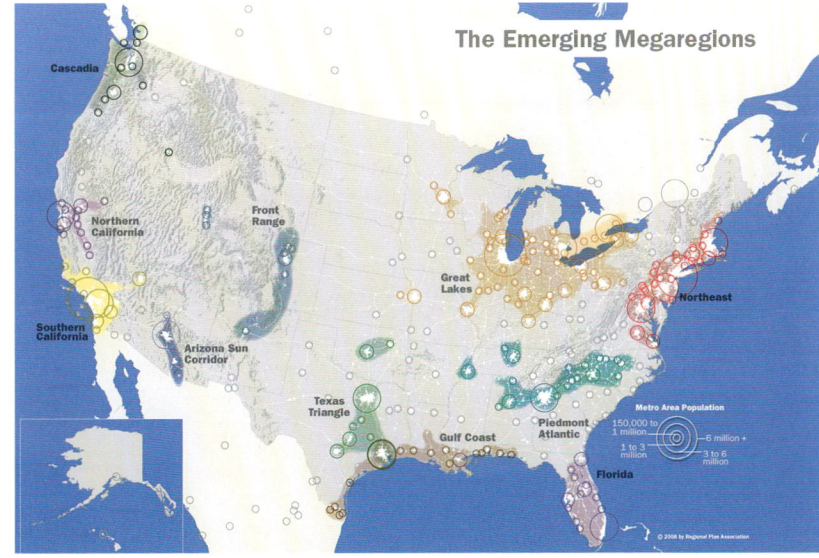

Emerging megaregions in the US
Regional Plan Association 2008

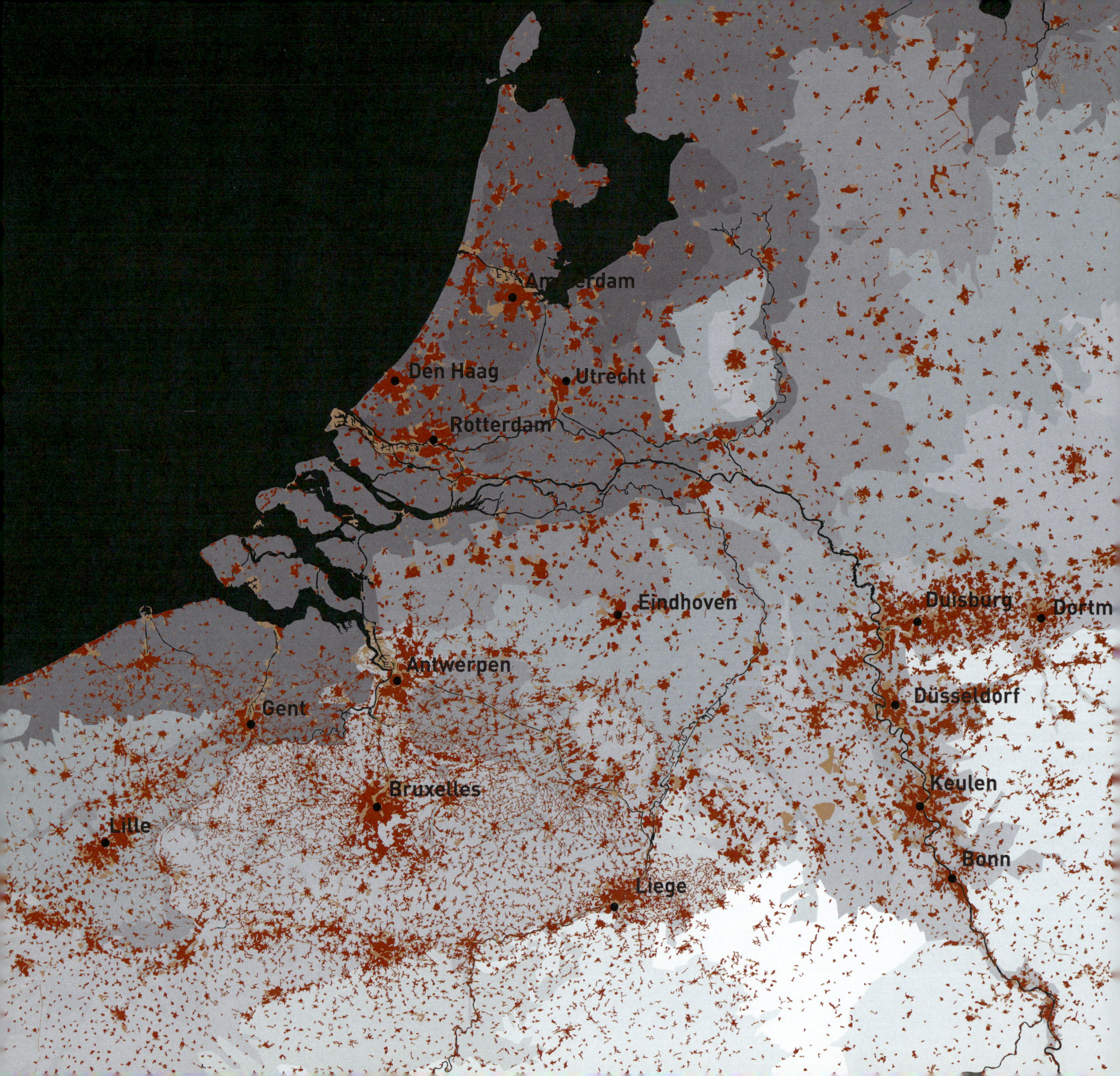

Amsterdam

Den Haag

Utrecht

Rotterdam

Eindhoven

Duisburg

Dortm

Antwerpen

Düsseldorf

Gent

Keulen

Bruxelles

Lille

Bonn

Liege

example of a megaregion is the American North-east, also called BosWash, the chain of cities on the east coast of the United States running from north of Boston to below Washington D.C. There are ten such megaregions which can be distinguished in the US. The megaregions have diverse configurations of subsystems: urban regions, metropolises and metropolitan regions, but also logistical complexes, ecological structures, energy regions, catchment areas of air travel hubs and tourist systems. A shared culture and history has also been listed as a distinguishing criterion.

Bob Yaro initiated the America 2050 project. With an eye to the great Erie Canal project, launched in 1808, and the plan for the first American Interstate Highways in 1908, it was proposed that a new step forward be taken in 2008, this time with sustainable development of megaregions. The America 2050 debate has been carried out by megaregion. At first these discussions revolved around 'smart growth'. Concentration of building activities around public transportation should prevent further 'urban sprawl' and the harm it caused to the landscape. In coastal regions the management of the effects of climate change was also an important issue. This involved not only physical threats, as seen in New Orleans and Florida, but also harm to unique ecological values in estuaries. The megaregion scale is also called for when it comes to the improvement of connections within megaregions, between the agglomerated

urban regions. The Japanese bullet train, Shinkansen, and the European high speed rail networks are often used as a point of reference for this. The implementation of a whole series of proposals from the 2050 debate has since been begun by the Obama administration.

Richard Florida also analysed Europe's megaregions in *The Rise of the Megaregion*.[15] He determined their extent by looking at night images taken from satellites. He named the contiguous urban region in North-west Europe, of which The Netherlands is a part, Am-Brus-Twerp. This megaregion has 59.3 million residents, and is -after Greater Tokyo, Bos-Wash and Chi-Pitts (Chicago-Pittsburgh) – the fourth largest economy in the world, as expressed in LRP (Light-based Regional Product). This is a happy thought-experiment, but the point of departure is not taken very seriously. In some countries the lighting on the motorways remains on all night, in others it is turned off. Nevertheless, it is interesting to look at this greater scale. In Europe there is no other region of comparable density, both in terms of population and in terms of metropolitan functions. Here we would suggest that this megaregion be called ABC, for Amsterdam-Brussels-Cologne, after its three central cores.

ABC

ABC spans areas in five countries and has a multiplicity of administrative constructions, but to an ever-increasing extent functions as one coherent spatial-economic system. The German state of North Rhine-Westphalia is the most important commercial partner for The Netherlands, and vice versa. Belgium – and in particular Flanders – is second. The Dutch hubs serve a large area, put primarily within this megaregion. That is true for the freight hub in that centres on Rotterdam's harbour, but also for the agricultural auctions in the Westland and Aalsmeer,

for the passenger and cargo hub of Schiphol, and for the information hub in the internet junction in Amsterdam's Watergraafsmeer.

ABC has a turbulent history. Far back in history the swarm of cities in the Low Countries formed the link between the economies of the Baltic Sea and the Mediterranean, with the Hanseatic cities along the rivers, and later cities like Bruges, Antwerp and Amsterdam in prominent roles. Braudel has shown how these cities grew up into centres for the world economy in the 16th and 17th centuries.[16]

From the early 19th century the mining of coal and the steel mills that used it became the basis for the development of an industrial economy of unprecedented scale. The emphasis now lay not on the flat part of the delta, but on the hills between it and the hinterland. It was there that coal and iron ore could be easily extracted. From this arose a string of coal mining towns and industrial cities from northern France, through Wallonia and South Limburg, to the Ruhr. In Germany this industrialization led to a total redistribution of the population. In the 19th and early 20th centuries millions of people from the hinterland settled in the Ruhr region. Within ABC this created a tension between the swarm of cities on the flat land of the delta and the mining and industrial cities on the slopes up to the central plateau.

The post-war *Wirtschaftswunder* and the extraction of oil and natural gas gave a new stimulus to ABC in the 1950s and '60s. In the wake of the production centres on the slopes, the cluster of cities on the flat delta also developed at a feverish pace, partly (the harbours at Amsterdam, Rotterdam, Antwerp and Zeebrugge) as a gateway to the production centres, and partly with specific products in niche markets such as shipbuilding, oil refining, foodstuffs, electronics and agribusiness. Moreover, the coast took on a completely new profile as the recreation centre for the population of the new cities.

Land use
▬	Urban land use
▬	Economic land use

Water
▬	Water

Height in metres
▬	<0
▬	0-5
▬	5-10
▬	10-20
▬	20-50
▬	50-100
▬	100-200
▬	200-300
▬	300-500

← **ABC Megaregion** *Amsterdam-Brussels-Cologne*
Sources: Alterra (2007), LANMAP-2 European Environmental Agency (EEA) (2011), Corine land cover 2000, version 15

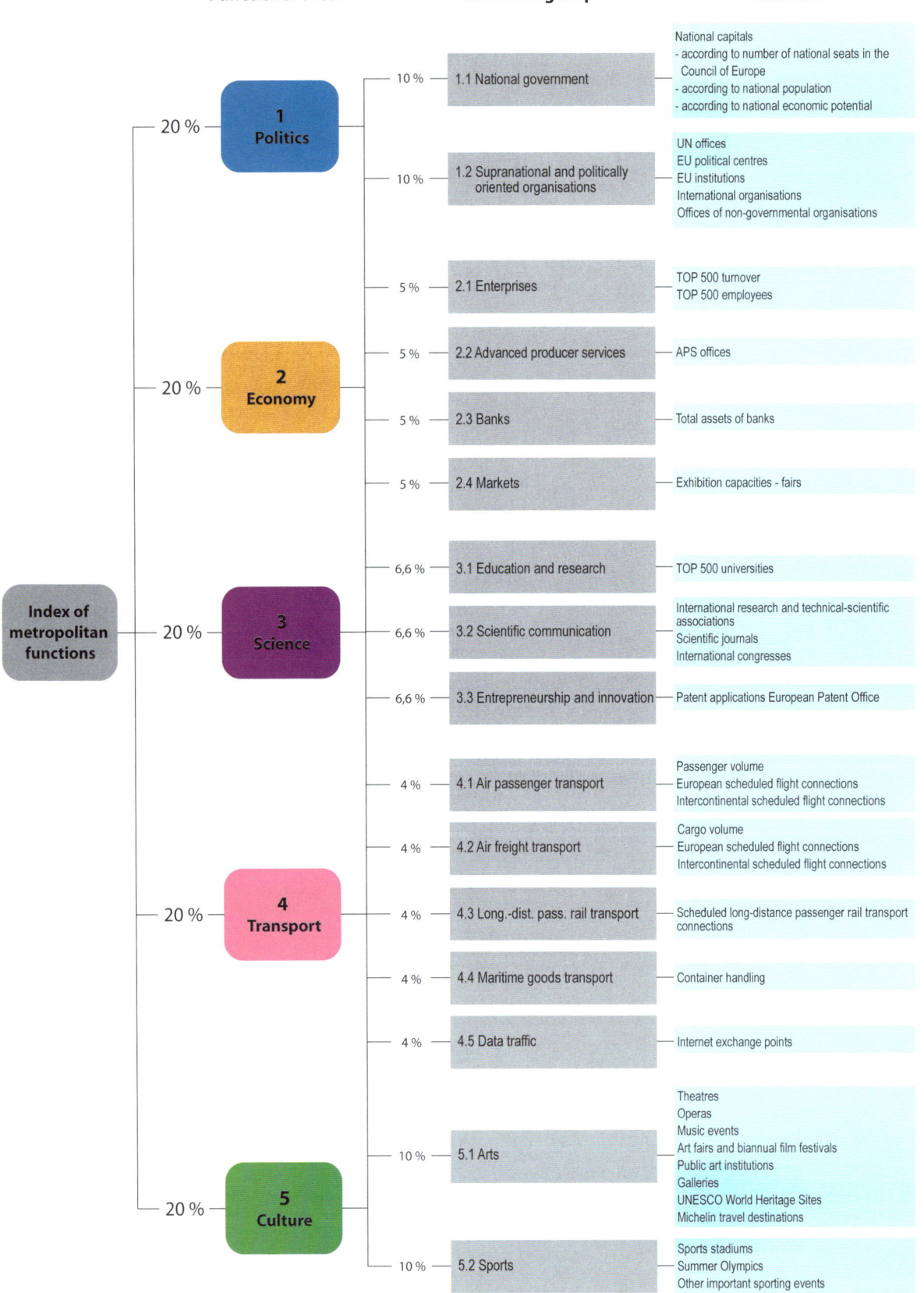

Functional area		Indicator group	Indicator
20 %	**1 Politics**	10 % — 1.1 National government	National capitals - according to number of national seats in the Council of Europe - according to national population - according to national economic potential
		10 % — 1.2 Supranational and politically oriented organisations	UN offices EU political centres EU institutions International organisations Offices of non-governmental organisations
20 %	**2 Economy**	5 % — 2.1 Enterprises	TOP 500 turnover TOP 500 employees
		5 % — 2.2 Advanced producer services	APS offices
		5 % — 2.3 Banks	Total assets of banks
		5 % — 2.4 Markets	Exhibition capacities - fairs
20 %	**3 Science**	6,6 % — 3.1 Education and research	TOP 500 universities
		6,6 % — 3.2 Scientific communication	International research and technical-scientific associations Scientific journals International congresses
		6,6 % — 3.3 Entrepreneurship and innovation	Patent applications European Patent Office
20 %	**4 Transport**	4 % — 4.1 Air passenger transport	Passenger volume European scheduled flight connections Intercontinental scheduled flight connections
		4 % — 4.2 Air freight transport	Cargo volume European scheduled flight connections Intercontinental scheduled flight connections
		4 % — 4.3 Long.-dist. pass. rail transport	Scheduled long-distance passenger rail transport connections
		4 % — 4.4 Maritime goods transport	Container handling
		4 % — 4.5 Data traffic	Internet exchange points
20 %	**5 Culture**	10 % — 5.1 Arts	Theatres Operas Music events Art fairs and biannual film festivals Public art institutions Galleries UNESCO World Heritage Sites Michelin travel destinations
		10 % — 5.2 Sports	Sports stadiums Summer Olympics Other important sporting events

Index of metropolitan functions

Since the 1970s there has been a radical economic transformation. The closing of the coal mines marked the end of the industrial era. Globalization and technological change, but also the reorganization of the 19th century nation states, has laid a completely new task before ABC since the beginning of the 1990s. Coal and steel have been replaced by chemicals and knowledge. Traditionally protected national markets, such as energy, are rapidly being integrated. PCs and the internet appeared. Europe acquired open internal borders, with the free movement of persons, goods, capital and information. While Brussels became the capital of a united Europe, after the fall of the Iron Curtain the German government moved from Bonn to Berlin.

The radius of the ABC megaregion is about 130 kilometres. About 45 million people live within that radius. That is not as many as Richard Florida's 60 million, but it is still a substantial number. It is an extremely dynamic area, in which the position of the cities and regions is constantly changing, both in regard to one another and in regard to greater networks. Unlike in the US, the megaregion here will not soon be adopting common policies. It is true that the Benelux parliament has had a Benelux structural vision drawn up, but that is not much more than a planning document reporting the present status quo. The role of the EU is also changing, but it is hard to imagine a European spatial policy; at the most, there may be a certain degree of policy coordination. Thus the concept of a megaregion here is primarily an analytic category. Studying the level of scale of the ABC megaregion helps understand the position of the Randstad better.

Schematic chart of indicators of metropolitan functions
BBSR 2010

18

Delta City Regions

Luuk Boelens has linked the dynamic of urbanization in ABC with the physical conditions of deltas. In a delta region you can only survive by working together. The *compagnie* or corporation is the social organizational model that the people of the Low Countries traditionally seized upon when it came to defending themselves against the water, reclaiming peat bogs, digging peat or discovering the world, religion, constructing housing, or selling milk, vegetables and flowers. It was, and in fact still is, a typical bottom-up society. The city is also a collaboration of free citizens.

Following from that, Boelens makes a sharp distinction between Capital City Regions, Delta City Regions and Pioneer City Regions.[17] Capital city regions, such as Beijing, Paris or Moscow, are in his view tightly centrally controlled urban systems. They develop from the top down. Urban regions like the Randstad are in his eyes characteristic delta city regions, highly diffuse and competitive bottom-up urban systems. New York and São Paulo are examples of pioneer city regions. These regions develop precisely because they are always attracting new groups of immigrants, who each leave their stamp on the area.

Developing this distinction further, it is interesting to compare the Dutch Randstad with other delta city regions. The maps on the following pages provide a picture of the structure of a number of European delta city regions: the Po delta with the Veneto and a part of Emilia Romagna, the Bouches du Rhône and a part of the department of Gard, the Scheldt delta with the Flemish cities and Brussels, and the Dutch Randstad. The maps are each on a 1:500,000 scale. For purposes of comparison, the Rhine-Ruhr region is included too. This is a typical pioneer city region.

The description of each of the five regions opens with some data from the BBSR research: the number of metropolitan areas and their ranking, the number of locations with metropolitan functions, and the type of metropolitan area. Next they deal with Natura 2000 regions, agrarian and logistical complexes, universities, convention and trade fair facilities, numbers of visitors and hotel occupancy in relation to UNESCO world heritage, and finally large-scale events.

The comparison will offer a first insight into the specific characteristics of the Randstad.

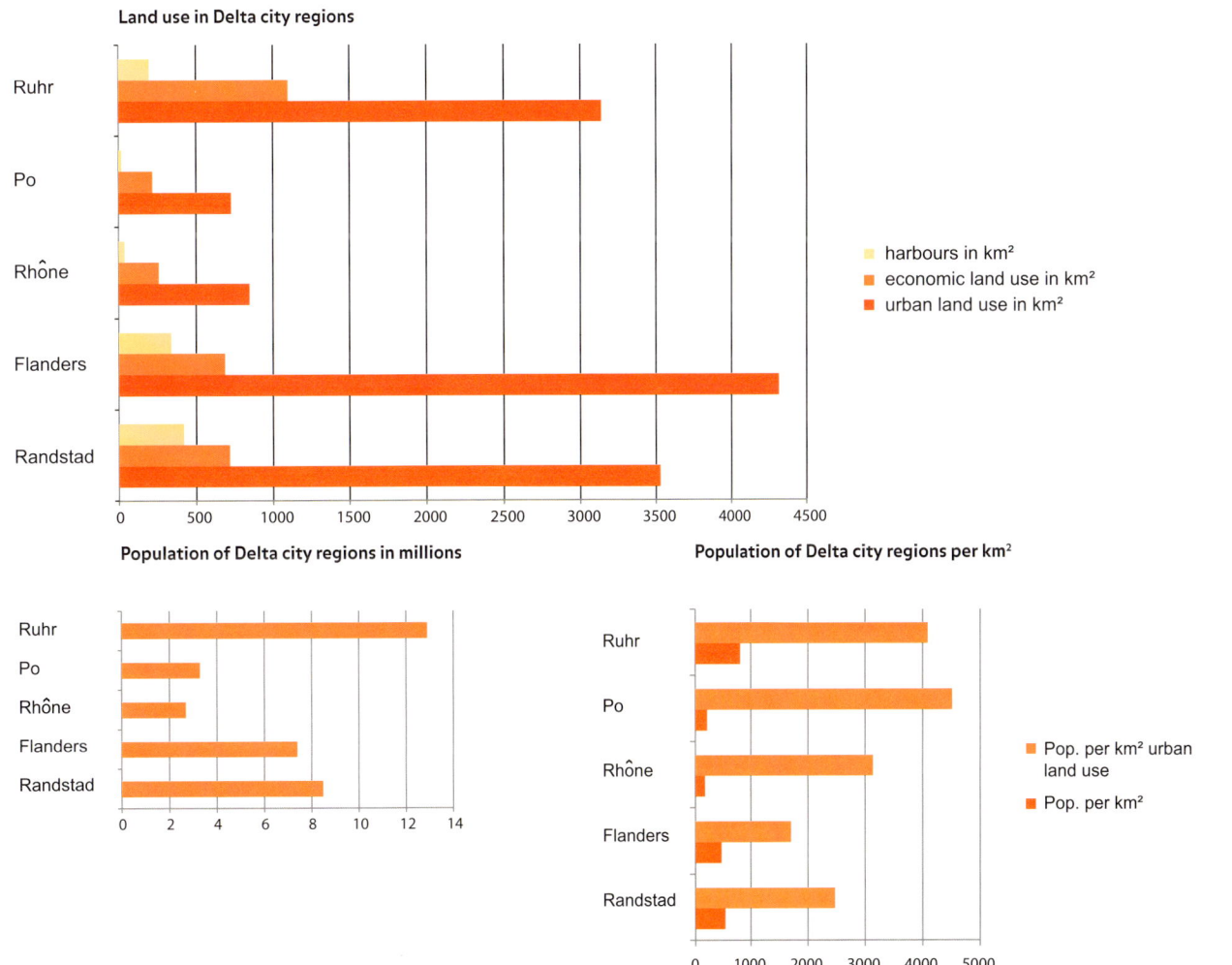

Land use in Delta city regions

Legend:
- harbours in km²
- economic land use in km²
- urban land use in km²

(Regions: Ruhr, Po, Rhône, Flanders, Randstad; x-axis 0–4500)

Population of Delta city regions in millions

(Regions: Ruhr, Po, Rhône, Flanders, Randstad; x-axis 0–14)

Population of Delta city regions per km²

Legend:
- Pop. per km² urban land use
- Pop. per km²

(Regions: Ruhr, Po, Rhône, Flanders, Randstad; x-axis 0–5000)

Veneto

The Veneto and Emilia-Romagna lie on either side of the Po. Four metropolitan areas can be seen in the map detail: Bologna (number 45 in the BBSR ranking, one location with metropolitan functions, Type 2 with moderate differentiation), Venice, (50, two locations, Venice and Padua, Type 3, limited differentiation), and Verona and Parma (74 and 84 respectively, each with one location, Type 3, limited differentiation). The number of residents in the detail is 3.3 million.

The Po delta and lagoon are the largest protected natural areas under the framework of Natura 2000: the lagoon with 55,206 and the bird's-foot delta with 25,362 hectare of protected natural areas.[18]

The Veneto and Emilia-Romagna are traditionally the breadbasket of North Italy, particularly for vegetables, fruit, maize and wine.

The occupation pattern is characterized by a large number of relatively small cities. The cities all have their origin in Roman times, and grew strongly in the early Middle Ages. An almost unbroken chain of urbanized areas stretches along the slopes on the south side of the delta, transected by roads and rail lines. On the north side the pattern is more fragmented. The centre, around the river, is rather open.

Venice is still an important port city, handling 26 million tons of cargo in 2011. The harbour and harbour industries lie in Mestre. Extensive wetlands there have made way for harbour basins and petrochemical plants. A channel is kept open through the lagoon. A busy cruise terminal lies in Venice itself. Ravenna, on the south side of the bird's-food delta, also has a harbour complex in the lagoon.

Bologna is the capital, and largest city, of Emilia-Romagna. It lies at the intersection of road and rail routes. There is a large transshipment emplacement. With regard to industry, it is the motor and auto industry that most appeals to the imagination, with brands such as Ducati, Ferrari and Lamborghini. The research centres of Enea, CNR and Cineca are located in Bologna. Bologna also has an enormous trade fair complex, with 18 large halls with a total of 375,000 m² in exhibition space, the largest of which were designed in the 1960s by Leonardo Benevolo and Kenzo Tange. A new convention centre has also been constructed on the site, with a hall accommodating 5000 people.

All the large cities of the Veneto and Emilia-Romagna have prestigious universities: Bologna, Ferrara, Modena, Parma, Venice, Verona and Vicenza. The university of Bologna is the oldest still functioning university in the world, and has branches in Ravenna and Rimini, among other places. The University of Bologna has at least 93 libraries. The University of Mantua was established only recently, in 1992.

The Veneto alone drew 14.6 million visitors in 2010, with 61 million overnight hotel stays. The city of Venice accounted for 4 million of these visitors (about 80% from foreign countries), with 9.1 million stays.[19] Many more visitors make day trips to Venice from other cities or from popular destinations on the *lidi,* the barrier islands that protect the lagoon. These are not counted in the visitor totals.

The city centres of five of the cities are on the UNESCO World Heritage list: in addition to Venice, also Mantua, Verona, Ferrara and Vicenza. Modena, Padua and Ravenna have individual buildings on the list. Venice and Bologna compete for festivals and events. Venice hosts the Biennale in the Giardini and the Arsenal. The focus in 2012 is architecture. David Chipperfield is the director. Bologna was the Cultural Capital of Europe in 2000.

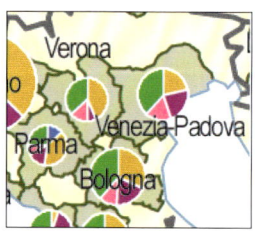

↑ **Metropolitan functions delta city region Veneto**
BBSR 2010

← **University building, University of Bologna**

→ **Delta city region Veneto**
Sources: Alterra (2007), LANMAP-2, Wageningen. European Environmental Agency (EEA) (2011), Corine land cover 2000, versie 15

Infrastructure
Roads
Railways

Land use
Urban land use
Business and industrial sites, mines, dumps and construction sites
Ports and airports

Coast
Wetlands
Estuaries and lagoons
Beaches and dunes

Water
Water

Height in metres
<0
0-5
5-10
10-20
20-50
50-100
100-200
200-300
300-500
500-700

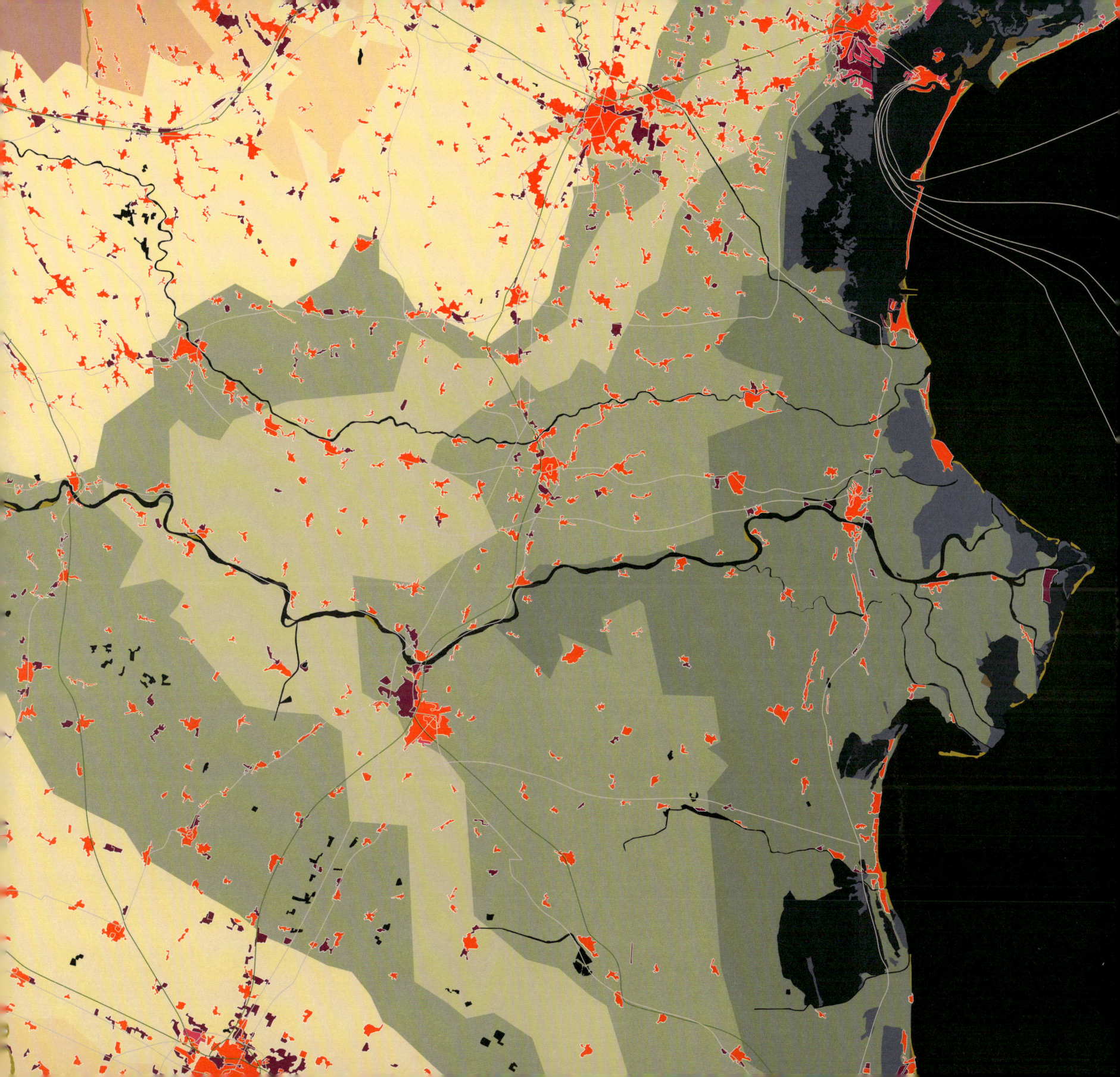

Bouches du Rhône

Two departments are included in the map detail: Bouches du Rhône and Gard. Metropolitan areas lie around the two main locations: Marseille and Montpellier (numbers 65 and 91, respectively, each with one location with metropolitan functions, Type 3, limited differentiation). The Rhône delta lies largely in the department of Bouches du Rhône. The number of residents in the detail is 2.7 million.

Extensive protected natural areas lie in the middle of the Rhône delta. The Camargue is the largest, with at least 221,062 hectare; the Petit Camargue measures 34,559 hectare, and the adjoining Crau 39,333 hectare.

The region is very fertile and is one of the greatest producers of vegetables, fruit, olives, wine and rice in France. Market gardening in plastic greenhouses lying in the flat sections is typical for it.

The occupation pattern is characterized by a limited number of cities and the rather open nature of the landscape. The cities are all of Roman origin, and grew rapidly in the early Middle Ages. Marseille lies just behind a ridge of hills, and became a major port and industrial city in the 19th century. An extensive urbanized zone lies along the roads and rail lines from the Rhône Valley to Marseille.

Large logistic complexes lie near Marseille. The old harbour close to the city is now used primarily by passenger services and cruises. Large new harbours have been created in Étang de Berre, Port du Bouc and Port St. Louis, in the middle of the lagoon. The port handled 88 million tons of freight in 2011. The Marseille Marignane airport also lines in the lagoon. It handled 7 million passengers in 2009. The large industrial complexes of the French/German Eurocopter, Shell and BP are also located there.

As of January 1, 2012, three universities merged to create the new Aix-Marseille Université, with five locations and 70,000 students. The city also advertises itself as a conference city, with a pair of large (900 and 1200 seats) and a large number of smaller conference facilities, and more than 100 hotels, with almost 6000 rooms.

Since the 1960s the population of Montpellier has more than doubled, to 270,000. It has become a growth city under the influence of a series of major investments by R&D businesses. The University of Montpellier was refounded in 1969.

The number of visitors to Bouches du Rhône was about 9 million in 2009, of whom only 15% came from foreign countries. The region is thus really a French vacation destination. In 2009 there were 43.3 million hotel stays, 13.6 million of which were in Marseille.[20] Tourist attractions on the UNESCO World Heritage list include the Roman monuments in Orange and Arles, the bridge over the Gard, and the episcopal palace in Avignon. Art tourism predominates. Aigues Mortes, La Grande Motte, Le Grau du Roi and Saintes Marie de la Mer are popular destinations.

Marseille is the Cultural Capital of Europe in 2013, and is carrying out a series of projects under the title Marseille-Euroméditerranée. The city's waterfront – over 480 hectare – is being radically renewed.

Plan Marseille-Euroméditerranée

Impression of Marseille-Euroméditerranée

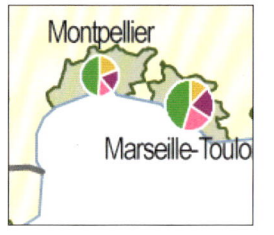

← **Metropolitan functions Bouches du Rhône** BBSR 2010

→ **Delta city region Bouches du Rhône**

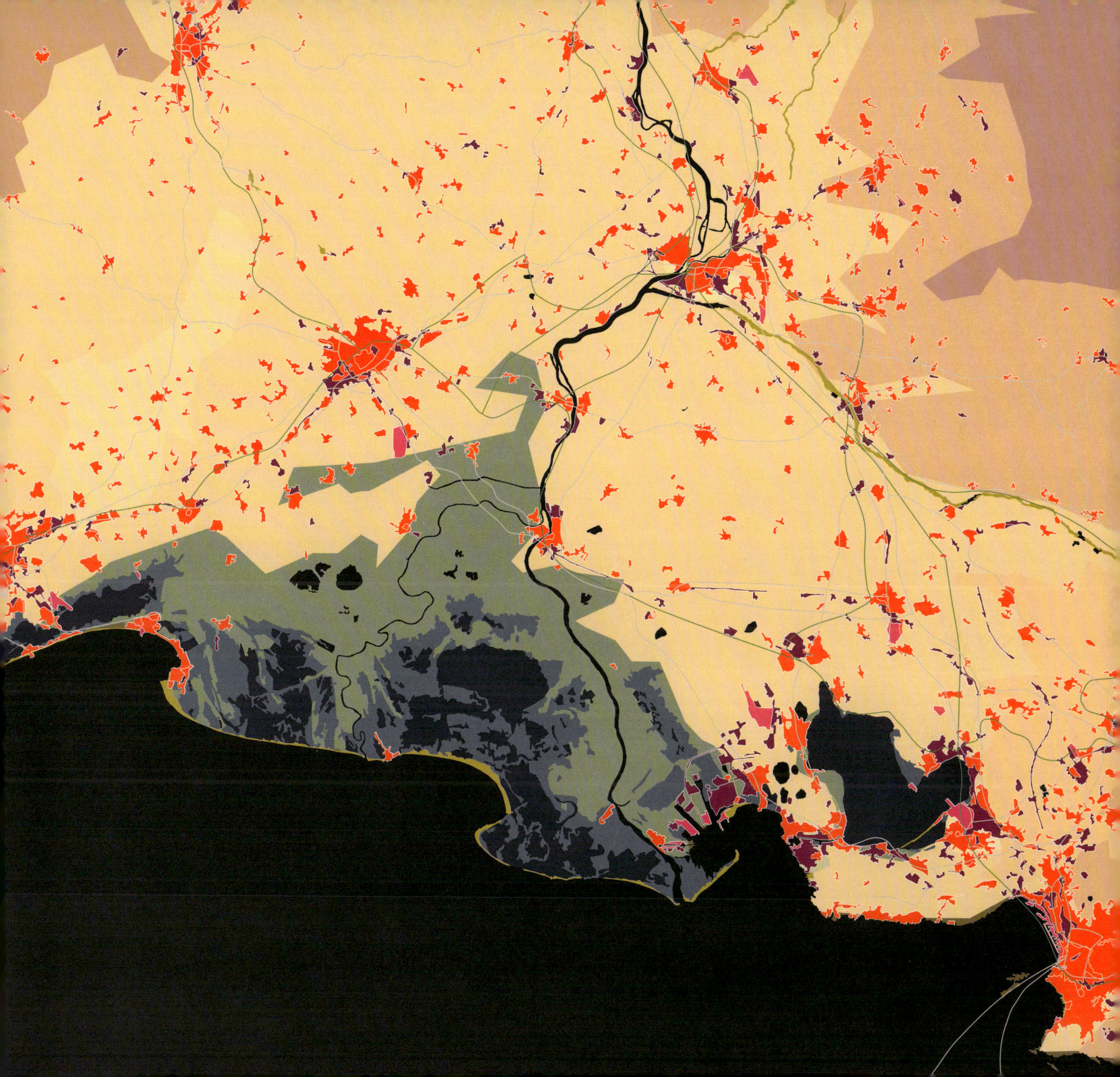

Flanders and Brussels

Flanders and Brussels have two metropolitan areas: Brussels (4, with four locations with metropolitan functions – Brussels, Antwerp, Louvain, Mechlin – Type 1, highly differentiated) and Ghent (54, with two locations with metropolitan functions – Ghent and Bruges – Type 3, limited differentiation). The number of residents within the map detail is 7.4 million.

The protected dune area, including the estuaries of the IJzer and Zwin, is not large, measuring only 3782 hectare. Other protected natural areas in the framework of Natura 2000 lie in Belgian territory, in the vicinity of harbour areas: the Polder Complex around Zeebrugge measures almost 10,000 hectare, the salt marshes and polders of the Lower Schelde 7085 hectare, and the waters and banks of the Schelde estuary 8957 hectare. Within Dutch territory, the whole of the Schelde basin is protected: 42,840 hectare, including several of the surrounding polders.

The agrarian sector is strong. Belgium produces an enormous tonnage of potatoes and beets.

Flanders has a highly diffuse pattern of urbanization, with a large number of relatively small cities, but primarily extended ribbon towns. Most of the cities date from the Middle Ages. Ghent, Antwerp and Brussels grew rapidly in the 19th century as a result of industrialization.

The harbours at Antwerp, Zeebrugge, Ghent, Vlissingen and Terneuzen together handled a total of 288 million tons of freight in 2010. Antwerp alone accounted for 178 million tons of this. In 2011 Zaventem Airport at Brussels handled 17 million passengers. Various conference and trade fair facilities are spread around Flanders: Flanders Expo in Ghent has a floor area of 54,000 m², and Brussels Expo, near the Atomium, 115,000 m².

Flanders and Brussels have five Dutch-language universities, in Brussels, Antwerp, Louvain and Ghent, and three French-speaking universities, at Brussels and Louvain-la-Neuve. A number of international organizations have their headquarters in Brussels, including the EU, Benelux, NATO, the World Customs Organization and Eurocontrol.

In 2010 28.5 million hotel stays were recorded, more or less equally divided over coastal, urban and regional tourism. Half of the visitors came from other countries, 4 million being from The Netherlands. Brussels itself recorded 5.5 million stays, 81% of which were international.[21] Flanders and Brussels count over 1500 hotels.

The heart of the city of Bruges, the Plantijn complex in Antwerp, the Begijnhof in Mechlin and the Grote Markt and the Art Nouveau houses by Victor Horta and Josef Hofmann in Brussels are on the UNESCO World Heritage list. A whole series of seaside resorts lies in the narrow strip with dunes and beach ridges along the North Sea.

Brussels was the Cultural Capital of Europe in 2000. In 2008 four employer's organizations launched the Business Route 2018 for Metropolitan Brussels, Brussels Metropolitan in short, with the aim of better utilizing Brussels's position as the capital of Europe in sustainable economic development, retaining talented individuals, and promoting growth in knowledge-intensive niches.

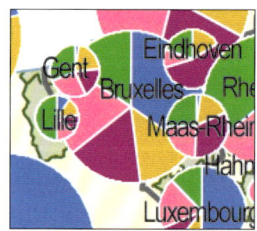

Metropolitan functions Flanders and Brussels
BBSR 2010

← **European Union building in Brussels**

→ **Delta city region Flanders and Brussels**

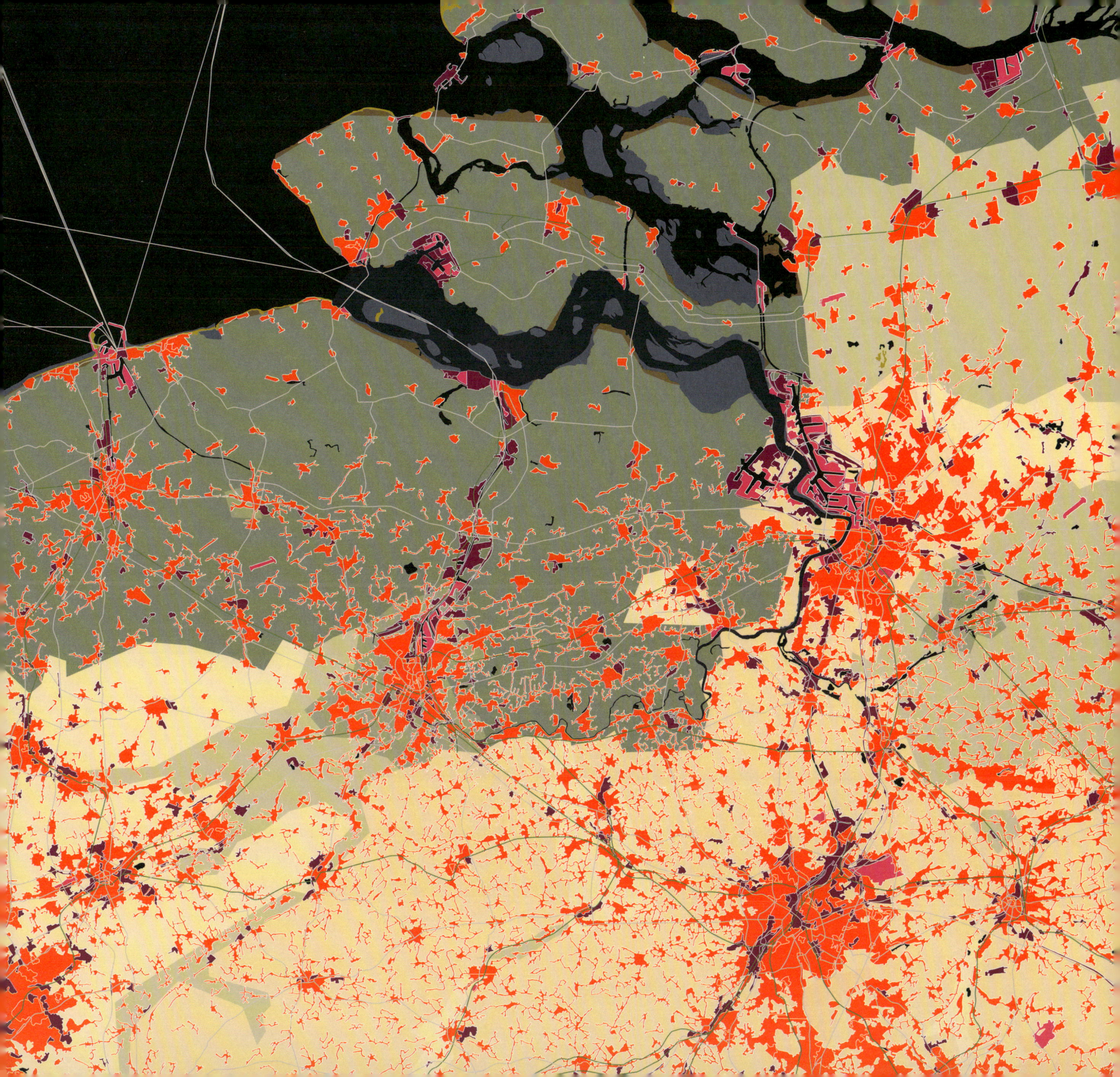

Rhine-Ruhr

Rhine-Ruhr (in fifth place) is one single metropolitan area with five locations with metropolitan functions – Cologne, Düsseldorf, Duisburg, Essen and Dortmund. Rhine-Ruhr is Type 1, with strongly differentiated metropolitan functions. The number of residents in the map detail is 12.9 million.

There are no Natura 2000 areas in the urbanized area in Rhine-Ruhr. However, several extensive bird sanctuaries lie immediately outside the urbanized area: Nieder-Rhein, of 25,809 hectare and Helleweg-börde, of 48,417 hectare.

The agrarian sector plays no significant role in the economy or in land use.

There is a major contrast in the urbanization pattern between the urban regions in the south and the Ruhr region in the north. Cologne has Roman roots, and has traditionally been the largest city. Düsseldorf also has an urban character. Many of the cores in the Ruhr region only developed during the 19th century, and are highly diffuse in nature. In fact, one can say there is a connected urbanized zone in the Ruhr area. Moreover, much of the historic construction disappeared as a result of heavy bombardment during the Second World War.

Duisburg is the largest internal port in Europe. The airport at Düsseldorf handled 19 million passengers in 2010, at Cologne 11 million. The Kölnmesse is one of the largest trade fair and conference centres in Germany, with 284,000 m² of exhibition space. It lies on the right bank, close to the city centre of Cologne. The Ruhr region was traditionally characterized by mining and heavy industry. Today most of the mines have closed and the spectrum of economic activities has become much broader. Among the large firms are E.ON, Thyssen-Krupp, Bayer and Henkel.

Cologne has the largest university in Germany, with 40,000 students. In addition there are universities at Düsseldorf, and since the 1960s in the Ruhr region at Bochum, Duisburg-Essen and Dortmund.

During the year 2010, in which it was the Cultural Capital of Europe, the Ruhr region was visited by 3.5 million people, good for 6.5 million overnight hotel stays, a sharp rise with respect to other years.

The cathedrals of Cologne and Aachen, the rococo castles at Augustusburg and Falkenlust, and the Zollverein complex in Essen are on the UNESCO World Heritage list. The Ruhr Museum, designed by O.M.A. and opened in 2010, and the ARKA Kulturwerkstatt are part of the Zollverein complex.

Germany has an interesting tradition of events with its IBAs, Internationale Bauausstellungen (Berlin, 1957 and 1984, Sachsen-Anhalt, 2000). The IBA Emscherpark took place between 1989 and 1999. Many abandoned industrial sites around the Emscher River were transformed into attractive landscape parks.

Metropolitan functions Rhine-Ruhr
BBSR 2010

← **Ruhr Museum**
Zollverein, design O.M.A.

→ **Delta city region Rhine-Ruhr**

Dutch Randstad

The BBSR regards the Dutch Randstad as one metropolitan area, and on their list it stands at third place in Europe, after Paris and London, with the strongest spread of metropolitan functions over at least seven locations – the four largest cities, the two university cities of Leiden and Delft, and Haarlemmermeer, with Schiphol airport. The Randstad is Type 1, with a strong differentiation in metropolitan functions. The number of residents within the map detail is 8.5 million, comparable with Flanders-Brussels, and larger than Rhine-Ruhr.

In the transport sector the Randstad is the strongest region in Europe, because of its enormous seaports and airports. Its scores in economy and science are comparable with London, but sharply slower than Paris. The Randstad has average scores in politics and culture.

Veneto and Emilia-Romagna and Bouches du Rhône and Gard have relatively low scores all across the board; the exceptions are specialized metropolitan functions such as the sciences, in which Bologna scores high, and culture, in which Venice and Marseille score high. Flanders and Brussels have a very high score in the field of politics because of the multiplicity of international organizations there, but otherwise have average scores. Rhine-Ruhr is strong in economy and culture, but average in the sciences and transport, and low in politics.

A number of Natura 2000 sites lie around the Randstad: 15,809 hectare surrounding the cities, 17,724 hectare along the west in the dunes along the coast, 33,181 hectare along the rivers to the south, 70,093 hectare to the north in the remnants of the lagoon (IJmeer and Markermeer), and 97,564 hectare to the east, in the Veluwe, for a total of 243,371 hectare (excluding the Voordelta and the IJsselmeer). The Natura 2000 regions are strongly cultivated, and in total smaller than the wide delta of the Camargue, but larger than the protected regions in the lagoon of the Veneto and the Po delta, and much larger than the 'scraps' in Flanders and Rhine-Ruhr.

The agrarian landscape of the Randstad is dominated by greenhouses for market gardening under glass. They have an industrial aura, certainly in comparison with the open-air agriculture in the Veneto and Rhône delta. The farming in the flower bulb producing region, and in Boskoop, have distinct identities of their own.

In terms of size, Amsterdam, Rotterdam and The Hague are comparable with cities like Bologna (380,000), Marseille (839,000), Antwerp (492,000), Brussels (951,000), Cologne (1,007,000) and Düsseldorf (588,000). Utrecht (300,000) belongs to the extensive list of middle-sized cities, with a population of between 100,000 and 250,000.[22]

In comparison with the occupation pattern in the Ruhr region and Flanders, the Randstad has rather great contrasts between urban areas and open landscapes. Dutch towns and cities are relatively compact.

The port of Rotterdam handled 430 million tons of goods and that of Amsterdam 75 million – together far more than the 26 million of Venice, 88 million of Marseille and 178 million of Antwerp put together. Comparable differences are found in air passenger totals. Schiphol processed 50 million passengers in 2011.

In 2011 the number of foreign visitors to The Netherlands was more than 11 million.[23] This largely involved 'city tourism'. Amsterdam's Ring Canals and the old defences of the Stelling van Amsterdam, the windmills at Kinderdijk, the Beemster and the Rietveld-Schröder House are all on the UNESCO World Heritage list.

Rotterdam was the Cultural Capital of Europe in 2001. Utrecht and The Hague are candidates for 2018. The Floriade exhibition was held in Venlo in 2012.

Conclusion

Fertile soil, fresh water and clear light, in combination with a moderate climate, make deltas perfectly suited for agricultural pursuits. That explains the small-scale settlement pattern, with diffuse farms, villages and market towns of all sizes and types, not only in the Delta City Regions analysed, but also in the deltas of the Mekong, Euphrates, Ganges and Nile. The plains of the Po, and the deltas of the Rhône, Schelde, Maas and Rhine feed many times the number of their inhabitants. The market gardening in the Randstad stands out through the very specialized nature of its products, and its almost industrial production methods.

The high agricultural production of the deltas, in combination with their favourable location at the mouths of rivers, also explains their importance in trade and transport. Traditionally harbours have been located in and around deltas, with storage and transshipment facilities near the sea, and a central core with a great annual fair more inland.

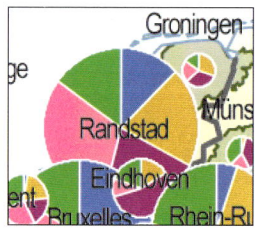

Metropolitan functions Randstad, Netherlands
BBSR 2010

← **Bulb growing region from the air**

→ **Delta city region Randstad, Netherlands**

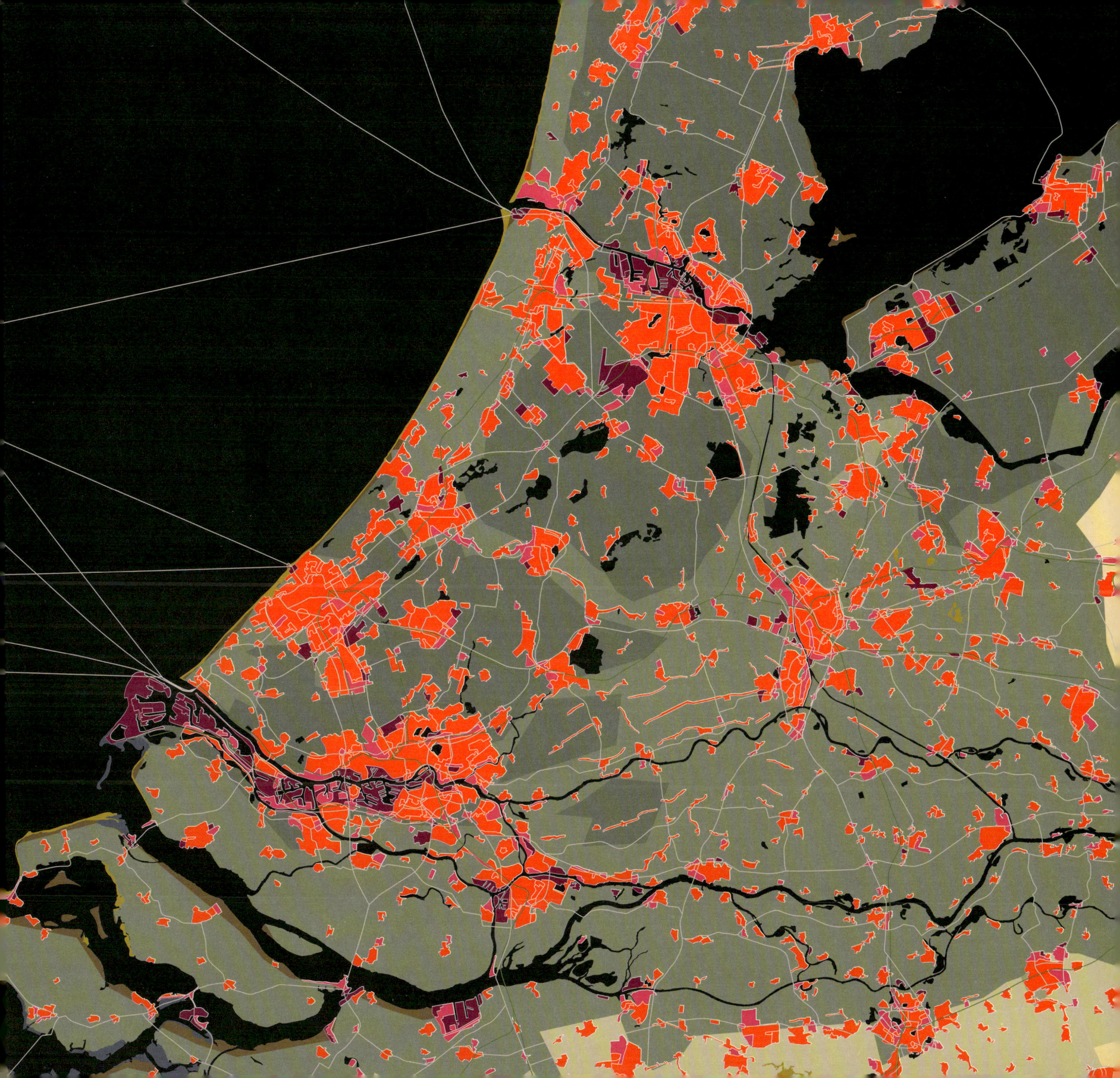

The combination of Alexandria and Cairo in the Nile Delta is the prototype for this. Milan-Venice around the Po and Lyon-Marseille around the Rhône are similar combinations. In the Flemish ports, Cologne also had an outpost on the sea. Amsterdam, and especially Rotterdam, later took over that role. Marseille and Venice lie on the sea, but to one side of the main channel of their rivers. In a certain sense that is also true for the Flemish ports. The Dutch ports, on the other hand, lie right in the middle of the delta. Their potential for expansion was created by manipulating the delta: re-routing rivers, digging canals, and damming off side arms, draining swamps and lakes, and building harbour facilities on landfill.

Although in the 19th and 20th century the expansion of the harbour facilities in the Rhône delta and Venetian lagoon came at the expense of natural areas, large, connected nature reserves remained. In the Randstad the contrast between natural areas and urban areas is great. In comparison with Flanders, however, the extent of the natural areas is much more substantial.

The cities in Delta City Regions owe their attraction in part to the role they played in European culture and history. Bologna is home to the oldest university, Cologne to the northernmost Dom. In the 15th, 16th and 17th centuries Venice, Bruges and Amsterdam were the world's economic centres.

The significance of Delta City Regions today is determined by the form and degree to which they have been able to expand and broaden their traditional delta economies, with the emphasis on agriculture and transport. Bologna and Marseille developed extensive industrial sectors, and Brussels politics and culture around international organizations. The strong position of the Dutch Randstad rests primarily on its seaports and airports. In other fields the Randstad's scores are only average. The great challenge which it faces is strengthening them.

Concepts for the development of metropolitan functions

In light of Luuk Boelens's distinctions, centralized control of a Delta City Region like the Randstad is a contradiction in terms. This also to a large extent explains the conceptual and administrative wrestling in the national policy with regard to the relation of the cities to one another, the relation of the large cities to their surrounding regions, to the Wings, and to a large or small Randstad. National policy is really only successful when there are financial resources for the cities connected with it. The national government traditionally has had a role in the construction of national and international transportation networks: seaports and airports, motorways, rail lines and utility networks. Since the appearance of the *Vierde Nota* in 1988, this general infrastructure has been related to spatial policy for the development of specific areas or functions. What is worth noting about this is that the 'port' metaphor is still being used. The best known instance is the policy around the 'mainports' of Schiphol and the Rotterdam harbour. This was followed in the *Nota Ruimte* policy surrounding 'greenports'. Enhancing the traditional elements of delta economies, horticulture and transport, played the main role here.

A variant is the policy regarding what have been called 'key projects', and the 'brainport' in Eindhoven. These involve investment in shaping the centres of the largest cities. At first sight the recent 'top sector' policy appears to usher in a new impetus for this strategy, but on further examination it has hardly any spatial component.

Mainport

Schiphol and the Rotterdam harbour are rightly regarded as the most important motors of the Dutch economy. These vital functions were further developed through the mainport strategy.

With respect to the mainport Schiphol, this involves two closely intertwined functions. 'First, it is an airport with a hub function: an interchange where many national, European and intercontinental connections come together. Second, it is a metropolitan area with a high quality climate for homes, daily life and investment, where many businesses operate competitively in international networks of production and consumption, and where many people live, work and seek entertainment.'[24] In this definition, Amsterdam is a part of the mainport.

The strategy is elaborated in the *Planologische Kernbeslissing* (PKB) *Schiphol en Omgeving*, issued in 1995. The total cost (including the South and East High Speed Rail lines) were estimated at about 30 billion guilders. The cost of the measures for expanding Schiphol itself were to be about 12 billion guilders. Three-and-a-half billion of this latter sum was contributed by the national government, primarily for financing roads, rail links and tunnels.[25]

The mainport Rotterdam Harbour was somewhat less handsomely financed. The mainport strategy there focused on the construction of the new Second Maasvlakte, and several large compensatory nature reserve projects. In addition, in and around the present harbour a series of projects involving intensification of existing activities and improving liveability were realised. The costs for construction of the Second Maasvlakte were estimated at 2.9 billion Euro. The national government contributed 571 million Euro to the financing of the public infrastructure, and in addition spent 500 million Euro on buying new shares in the Port of Rotterdam.

Greenport

Investment around greenports is less sizeable, but developments in the trade and distribution in market gardening are nevertheless of great importance. The concept was launched in 2004 in the *Nota Ruimte*. A greenport is a complex of horticultural businesses, auctions, marketing organizations, trading companies, exporters and horticultural suppliers. Often there are also plant breeders and propagators and seed companies involved, and there are links to knowledge institutions and banks. In the *Nota Ruimte* there are five areas designated as greenports: the Dune and Flower Bulb region, Westland/Oostland, Venlo, Boskoop and Aalsmeer. The policy focuses on stimulating and facilitating restructuring and improved accessibility.

In the meantime the concept of Greenport Holland has been coined, and there is a collective development strategy for the sector as a whole.[26] The background for this is an unlikely concentration which took place in the trade in vegetables and fruit, and in plants and flowers. Over a couple of decades almost all local auctions have merged into several large, cooperative trade organizations like The Greenery and Flora Holland. These have their most important locations in Barendrecht, Bleiswijk and Venlo, and in Naaldwijk, Rijnsburg and Aalsmeer, in the middle of their respective production areas.

Presently, in addition to the focus on investment and infrastructure surrounding the auctions, the stimulus policies are also directed toward promotion and research. As part of the top sector policy, the aim is to have a budget of 355 million Euro in 2012, toward which the government will provide a contribution of 152 million for knowledge and innovation.

Brainport

A Brainport – the Eindhoven/South-east Brabant region – was also introduced in the *Nota Ruimte*. 'Brainport Eindhoven is one of the top ten innovative regions in Europe, with high-quality activities in the field of research and development, innovative knowledge and production industries and the educational facilities and research and design institutions to support them. Continued efforts to support the knowledge industry can enable it to hold its own against international competition. The

climate for recruitment and relocation of highly qualified firms and employees must therefore be attractive, with well developed cities and quality surroundings, to maintain the competitive position in the future.'[27]

To this end the Eindhoven urban region developed a large number of projects, including an extensive 'campus landscape' around the reconstructed A2 motorway/Brainport Avenue. The national government contributed 75 million Euro, not only for connections to the A2, but also for a network of bicycle paths and for landscape development, the Slowlane and the Parkplateau.

Such spatial projects fit into the approach of what are termed Key Projects, which the national authorities have been carrying out since the Fourth Memorandum.

Key Projects

The first generation of Key Projects in the early 1990s were public-private partnerships in the cities, oriented toward 'intensifying and completing the existing city, high-quality planning, development of an internationally competitive environment for business location, and curtailing and channelling mobility.'[28] A whole series of restructuring projects were selected to accomplish this: the Central City District (Amersfoort), Céramique (Maastricht), Kop van Zuid (Rotterdam), the Eastern Harbour District (Amsterdam), the Station District North-west (Groningen), New Centre (The Hague), Brabantse Poort (Nijmegen) and the Eindhoven-Veldhoven-Welschap Corridor. Two projects eventually dropped away (IJ Banks, Amsterdam, and Noordrand, Rotterdam), and one was slid back into the second generation of key projects (Utrecht City Project, around Central Station). The programmes for these projects were highly diverse, from residential construction on difficult transformation locations, through high-quality public transit connections, to renewal and expansion of city centres.

In the second generation, around the millennium, the focus shifted to new High Speed Rail stations and their vicinity. The intention was to achieve a maximum spin-off from the investment in the six station sites, to shape attractive urban core areas. In addition to the infrastructure itself contributions were therefore planned toward fitting the stations into the districts around them, and the public space around them. The national government contributed a total of 1.4 billion Euro for this. This second generation of projects include the South Axis, Amsterdam, Rotterdam Central Station, New Central Station, The Hague, Utrecht Central Station, Arnhem Central Station and the Breda Station District.

Top Sectors

The central slogan in the spatial-economic policy of the 2008 governmental memorandum *Randstad 2040* is 'strengthen what is already strong'. That quickly led to the familiar list of mainports, greenports and brainports. Buck Consultants correctly noted in the study report *Uitvoeringsstrategie duurzame internationale concurrentiepositie Randstad 2040* that it is important to look at the development cycle of economic sectors (see graph on page 32).[29] Buck distinguished 32 sectors in the economy of the Randstad, and placed these in a cycle of start-up, development and adulthood. Some of the 'strong' adult sectors will inevitably stabilize or shrink. Small but promising rising sectors can grow stronger, and therefore deserve focused support. For other 'strong' adult sectors the question must be asked how much more continued growth is possible. In all cases, however, it is necessary to have a specific policy for each sector or segment.

This commentary has been reflected in the policy. In the spring of 2011, in what was called the *Bedrijfslevenbrief*, the Rutte-Verhagen Cabinet launched a new set of instruments for making the Dutch economy more competitive. The task is 'to put The Netherlands in a strong position in rapidly growing sales markets, and find innovative solutions for our social questions.'[30] By challenging nine Top Sectors to come up with proposals for enhancement and growth the ball was tossed into the private sector's court, to find ways to make a leap forward. The nine sectors were AgroFood, Horticulture, High Tech, Energy, Logistics, Creative Industry, Life Sciences, Chemicals and Water. In addition, separate attention was given to Corporate Headquarters.

In 2012 the national government made 1.5 billion Euro available for the Top Sectors. That sum will grow to 2 billion in 2015. Top teams, under the leadership of a standard bearer from the sector, have drawn up action agendas, and by the time this is being written, most of the sectors have signed 'innovation contracts'.

There are, however, a number of questions which can be raised about the selection of the sectors. The choice was made on the basis of their market and export position, intensity of knowledge, cooperation among entrepreneurs and knowledge institutions, and capacity to make an innovative contribution to social challenges. The *Bedrijfslevenbrief* includes a table of

their percentage of the GNP and investment in R&D.

Yet there are a number of important sectors missing from the Top Sector policy. In background studies there has been extensive discussion of business service providers, international law and peace, and ICT and broadband services.[31] In addition – remarkably enough – the tourism and convention sector is also absent.

Moreover, although most of the action agendas discuss the spatial clustering of activities in the sector, in no single case is there any discussion of concrete spatial projects which would provide higher quality, better accessibility or stronger internal cohesion for a particular cluster. Most of the proposals involve – as we already saw in the horticultural sector, above – knowledge and innovation, enhancing entrepreneurship and reducing government regulations.

The suggestion is made, though, that for investment in spatial-economic development priority be given to the urban regions around Amsterdam, Rotterdam and Eindhoven. That is a rather meagre policy commitment.

Cluster-forming and interaction environments

Clusters and cluster-forming play an important role in economic theory. Reference is often made to the pioneering work of Michael Porter in *The Competitive Advantage of Nations*, published in 1990.[32] Although the term cluster has a spatial connotation, it is a concept which is hardly operationalized in urban planning or planning theory.

In economic theory a cluster is a collection of similar economic activities which complement one another. Cluster-forming offers advantages because they can all make use of the same suppliers and clients, the pool of trained workers and the collection of knowledge they represent, and the same facilities for distributing products.

In much of the research and theory arising from it, the regional level is central. The Flower Bulb Region in Holland and Silicon Valley are familiar examples. But clusters can also be identified at the urban level: one can think of concentrations of office buildings, stores or university buildings.

The facilities that clusters of economic activities share to exchange products (more generally, persons, goods, capital and information) have a spatial component. In the example of the Schiphol mainport cited above, this is the airport's terminal complex; in the greenports, the auctions. In this study, the areas where these built facilities are found will be termed an *interaction environment*.

An interaction environment is to be understood as a spatial environment with facilities for encounters and for the exchange of persons, goods, capital and/ or information. Interaction environments are sharply distinguished from other urban environments, such as living or production environments. Interaction environments have ever-changing groups of users, and specialized facilities. In many cases they involve what have traditionally been labelled as 'centres'; business centres, museum districts, shopping centres or entertainment centres.[33] It is true that most

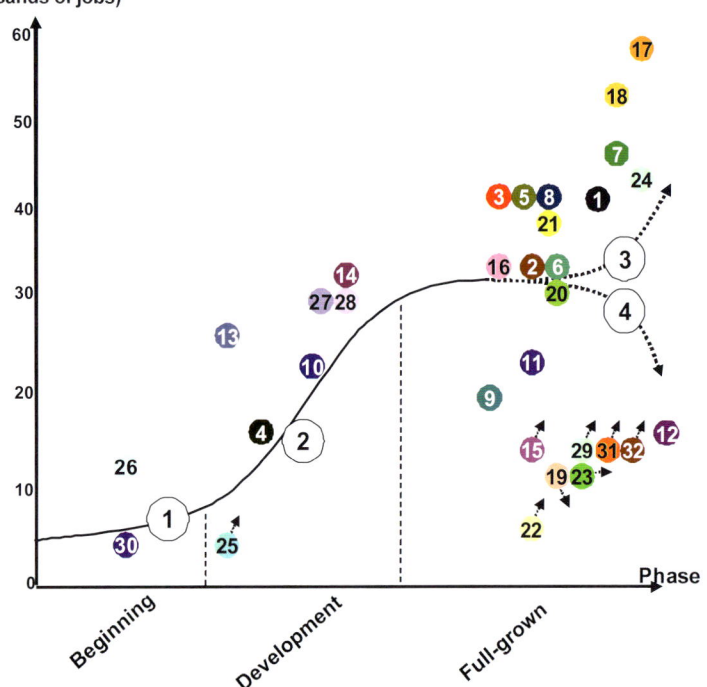

Sectors of international scale in the Randstad (by thousands of jobs)

1 ICT
2 Financial
3 Int. Offices
4 Media/Creative
5 Fashion/lifestyle
6 Consultancy
7 Tourism
8 Conferences
9 Aerospace
10 Medical
11 Petrochemical
12 Other chemicals
13 Biobased
14 Energy
15 Transshipment
16 Distribution
17 Maritime technical
18 Cut Flowers/plants
19 Flower bulbs
20 Fresh
21 Tree nurseries
22 Peace and security
23 Int. management
24 Food/ingredients
25 Materials
26 Nanotechnology
27 Life sciences/pharma
28 High tech systems
29 Space
30 Water (delta)
31 Legal services
32 Architecture

Phase: Beginning — Development — Full-grown

Size and stage of development of economic sectors in the Randstad
Buck Consultants International 2008

interaction environments still lie in the historic heart of the city, but in the modern network city that is no longer always the case. That applies absolutely to the harbours, airports and auctions mentioned above, but also for seaside resorts, festival sites, internet exchanges, campuses, sports stadiums, concert halls and fair complexes. An interaction environment is a broader and more neutral term than the old 'city centre'.

A *metropolitan interaction environment* is an interaction environment with a wide international reach. A metropolis is to be distinguished from a 'big city' perhaps precisely through its large number of visitors: people on business trips, foreign and domestic tourists, convention attendees, residents of the region who come to shop, visit a museum or conference, or just wander through the city and go out for a meal – or combinations of these. Refugees, students and expats are also 'visitors', although they may stay for some years.

This definition of a metropolis builds on the German studies previously mentioned, when we referred to *Metropolregionen*. Metropolitan interaction environments form the spatial milieu for metropolitan functions. Metropolitan functions are the 'hubs' in the flows of persons, goods, capital and information, and their strength determines the international position of cities and regions. It is here assumed that, in addition to their number and extent, that the quality of these interaction environments also matters in the international context. This quality is in part determined by the attractiveness of a city or region as a prospective business location, or as a travel destination. Therefore it is relevant to look at the spatial and functional structure of these interaction environments, at their location in the regions and in relation to one another, and at the way in which they have developed.

This interpretation of the concept of a metropolis clearly separates itself from definitions based on the number of residents, the economic power of the core, and living/work relations, as in the theories surrounding Functional Urban Regions. But it also takes a step beyond the German research surrounding metropolitan functions. A ranking affords insight into the size and 'strength' of metropolitan functions, into where we stand. Now our task is to find keys to the metropolis, and how they can be applied.

The spatial arrangement of Schiphol provides a good example. The success of the airport is closely linked with its hub function in the network of Air France/KLM, and the number of passengers. But the one-roof concept of the terminal complex is crucial for this. Through the particular spatial configuration of the terminals, with a central hall on the land side and transfer possibilities on the air side, Schiphol offers comfort that many other airports lack. To enhance the quality of the metropolis we have to search for more smart and smoothly functioning concepts of this sort.

Typology

Precision is necessary for quality: precision in intended economic effects, but also precision in a spatial sense. What are the usable design solutions for improving the quality of a particular interaction environment? Constructing a typology is a suitable means for this.

For retail interaction environments one can, for instance, construct a simple series running from the 'corner store' through the shopping street, shopping square or shopping district, to the passage, shopping centre, boulevard, mall and super mall.[34] A typology of this sort revolves around diverse forms of clustering of facilities, coupled with a specific spatial form. Customer access, delivery of supplies, the degree of blending with the supporting programme and with other urban functions will also differ. In the series the degree of concentration and specialization increases, while the extent of their public nature decreases. The coupling to specific spatial forms, such as the passage or shopping square, enriches the typology and makes it more interesting as part of a qualitative approach.[35]

It is worth noting that in everyday language many terms for certain types of interaction environments are in circulation, without ever being well defined in the professional literature. One might think of 'medical centre', 'shopping quarter', 'culture park', 'entertainment district', 'fairgrounds', 'central business districts', etc. This study will in part focus on supplying this lack, and thus providing an alternative for the haphazard use of terms such as 'port' and 'campus'.

Metropolitan quality

Horticulture and transport play an important role in the economy of Delta City Regions. Over the past few decades an increasingly strong emphasis has been placed on these sectors in the policy for the development of the Randstad. With the Key Projects surrounding the major stations and the development of the Eindhoven Brainport, this has broadened out. In the national government's recent Top Sector Policy, attracting the corporate head offices of internationally operating concerns is mentioned as a specific commitment. All of the top sectors would profit from this. In addition to fiscal measures, relaxing rules for expats, and promotion, the development of an attractive location for businesses in the vicinity of Schiphol was regarded as of paramount importance for the development of the Randstad, and the Dutch economy. In what the Cabinet entitled its Amsterdam Letter, which appeared at the same time as the *Bedrijfslevenbrief* mentioned above, they announced further research into expanding and improving the quality of Amsterdam's South Axis. The South Axis must become the Central Business District (CBD) for the whole of The Netherlands.

Traditionally, the development of an attractive CBD around a stock exchange was seen as an effective means of drawing the corporate head-quarters of international firms. Wall Street, London's City and the Nihonbashi district in Tokyo are the basic models for this. This concept is expanded in the theories about Global cities. Research suggests that, in addition to the Exchange, over the last decades it was precisely a whole range of services termed the Advanced Producer Services – banks, insurance companies, advertising agencies, law offices and accountants – which were the deciding factors in attracting the corporate headquarters of inter-national businesses.[36] Some of these services do in fact prefer an environment like Wall Street or its variants such as La Défense or the Docklands, while others, like advertising agencies, on the other hand, seek out more lively urban milieus.

The credit crisis has relativized the importance of high-quality business services and corporate headquarters in shaping the metropolis. But in a scientific perspective, the emphasis on high-quality services is also limiting. Following the five *Metropol-bereiche* of the German Bundesinstitut für Bau-, Stadt- und Raumforschung (BBSR), the strongest cities are, rather, the most versatile cities. They excel in an economic sense, but also politically, acade-mically, in transport and culture.[37] In addition to the facilities for business interaction in the CBDs, this also calls for environments in which international organizations thrive, for top universities, for airports with an intercontinental network, and for high-quality facilities for cultural interaction and the exchange of knowledge. It is precisely its palette of interaction environments that gives a metropolis its colour.

Culture – convention – knowledge

In this book, the facilities and interaction environ-ments for the cultural, convention and knowledge sectors will be central.

We previously noted that a metropolis is to be distinguished from what is merely a big city primarily by its large number of visitors. In recent decades the tourism and conference sector in The Netherlands has undergone massive growth. Particularly city tourism is of great importance for the international position of The Netherlands. Visits to cultural institutions play an increasingly large role in recreational city tourism; in business tourism, that role is fulfilled by visits to conferences.

The importance of the knowledge sector is beyond dispute. Unlike in the Top Sector policy, here there is a focus on the quality of the interaction environments in which knowledge is produced: university campuses and R&D centres of institutions and businesses.

For *The Dutch Metropolis* research was done into the extent and quality of the facilities and interac-tion environments for culture, conferences and knowledge in the Randstad. In presenting this, the same approach is taken for each of these three sectors:

• *Development* – the main lines of the development of the sector are analysed on the basis of literature research and conversations with experts.

• *Clusters and interaction environments* – next the locations where the most important facilities are to be found are mapped out, and we sketch which clusters stand out, and how they are embedded in their surroundings and in interaction environments. The analysis focuses on the four largest cities. When examining the knowledge sector, Leiden and Delft are also included.

• *Typology* – on the basis of comparisons with other Dutch cities and foreign cities, the types of interac-tion environments are identified: their location, size, programme and spatial form.

• *Relations* – how the interaction environments relate to each other, to other clusters of facilities for interaction in their cities, and to similar environ-ments in the rest of The Netherlands is examined. With regard to culture, this will chiefly involve shopping, entertainment and art tourism. With regard to conventions, the relations with hotels, business interaction environments and sports are important. For knowledge, it is interesting to look at the differences between institutions in and outside the cities. Specifically for The Hague, the relations with government ministries, governmental administration and international organizations will also be examined.

• *Perspective* – against the background of their position in the developmental cycle, diverse perspectives can be conceived for the separate interaction environments; design studies from planning practice, academic dissertations and theses, and further design research are called upon to illustrate them.

Structure of the book

Chapters 2, 3 and 4 are the core of the book, with material on interaction environments in the cultural, convention and knowledge sectors in the Dutch metropolis.

Chapter 5 explores a more integral perspective. Here we will first deal with logistic interaction environments from the horticultural and transport sectors. Next, the material is summarized in maps, with all the existing and with the up and coming metropolitan interaction environments in the four largest cities.

Further, from the material it becomes clear that the design discipline has at its disposal a wide but still hardly utilized repertoire of types of interaction environments. Here there are worlds still to conquer.

Against the background of its international position, the book closes with a sketch of the development perspective for the Dutch Metropolis.

→ **High Tech Campus, Eindhoven, The Strip**

35

Culture clusters

The year 1970 marked a breakthrough for modern city tourism in The Netherlands. To mark the 25th anniversary of liberation from the German occupation, in the summer of that year C'70 took place, a broadly conceived event around the theme of communication. A whole series of individual events, including the famous pop festival in the Kralingse Bos and the first edition of Poetry International, were organized, running from May to September. In addition a whole series of temporary attractions, such as a monorail, a dolphinarium, a fun fair and an enormous maquette of the harbour area, were built in and around the heart of the city. The Schouwburgplein was redesigned, and the Euromast given a new, higher tip. Pavilions along the city's wide boulevards provided space for cafés, snack bars and restaurants. Hundreds of thousands of visitors came to the event – and not just Rotterdammers.

Five years later Amsterdam-700 followed, with the slogan 'living, working, playing'. The city opened a series of new cultural buildings, including the Amsterdam Historical Museum in the former Municipal Orphanage. Furthermore, according to the official count, residents and visitors were treated to no less than 260 events. In the years that followed, many of these events became traditions: Sail, the Jordaan Festival, the Amsterdam Marathon, the Amsterdam Tournament and the Kwakoe Festival.

In this chapter city tourism in The Netherlands will be analysed, and we will focus in on existing and new clusters of cultural institutions in the four largest cities. We will investigate how these have developed and how they are embedded in the cities. Next we will look at how city tourism relates to other tourist sectors, including coastal tourism and visits to attractions. Finally, against this background we will sketch future perspectives for the Holland Cluster.

The IJ during Sail 2010

Development of tourism in The Netherlands

In The Netherlands, tourism was long an activity for the elite. According to a 1906 report from the Labour Council, less than 12% of the workers questioned had vacation rights. Many of these vacations were not more than one to three days in length.[1] These were mostly used for day trips, such as a day out at the zoo. The number of vacation days rose steadily in the ensuring decades. In 1962 most workers had Saturday free, and an average of 13 vacation days per year. Tourism became democratized.

This enormous expansion led to vacations involving stays of several days or more joining day tourism, to create an extensive economic sector. In 1954 2.8 million adult Dutchmen went on vacation. Of them, 2.2 remained in The Netherlands; the other 600,000 went abroad. Ten years later, in 1963, the number of vacationers had risen to 4.3 million, of whom 1.7 million went abroad.

In addition to traditional destinations such as the Veluwe and South Limburg, the domestic vacations were concentrated on the North Sea resorts along the coasts of Holland and Zeeland, and the Wadden Islands. A quarter of the day trips form the cities were also in the direction of the coast.

In this period however the pressure on the coast rose primarily as a result of sharp growth in the

Poster for the year-long event Amsterdam 700
Michael Toner 1975

Development of vacations by Netherlanders in and outside The Netherlands between 1970 and 2009
CBS Statline

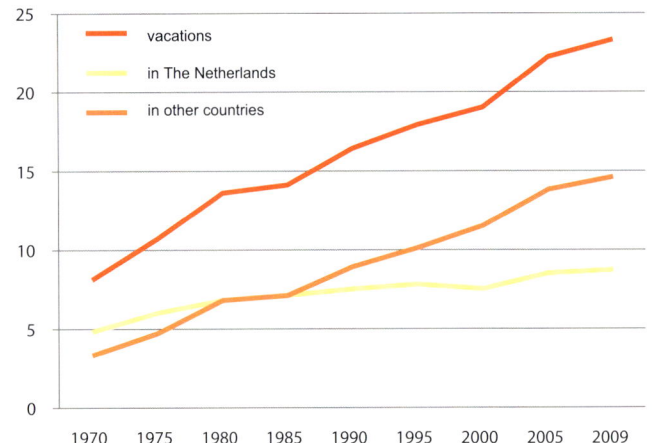

Kurhaus and beach at Scheveningen

number of foreign vacationers, the largest group from Germany. Between 1957 and 1962 the number of foreign hotel guests rose by 10% per year, and the number of foreign bed-and-breakfast guests by at least 30%. In the summer of 1962 1.4 million foreigners stayed in The Netherlands, 600,000 of whom were Germans. In 1999 this ultimately hit a peak, with over 3 million German visitors.

While the Germans were particularly attracted to the coast, other foreigners stayed chiefly in the cities. More than 50% of the foreigners overnighting in hotels in The Netherlands in 1962 were visitors to the four largest cities: 710,000. Compared to that, the numbers of Dutchmen staying in hotels in the largest cities was negligible: less than 9000.

This picture changed radically after the 1970s, under the influence of growing world-wide prosperity. In 1990 the number of foreign visitors had already grown to 5.8 million, and doubled to more than 10 million in 2009. In that year, that was good for 25 million overnight hotel stays.[2] This largely involved 'city tourism': for instance, the number of guests in Amsterdam hotels rose from 1.8 million in 1990 to 4.6 million in 2009, good for 8.6 million overnight stays.[3] In recent years the number of Dutchmen overnighting in hotels also grew explosively: from 110,000 in 1990, through 150,000

in 1995, to more than one million in 2009.

The growth of day tourism in The Netherlands since the 1960s was proportionate. In recent years there has however been a certain decline.[4] That comes primarily from the decline in 'traditional' day tourist activities such as 'picnicking, swimming, sunbathing, hiking and cycling', and – especially – 'going for a ride'. 'Theatre visits, eating out and dancing' remained more or less stable. The growth areas have been 'fun shopping', and 'visiting events, attractions and places of interest'.[5] In 2007 Dutchmen took a total of 134 million days out for shopping – an average of eight times a year! – and 119 million day trips were made to events, attractions and places of interest – an average of seven times per year. Compared with 1995, the growth in visits to events was more than 30%.[6] Rotterdam is the city for events, par excellence. In 2005 more than 17.5 million day trippers came to the city.

Thus there are three sectors which can be clearly distinguished: the traditional regional tourism, oriented to domestic visitors; coastal tourism, in which German visitors also play a role, and city tourism, oriented to both Dutch and international visitors. This last sector has seen the strongest growth in recent years.

The rise of city tourism in The Netherlands is part

of the growth of the tourist sector as a whole. In 1950 the World Tourism Organization (WTO) counted only 25 million tourists world wide; in 2008 that was 922 million.[7] It is expected that this number will continue to grow strongly. It should not be surprising, then, that tourism has become a vital sector in the Dutch economy. In 2008 the sector accounted for about 400,000 jobs in The Netherlands, and produced incomes of 37 billion Euro, 3% of the Dutch GNP. If one looks at leisure time activities and tourism as a whole, then these figures are much higher.[8] In the Amsterdam region, the number of persons working in the tourism sector, at 100,000, is almost equal to those in ICT, and considerably larger than in the creative industries. And, these are almost all jobs for those with lower educational levels. Thus tourism provides a contribution to the mixed labour situation in the region.

Differences among the largest cities

The table below gives a picture of the enormous growth in the tourist sector in The Netherlands and in Amsterdam over the past decades. An important percentage of the growth in city tourism is concentrated in Amsterdam. In 2010 Amsterdam drew 5.3 million hotel visitors. The Hague (680,000),

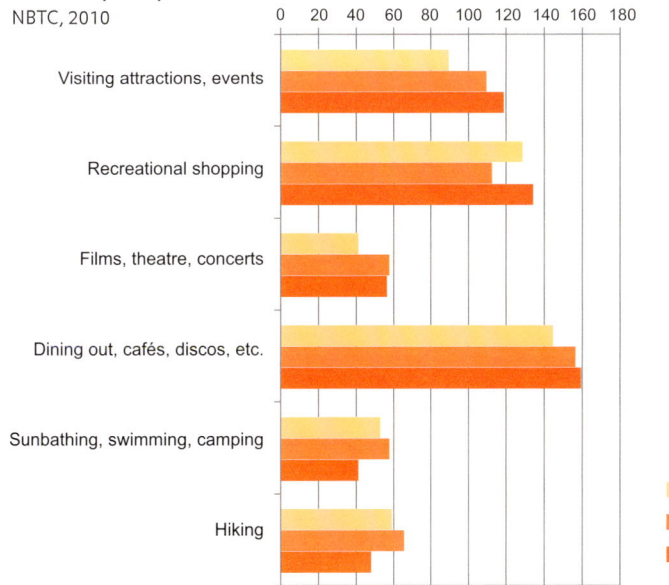

Development in popular day activities 1995-2007 in millions of participants
NBTC, 2010

Legend:
- 1995-1996
- 2001-2002
- 2006-2007

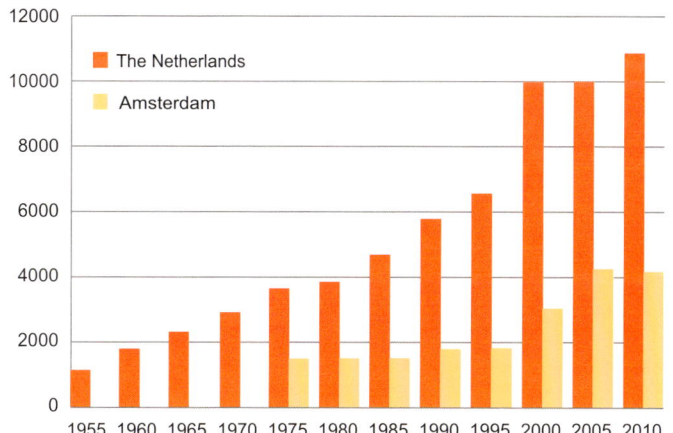

Development in numbers of foreign visitors to The Netherlands and Amsterdam 1955-2010
CBS and O+S Amsterdam

Legend:
- The Netherlands
- Amsterdam

Rotterdam (630,000) and Utrecht (290,000) lagged far behind. Tourism in Amsterdam is also much more international. While the share of Dutch visitors to the other cities is about 50%, in Amsterdam it is only 20%. The foreign tourists to Amsterdam also come from farther away: Japan, the U.S. and Australia are strongly represented. The reasons for their visits are also more diverse. In 2005, 40% of the tourists to Amsterdam came for business reasons.[9] That is much higher than in the other cities.

The tourist infrastructure in the city reflects its international attraction. Not only does Amsterdam have far and away the largest number of top attractions and the most heavily visited museums in the country, but the city also has the most supporting facilities. Roughly 70% of the hotels in the four largest cities are found in Amsterdam. The number of cafés, coffee shops and restaurants is also exceptionally high. Although Amsterdam is not known as an international shopping destination, the selection of stores in the luxury and specialist leisure sector is the widest. Finally, the large number of taxis in the city can be explained by the number of tourists (including those visiting for business reasons). The strong position of the city makes Amsterdam the core region for Dutch city tourism.

Score per function

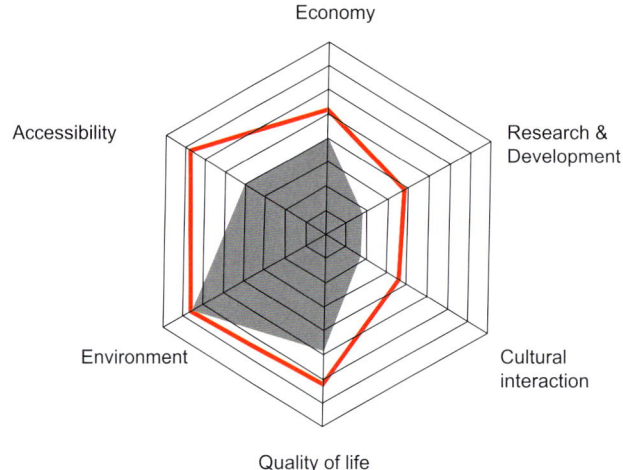

Amsterdam's scores by function and by actor in the *Global Power City Index 2012*

Score per actor

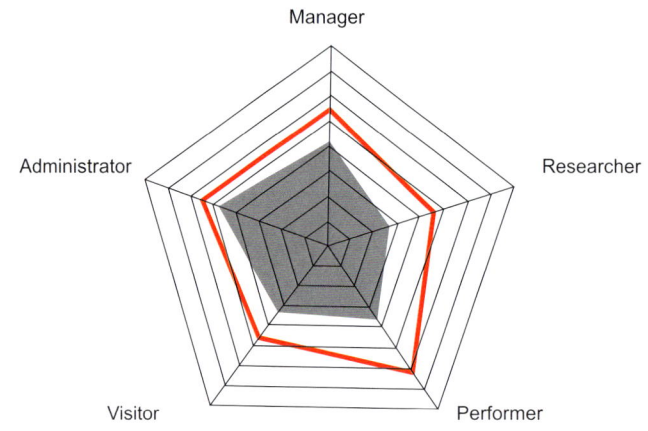

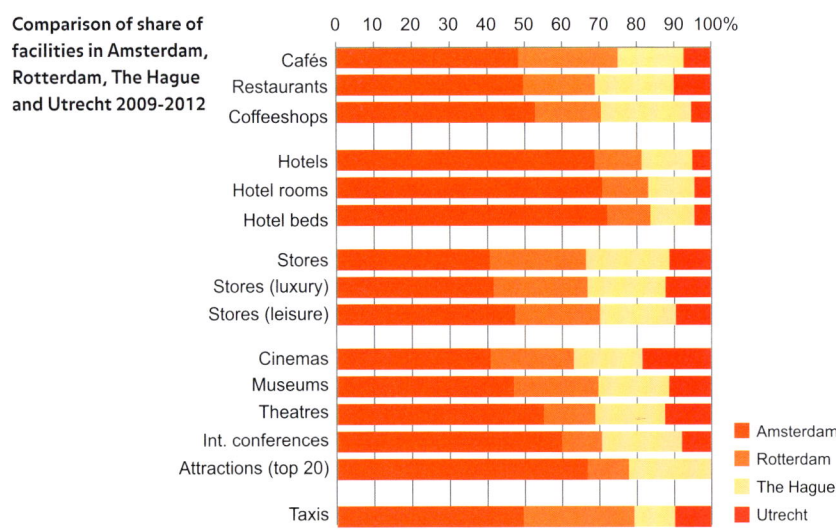

Comparison of share of facilities in Amsterdam, Rotterdam, The Hague and Utrecht 2009-2012

- Amsterdam
- Rotterdam
- The Hague
- Utrecht

New round, new challenges

Within Europe, the position of Amsterdam is more open to challenge than it is at the national level. It is true that for years now Amsterdam has played a role in the top ten European destinations, but the growth of tourism in other, particularly Eastern and Southern European cities has been much greater.[10] On the basis of Toumis's data, the number of overnight stays in Amsterdam in 2009 was comparable with cities such as Vienna, Munich and Hamburg,

Culture clusters in the four largest cities

while cities such as Barcelona, Madrid and Prague lie far ahead of the city.[11]

The conclusions of the Japanese Global Power City Index are interesting in this regard.[12] In that research, 35 world cities are ranked on the basis of 69 indicators. At first glance, Amsterdam appears to do well. It stands in seventh place in the world, and fourth in Europe, and together with Berlin, Vienna, Zurich, Frankfurt and Madrid forms the upper-middle group of Europe (the frontrunners being London and Paris).[13] Against this general high score however stands its low ranking with regard to visitors. Further examination shows that Amsterdam chiefly scores high on liveability, environmental issues and accessibility (infrastructure), but has relatively few 'cultural interactions'.

By 'cultural interactions' the Japanese researchers mean 'trendsetting potential' (Amsterdam comes in at 12th place), 'accommodation environment' (26th), 'resources for attracting visitors' (7th), 'shopping and dining' (29th), and 'volume of interaction' (22nd). Amsterdam scores relatively low in comparison with other European cities such as Vienna and Berlin. Thus, in contrast to what the growth in tourism might lead one to expect, Amsterdam has no strong tourist infrastructure. There is a danger that the city profits from the drawing power of the Ring Canals, its Old Masters and tolerant drug policy, but will fail to invest in its attractiveness, in terms of the supporting facilities (hotels, cuisine, shops, public transit) and in the possibilities for interaction. It is therefore of the utmost importance to stimulate cultural interaction.[14] To get a sharp picture of the present state of affairs, and of developments, in the following sections we will survey the city's tourist interaction environments. The analysis will not be limited to Amsterdam, but also involve the other three largest cities.

The largest cities of The Netherlands have an immense range of cultural attractions, which are difficult to assign to obvious categories. The Cultural Council, for instance, distinguishes at least fourteen sectors.[15] Far from all of these sectors require specific buildings. That is true for the performing arts and film (auditoriums), the visual arts (museums and galleries) and for libraries and archives (depots). Performances are generally given in the evening; exhibitions, libraries and archives are for the most part open in the daytime. Museums have the greatest reach. In addition to local and regional visitors, they draw national and international visitors. Museums therefore form the core of the culture selection, in the perspective of stimulating city tourism, and are a good starting point for an analysis of culture clusters.

The oldest still existing museum in the Netherlands is Teyler's Museum, in Haarlem. The museum was founded in 1784 from the legacy of Pieter Teyler van der Hulst, and displays a magnificent collection of 'objects of science and art'. The next apex came with the opening of the Rijksmuseum on Amsterdam's Museumplein in 1885. Amsterdam's Stedelijk Museum followed in 1895. Municipal museums were also opened in the other lager cities. The Gemeentemuseum in The Hague opened in 1935 with the Mondrians from Slijper's collection. In the same year the Boijmans collection, which had been housed in the Schielandhuis since 1849, was moved to the new building of Rotterdam's Boijmans-Van Beuningen Museum on the Witte de Withstraat. Other large private collections formed the basis for a whole series of later national museums, including the Palace Het Loo, the Mauritshuis, the Mesdag Collection and the Kröller-Müller Museum. In the 1980s and 1990s the number of museums in The Netherlands increased sharply, to at least 942 in 1997. Since then the total has fallen back to 773, in 2007.[16]

The illustration on page 42 shows where the 50 largest museums in The Netherlands are located. The four large cities in the Randstad – Amsterdam, Rotterdam, The Hague and Utrecht – each have three or more of these museums. Amsterdam stands out above the others with 12 of the 50 largest museums. (Actually, thirteen, because in 2009, the Stedelijk Museum, which normally would have been on the list, was temporarily closed for rebuilding.) Moreover, Amsterdam has all five of the largest museums on the list.

Many of the museums are part of a cluster of cultural amenities. The oldest culture cluster in The Netherlands is Amsterdam's Museumplein. With the 1885 opening of the Rijksmuseum, designed by the architect P.J.H. Cuypers, the collections of the royal family, the City of Amsterdam and the National Print Cabinet were merged into a collection that give a picture of 'Dutch culture'. The site around it was used for international exhibitions in 1883, 1887 and 1895. In part as a result of the success of these events, the site was kept open and, with the construction of the Concertgebouw (A.L. Van Gendt, architect, 1888) and the Stedelijk Museum (A.W. Weissman, architect, 1895) subsequently developed into a culture plaza. After countless plans for new cultural functions, such as an opera house, the Van Gogh Museum followed in 1973, in a building designed by Gerrit Rietveld.

In recent decades there has once again been heavy investment in the Museumplein. After the realization of a new foyer and entry for the Concertgebouw (Pi de Bruijn, architect, 1988), the 1995 redesign of the open space according to plans by the Danish landscape architect Anderson provided a powerful stimulus for the renewal of the cultural buildings surrounding it. The 'shortest motorway' running through the site disappeared, and the Van Gogh Museum was the first to expand with a new wing (Kisho Kurokawa, architect, 1998). The

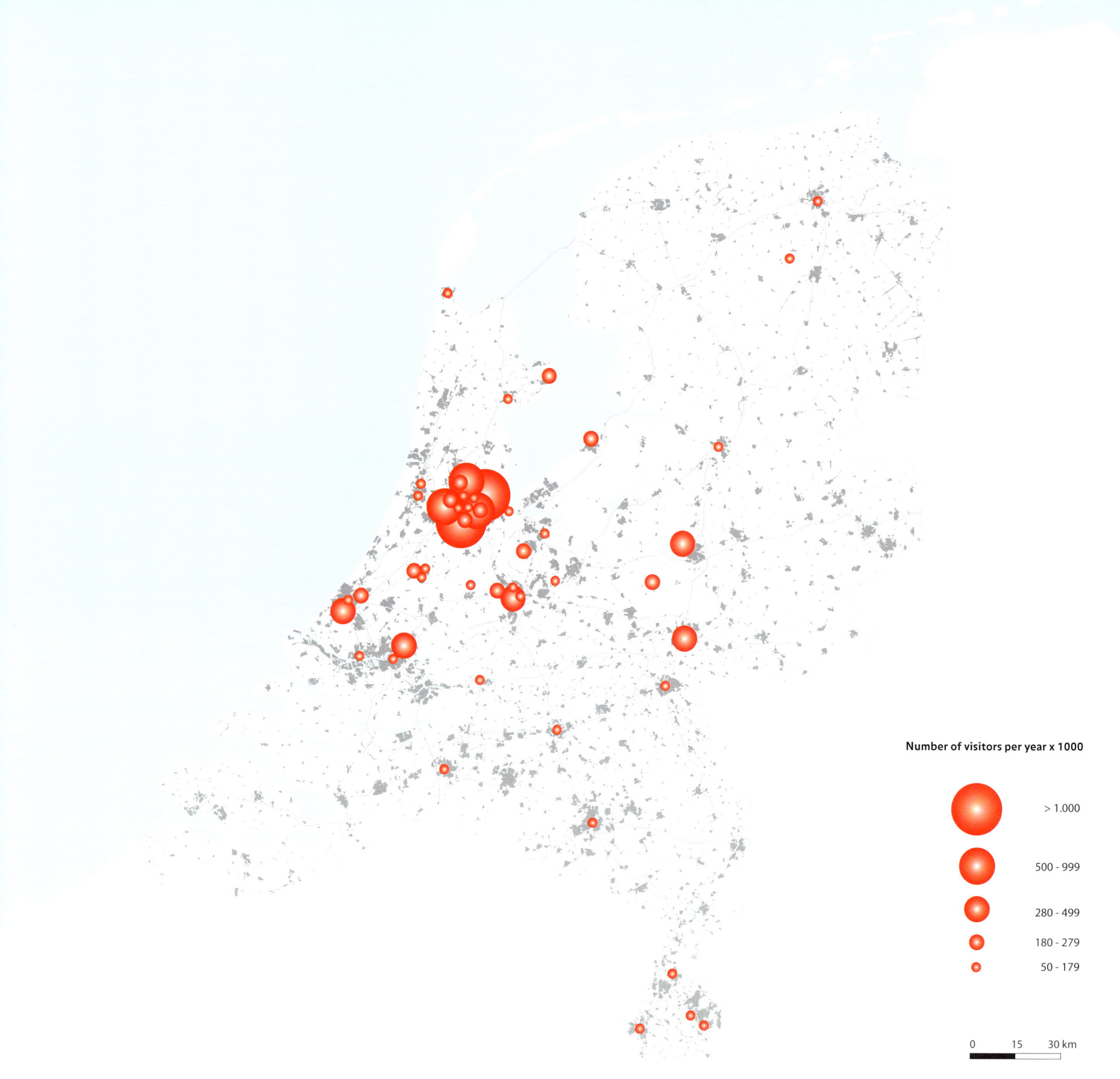

Number of visitors per year x 1000

> 1.000

500 - 999

280 - 499

180 - 279

50 - 179

0   15   30 km

Top 50 Museums (visitor numbers)	G4	Holland	Other
1 Van Gogh Museum	1,432,500		
2 Anne Frank House	1,050,000		
3 Rijksmuseum	900,000		
4 Hermitage Amsterdam	650,000		
5 NEMO	504,000		
6 Netherlands Open Air Museum			440,000
7 Netherlands Railway Museum	350,000		
8 Palace Het Loo			320,900
9 Boijmans van Beuningen Museum	300,000		
10 Hague Gemeentemuseum	290,000		
11 Kröller Müller Museum			275,000
12 Naturalis		270,000	
13 Mauritshuis	233,400		
14 ZuiderzeeMuseum		221,000	
15 Castle de Haar			201,213
16 Amsterdam Historical Museum	201,000		
17 National Air Museum Aviodrome			200,500
18 Rembrandthuis	200,000		
19 Inst. for Sound and Vision			200,000
20 Tropical Museum	197,000		
21 FOAM	180,000		
22 Museon	175,000		
23 Singer Laren	152,750		
24 Castle Hoensbroek			145,150
25 Military Aviation Museum			145,000
26 Centraal Museum Utrecht	135,000		
27 Oude Kerk	133,250		
28 Maritiem Museum Rotterdam	132,000		
29 National Antiquities Museum		130,000	
30 Jewish Historical Museum	130,000		
31 Museum de Fundatie			130,000
32 Van Abbe Museum			121,761
33 Museum Slot Loevestein			120,000
34 Steam Tram Museum Hoorn Medemblik		120,000	
35 Muiderslot		115,000	
36 Liberty Park			111,000
37 Nat. Museum v. Speelklok tot Pierement	110,000		
38 Teylers Museum		109,500	
39 De Nieuwe Kerk	108,000		
40 Hortus Botanicus		108,000	
41 National Prison Museum			106,100
42 Bonnefanten Museum			102,000
43 Museum Volkenkunde		100,000	
44 Discovery Center Continium			92,500
45 Breda Museum			92,000
46 Frans Hals Museum		90,000	
47 North Brabant Museum			86,000
48 Stedelijk Museum Schiedam		83,100	
49 Museum Het Vlakhof			82,500
50 Marinemuseum		80,000	

Top-50 Museums 2010 [17]

Stedelijk Museum (Benthem-Crouwel, architects, 2012) and the Rijksmuseum (Cruz & Ortis, architects, 2013) were also thoroughly renovated and expanded. After these museums reopen, it is expected that the cultural institutions around the Museumplein will attract four million visitors per year. With that, the cluster will rival the Efteling amusement park as the leading attraction in The Netherlands.

The importance of the Museumplein is underscored by the large number of events held there. Fine examples from the past are the three international exhibitions. More recently the Museumplein has provided a site for countless festivals, demonstrations and performances. The Boulevard of Broken Dreams, the Uitmarkt, the anti-cruise missile demonstration of 1981, and the mass welcome of the victorious Ajax football club and the Dutch championship team have become the stuff of legend. If the events on Museumplein are counted into visitor numbers, then it is unarguably the most popular destination, and largest culture cluster in The Netherlands.

The introduction of cluster strategies

The rise of cluster strategies in the cultural sector in The Netherlands and Europe as part of urban revitalization practice has been comprehensively described by Hans Mommaas.[18] In the 1990s countless city planners seized upon now empty industrial and harbour complexes to develop combinations of new cultural facilities. Familiar examples include the Westergasfabriek in Amsterdam, the Verkade Factory in Den Bosch, the Muller Pier in Rotterdam and the Caballero Factory in The Hague. Some focused explicitly on visitors and the expansion of cultural life and entertainment, while others focused more on attracting creative industries, and are therefore often combined with facilities for culture production and business spaces.[19]

Rotterdam was the first to discover the potential of new culture clusters. Rotterdam had had a maritime museum since 1873. The collection however floated around the city until the Maritime Museum, designed by Wim Quist, opened in 1986 on the Leuvehaven. Together with the Harbour Museum on the quay of the Leuvehaven, realized at the same time, and the IMAX theatre, it formed an appealing new culture cluster. In it, the square at the head of the Leuvehaven, designated as the 'window on the river' in the Basic Plan for the city's postwar reconstruction, with its dramatic sculpture by Zadkine, The Destroyed City, obtained a new function. It became a 'window on the past'. This culture cluster attracts about 250,000 visitors annually.[20]

In the years that followed a second culture cluster was developed in conjunction with the existing Boijmans-Van Beuningen Museum, designed by A. van der Steur.[21] In what has come to be called Museumpark, next to the Boijmans, a whole series of new institutions were realized: the NAi (Coenen, 1993), the Kunsthal (OMA, 1992), the Natural History Museum (Mecanoo/Erick van Egeraat, 1990-1995), and the Chabot Museum (Baas and Stokla, 1938, converted to a museum 1993). The park itself was designed by Rem Koolhaas and Yves Brunier, and was also delivered in 1993.

The proposal for the construction of the Museumpark was launched in the Binnenstadsplan Rotterdam 1985-1995. It designated three development sites: the Centre, the Water City and the Park Triangle. The Museumpark is part of the Park Triangle, and is connected with the centre by the Westersingel and the Witte de Withstraat. The cultural function was enhanced by the construction of new museums in and around the Park. At the same time the Park provides space for open-air festivals, such as Poetry International. Rotterdam embraced city tourism.[22]

← **Locations of the top 50 Dutch museums**
(in terms of visitor numbers)
Nederlandse Museumvereniging 2010

The development of the Museumpark built upon a series of successful events on the Land van Hoboken in the 1950s. The Land van Hoboken was originally a private estate on the Westzeedijk, around the country home Dijkzigt. The City of Rotterdam purchased the site in 1924. The green wedge connecting the city centre with the 19th century Park aan de Maas, designed by Zocher, is characteristic of the 1927 urban development plan by the city architect Witteveen. To finance the purchase, part of the land was already built upon prior to World War II.[23] After the War, to meet the demand for amusement and relaxation the Land van Hoboken was used for temporary events. The Nenijtohal was rebuilt again for this purpose.[24] The AHOY' harbour exhibition in the summer of 1950 drew at least 1.5 million visitors in two months. The

↑ **Kunsthal, in the Museumpark in Rotterdam**
Design: O.M.A.

← **Post card of the aerial tram and maquette during C'70 in Rotterdam**

44

E'55 National Energy Manifestation followed in 1955, the first Floriade in 1960. With the development of the Museumpark in the 1990s this site in the city received a more permanent significance as a culture cluster.

The fourth great event in Rotterdam was C'70, which was mentioned in the introduction to this chapter, with the theme of communication. Although the famous pop festival was held in the Kralingse Bos, the newly reconstructed city centre was the foremost stage. The magnificent but 'cold' boulevards like the Coolsingel and Weena were completely redesigned with pedestrian spaces and pavilions for exhibitions, corporate presentations and cafés and restaurants, and, to complete the attractions, a dolphinarium and a fun fair. An aerial cable-way afforded a wonderful overview of an enormous maquette of the harbour expansions in Botlek and Europoort. The shopping precincts were thus converted into a tourist destination.

In the course of the 1970s and '80s this expansion of the programme of the city centre became a central element in the policy of many cities. In the 1990s a boom in new cultural buildings and investment in culture clusters followed. The numbers of visitors rose correspondingly.

The rise of the event

The increase in the number of visitors to events was at least as spectacular.[25] In 2005 a total of more than two million visitors came to the Uitmarkt, the Queen's Birthday, the Bloemencorso, Gay Pride and the Holland Festival in Amsterdam. Sail, with an estimated 2.5 million visitors, is not included in this count. The number of visitors for the Queen's Birthday in Amsterdam almost doubled between 2003 and 2005. Smaller festivals also grew rapidly. For instance, in 2001 20,000 visitors came for the Jordaan Festival, in 2005 60,000.

Various explanations for the growth in the number of events can be found in the literature.[26] The increase in spendable income and the rising percentage of one and two person households encourages spending more leisure time outside of the home. Moreover, after 1985 free time became scarcer. In 2005 the average Dutchman had 44.7 hours of free time per week, over four hours less than in 1985.[27] With this, the increase in free time described in the introductory chapter saw its first cautious downturn. The scarcity of free time encourages money-intensive and time-extensive leisure activities. Visits to events fit perfectly with that trend.

The illustration on page 46 shows where the 100 largest events in The Netherlands are held. Here too there is clearly a concentration in the Randstad.[28] While the largest museums in The Netherlands draw the highest percentage of foreign visitors, that is not the case for the largest events. Massive events like the Tilburg Carnival chiefly draw domestic visitors. The Rotterdam summer Carnival and the Dunya Festival are also visited primarily by Dutchmen.

There are major differences in the way in which events are woven into the city. Many large music festivals, like Lowlands and Dance Valley, take place on specialized sites on the edge of, or outside the cities. Some of these sites, like the Westergasfabriek and the NDSM site in Amsterdam, have developed into multi-faceted culture clusters. Other events, such as the Uitmarkt, the parade welcoming St. Nicholas, and the Canal Parade, are integrated right into the city.

In terms of their form, events can be categorized as point, line and plane events. Point events take place around indoor and outdoor stages, in spacious areas such as squares and open fields, and in stadiums or similar facilities. Because public attention is focused on one point, obstacles are very disruptive. A line event is an event which moves along a previously planned route. Visitors are generally spread along the whole course, but there are often concentrations at the starting point and end of the route. Marathons, auto races, the Canal Parade, carnival parades, demonstrations and flower

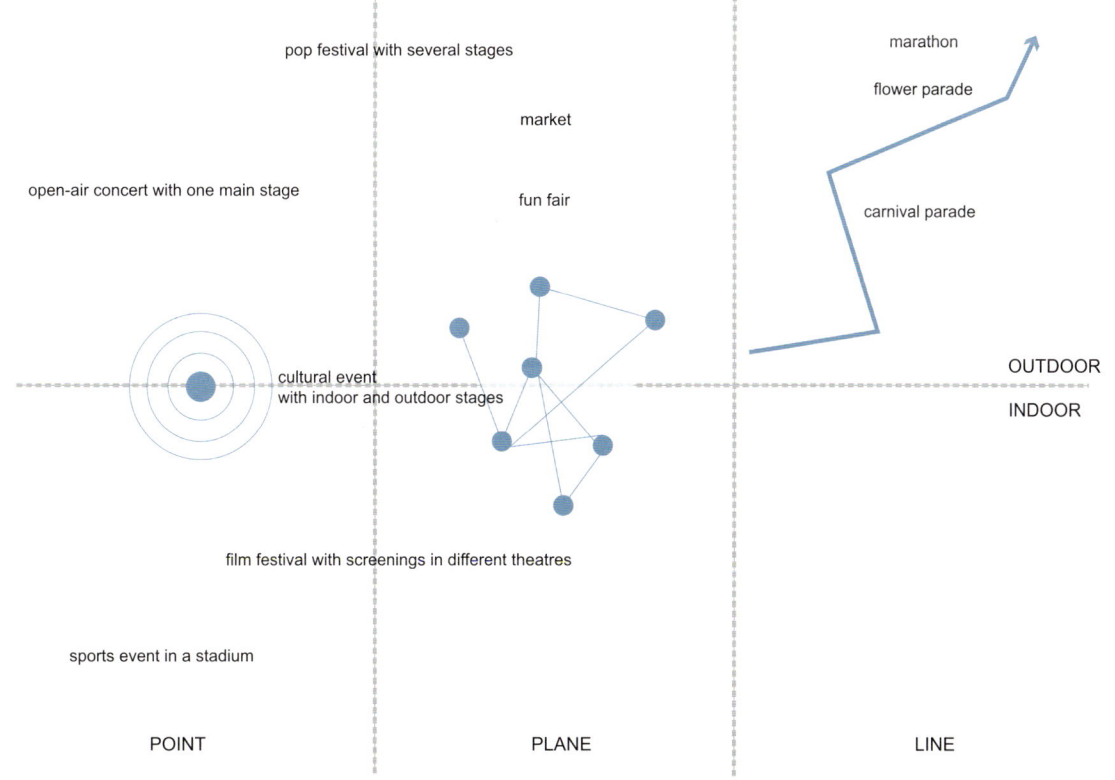

Types of indoor and outdoor events: point, plane, line

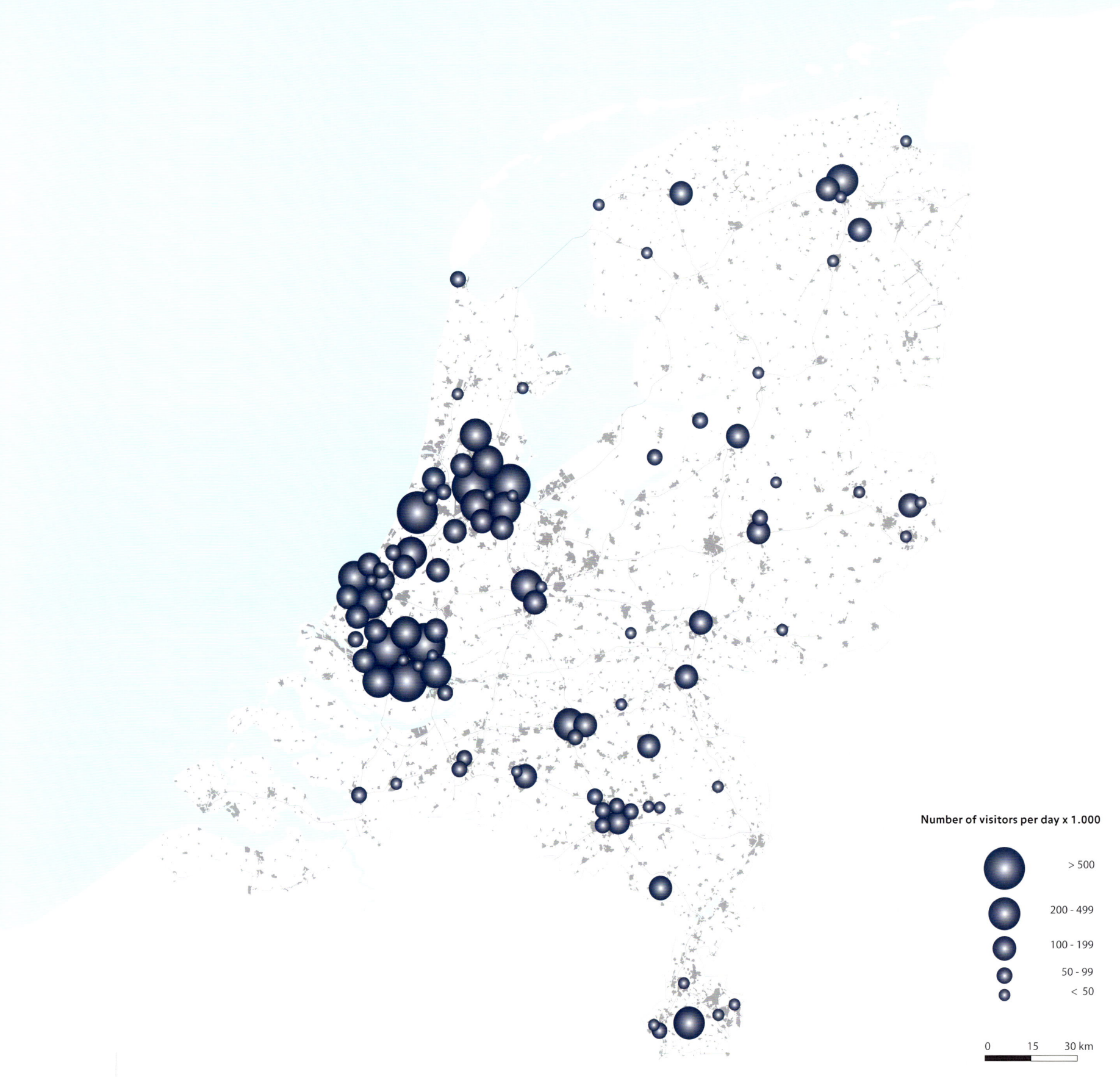

Number of visitors per day x 1.000

> 500

200 - 499

100 - 199

50 - 99

< 50

0   15   30 km

pageants are examples of line events. They extend through a large area, and the impact on the use and accessibility of the area where the line event is taking place is therefore considerable. In plane events, it is the visitors who move. Markets, carnivals and The Parade are examples of plane events. Plane events require a large, continuous spaces or clearly defined routes between different places. Museum Nights and the Canal Festival cover a large area; Oerol even covers a whole Wadden island.

Point and plane events often take place within culture clusters. They can enrich the programme, but they sometimes also will conflict with the use and atmosphere of the surrounding facilities. Line events often cover a larger area. In many cases the larger public spaces in culture clusters will function as beginning or end points.

Culture clusters in the four largest cities
In order to obtain insight into the structure and functioning of culture clusters, an analysis has been made of the location of all the major cultural institutions in the four largest cities: museums, theatres, music venues, discussion centres and libraries. Subsequently clusters are distinguished. The point of departure for this is a strict definition of culture clusters: a culture cluster has at least three cultural institutions within a walking distance of not more than five minutes from each other, and draws at least 500,000 visitors per year. Visitors to events are not counted into this figure.

According to this definition there are 18 culture clusters in the four largest cities: two in Utrecht, three in The Hague, four in Rotterdam, and nine in Amsterdam. For each city we examine aspects such as the location and structure of the clusters in the city, their domestic and international visitor numbers, and daytime and evening use. Ester Heiman of Stipo – Team for Urban Development – has received a commission from the Ministry of Infrastructure and the Environment to investigate how the clusters are used and experienced. The method used is explained in the text in the box below. An impression of the results is given for each city. The first conclusion in Chapter 5 is drawn from this research.

Urban anthropology: the everyday experience of culture clusters

The reality of a map is different from that of the street. Surfacing the stories from everyday reality, the lived-in city, and connecting this with the reality of professionals from the planned city, is the work of urban anthropology. It is precisely these stories which can refine the thinking about culture clusters and provide it with more colour. It is then the combination of knowledge from the planned city and insights from the lived-in city that provides ammunition for a strong development strategy for culture clusters.

For this reason the Ministry of Infrastructure and the Environment asked Stipo to complement the research by the TU Delft with an urban anthropological dimension. To do this, Stipo organized the Anthropologist in your Own City event. A total of 150 professionals went out on the streets of the four largest cities to survey visitors personally, to determine how the visitors experienced the culture clusters. How did they find their way there? How did they organize their day programme? Did it make a difference that the institutions were close to one another? What led them to appreciate their visit to the city and the cluster, and come back again?

The anthropological field work took place in the form of four 'relays' on four successive Fridays in February. In each city three shifts of local professionals went out on the streets, from early morning to late evening. A short crash course in urban anthropology research methods, such as making mental maps, conducting street interviews and being a participant observer, guaranteed that all the members of the teams were trained for their work. In each city there was a focus on one, or sometimes two culture clusters. In Utrecht that was the Museum Quarter and the connection with the city centre. In Amsterdam it was the connection between the Oosterdok, Waterlooplein and Plantage cluster. In The Hague the focus was on the Spuiplein cluster and its connection with the rest of the city. In Rotterdam the focus was on Museumpark and its relation with the immediate vicinity.

The following pages display a selection of the results from the fieldwork in the form of a logbook, which brings the culture clusters to life, as it were. On the one hand, the portraits of the visitors make it clear how diverse and capricious the behaviour and motivations of the visitors is. At the same time the threads which run through their stories can be disentangled to provide a typical picture for each city, which evokes questions and new directions in the thinking about development strategies for the various clusters.

← Locations of the top 100 events, with the highest number of visitors per day

Legend for pages 48-66

- cultural institutions
- cafés, restaurants
- retail stores
- hotels
- art education
- walking distance: core 2 min. ring 5 min.

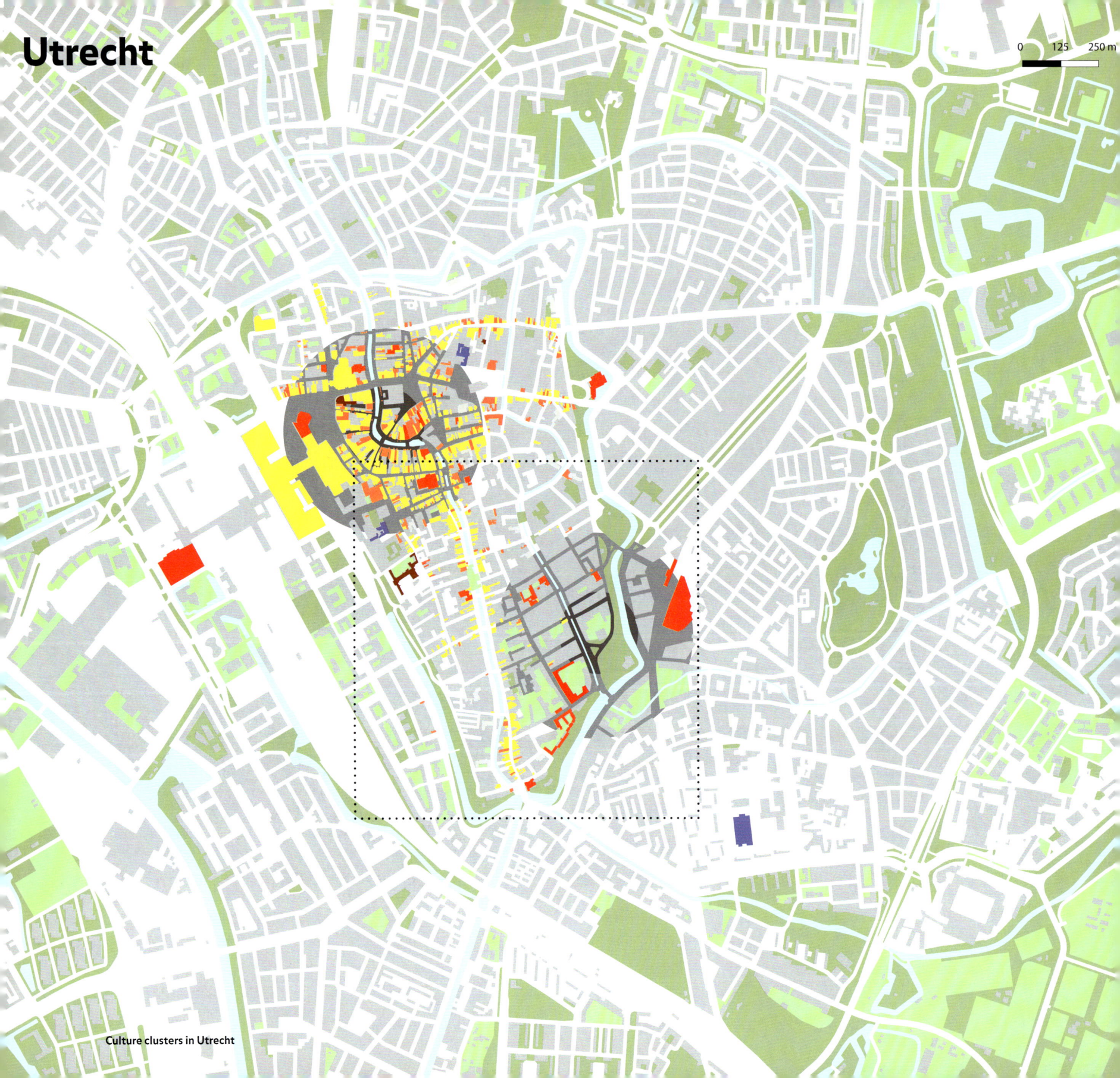

Utrecht

0   125   250 m

Culture clusters in Utrecht

Utrecht logbook

Convenient for wandering

9:30 a.m. Central Station People walking to the Museum Quarter sometimes deliberately wander off the route recommended by the directional signs. They turn into a narrow alleyway or discover the hidden beauties of medieval courtyards, while the tower of the Dom looming over the city assures that they never lose their bearings. This convenience in wandering was listed by many visitors as the most attractive thing about their visit.

100% Dutch?

10:50 a.m. Lange Nieuwstraat Today it is primarily Dutch senior citizens visiting the Museum Quarter. A bit further up, near the Dom, we found a Swiss, who didn't know that there were museums in Utrecht. The international visitors who we encounter in the Museum Quarter are almost all Asians, who come specifically for the Dick Bruna House, because of the popularity of Nijntje in their own countries. The fact that there are fewer tourists than in Amsterdam is something that both Dutch and foreign visitors appreciate about Utrecht.

Railway Museum: a stand-alone?

1:50 p.m. Railway Museum We speak primarily with families who have come by car or the shuttle train, and are going home directly after their visit to the museum. They think that the museum is a long way from the city centre. Yet some do decide to walk back to the Central Station, as the shuttle train only runs once an hour. Would more people walk back to the centre if there were, for instance, a Nijntje -hunt from the Railway Museum that would lead past the Dick Bruna House on the way to Central Station?

Sleeping over in Utrecht

9:30 p.m. Rechtbank Hotel The visitors which we uncover with some difficulty in the cafés and hotel lobbies are invited for a lecture series at the University, and an exchange student with his friends from Colombia. Most of the visitors came for one day, and because of the good train connections are snug at home, or have gone to another city to overnight.

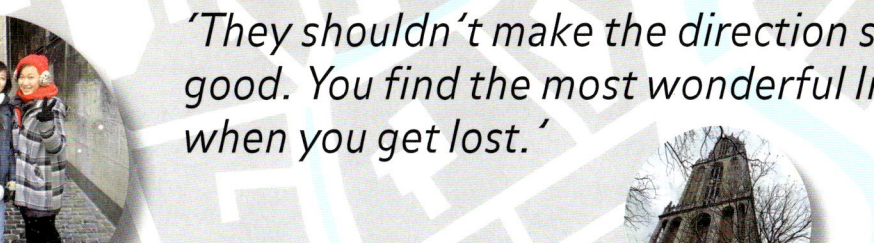

'They shouldn't make the direction signs too good. You find the most wonderful little streets when you get lost.'

'In Amsterdam everything is so massive and there are tourists everywhere. Here it's nice and quiet.'

'I want to decide for myself if I go the shortest or nicest way. These signs are too coercive.'

'My husband and son are going to the Railway Museum and my daughter and I to Hoog Catharijne.'

'All the exciting things in Utrecht happen outside the centre.'

On the basis of the working definition, two culture clusters can be distinguished in Utrecht. The cultural institutions in the heart of the city form the Vredenburg Cluster, and the institutions in the southern corner of the old city the second, the Museum Quarter. There are three separate major institutions which lie outside these clusters: the Beatrix Theatre, Tivoli and the Stadsschouwburg. The latter two attract less than 300,000 visitors each. The Beatrix Theatre often has more than 600,000 visitors per year.

VREDENBURGCLUSTER

The cultural institutions in the heart of the city are subordinate to the many stores and cafés and restaurants. Nor do they lie together in one location, but are spread through the area. They appear to profit more from interaction with the other functions than they do from the other nearby cultural institutions. The cluster will thus not easily be experienced as a culture cluster. Their integration into the city is optimal, but better profiling of the cultural institutions could perhaps strengthen the interaction between the city and the institutions even more.

The Vredenburg Music Centre is the largest institution, and stands on a square with the same name. It can be reached through the Hoog Catharijne shopping centre. As a matter of course, visitors from outside the city who come by train will not make use of the square. The Music Centre is an evening function. Interaction with cafés and restaurants is an obvious possibility, but hardly appears to be realized. On the other hand, the national Speelklok Museum, Dom Tower and Aboriginal Art Museum are institutions which function during the day. Theatre Kikker and the Werftheater are also found in this cluster. Together they attract a respectable 500,000 visitors per year. The well-patronized Central Library is also in this cluster. It accounts for about half the visitors. International visitors come chiefly for the Dom Tower, and hardly if any go to the Music Centre.

MUSEUM QUARTER

The various institutions in the Museum Quarter are also spread out. Unlike the heart of the city, the shopping and dining programme here is limited. The Railway Museum, the largest institution in the cluster, tends to stand alone. The Oude Gracht could function as a strong link between the cluster and the city. Strengthening the shopping and dining functions along this route, and good hookups between the institutions on it, appear to offer better possibilities than adding functions through the whole Quarter. The functions are all museums, thus are oriented to day visitors. The cluster attracts relatively few visitors, about 550,000 per year, of whom foreign visitors are a negligible number. For instance, only 1% of the Railway Museum's visitors are foreigners.

Vredenburg cluster

Museum quarter

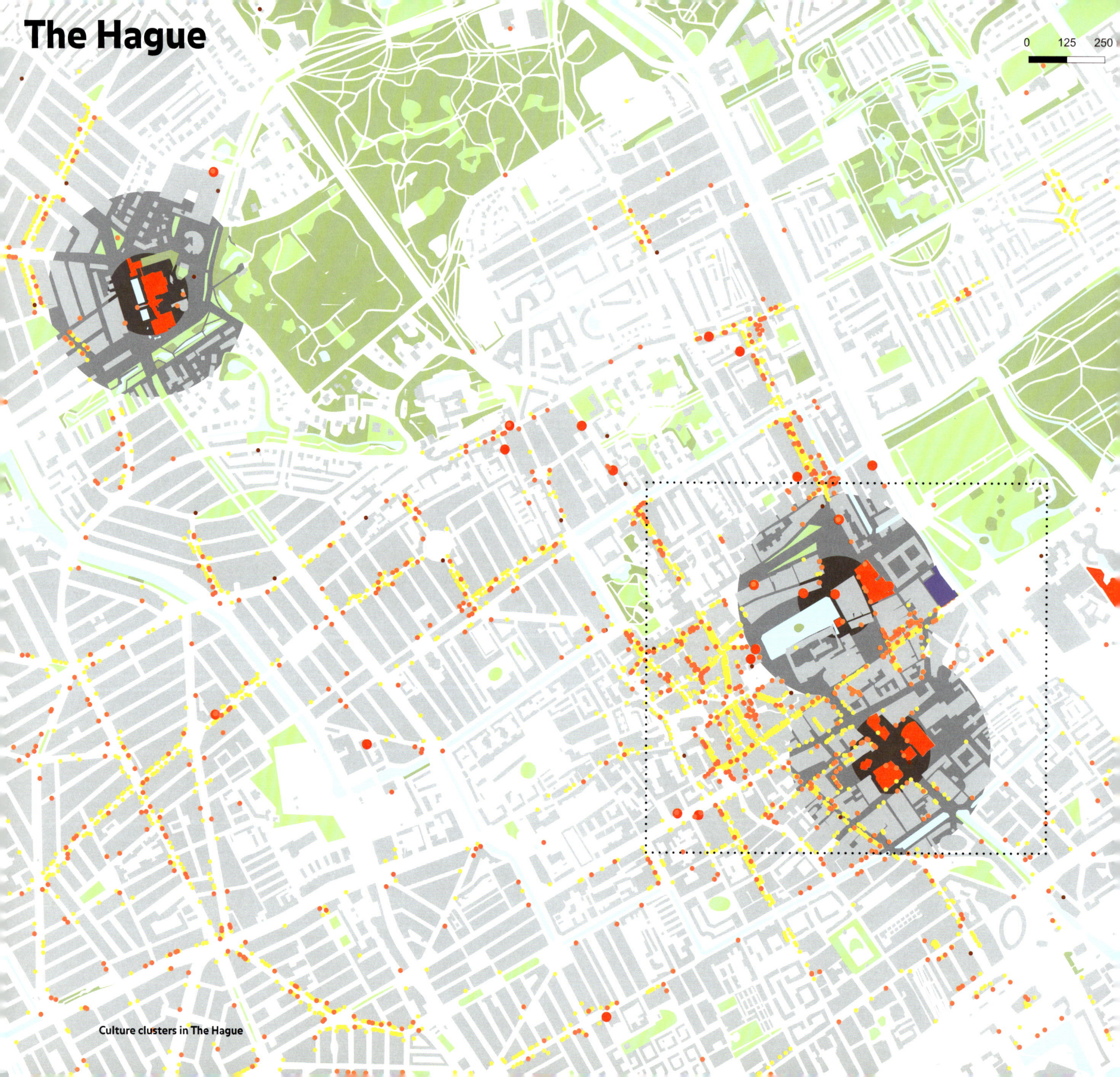

The Hague

0 125 250

Culture clusters in The Hague

The Hague Logbook

Bits of the city

10:13 a.m. Turfmarkt A woman from Nijmegen is looking around her, map in hand. This is not her first visit, but she still does not understand 'how the different pieces of the city fit together'. We often hear that visitors get lost on their way to their destinations. However, it is never for long, and is rarely experienced as frustrating – the distances are too short for that.

There is a feeling that there is little spontaneous 'wandering'; everyone is on their way to their destination in one of the 'bits of the city'. One person comes specifically for the Binnenhof and the Mauritshuis, another to go shopping around the Grote Markt. In the evening, some people come specifically for the theatre on the Spuiplein, others for fish dinners on the beach at Scheveningen. If you ask people where the heart of The Hague is, you get different answers, chiefly reflecting their destination.

Surprising mix

7:30 p.m. Spui Where the Spui is quiet through the day, used primarily as a short cut or for skating, in the evening it is a good bit more lively. A couple from Amsterdam came to The Hague specifically for a theatre performance, but will certainly come back again to see more of the city. We speak with a number of other people who are surprised by what The Hague has to offer. Its image of a stately, dignified city with a lot of cultural history remains the biggest draw. Visitors come here from all over the world, and that is also what they respond to the most. The diversity of residents and expats, the mix between old and new architecture, and a versatile selection of shops and restaurants then guarantees that visitors will be surprised by the city.

'The Hague has three centres: historic (Binnenhof), cultural (Spuiplein) and economic (Grote Markt).'

'This is where the government is. If you haven't come here, you can't have your say.'

'There is something to do everywhere, but how you get there is not always clear.'

'We had no idea how much there is to do here. We're coming back!'

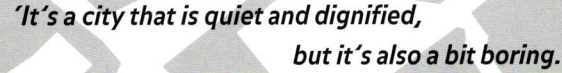

'The Hague is a lot of disconnected pieces.'

'It's a city that is quiet and dignified, but it's also a bit boring.'

The Hague has three culture clusters, two in the centre and one lying eccentrically in the International Zone. In addition, the Circus Theatre attracts a large number of visitors to Scheveningen with its musicals.

BINNENHOF CLUSTER

There are various cultural institutions to be visited around the Binnenhof. During the day there is the Mauritshuis, Escher in 't Paleis, Gevangenpoort, the Hague Historical Museum and Museum Bredius; in the evening the Royal Schouwburg. The cluster is connected with the shopping district in the heart of the city by the Lange and Korte Poten. The character of the cluster is defined by the complex of government buildings, the parliament and the court.

In total, the culture cluster attracts a bit over 500,000 visitors. The Mauritshuis has the most visitors, 51% of them coming from other countries. The other institutions could benefit from that. Spatially, the cluster is a hybrid. The Royal Schouwburg and Escher in 't Paleis lie on the Voorhout; the other institutions are spread out more. Den Haag Sculptuur, the annual sculpture exhibition around the promenade on the Lange Voorhout, is a unique cultural event.

Binnenhof cluster

Mauritshuis

Spuiplein cluster

Together, the cultural institutions around the Spuiplein attract 220,000 visitors per year. That this area still counts as a culture cluster is due to the Central Library, which enlivens the cluster considerably with its one million visitors per year. Together with the Nieuwe Kerk, it attracts its public primarily through the day and in the early evening. With their performances, the other cultural institutions chiefly draw an evening and weekend audience. The share of foreign visitors to the institutions in this cluster is limited.

All the institutions have their front doors on the Spuiplein. Like the Binnenhof cluster, this cluster adjoins the central shopping and dining area of the city. The two clusters overlap. With better connections the two could strengthen each other.

Museum cluster

Various cultural institutions lie along the stately Stadhouderslaan: the Municipal Museum, Omniversum and the Fotomuseum. They are very close to one another, but do not have a collective outdoor space where visitors can linger. There are also very few supporting amenities in the vicinity. There is no obvious connection with the Frederik Hendriklaan, with its shops and restaurants. This is surprising, as the cluster attracts an average of 700,000 visitors per year. Moreover, 10% of the visitors to the Municipal Museum come from other countries. That is strikingly high for a cluster which stands so much by itself. The Worldforum Conference Centre is also in the immediate vicinity. In Chapter 3 we will discuss the relations between these institutions. The Omniversum also attracts evening visitors; the other functions, all museums, can only be visited during the day.

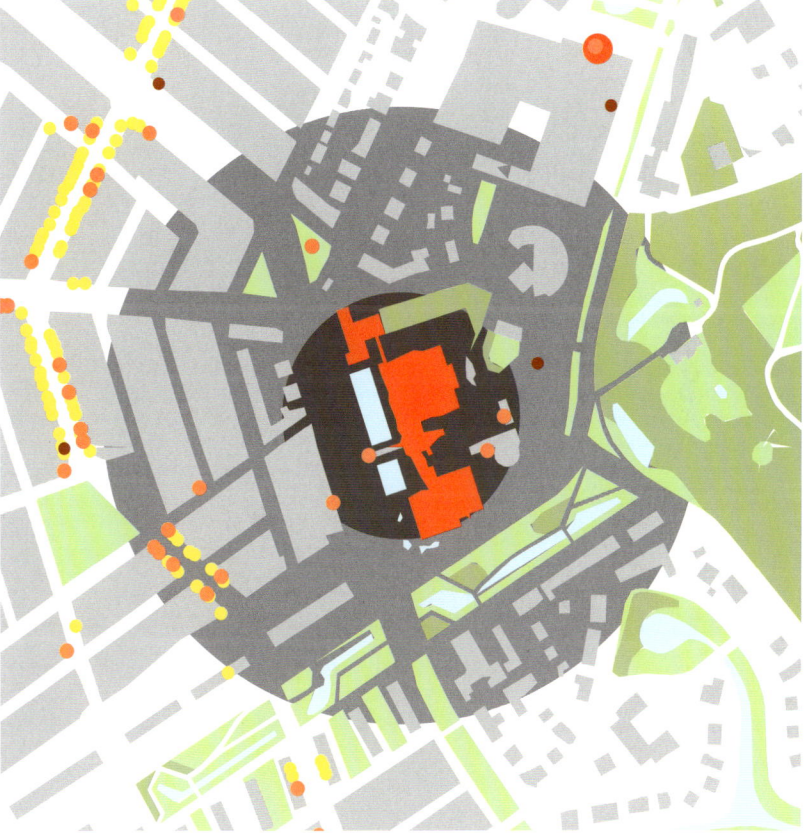

Spuiplein cluster

Museum cluster

Rotterdam

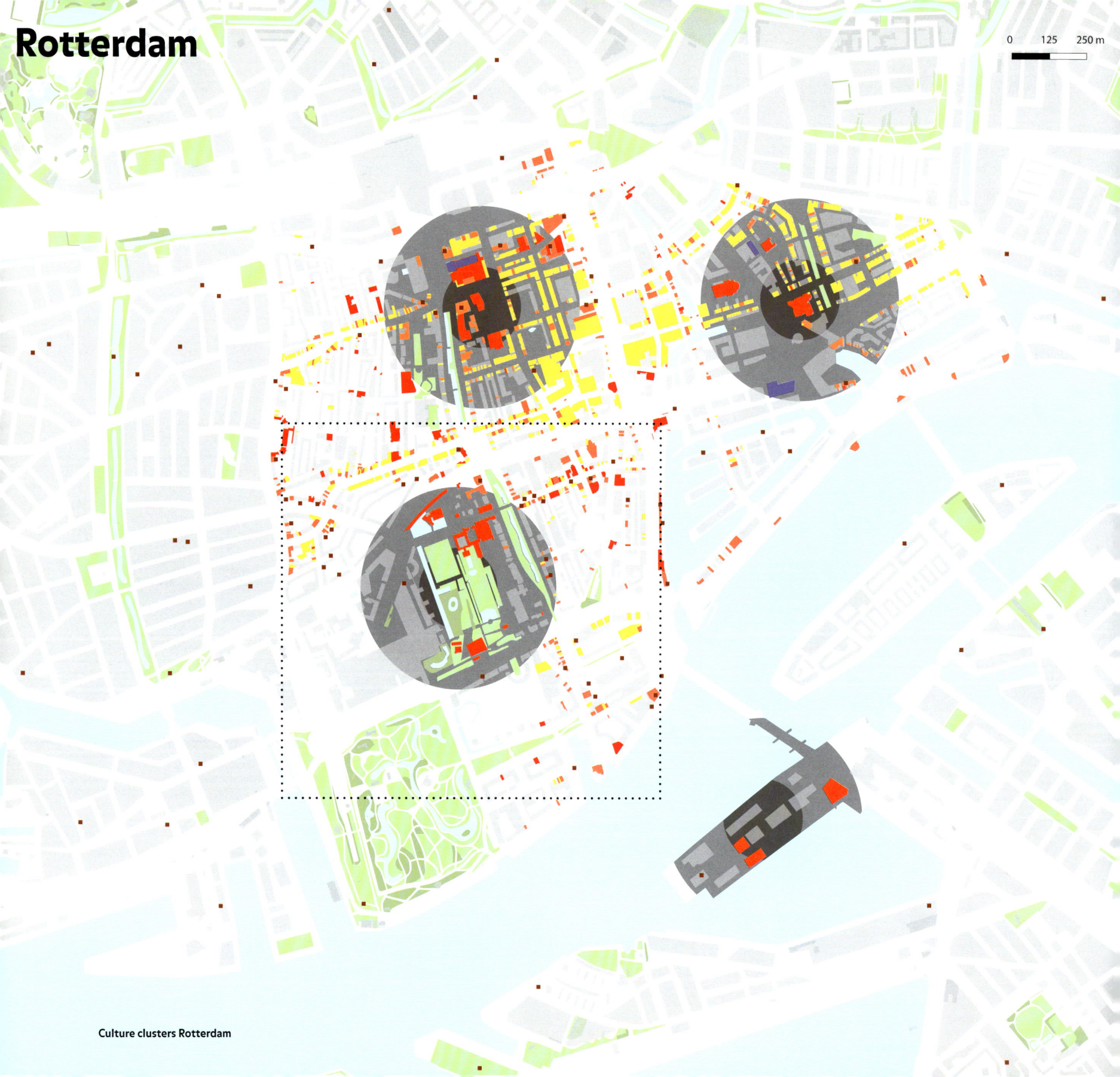

0   125   250 m

Culture clusters Rotterdam

Rotterdam logbook

Museum island?

9:50 a.m. Museumpark Several tourists are roaming around; the museums are apparently not open yet. One tourist asks where the park is. A visitor from Belgium thinks that the site for large public events is a helicopter platform the the adjoining hospital. Later in the day we also speak with many people who do not experience the Museumpark as a park: there is no grass. Anyway, the name Museumpark means little to most people, and how you get to and from it is not obvious to many visitors. The fact that there are several museums close to one another is well known, although the Boijmans and Kunsthal, and sometimes the NAi, are the only ones people are likely to know by name. People who do experience the Museumpark as a park often refer to events they have attended there, like the Parade, or the Pleinbioscoop. Apparently even after they are over, events still affect the experience of a place.

Swiss cheese city

7:45 p.m. Sneaker Shop, Witte de With-straat The owner of this sports shoe store gives directions to lots of people who are on their way from one 'district' to another. She finds that that just goes with living in Rotterdam: you have to do your best to get to know this 'Swiss cheese city', with its sometimes considerable distances between one destination and another. A Belgian family illustrates this nicely: they experience the half hour walk across the Erasmus Bridge from Hotel New York to the Kunsthal as 'typically Rotterdam'.

Old and new

9:15 p.m. Nieuwe Binnenweg A tourist from Oslo comes back every two years to see what new buildings have gone up. Like many international visitors, he comes specifically for the modern architecture. At the same time, many people admit that they are surprised by how much of Rotterdam's history is still there too, and say that it precisely that combination of old and new that makes the city exciting.

'Museumpark parking garage exit: Is this Museumpark? And where is Boijmans?'

'It was only when I started visiting a friend here that I learned how nice Rotterdam is.'

'Why are there no signs in Rotterdam that tell you about its history?'

'Because we got lost, we discovered how beautifully the old and new blend together in Rotterdam.'

'In Rotterdam I know precisely what I want to see and where I am going. In Amsterdam I wander around more.'

Rotterdam has four clusters that are spread around the city.

SCHOUWBURGPLEIN CLUSTER
The Rotterdam Schouwburg, the Doelen and the Pathé cinema are the large institutions in the Schouwburgplein cluster. Shops and restaurants around the edges of the square form the transition to the shopping area around the Lijnbaan. The Old Luxor Theatre lies in a side street. The concert halls of the Doelen and the Schouwburg primarily have an evening function. The square is also kept quite lively during the day with passers-by, the surrounding cafés and restaurants, and the audiences for afternoon screenings at the cinema. In the evening the square is transformed into an entertainment centre. The institutions in this cluster attract few foreigners, less than 1% of the over 600,000 visitors per year.

MUSEUMPARK
The institutions in this cluster lie around a park. Trees, grass and water define the atmosphere. The garden of the Boijmans-Van Beuningen Museum flows into the park. With the arrival of the NAi, the Kunsthal and the Natural History Museum in the early 1990s, it became a fully-fledged culture cluster. The cluster draws a relatively high number of foreign visitors. Depending on the exhibitions, they comprise 15 to 20% of the visitors to the Boijmans. The cluster has hardly any supplementary functions, but the Witte de Withstraat, with cafés, restaurants, shops and smaller cultural institutions lies nearby. Along with the Westersingel, it is also the most important connection with the city centre. The museums and park draw visitors during the day; in the evening it is quiet.

Schouwburgplein cluster

Museumpark

58

Binnenrotte cluster

The Binnenrotte cluster lies in the middle of the pre-Second World War city centre of Rotterdam. The library stands at the edge of the open plane and is the most important drawing factor. The other institutions are more widely spread. The National Education Museum, the St. Laurenskerk and the Mariners Museum are relatively small institutions, with something less than 50,000 visitors per year. The vicinity of the library is therefore not experienced as a cluster. The dominant function is the massive open-air market on Tuesdays and Saturdays, with over 450 stalls. The construction of a roofed-over market designed by MVRDV will reinforce this market function. The cluster lies at the end of the shopping district on the Hoogstraat. The many visitors to the market and library provide a great opportunity to strengthen this cluster.

Wilhelmina Pier

The Wilhelmina Pier cluster is the most recent cluster to fulfil the definition, thanks to the opening of the LantarenVenster film theatre, moved there from the city centre. In addition the Luxor theatre and the Nederlands Fotomuseum are part of the cluster. There are hardly any shops in the cluster and its immediate vicinity, although there is a hotel and several cafés and restaurants. The city centre is some distance away. The cluster primarily attracts domestic visitors. Only the Fotomuseum draws visitors during the day, the other institutions primarily in the evening.

Binnenrotte cluster

Wilhelmina Pier

Amsterdam

0   125   250 m

Culture clusters in Amsterdam

Amsterdam logbook

A rambling city

11:30 a.m. Waterlooplein A group of young people are just knocking around through the city. The people we speak to around the Waterlooplein appear to be sort of tourists who 'just follow their nose', people who have no preconceived plan, but allow themselves to be led by what the city has to offer them. The greater the concentration of institutions and facilities, the more tourists like this we encounter. On the other side of the Mr. Visserplein, in the Plantage neighbourhood and around the Hermitage, they are no longer to be found. There we speak primarily with tourists who have an itinerary in mind: people who come for a specific institution, and then go on to their next destination.

A quiet, hidden strength

3:45 p.m. Plantage Middenlaan A pair of Scots come out of their hotel and get right on the tram to 'the city'. They say there is nothing to do in the Plantage neighbourhood. The people who do come here have a specific reason: the French botanist who is on her way to the Hortus, or a Jewish man who is walking the first stage of the Westerbork Path. The people we speak to outside the Plantage seldom know what this neighbourhood has to offer, and that it is so close to the centre.

Ambassadors for the city

9:30 p.m. Café Hooischip, corner of Blauwbrug The bartender at this café gives about thirty people a day directions to the Hermitage. A map and the directional signs don't appear to be adequate. The owner of a smart shop around on the Waterlooplein points his clients in the direction of the most authentic places in the city. On the other hand, hotel staff don't get much beyond recommending the Anne Frank House and the Van Gogh Museum. In Amsterdam we discover the strength of these 'hidden visitors' bureaus' for the city, who have more influence for some tourists than any map or guidebook.

'We don´t want Lonely Planet, we don´t want a plan; we just want to experience the city.'

'If we ask directions from someone, it seems everyone is a tourist.'

'I like going to the Plantage, because it is not as busy and touristy as the centre.'

'I will particularly remember my meetings and conversations with Amsterdammers.'

'Bicycling in Amsterdam is fantastic. Then it turns out the city is really not so big!'

According to the working definition, Amsterdam has nine clusters. All lie in, or right next to the historic city centre.

1012

Within the 1012 cluster there is a distinction to be made between the Sex Museum and the Berlage Beurs, which are located prominently on the Damrak, and the Oude Kerk, Ons Lieve Heer op Zolder and W139, in the middle of the Wallen. The cultural institutions primarily attract visitors during the day. The area is however dominated by shops and eating places, which chiefly draw their visitors, many of them foreign, in the evening and at night. The location right across from Central Station plays an important role in this. About 90% of the visitors to the Sex Museum are foreign tourists.

Dam cluster

The Dam cluster overlaps with the 1012 cluster. Although the greatest cultural institutions – Nieuwe Kerk, the Palace, Madam Tussauds – lie around Dam Square, the atmosphere is defined more by the shoppers. The Dam is a nexus for day functions; the Nes, with its various theatres, chiefly draws an evening audience. About 60% of the visitors to Madam Tussauds are international visitors. For the theatres on the Nes, that percentage is much lower.

Jordaan cluster

The Anne Frank House is the most important drawing card in the Jordaan cluster. All by itself it has about a million visitors a year. 98% of whom come from outside The Netherlands. The other cultural institutions in the cluster include the Rode Hoed Theatre, Felix Meritis and the Westerkerk, but also

the scattered art galleries of the Jordaan. The cluster has good connections with the city through the Nieuwe Leliegracht and the Raadhuisstraat. There are also shops and a variety of restaurants and cafés to be found. In the Jordaan itself they are spread all through the small-scale urban fabric.

Oosterdok cluster

A new cluster has developed around the Oosterdok. Nemo, the Muziekgebouw, Bimhuis and the Central Library all lie around a notional middle point in the water of the Oosterdok. Arcam and the Scheepvaart Museum also lie on the Oosterdok, but are not within five minutes walking distance. The cluster has surprisingly few stores and eating establishments. Because of the water in the middle, access from one institution to another, and connections with the city, are less obvious. Moreover, the rail line complicates the connections with the Muziekgebouw and Bimhuis. This separation is also a difference between a day and evening audience. The museums on the Oosterdok are open during the day, the Muziek-gebouw and Bimhuis primarily in the evening. The cluster does not draw many foreign visitors, as the location near Central Station might lead one to expect. At Nemo they account for only about 10% of the visitors.

Jordaan cluster

Oosterdok cluster

Canal cluster

The Canal cluster is also a new cluster in the city centre. There are many cultural institutions on the Ring Canals, such as FOAM, the Kleine Komedie, Museum van Loon, Tassenmuseum Hendrikje and the Geelvinck Hinlopenhuis Museum. When the Municipal Archive moved into the area, for the first time it received more than 500,000 visitors. This cluster too has no obvious orientation point. The most famous square in the cluster, Rembrandtplein, has no cultural institutions. It is an entertainment centre *pur sang*, dominated by restaurants, cafés and pubs. Most of the performances at the Kleine Komedie are in the evening, the other institutions are open in the daytime. In principle, the cluster is well connected with its surroundings, but most of the cultural institutions lie just off the familiar routes. Yet about 30% of FOAM's visitors, for instance, are foreigners.

Waterlooplein cluster

The Waterlooplein cluster is not new, but received a major boost with the addition of the Hermitage in 2009. The number of visitors to this cluster immediately doubled. In its first year, 20% of the visitors to the Hermitage were international. The Muziektheater, Rembrandt House, Jewish Historical Museum and Willet-Holthuysen Museum are also in the cluster. It does not have any clear form. Because

Ring canal cluster   **Waterlooplein cluster**

the urban structure is difficult to read in this part of the city, visitors often get lost. A clearer connection to, for instance, the shopping area on the Utrechtsestraat, or the Rembrandtplein would be desirable.

LEIDSEPLEIN
The Leidseplein is an entertainment centre, but unlike the Rembrandtplein the cultural institutions which lie around it or in the neighbourhood contribute strongly to the character and atmosphere of the entertainment venues. With Paradiso, Melkweg, the Stadsschouwburg, Boom Chicago/Leidsepleintheater, Bellevue Theatre, de Balie, the youth theatre Krakeling and the Nieuwe de La Mar Theatre, this spot offers a highly diverse evening programme. The visitors to these institutions are mostly domestic – more than 90% at Paradiso, for instance. This is striking, because the restaurants in the streets off the Leidseplein are patronized heavily by international tourists.

MUSEUMPLEIN
The Museumplein has the largest number of visitors of any of the culture clusters in The Netherlands. More than 3.3 million visitors per year come for the Van Gogh Museum, Rijksmuseum, Stedelijk Museum and Concertgebouw. With so many visitors the lack of cafés and restaurants in the immediate vicinity is beyond comprehension. The share of foreign visitors is high – from 65 to 80% for the museums. Surprisingly enough, the Concertgebouw is an exception: less than 1% of its audiences are foreign visitors.

Leidseplein

Museumplein

Comparison and definition

PLANTAGE CLUSTER

The Artis Zoo draws the largest number of visitors in the Plantage cluster, with 1.2 million per year. In addition, the Hortus Botanicus, Resistance Museum, and Trade Union Museum are in this cluster. It chiefly draws day visitors. There are several eating establishments immediately around the Artis; farther away from it, the support facilities are limited. The cluster immediately adjoins the Waterlooplein cluster and the Oosterdok cluster. The institutions therefore present themselves, together with other institutions in the east of the city centre, as Plantage on the Water.

The five largest clusters in Amsterdam each draw more than one million visitors, and have a strong profile both domestically and internationally. The Binnenhof and Municipal Museum cluster in The Hague and the Museumpark in Rotterdam also draw both domestic and international visitors, but far fewer than the top five in Amsterdam.

The other Utrecht, Hague and Rotterdam clusters generally draw just around 500,000 visitors, the Vredenburg, Spuiplein and Binnenrotte clusters thanks to the central libraries being located there. These clusters have a primarily city-wide or regional significance.

The point of departure of looking at cultural institutions within a radius of five minutes walking distance makes it possible to make a clear and meaningful distinction between clusters. The differences between the cities also emerge clearly. The boundaries are however rather arbitrary. Sometimes the institutions lie very close to one another, others are widely spread out. Some clusters are isolated, others adjoin one another, and in this way enhance each other. Some are thoroughly mixed, while others are specialized.

Five minutes walking time is the equivalent of about 350 to 450 metres. In Dutch, the area that lies within that is generally designated as a neighbourhood or a quarter, and double that distance as a neighbourhood or district. If a ten minute walk was the criterion, then Utrecht, The Hague and Rotterdam each have one city centre district with more than one million visitors. Within this area there is a strong mixture of functions. The Municipal Museum cluster in The Hague and the Wilhelmina Pier in Rotterdam both fall outside these districts, and are rather peripheral. Amsterdam would have three such districts.

If the scale were stretched to a 20 minute walk or ten minutes by bicycle, then the cultural institutions in and around the centre of Amsterdam form one 'super district', with something more than 10 million visitors per year. The Muziekgebouw on the IJ and the Concertgebouw on the Museumplein still fall outside this circle.

This approach is strongly quantitative in nature. In order to obtain a sharper insight into the nature of the differences in the culture clusters it will be helpful to work in a more qualitative fashion.

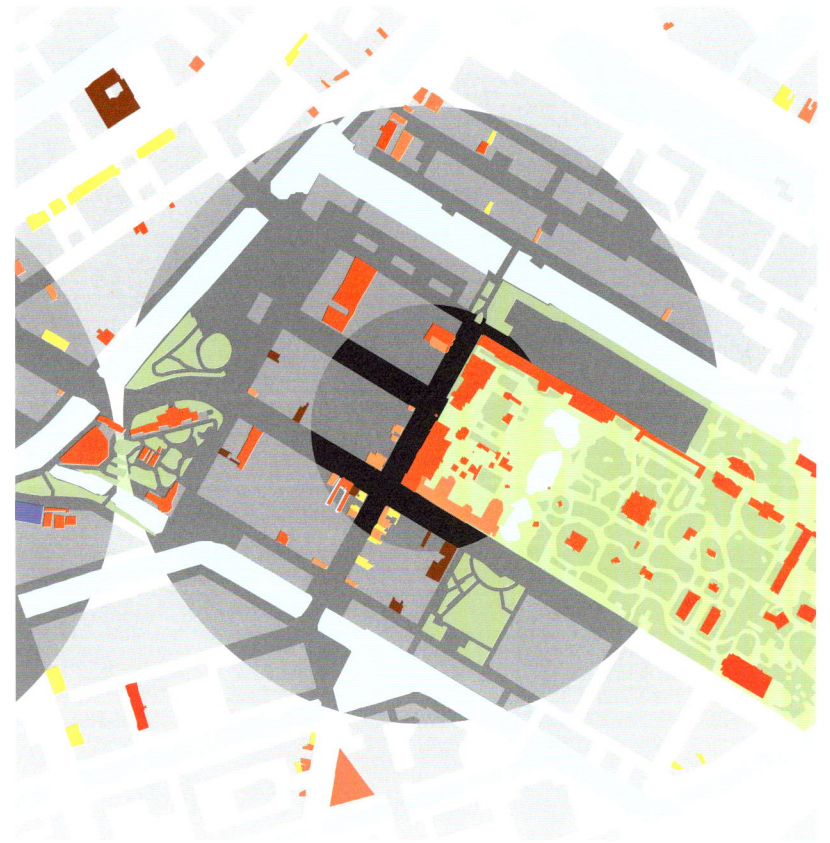

Plantage cluster

Scheepvaartmuseum, Amsterdam

Typology of culture clusters

The LA Group Leisure & Arts Consulting distinguishes various sorts of clusters: 'virtual', 'culture square', 'apart under one roof' and 'together under one roof'.[29]

Virtual clusters share a website. In Amsterdam Plantage on the Water, the collaboration of the cultural institutions on the east side of the city centre, profiles itself as 'a unique place in the heart of Amsterdam where nature, culture, history and science go hand in hand. An ideal place for a day out in Amsterdam. Come and spend a day lazing in one of the beautiful parks, visit one of the prominent museums, wander past centuries-old warehouses, and close your day with a drink on that magnificent terrace on the water.'

The Museumplein, with its great cultural institutions around it, is an example of a culture plaza. Apart and together under one roof are at first sight forms of clustering that would be primarily of interest to smaller cultural institutions which would reap advantages from sharing facilities. In The Netherlands there are various clusters to be found in one building. For instance, the Verkade Factory in Den Bosch, with, in addition to a large film auditorium, several film screening rooms, a theatre production house, visual arts institutions and eating establishments. Often the visitors to these smaller institutions come from the place itself or the region. The Centre Beaubourg in Paris is a much larger and more internationally oriented cultural centre.

If we look at the culture clusters in the four largest cities from this qualitative perspective, then several more types can be distinguished. Based on an analysis of the culture clusters on aspects such as their programme, the form of the public space, intensity and time of usage, and functioning, and informed by international examples, a distinction can be made among seven types: cultural centres, culture streets, culture squares, culture quarters, culture parks, culture wharfs and culture gardens.

Cultural centres

The most compact configuration for cultural facilities is the cultural centre, a building that accommodates various institutions under one roof.

David Chipperfield has realized such a cultural centre with the renovations of the museums on Berlin's Museuminsel. The separate museums are linked underground to form one connected museum complex, which is accessed by the new reception building, the James Simon Gallery, next to the Neue Museum. With it, it is expected that as many as four million visitors a year can be handled efficiently. The new entrance does deprive the Kolonadenhof, surrounded by its magnificent colonnade, of some of its significance, now taking on more of the character of an internal courtyard.

The Beaubourg centre in Paris, designed in the 1970s by Richard Rogers and Renzo Piano, is also an interesting example of a cultural centre. In addition to the museum for modern art, the Beaubourg, officially known as the Centre national d'Art et de Culture Georges Pompidou, accommodates a large public library, a cinema, the Brancusi atelier and Ircam, the Institut de recherche de coordination acoustique/musique. The square in front of the centre, the Stravinsky fountain with the sculptures by Jean Tinguely and Niki de Saint-Phalle, and the terraces around it give the environs of Beaubourg a special identity.

In the four largest cities in The Netherlands, only the Hague has a comparable compact collection, with its Museum cluster (Municipal Museum, Museon, Omniversum, Fotomuseum). The museums are not, however, linked with one another. Only the colour scheme and selection of building materials indicate their relationship. The cluster also has no obvious public space toward which the institutions are oriented. The water feature in front of the Municipal Museum, with the pergola near the entrance to the museum, has the effect of separating rather than

uniting: you leave the city, and enter the museum.

Different institutions are more thoroughly integrated in the Muziekgebouw on the IJ, a part of the Oosterdok cluster. The concert hall, Bimhuis, the café and the acoustic playground are accessible from a shared interior space. The relationship with the adjoining hotel and cruise ship terminal lies primarily in the shared parking facilities and the façade materials. The 'panorama decks' on the second layer are hardly uninterrupted.

Both the Haagse Museum complex and the Muziekgebouw with its adjoining functions are extremely compact. They cover three, and one-and-a-half hectare, respectively, within a radius of less than a hundred metres.

In Utrecht the Vredenburg Music Centre is being reconstructed as the Music Palace. When it opens in 2014 this new cultural centre will accommodate the present Vredenburg Music Centre, the pop centre Tivoli, and the SJU Jazz Podium. To a greater extent than in the present situation, Vredenburg will serve as an outdoor space with cafés and terraces.

The classic culture square

The Dam in Amsterdam is a characteristic example of a 'classic culture square'. Dam Square lies in the midst of the central shopping area of the city. In 1975 the Amsterdam 700 event planted the seed for the culture cluster around the square, with the opening of the Amsterdam Historical Museum, the Bible Museum in the Cromhout houses, and the summer opening of the Palace on the Dam. The Allard Pierson Museum on the Rokin opened a year later. Tourist attractions such as Madam Tussauds (1971), the Nieuwe Kerk (1979), the Amsterdam Dungeon and the Hash, Marijuana & Hemp Museum (1985) complete the cluster. The institutions are pitched primarily toward random passers-by.

The Museumplein in Amsterdam is not a real square; actually it is a plaza. Four classic cultural

James Simon Gallery, Museumsinsel Berlin
Design: David Chipperfield
(© Stiftung Preußischer Kulturbesitz / Imaging)

Trafalgar Square, London
Redesigned by Foster + Partners

institutions stand around the grand open space of the Museumplein: three museums and the Concertgebouw. They dominate the space and the programme around the plaza. The degree of mixing with other urban functions is limited. The structure of the plaza does however offer diverse possibilities for temporary use and events.

The spectrum of temporary uses of the Dam – from the National Commemoration Day observance to fun fairs – is wider than that of Museumplein. The Museumplein is a much more highly specialized culture plaza.

Examples of culture squares in other countries include Trafalgar Square in London, with the adjoining National Gallery, and Place de la Concorde in Paris, with the Petit Palais and Grand Palais. These squares also contain countless references to the 'big events' of their nation-state's history, such as Nelson's Column and the Luxor obelisk. The National Monument on the Dam and the monument for the Women of Ravensbruck on the Museumplein fit in this tradition.

All the important buildings of the Dam cluster lie within a radius of 150 metres. The distance is greater at the Museumplein: 300 metres.

There are countless variants on the classical culture square in other countries. Paseo del Prado in Madrid and Museum Mile along Fifth Avenue in New York are examples of 'culture boulevards'. Here demonstrations and parades are the complementary events.

The modern culture square

The 'modern culture square' is also a variant of the classic culture square. Sometimes the former has arisen from the latter. The cultural institutions around these squares have a different profile than the institutions around the classic square. Here you will chiefly find theatre, music, film, jazz and pop. In contrast to the classic square, the modern culture square is busiest at night. That is also true for the multitude of restaurants, cafés, terraces, coffee shops, discos and snack bars which you find on and around the modern culture square. Among the newer entries in the field are the discussion centres and concept stores.

The best known examples in the largest cities are the Leidseplein in Amsterdam, the Schouwburgplein in Rotterdam, and the Spuiplein in The Hague. Most of these modern culture squares have a primarily regional importance. The Spuiplein distinguishes itself from the others because it is also busy during the day, because of the combination with city hall and public library on it. In the case of all these modern culture squares, the square itself and the buildings surrounding it are all within a radius of 150 metres.

Although at first glance the Vredenburg in Utrecht looks like a culture square – or might become one through the construction of the Muziekpaleis –

The Dam, Amsterdam

there the shopping facilities are dominant, and the cultural functions are diffused. Rather, the Vredenburg cluster is a mixed shopping quarter which includes institutions such as the Speelklok Museum, Dom Tower, Central Library, Kikker Theatre, Aboriginal Art Museum and Werftheater. In the same way, the Amsterdam Wallen – here designated by their postal code, 1012 – are an entertainment quarter which includes diffusely distributed cultural institutions such as the Oude Kerk, Beurs van Berlage and Sex Museum. In the next section we will examine such mixed clusters more closely.

Another variant of the modern culture square lies around the large-scale venues on the periphery of the city, such as Amsterdam's ArenA-Boulevard. The ArenA was constructed in 1996 as a multifunctional stadium and has a capacity of 50,000 visitors for concerts. The Heineken Music Hall, with a capacity of 5500, the Ziggo Dome for 15,000 visitors, and a mega-cinema also lie on the ArenA-Boulevard. The supporting selection of cafés and restaurants around these venues is limited. On the other hand, large-scale retailers, a furniture boulevard and the studios and editorial facilities of Endemol assure that the ArenA-Boulevard is also busy during the day, making it a more attractive destination.

Ahoy, in Rotterdam, was built in the 1970s and offers space for 15,000 visitors for large-scale concerts, but in fact has no public life around it. The same is true for the Beatrix Theatre in Utrecht. Supporting facilities are slowly developing around the Circus Theatre, Palace- and Kurhausplein in Scheveningen, but it is not yet clear that this should be designated as an entertainment quarter.

Times Square in New York and Leicester Square in London are the best known international examples of the modern culture square. Both are parts of extensive theatre districts, and over the course of time developed, by processes of downgrading and upgrading, from classic culture squares into strongly differentiated cultural areas.[30]

Culture quarter

We also encounter several mixed culture clusters in the centres of Amsterdam and Utrecht, in which residential and work functions predominate: the Jordaan and Plantage in Amsterdam, and the Museum Quarter in Utrecht. The term 'quarter' is a perfect description for these areas. They are clearly defined areas with a strong spatial identity, imposed by the street plan and architecture. The cultural institutions are spread through the quarter, and often have no functional or visual relation with each other. The quarters have a radius of 300 to 400 metres, in conformity with what post-war Dutch urban planning practice termed a neighbourhood (buurt). They are characterized by the strong mixture of functions. In addition to apartments, and often small offices, to a greater or lesser degree you find specialist businesses, galleries and unusual restaurants and cafés. The culture quarters are the sort of urban areas ideal for strolling, where you can encounter locals and inhale culture, precisely because they are off the beaten track, away from large tourist attractions and chain stores.

The development of SoHo in New York is often cited as a reference for culture quarters. Since the 1960s SoHo has undergone a remarkable evolution,

Leicester Square, London

from a dilapidated, small scale industrial neighbourhood, through an artists' colony, to a hip and extremely expensive residential and entertainment quarter.[31] The gentrification process has taken on grotesque forms. SoHo has not nine, but some thirty small streets on which all the fashion chains have outlets, and the prices are astronomically high. As of June, 2011, the average price for an apartment is 2.8 million dollars, as opposed to only 1 million for Manhattan as a whole. In comparison, the development (and prices) in Amsterdam are modest. The average real estate tax assessment in the Jordaan lies around 300,000 Euro per apartment, while the average transaction price in the whole of Amsterdam in 2009 was 238,500 Euro.[32]

The Binnenhof cluster in The Hague stands apart from the others because it was originally a chic residential area, around the court of the Counts of Holland and – later – the Staten-Generaal and the royal palaces. Here you do not encounter locals, but politicians. The stately ensembles of urban spaces take on special significance from the rituals which take place there, for instance surrounding the opening of Parliament.

The Binnenrotte cluster in Rotterdam and the Waterlooplein cluster in Amsterdam are unique variants of the culture quarter. Both are also examples of districts in transition, after the bombardment and urban renewal and being cut through with multi-lane access roads, respectively.

In Rotterdam, after the bombardment the shopping precincts shifted from the Hoogstraat to the Lijnbaan. The Laurenskerk, the public library and the market on Tuesday and Saturday give the Binnenrotte cluster a strong local flavour.

On the other hand, the Stopera, Hermitage, Jewish Historical Museum, Rembrandt House and flea market on and around Waterlooplein give the cluster a strong touristy atmosphere. This quarter also accommodates the art training programmes of the Amsterdam Hogeschool voor de Kunsten, Theaterschool, Filmacademie, Academie van Bouwkunst and Academie van Beeldende Vorming.

In some quarters certain streets have more specialized cultural functions. The Nes, in the university quarter on the south-east of the city centre, is a typical culture street, with three theatres, the Brakke Grond, Frascati and the Comedy Theatre.

Waterfront

A unique variant of the culture quarter is the waterfront. In many cities the world-wide rise of city tourism in the late 1970s coincided with the renewal of old harbour areas. The American 'city doctor' James Rouse developed a frequently copied formula for this.[33] In addition to new cultural facilities such as a science museum or concert hall, the formula chiefly revolves around commercial leisure facilities, to bring numbers of people who had fled to the suburbs 'back to the city'. Baltimore, Genoa and Sydney all

SoHo, New York City

Jordaan, Amsterdam, Anne Frank House

Parc de la Vilette, Paris
Design: Bernard Tschumi

received an aquarium, a festival site, a shopping mall, an IMAX theatre, a food court, a replica of an historic ship, and a promenade along the water.[34]

The Netherlands too experimented with this formula, but the waterfront development in Rotterdam and Amsterdam lagged far behind these examples. The first experience with waterfront development in Rotterdam came in the early 1980s with the development of the Museumhaven around the Leuvehaven, discussed above. In 1986 the planning for the Kop van Zuid began with the presentation of the plans for the Erasmus Bridge. Although the bridge has become an icon for the city, the transformation project has proved more problematic than expected. The waterfront cluster includes Hotel New York, the Entrepot, the Passenger Terminal, Luxor Theatre, Nederlands Fotomuseum in Las Palmas, and the music and film theatre LantarenVenster. This cluster draws more visitors than the Leuvehaven, especially if you count in the large-scale events which take place on and around the Erasmus Bridge and Boompjes. The

distance from the metro station at Wilhelminaplein and Hotel New York is almost 600 metres; the Entrepot is a 500 metre walk. The Wilhelmina Pier is itself more compact.

Amsterdam too developed its waterfront. After the success of Sail in 1975 as a part of Amsterdam-700, in 1983 Amsterdam held what was called the Oosterdok Competition, as a start for the redevelopment of the banks of the IJ. The basis for the waterfront cluster that developed in the years that followed was the Scheepvaart Museum that had opened in 1973. After eight editions of Sail, Oosterdok is still a building site. It is true that in 1985 the replica of the VOC ship Amsterdam has been tied up there, and Nemo, the science museum designed by Renzo Piano, opened in 1997, but it was only in 2005 that the Muziekgebouw on the IJ and the Passenger Terminal followed. The other new construction on Oosterdok Island and the renewal of central station is still to be completed. In the meantime the opening of the new Public Library in 2009 did provide a new drawing card for the cluster,

and assured an interesting mix of national and local visitors. Most of the buildings are within a radius of 500 metres of Nemo as a crow flies, but the actual walking distances are much greater.

The long distances set both the Dutch waterfronts apart from their foreign models, which are much more compact. Around the Porto Antico in Genoa all the attractions lie within a radius of 200 metres!

Scheveningen-Bad is also a waterfront, in this case a seafront with a beach, will all the specific spatial elements and facilities that go with that: a boulevard, boardwalk, parallel street, hotels and beach pavilions. Although there are several buildings which remain from the period before the Second World War, Scheveningen is not a classic beach resort. Much of it was destroyed during the war. After the war, all sorts of new spatial elements and amenities were introduced, during the reconstruction plan and again in the 1980s and 1990s, without any strong coherence. The construction of the Circus Theatre and the popularity of the beach pavilions

75

marked a broadening in use. Scheveningen-Bad became a beach resort more oriented to the city. The seafront has the form of a strip – in this case, almost 600 metres long and 200 metres wide, including the beach.

Culture park

One of the most interesting new types is the 'culture park'. The origin for it is the Parc de la Villette in Paris. Unlike the commercial American model, from its inception 'education' and 'relaxation' in the broadest senses of those words stood at the heart of the planning. Since the 19th century the area had been in use as a cattle market and slaughterhouse. In the 1960s it became outdated, and it was closed in 1974. The French state acquired the title. After a competition to select a concept, in 1979 it was decided to develop the site as a park with a museum and music centre. Giscard d'Estaing, and later Mitterrand, embraced the plan as a *Grand Projet*.

In June, 1982, the Etablissement Public du Parc de la Villette announced an international design competition. In the programme for the contest, considerable attention was devoted to the function and significance of the new park. It should become the focus for urban life; unlike many existing Parisian parks, used primarily by children and the elderly, it should be used intensively and constantly.[35] The designers were expressly asked to devote attention to the symbolic function of the park, with themes such as 'pluralism', 'dialogue between technology and culture', and 'integration of the park and surrounding neighbourhoods'. The 'separation between knowing and doing' should also be abolished by offering space for events in the restored Grand Halle and for all kinds of experiments in ateliers for technology, music, film, expression and theatre. The challenge to make a park for the twenty-first century inspired lots of designers; over 470 teams made submissions. After a second round

Westerpark, Amsterdam
Design for park extension: Kathryn Gustafson

among the nine winners Bernard Tschumi captured the first prize. The new park opened for the public in 1986.

Like Rouse's waterfront formula, this culture park formula acquired imitators worldwide. In The Netherlands the Museumpark in Rotterdam and the Westergasfabriek in Amsterdam are the most appealing examples. We have previously discussed the Museumpark in Rotterdam. The expansion of the Westerpark in Amsterdam with the western gas works site in Amsterdam followed the Parisian model more closely, albeit that its realization took nearly fifteen years (1990-2003) because of the need to decontaminate the soil.[36] On the other hand, that meant that all sorts of experiments could be made in existing buildings on the edges of the site to

determine their viability for the future. The landscape plan is the design of Kathryn Gustafson. The buildings of the Westergasfabriek itself, such as the Zuiveringshal, the Kettelhuis and the Gashouder, designed in 1883 by Isaac Gosschalk, were renovated by a series of architects, based on the winning 1999 competition submission from Francine Houben (Mecanoo). They accommodate creative industries and a large number of extremely flexible exhibition and event spaces. The Westergasfabriek has an enormous stature, chiefly as a result of a number of well-visited annual events such as Awakenings, Kunstvlaai, the winter carnival and Fashion Week.

The buildings around Rotterdam's Museumpark all lie within a radius of 250 metres. From the Witte de Withstraat it is, however, it rapidly becomes a 400 metre hike to the Kunsthal. The Westergasfabriek is somewhat larger, and has a main entrance placed eccentrically. Its central 'street' is almost 600 metres long.

Culture wharf

The NDSM (Netherlands Dock and Shipbuilding Company) site in Amsterdam North can be regarded as an organic, rough around the edges little brother to the culture parks. At the 'culture wharf' there is an even greater emphasis on events. The site is somewhat larger than the Westergasfabriek, and has a radius of 400 metres. It is a complete neighbourhood in itself. Île de Nantes is an interesting foreign exemplar.

After the bankruptcy of the shipyards in the early 1980s, its wharves long lay in the lee of urban development. Artists and theatre-makers, including the Dogtroep, settled in. They discovered the power of the rough area with enormous contrasts and artefacts which appealed to the imagination such as

harbour cranes, slipways and docks, all exquisite opportunities for experimental theatre on location.

After a competition for temporary use of the 20,000 m² NDSM work hall, it was transformed into 'Art City'.[37] The site became more widely known to a larger audience through a series of much-talked about festivals, such as Lara aan het IJ, and VOLLT. The opening of cafés and restaurants, student housing and a ferry connection to Central Station did the rest. In 2008 the transformation of a part of the site into a 'media wharf' began, with ground-breaking new structures such as the Kraanspoor for media firms like MTV Benelux, IDTV and Discovery Channel. The head offices of Hema, VNU and Red Bull and the creative industry department of the Amsterdam ROC followed.

Now that residential development is also being considered, it has become a question whether the 'culture wharf' formula is still tenable. Large-scale dance events are not particularly compatible with homes.

Culture garden

The private variant of the culture park is the 'culture garden'. Tivoli in Copenhagen is a famous example. The garden is only eight hectare in area, but draws three million visitors in the summer season. Tivoli opened in 1843 just outside the old city, modelled on the 17th century Vauxhall Pleasure Gardens just outside London. These gardens were famous for their concerts and gay lighting. They closed after bankruptcy in 1859, and largely became building lots. Tivoli is however still going strong. You buy a ticket at one of the entrances to the gardens, and look to see what is to your taste. There is lots of music: daily performances by the Tivoli Big Band, and a pop concert and a classical concert weekly by the Tivoli Symphony Orchestra in the large concert hall, seating 1800, built in 1956. The 2011 summer festival offered at least 47 concerts with music from Beethoven and Chopin to Ravel and Britten. But there are also 26 'rides', an aquarium, countless restaurants, and since 2010 a theme park à la Disney

NDSM site, Amsterdam

Culture garden Tivoli, Copenhagen

World: Petzi Park, based around the popular Danish comic character Rasmus Klump.

There were also countless 'pleasure gardens' around the cities in 17th century Holland, with attractions such as peacocks, pall-mall, bear baiting, mazes, grottoes and, undoubtedly, strong drink and prostitutes. The Plantage, with the Hortus Botanicus (1638) and a whole series of private tea and pleasure gardens, lay within the walls of Amsterdam. Many of these gardens had a function comparable with the gardens outside the city. Moreover, in the 19th century various theatres, societies for rural pursuits, concert halls and a panorama arose, and in 1838 the first public zoo in Europe, the Artis, was established, initially on a plot of 60 by 80 metres.[38] The Zoological Society Natura Artis Magistra did honour to its name – 'nature is the instructor of art' – by expanding the menagerie and by exhibiting all sorts of 'products of nature', the basis for the later Zoological Museum. At the same time, concerts took place in the zoological gardens, and two large banquet rooms were included in the new building for the 'Groote Museum' (1852): the Koningszaal and the Tijgerzaal.

The double aims of 'education and pleasure' have been rediscovered in recent years through the reconstruction and expansion of the zoo, and moving the Planetarium from the Gaasperpark to the Artis, but also by a series of summer evening concerts, the appointment of an Artis professor, renovation of the Parkzalen, and renting out buildings as recording studios – the Plantage Studios, familiar from all sorts of talk shows on radio and TV. Thus the Artis is once again firmly anchored in the public life of the city. Artis now measures 15 hectare.

Strictly speaking, a 'culture garden' is not a culture cluster by the definition we are using here. But because of the peculiar combination of activities the Artis is more than an attraction park. One could also say that the attraction is part of the Plantage 'culture quarter'. The Hortus, the Resistance Museum, the Labour Union Museum, in its building once designed by Berlage for the Diamond Workers Union, and the Hollandse Schouwburg are all just a stone's throw away.[39]

Work in progress

At the moment, all four of the largest cities are investing heavily in the further development of their culture clusters. In Rotterdam the NAi was recently renovated, and access to the Museum Park was improved by realization of a large underground car park. After the renovation of Las Palmas was completed in 2007 for the Nederlands Fotomuseum, in the spring of 2010 LantarenVenster strengthened the selection in the Wilhelmina Pier cluster by its relocation there.

In mid-2012 the final decisions will be made regarding the construction of a new dance and music centre on the Spuiplein in The Hague. The new complex would be realized on the present site of the Lucent Dance theatre and the Dr. Anton Philips Hall, and would be used by the Netherlands Dance Theatre, the Residentieorkest and the Royal Conservatory. Considerable attention is also being given to the future of Scheveningen-Bad and the development of this peripheral cluster into a fully-fledged, broader culture cluster.

In Utrecht investment is being concentrated on the renewal of the heart of the city, around Hoog Catharijne. The Vredenburg Music Centre is being transformed into the Music Palace. In 2014 the new complex will accommodate the present Vredenburg Music Centre, the pop centre Tivoli, and the SJU Jazz Podium. In this way, peripheral facilities will be clustered. Remarkably enough, the new Central Library is being realized somewhat to one side of the cluster, on the Smakkelaarsveld. The expansion of the programme around the Jaarbeurs on the west side of Central Station is also of interest. Next to the renovated Beatrix Theatre the municipal offices, a casino, mega-cinema and a hotel are springing up. The entry to the Jaarbeurs is being provided with a food court. This could create a third cluster.

Amsterdam is investing heavily in the Museumplein cluster (366 million in the Rijksmuseum, 61 million in the Stedelijk Museum). Even before the renovated and expanded museums have been delivered, a discussion has arisen about the use and character of this place in the city. With the 538 Queen's Birthday concert, the Liberation Festival, the start of the Giro, the welcome for the Dutch football team and the Uitmarkt all in 2010, many feel that Museumplein reached its annual quota of events. The events have little do to with the cultural institutions on either side of it, and after a big event the square always looks somewhat the worse for the wear. In 2010 the big Queen's Birthday concert was moved to the forecourt of the RAI. The development of other clusters, such as the Oosterdok cluster with the new central library and renovated Scheepvaart Museum, can perhaps divert some of the pressure away from Museumplein. Also the development of new types of culture clusters which are more resistant to events, such as the culture park or culture wharf, could be an answer to the contradiction.

Size and character of the clusters

It clearly emerges that there are great differences between the clusters with regard to size and character. The cultural centre is the most compact, with a radius of 100 metres. Most culture squares have a radius of 150 metres, with an exception in the case of the Museumplein in Amsterdam, at 300 metres. This is almost the format of a culture quarter, with its radius of 350 to 400 metres. The culture park and culture wharf are similar. The two waterfronts are rather expansive, compared with foreign examples.

A single-purpose theatre or culture district, like one has around Times Square, is not to be found in The Netherlands. The city centre districts around the Dam in Amsterdam, the Beursplein in Rotterdam, the Grote Markt in The Hague and Vredenburg in Utrecht are strongly mixed and dominated by stores. The eastern side of the city centre of Amsterdam, with Nieuwmarkt, Waterlooplein, Oosterdok and the Plantage comes closest to being a culture district, but has a strongly composite character. It is, rather, perhaps a district in the making. That is also true for the 'double cluster' of Leidseplein and Museumplein.

Relations with other tourist activities

A visit to a culture cluster is a standard part of a visit to any one of the largest cities. That has long been the practice for visitors staying for a couple of days, who combine different activities; it is increasingly true for day trippers as well.

Day trips are part of what Continu Vrije Tijds Onderzoek (CVTO) called 'free time activities': all daytime recreational activities that are undertaken outside one's own home, which take one away from home for a minimum of one hour (including travel time), but do not keep one away overnight. Visits to family, friends and acquaintances and activities undertaken during vacations are not included in this consideration.[40]

CVTO lists eleven clusters of day recreational activities. Outdoor recreation, sports, club activities, beauty and wellness activities and water recreation are activities undertaken either in the immediate vicinity of one's home, or outside the city. The other day recreational activities – fun shopping, entertainment and visiting events, cultural activities, attractions and sports competitions – are almost all city tourism activities. It is precisely these activities

which have been on the increase over the last decades, and many people combine them.

That is easier in some clusters than in others. From the survey of culture clusters a sharp distinction emerges between specialized and mixed culture clusters. The Municipal Museum cluster in The Hague, the Museumpark in Rotterdam, and the Museumplein, NDSM wharf and Westergasfabriek in Amsterdam are specialized clusters. In and around the other culture clusters in the four largest cities lie many other tourist destinations: shops, hotels, restaurants and cafés, cinemas. Activities are easy to combine in these mixed clusters.

Shopping

The city centres of Amsterdam and Utrecht have an attractive mix of retail stores, restaurants and cafés and culture. The illustration on page 80 shows the retail shopping concentrations in Amsterdam (not including food items). The characteristic form of shopping concentrations in Amsterdam are shopping streets, with the ultimate example being the continuous route from the Haarlemmerstraat, via Nieuwendijk, Kalverstraat and Reguliersbreestraat, to the Utrechtsestraat. At angles to that lie Heiligeweg and Leidsestraat, the shopping streets leading to the Leidseplein. All sorts of cultural institutions are spread in and around these shopping streets, such as the Amsterdam Historical Museum. The culture square of the Dam is an important link in this chain. It is the obvious middle point.

Around the series of shopping streets also lie the shopping quarters of the Nine Streets, the Jordaan and the Nieuwmarkt. Taken all together, this shopping area forms a complete 'shopping district', with a radius of 750 metres and over 1000 stores. Just off the Museumplein lie the chic P.C. Hooft-straat and Van Baerlestraat, with 144 stores. They are poorly connected with the central shopping district.

Seen from an international perspective, the maximum store rentals in Amsterdam are in the middle bracket. In London and Paris the maximum store rentals are around 7500 Euro per square metre per year. After Frankfurt, Moscow, Milan and Rome, with maximum rentals of around 3000 Euro, follow Amsterdam and Berlin, with 2800.

In the other three largest cities the central shopping areas have a radius of about 400 metres; they are 'shopping quarters' with considerably fewer stores. The highest store rentals in Rotterdam lie around 1700 Euro per square metre per year. In Utrecht that is 1635, and in The Hague 1400. The centre of Utrecht is a good example of a mixed shopping quarter, with 130 stores.[41] The diffused cultural institutions give the city centre colour. In contrast, Hoog Catharijne is a closed box with stores. In terms of programme, it is in fact a super mall with a floor area of 42,000 m² and 160 stores, but cannot duplicate the aura of more illustrious examples in other countries.[42]

The Rotterdam shopping quarter around the Beursplein is larger in terms of area, but has fewer stores; 70 stores are members of the Beursplein business association. It also has few other functions. The Schouwburgplein and Leuvehaven culture clusters lie on the edges; Museumpark is at some distance. The Binnenrotte and Hoogstraat, the old city centre from before the bombardment, assume a subordinate position today. Aside from the city library, the market on Tuesday and Saturday is the main draw.

The Hague's shopping quarter around the Lange Poten and Grote Marktstraat is also relatively specialized in retailing. The Spuiplein and the Binnenhof clusters lie on its edges.

A culture cluster is developing in the ArenA area, which, in addition to culture also has sports and large-scale retailing. Further integration with the more close-knit shopping area of Amsterdamse

Amsterdam

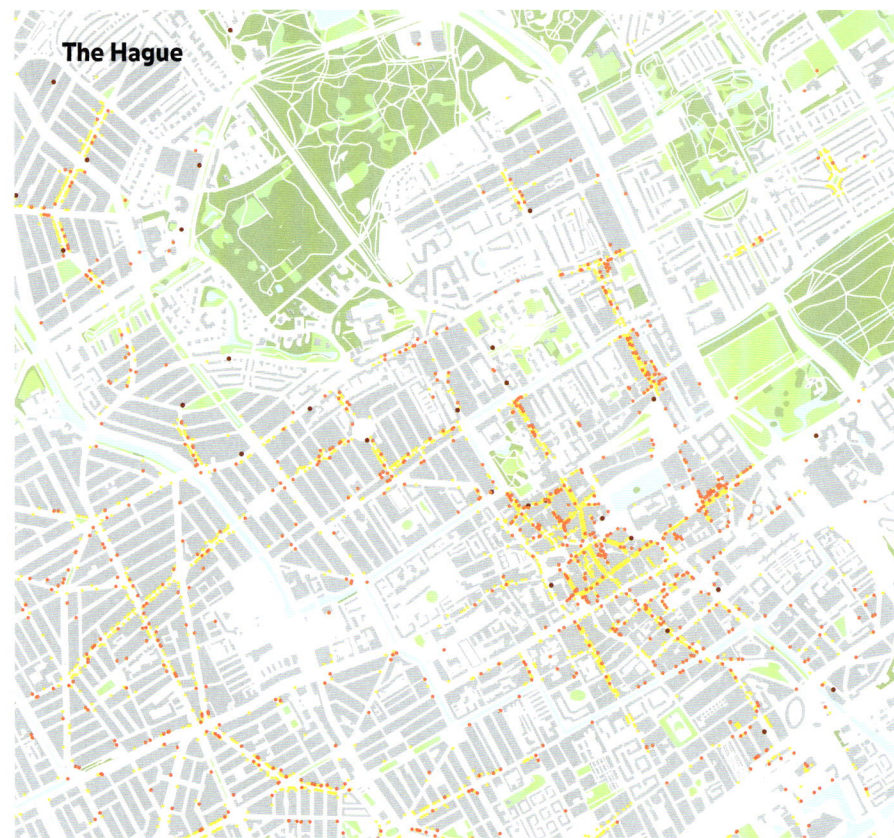

The Hague

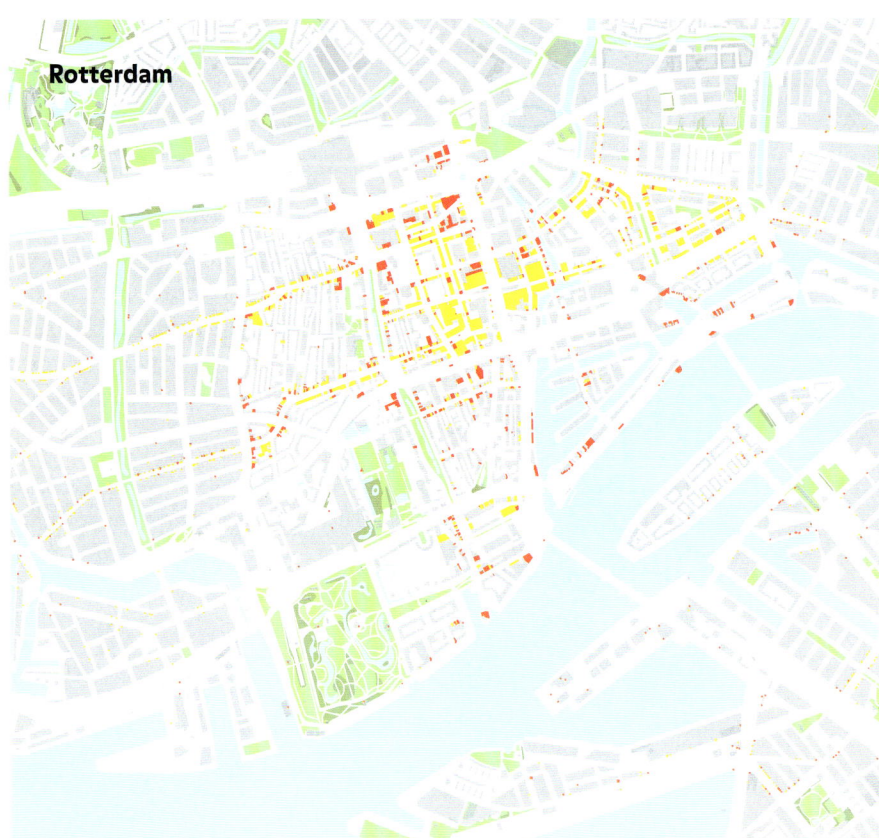

Rotterdam

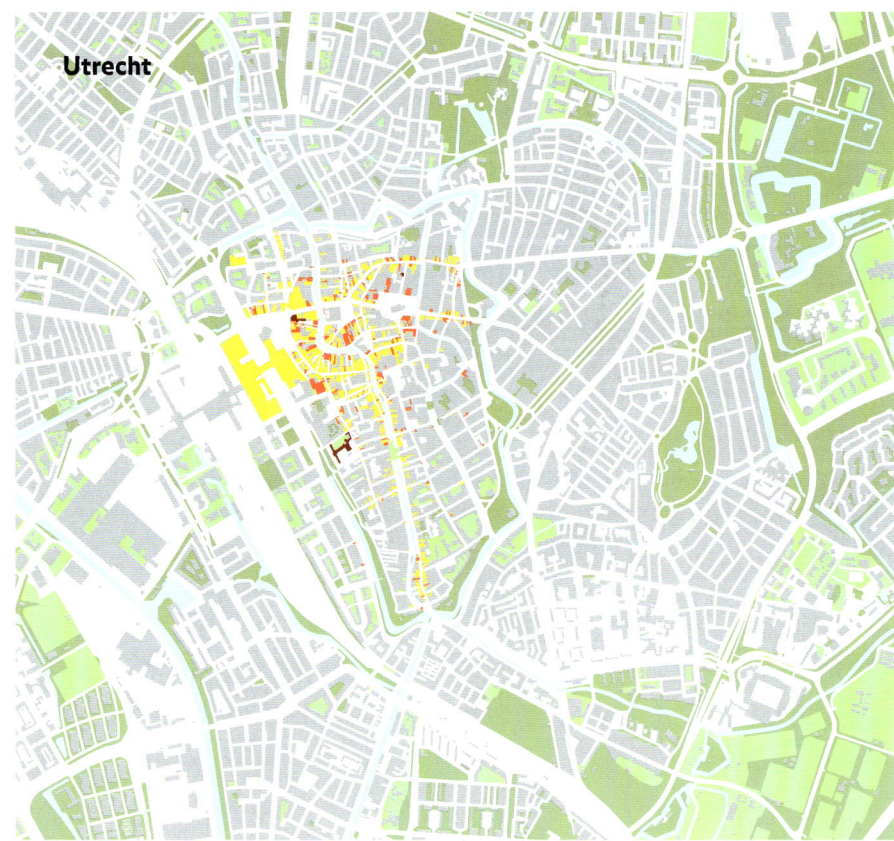

Utrecht

Poort, on the other side of the rail line, could here provide a more diverse area. An important step has already been made with the complete renovation of the Bijlmer-ArenA Station.

Entertainment

We encounter all kinds of entertainment functions on and around the modern culture squares with evening programming: cafés, restaurants, cinemas. The Leidseplein is the vital hub of an entertainment area with at least 120 eating establishments within a radius of about 250 metres. Rembrandtplein is a specialized entertainment square with extensions in the surrounding streets. In 1012 the entertainment function is so dominant that it has also become a specialized entertainment quarter. In addition to the traditional cafés and restaurants there are also gambling halls, fast food, coffee shops and countless other leisure activities. The cultural institutions in a way counterbalance this.

On and around other culture squares like the Schouwburgplein and the Spuiplein there are fewer cafés and restaurants. There such establishments are a support for the cultural functions around the squares. That is also true for the recently developed waterfronts in Amsterdam and Rotterdam. The ArenA area in Amsterdam, and soon the Jaarbeursplein in Utrecht, each have a mega-cinema, but only limited opportunities for eating out.

In The Hague, on the other hand, concentrations of cafés and restaurants lie in the culture quarter of the Binnenhof cluster, around the Plein and the Buitenhof. Many of the hotels and clubs in this quarter also have restaurants. In Utrecht the widely distributed dining cafés and restaurants contribute to the quality of the mixed central city quarter.

Hotels

Many hotels lie around the culture squares and in the culture quarters. In Amsterdam most of the hotels are distributed around the city centre and in the area between the Museumplein and Leidseplein. Hotels however play a definitive role in the image and use of many culture squares, in part because of their grand cafés, restaurants and meeting facilities. The great Hotel Krasnapolsky lies on Dam Square itself, and in addition to the American Hotel, Leidseplein has a Marriot Hotel and the NH Center Hotel. Recently the former conservatory near the Museumplein opened as the Conservatorium Hotel. On Rembrandtplein there are no less than six hotels, including the Schiller.

It is true that the other cities have fewer hotels, but there too the hotels, with their cafés, restaurants and meeting facilities contribute to the atmosphere and use of the culture clusters. That is true for Rotterdam, for instance with the Park Hotel near the Museumpark, and with Hotel New York, one of the pioneers in the development of the Wilhelmina Pier. In Utrecht there are several hotels near Vredenburg, but most of the hotels are spread out through the Museum quarter. The hotels are the most definitive factor in The Hague. That is the case for the Binnenhof quarter, with its famous establishments like the Hotel des Indes on the Lange Voorhout, but of course most of all for Scheveningen. The Kurhaus is literally the centre point of the culture cluster in Scheveningen-Bad.

Combinations

In the four largest cities, cultural functions are combined with other tourist interaction environments in diverse ways.[43] Amsterdam has an extensive and mixed shopping district in the heart of the city. Distributed through the district lie all sorts of cultural functions. There are five concentrations of cultural functions in and around this shopping district. The classic culture square of the Dam, the culture street Nes, and the entertainment quarter of Rembrandtplein lie in its midst. The 1012 and Leidseplein entertainment quarters bound on it. The culture square and entertainment quarter around the Leidseplein, the Museumplein culture cluster, the chic shops in the P.C. Hooftstraat and Van Baerlestraat lie close to each other, and form a rising culture district. The same is true for the east of the central city, with the clusters around the Oosterdok, in the Plantage, and around Waterlooplein. This is also a mixed district with a large number of hotels, but it has fewer entertainment venues. It is only on and around the Nieuwmarkt that one finds many cafés and restaurants.

The contrast between the mixed quarters in the old city centre, with their opportunities to wander and stroll, and the closed world of the Hoog Catharijne super mall typifies Utrecht. The Beatrix cluster will also be highly specialized.

In part as a consequence of the modernist reconstruction plans for the city centre after the war, Rotterdam has a specialized shopping quarter around the Lijnbaan, Binnenwegplein and Beursplein. 'Tentacles' of shopping streets link the Lijnbaan with the entertainment venues around the Schouwburgplein and the 'old' heart of the city around the Binnenrotte. The culture clusters around the Leuvehaven and Museumpark are not obviously connected with the central shopping area. The Hague too has a rather highly specialized shopping quarter around the Korte and Lange Poten. It is somewhat more strongly mixed with places to eat out and apartments than the Lijnbaan quarter in Rotterdam is. There are also direct links with the culture cluster around the Spuiplein and with the mixed culture quarter around the Binnenhof. Scheveningen-Bad is a leisure quarter that is dominated by the beach facilities, but is taking on an increasingly mixed character.

Retail concentrations in Amsterdam, Rotterdam, The Hague and Utrecht

Legend

■ cafés, restaurants
□ retail stores
■ hotels

0   100   200 m

Dunes, near Egmond

Hotel and conference centre Huis ter Duin, Noordwijk

Holland cluster

In addition to city tourism, at the level of The Netherlands as a whole coastal and regional tourism has traditionally been important. People seek out the coast, the Veluwe, Drente or South Limburg for a day out, weekends, or vacations. The North Sea resorts on the Dutch coast are the prime destination for foreign vacationers: 2 million in 2011.[44]

Coastal tourism

An almost continuous chain of dunes some 250 kilometres long lie along the Dutch coast. That is a major recommendation, in comparison with the coasts of Flanders, or Los Angeles. There the coast is thoroughly urbanized, with a series of residential areas, seaside resorts, harbours, industry and generating plants succeeding one another. Thanks to the Amsterdamse Duinwatermaatschappij, the Duinwaterleiding in The Hague and the PWN in North Holland, extensive nature reserves dominate the coast here. These dune parks play an important role in providing the drinking water for the Randstad. Organizations such as the Natuurmonumenten (since 1905) and Noord-Hollands Landschap (since 1935)

are devoted to the protection of the dune areas. In 2007 South Kennemerland was finally designated a National Park. It covers an area of at least 3800 hectare.

Considered more closely, the Dutch coast is made up of three parts: the Wadden Islands in the north, a continuous coast in Holland, and the Zeeuwse delta, dominated by estuaries, in the south. This division very much defines the forms of coastal tourism.

Over the course of time the influence of the sea has been pushed back from both the northern and southern sections of the closed coast of the middle. Already in the 17th century the construction of the Hondsbossche sea defences and the draining of the Zijpe polder added the islands of Callantsoog and Huisduinen to the closed coastline. In the 20th century the construction of the Afsluitdijk forced the sea and its influence still further back. Plans to close the tidal channels between the Wadden Islands have never been carried out. The Wadden Sea is the largest contiguous nature reserve in The Netherlands, and since 2009 has been on the UNESCO World Heritage list.

After the Great Flood of 1953, as part of the Delta Works, the decision was made to shorten the

coastline in Zeeland too. On both the sea and land sides the Zeeuwse islands were connected to one another by dams and bridges. Grevelingen and Volkerak became complete inland lakes. The tidal flow in the Haringvliet and Oosterschelde was limited. Offshore the extensive Voordelta has formed, and in the Oosterschelde an archipelago of mudflats and salt marshes.

At the end of the 19th century the Dutch coast was discovered by foreigners – largely Germans – as a place for recuperation, relaxation and pleasure. New elements like the Kurhotel, the pier and the boulevard made their appearance. In just a few short years Scheveningen, Zandvoort and Domburg were radically transformed. In the early 20th century Noordwijk, Katwijk and Egmond aan Zee followed in their wake with the construction of their own beach boulevards.

Even before the Second World War the rise of the middle class and the gradual democratization of free time led to a stratification of seaside resorts. Scheveningen and Noordwijk remained the domain of the elite, Domburg, Egmond aan Zee and Katwijk of the middle class, while Hoek van Holland, Oostvoorne and Bakkum were primarily patronized by the working class. Zandvoort took on a mixed profile.[45] 'New' resorts, like Bergen aan Zee, were modelled on English villa parks and Belgian dune villages in designs produced by the landscape architect Springer. In 1921 Springer also designed the new Zeeweg through the dunes of Haarlem, to Bloemendaal aan Zee.

The Second World War had an immense impact on Dutch seaside resorts. In 1942 the German army began the construction of the Atlantic Wall, a defence line from Norway to the Spanish border, to prevent Allied landings. In The Netherlands almost all buildings along the sea were demolished, to free up places for extensive complexes of defensive works. Scheveningen, Zandvoort and Katwijk were hit the hardest. The Kurhaus in Scheveningen was retained, but in Zandvoort the monumental passage between the station and the beach disappeared. In Katwijk, half the town, with 580 dwellings, hotels and schools, was demolished. The old village church and the lighthouse remained behind, isolated in a desolate defensive landscape.[46]

The reconstruction of the resorts was approached in a coordinated manner already during the war. An agent and a supervisor were appointed for each resort. In 1947 the National Plan Agency published the memorandum Considerations Regarding the Reconstruction of North Sea Resorts, with a series of guidelines for diverse categories of resorts: luxury resorts with fashionable diversions, vacation resorts, resorts with vacation bungalows, and finally, resorts for mass day visits. Scheveningen and Noordwijk belonged to the first category; the other resorts became hybrids.[47]

The development of mass tourism picked up steam in the early 1960s as a result of increasing prosperity, increases in vacation time, and particularly the German Wirtschaftswunder. The coast became crowded. A special SER commission chaired by the sociologist Hilda Verwey-Jonker presented its advice in 1964 on the possibilities for spreading out vacations. The report is a treasure trove of data.[48] For instance: in the summer of 1960 22,000 Dutch and 104,000 foreign guests were received by hotels along the coast (excluding the Wadden Islands), several times more staying in bed-and-breakfasts and on camp sites.

Massive new hotels arose along the recon-structed boulevards (Huis ter Duin, Palace, Hotels van Oranje, Bouwes, Zuiderduin). In addition, the interaction environment of the resorts was enhanced with all sorts of 'attractions'. In addition to a new pier, Scheveningen received an aquarium, Sea Life, and a shopping mall. Beginning in 1958 the Grand Prix on the new race circuit in Zandvoort became a part of the Formula 1 world championship. In 1976 the first Holland Casino opened there. Lunch rooms,

ice cream parlours and souvenir shops opened in the villages, on the edges of immense parking fields, Diffuse attractions like the Keukenhof, Madurodam and Duinrell widened the selection.

Trends

This picture has radically altered since the 1980s. Inexpensive charter flights turned the countries around the Mediterranean Sea and the Caribbean islands into popular vacation destinations.[49] After the Wende Germans flocked to their own Baltic Sea coast. This caused coast tourism to change strongly in nature. It is true that a million Germans a year still come to spend several days on the Dutch coast (NBTC), but with increasing frequency they are choosing destinations in the Delta, or the Wadden Islands. These are less crowded, and therefore more interesting for longer or shorter vacations. Moreover, luxury camping sites and bungalow parks increasingly offer forms of recreation which are independent of the season, with all sorts indoor facilities right on site: restaurants, super markets, swimming pools, fitness centres, hobby spaces, tennis courts and bowling. In the Zeeuwse islands these resorts are often combined with marinas and docking facilities. De Roompot, Aquadelta, Zeeland Village, Port Scaldis and Port Zélande are the most extreme examples of this.

Some of the traditional interaction on and around the beach boulevards in the towns and resorts on the islands of Zeeland and the Wadden Islands has been redirected to the mind and senses. The Oerol Festival 'for theatre on location and landscape art' on Terschelling is a scintillating counterpoise, drawing more than 50,000 visitors, who often stay several days. Vlissingen and Domburg keep a public tradition going with festivals like Onderstroom and Jazz by the Sea.

The Dutch resorts are also increasingly orienting themselves toward day-trippers from the cities. In 2007 Scheveningen alone drew 11.7 million visitors in the year, and 430,000 on the busiest day. There are

2.2 million people who are within an hour's drive of Scheveningen; 4.2 million can reach the coast within an hour by public transit.[50]

In terms of use, this shifts the focus from the towns to the beach, with an ever wider selection of pavilions and events. Scheveningen now has 65 beach pavilions, far more than any other seaside resort.[51] Between 1999 and 2009 the number of seasonal snack bars and other commercial facilities on beaches in The Netherlands as a whole rose by 7%, to 365.[52]

The beaches at Bloemendaal, Hoek van Holland and Scheveningen have developed into new culture and entertainment centres on the sea, with events like Love Generation, Intuition, House Classics, Bamboo and the Royal Beach Concert. Sports events like the North Sea Regatta and beach volleyball tournaments draw many thousands of visitors. Towns in the dunes like Bergen and Noordwijk separate themselves from the pack with festivals like a ten-day arts festival and Opera on the Sea, with conference facilities and fitness activities, and exclusive restaurants.

At the same time, almost all the camping sites along the Dutch coast have been rebuilt as bungalow parks over the last couple of decades. As a result, the inner edge of the dunes along the coast has developed into a complete weekend city of second and vacation homes.

The contrast between the central Dutch cost, oriented to the metropolitan centres, and the Wadden Islands and the coast of Zeeland, more oriented to vacations, is becoming ever greater.

Regional tourism

With regard to the number of domestic vacationers, Zeeland and the Wadden Islands are in the middle bracket of regions in The Netherlands. Even before the Second World War the Veluwe, Salland and South Limburg had developed as popular vacation destinations from the big cities in the west of the

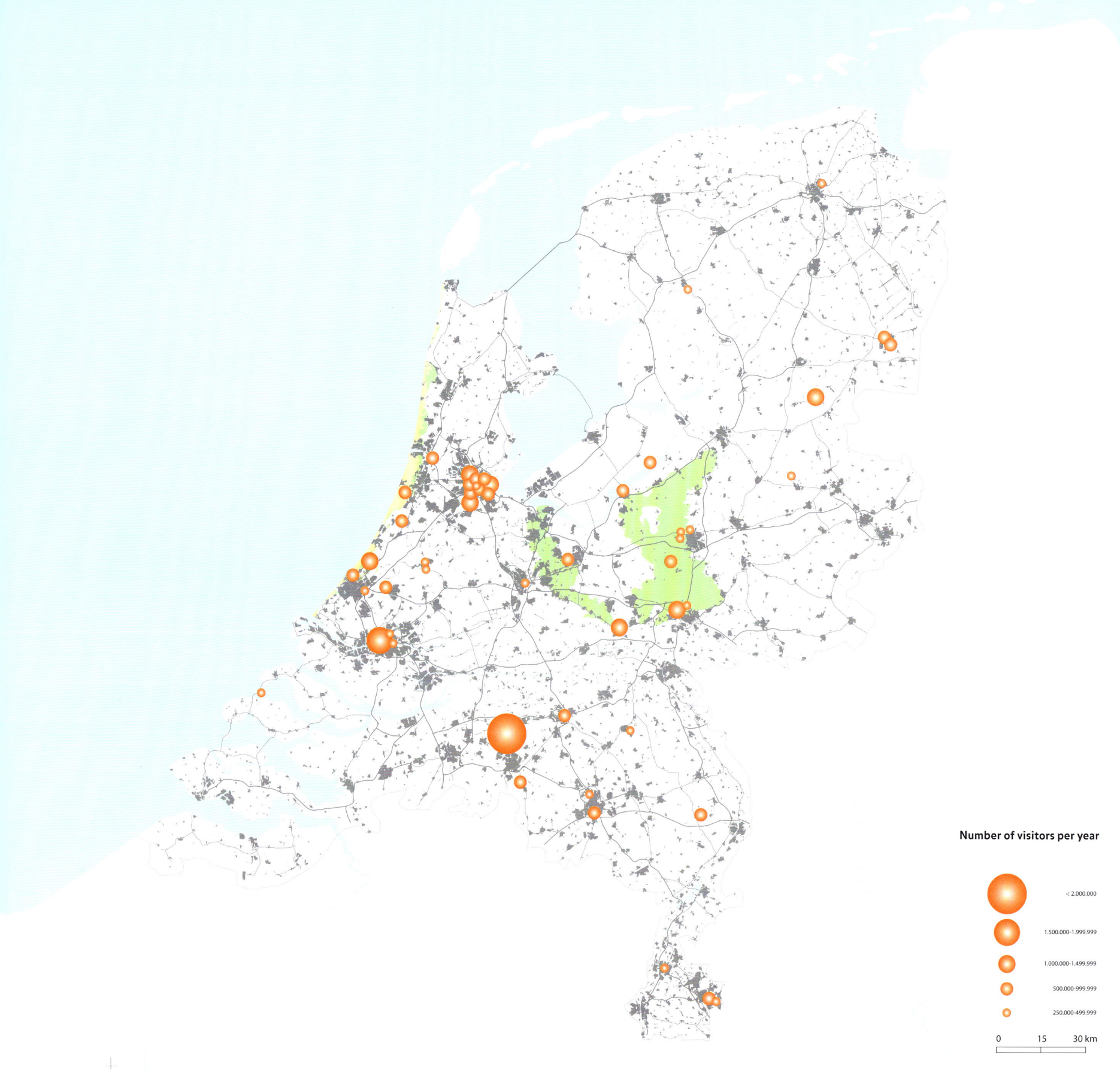

Number of visitors per year

< 2.000.000

1.500.000-1.999.999

1.000.000-1.499.999

500.000-999.999

250.000-499.999

0   15   30 km

Top 50 Attractions (number of visitors) G4		Holland	Other
1 Efteling			3,900,000
2 Blijdorp	1,551,707		
3 Burgers' Zoo			1,470,000
4 Slagharen Amusement Park			1,469,800
5 Van Gogh Museum	1,429,854		
6 Duinrell Amusement Park		1,358,110	
7 Natura Artis Magistra	1,135,003		
8 Anne Frank House	1,050,339		
9 Ouwehands Dierenpark			905,000
10 Rijksmuseum Amsterdam	892,536		
11 National Swimming Centre de Tongelreep			870,000
12 Sportiom			800,000
13 Beekse Bergen Safari Park			800,000
14 Keukenhof		787,000	
15 Dolphinarium Harderwijk			780,000
16 Walibi Holland			767,000
17 Amsterdam drinking water supply dunes		750,000	
18 Emmen Zoo			700,000
19 Amersfoort Zoo			673,500
20 Hermitage Amsterdam		650,000	
21 Snowworld Landgraaf			650,000
22 Snowworld Zoetermeer		650,000	
23 Madurodam	626,000		
24 Jaap Edenbaan	600,000		
25 Madame Tussauds Amsterdam	587,000		
26 Aquarena Swimming Pool			557,500
27 Sex Museum Amsterdam "Venus Temple"	510,133		
28 NEMO Science Center	508,601		
29 Hoge Veluwe National Park			505,000
30 Snowplanet		500,000	
31 Toverland			495,000
32 Ir Otten Swimming Pool			475,000
33 Queen Juliana Tower			450,000
34 Netherlands Open-air Museum			436,730
35 Heineken Experience		435,000	
36 Apenheul			402,500
37 Adventure Park Hellendoorn			400,000
38 Spido (Harbour boat tour, Rotterdam)	399,865		
39 GaiaPark Kerkrade Zoo			375,000
40 Kardinge Sports Centre			370,000
41 Railway Museum Utrecht	354,000		
42 Sport and Recreation Centre Thialf			350,000
43 Drievliet Family Park		350,000	
44 Boijmans van Beuningen Museum	324,121		
45 Palace Het Loo			323,083
46 Vogelpark Avifauna		321,060	
47 Deltapark Neeltje Jans			304,000
48 Glanerbrook Sports Centre			300,000
49 Archeon		295,000	
50 BillyBird Park Hemelrijk			291,117

country. Particularly in the Veluwe and Salland there were numerous pensions, camp grounds and bungalow parks. Recently Drente, Friesland and Brabant have also developed as vacation destinations. All these regions have beautiful nature reserves, often with high points and views which are spectacular by Dutch standards.

Traditionally interaction took place in several typical 'vacation towns' with a wide assortment of hotels, stores and dining establishments in season: Valkenburg, Ommen, Otterloo, Gieten. More than has been the case along the coast, in recent years attractions have played an important role in regional tourism. They are rapidly elbowing out the towns as the place for interaction.

Every year some 36 million people in The Netherlands visit a day attraction. Except for the previously discussed great museums, Madurodam and the zoos, most of the attractions in the top 50 lie outside the cities – often at a considerable distance. Duinrell, Drievliet, Snowplanet, Avifauna, Archeon and SnowWorld Zoetermeer lie in the Randstad; the real top attractions, like Efteling, Burgers' Zoo, Ouwehands Zoo and Slagharen all lie outside it.

Many of the attractions use the word 'park' for themselves, but in terms of typology appear to be closer to what was discussed under the heading 'culture garden'. They often have only one entrance, and their ticket prices are steep. The difference between a garden and park is also one of scale: After its recent expansion Artis grew from 10 to 14 hectare; Ouwehands is 22 hectare, and Burgers' Zoo 45. Efteling is 72 hectare in size, and moreover, is surrounded by 11 hectare of parking fields.

Two 'urban' clusters of attractions stand out in the top 50: Arnhem (1.8 million), with important

Duinrell amusement park

attractions like Burgers' Zoo and the Open Air Museum, and Apeldoorn (1.2 million), with the Queen Juliana tower, Apenheul in the Berg en Bos nature park, and Het Loo palace. The Hoge Veluwe National Park (505,000), with the Kröller-Müller Museum, is easily accessible from either Arnhem or Apeldoorn.

The attractions in and around the Veluwe could also be regarded as a 'regional' cluster. The Ouwehands Zoo, the Dolphinarium at Harderwijk, Walibi Biddinghuizen and Amersfoort zoo would belong to it. In total, the top-50 attractions in this Veluwe cluster draw 6.6 million visitors per year.

Brabant has two very big attractions, Efteling in Kaatsheuvel and the Beekse Bergen in Hilvarenbeek. Together, they draw 4.7 million visitors per year. Including the big swimming attractions – Sportiom in Den Bosch, Tongelreep and the Ir. Ottenbad in Eindhoven – and the Hemelrijk family park in Volkel, the regional cluster in Brabant even tops the Veluwe, at 7.9 million visitors.

Compared with the Veluwe and Brabant, South Limburg, with SnowWorld Landgraaf, Gaiapark Kerkrade Zoo and the Glanerbrook Sports Centre in Geleen, and Salland with Ponypark Slagharen and Adventure Park Hellendoorn, score considerably lower.

Improvements in the motorway and railway network over the last decades have made the attractions in the Veluwe and Brabant easier to reach for day trips from the largest cities. The distance from the cities in the Randstad to Apeldoorn, Arnhem and Tilburg is 70 to 100 kilometres, an hour's drive.

Integration of city tourism, attractions and coastal tourism

Over the past decades the greatest growth and internationalization has taken place in city tourism. Coastal tourism and a certain 'typically Dutch segment of regional tourism appear to be hooking up with it. Many international visitors combine a visit to the cities with a visit to attractions like Volendam or Marken, the Zaanse Schans, the Alkmaar cheese market, Keukenhof, Madurodam, the Porceleyne Fles in Delft, or the windmills at Kinderdijk. These are all within a reasonable distance from the Randstad, and in various combinations can be visited in a half day or a day. Tightly choreographed excursions to them are also available, departing from the cities.

Only the Keukenhof and Madurodam also draw numbers of Dutch visitors. Remarkably enough, the other attractions pitched toward international visitors do not appear on the list of the top 50 day attractions which the NBTC publishes annually. Most can, of course, be visited for free. The Zaanse Schans, with 850,000 visitors, should also belong to the top; the Porceleyne Fles, with 120,000 visitors in 2010, would seem to be focusing on a niche market.

If the attractions and coastal tourist facilities are included in the analysis of the city tourism in the four largest cities, then the picture changes, particularly for The Hague. The tourist pattern is much more diffuse yet than emerged from the analysis of the culture clusters. The Kurhausplein is the heart of an extensive entertainment quarter on the sea. The pier alone has a length of 350 metres. The strip of tourist

Legend

- cafés, restaurants
- retail stores
- hotels
- Madurodam
- Duinrell Amusement Park
- Drievliet Family Park

facilities along the beach boulevard, from the Havenhoofd to the Zwarte Pad, is no less than 2.5 kilometres long. The central part of Scheveningen-Bad is shorter: almost 600 metres. In cluster terms, this is therefore an entertainment district. With the hotels, cultural facilities, the old village, the wholesale fish market and a large number of dwellings, this district has a mixed character. In contrast, Madurodam and Duinrell are stand-alones.

Regarded on a larger scale, a coastal cluster emerges, a band 90 kilometres long and ten kilometres wide along the coast. Within it lie the heavily visited resorts of Hoek van Holland, Scheveningen, Katwijk, Noordwijk, Zandvoort, IJmuiden and Bergen and the extensive dune parks, mixed with a series of compact cities, attractions, and a sea of weekend homes.

Recent changes in the use of the seaside resorts, with a greater emphasis on day visits, provides for stronger relations between this coastal cluster and the city. The Hague was traditionally linked with Scheveningen and the coast. That is also true now to an increasing degree for Amsterdam and Rotterdam. The events and attractions contribute to this, but it would also be interesting to know where the residents of the weekend city on the inner edge of the dunes come from. Is this an up-scale, contemporary equivalent of an allotment garden?

Holland cluster

As far as Dutch and international visitors are concerned, the centre of Amsterdam, with its extensions to the IJ and the Museumplein, is the core of the Dutch metropolis. The coastal cluster with The Hague comes in a good second. The clusters of Rotterdam and Utrecht lag far behind, but all together they form a strong, mixed Holland cluster.

The Amsterdam core is oriented toward regional, national and international visitors, and is supported by a differentiated shopping district, with adjoining entertainment quarters and culture squares. Around Leidseplein and Museumplein, and in the east of the central city, rising culture districts are emerging. On the periphery of the city the NDSM Wharf, Westergasfabriek and ArenA-Boulevard are rapidly developing into more specialized culture clusters, focused primarily on events.

The coastal cluster has traditionally been of greatest significance for Dutch and German visitors, but this is changing. In recent years the seaside resorts have been reorienting toward day visits – or better, evening and night visits – related to the cities. Scheveningen has gone the farthest in this, with an enormous growth of events, a doubling of the number of beach pavilions, and a top-rank musical theatre.

The Hague, Rotterdam and Utrecht all have a central shopping quarter with a regional function. There are, however, major differences. Utrecht has a sharp contrast between the specialized, large-scale shopping mall of Hoog Catharijne and the mixed, small scale shopping quarter in the old city centre, with many cultural functions and places to eat. With the realization of the Master Plan for the Station district the two areas will become more integrated. However, with the Music Palace an internally oriented cultural centre will once again be 'implanted'.

Because of the peripheral locations of the Museum cluster and the Scheveningen entertainment district, the shopping quarter of The Hague is less mixed. The City Hall and library form a strong link between the shopping quarter and the entertainment area around the Spuiplein.

The Rotterdam shopping area around the Lijnbaan is highly specialized. The development of the Wilhelmina Pier appears to reinforce this specialization. Vital cultural functions such as the Luxor Theatre and LantarenVenster have been transplanted to this new cluster.

Stimuli

Investing in touristic interaction environments

In 2011 a broad coalition of tourism organizations presented the Future Agenda for Free Time and Tourism, under the title *Innovatieprogramma voor Gastvrijheid van Wereldklasse*. Among the participants in the Initiative Group were the ANWB, NBTC, the Forestry Commission, Recron, Gastvrij Nederland, and a number of knowledge and innovation centres.[53]

According to the Future Agenda, the important challenges for free time and tourism are 'citizens who are becoming ever more demanding, new markets created by emerging economies, and rising international competition.' When citizens and tourists decide where they want to go, 'factors such as quality, singularity, authenticity, safety and intensity of experience play a large role. That demands much of suppliers. Visionary and socially engaged entrepreneurs, working along with governmental authorities, social organizations and researchers, are necessary in order to create a demand-oriented, multifaceted and distinctive supply. If we succeed in realizing that, we can spend our free time more pleasantly, increase our contribution to the GNP to 5% and that to employment opportunities to 6%, and further enhance the quality of the environment. If we do nothing, the opposite will occur.'

In order to offer 'World Class Hospitality' by 2025, the values of all regions of The Netherlands must be better exploited, across the whole spectrum of quality and supply, but it is also necessary to more sharply guard the values of hospitality and business principles: connecting with demand, increasing profit and economic impact.

The means that organizations will employ to achieve this is derived from the programme for stimulating competition that Logistiek Nederland initiated between top logistic regions. In 2010 and 2011 the Venlo region was declared *the* Dutch hot

Results of the anthropological fieldwork

Visit and search behaviour: metropolitan flow

Interviews with visitors during the fieldwork made it clear that the attractiveness of a city lies in a combination of strong destinations and the possibility to enjoy wandering and exploring. Are the museums and institutions attractive enough to make a specific trip worthwhile, do you go out of your way, or do you go there only if you happen to be in the neighbourhood? On the other hand, there is the question of whether visitors can easily find their way, and whether visitors can be tempted to spend a little more time, or even come back again, by the strong selection of amenities and surprising discoveries.

The fieldwork also made it clear that it is precisely during their wandering around that people have the experiences that they remember and that make their visit worthwhile. You could call this 'metropolitan flow'. Does the city succeed in getting people to surrender themselves to the flow of the city? Does it give them the feeling that there is always something to experience or discover, and provide them with an attractive destination at the right moment?

Identity: one flow is not another

Metropolitan flow must be tailor-made. Every city must zoom in on its own urban structure, its own identity and visitor profile, per district. The fieldwork provided a number of insights and considerations for this task, for each city.

With its Ring Canals and fine-mesh urban structure, in combination with the density of its facilities and institutions, Amsterdam is a wanderer's paradise. However, there is a risk of having too many visitors roaming about, so that other visitors begin experience it as too crowded, and too touristy.

Utrecht is a very convenient and quiet city for roaming around, where people can almost experience the old city itself as a museum. The challenge is to tempt visitors to go outside the city walls and discover the other Utrecht, outside the centre.

The Hague is a city of little islands which people will visit, as long as they have a strong statement to make. The Spui could use a stronger statement of its own, perhaps with the arrival of the new music and dance centre. If The Hague wants to surprise visitors with its many faces, it must guard against the areas between the 'islands' being abandoned to their fate.

Rotterdam is not the classical city for wandering: between the different destinations there are great distances to travel and busy streets to cross. The question is whether Rotterdam should close these 'holes' or whether it should regard them as a strength and promote them, for instance by using alternative strategies which fit with the city's adventurous and raw identity to tempt and lead people from one place to another efficiently and enjoyably.

On the street

Despite its limited extent, the anthropological fieldwork shows that in interviews, visitors divulge details about their motivations and experiences which you could never conceive sitting at a desk. Together with the analysis from the maps of the culture clusters and the coalition that was formed during this project, it has supplied the ingredients for a strong development strategy for culture clusters. It has provided input for the four cities individually, but also for conversations about what the cities can learn from one another in this field.

---

spot.[54] By linking the designation of hot spots to initiating processes focused on the development of hot spots, the coalition expects to be able to develop ten Leisure Hotspots of international status by 2025. Collaboration among entrepreneurs, governmental authorities, organizations and researchers is seen as being crucial for achieving that goal.

It is going to be quite a task to define the regions. Will it be done on the basis of cities and geographic regions, of provinces, or perhaps on the basis of metropolitan regions, or the top regions from governmental policy?

What is certain is that in an international perspective, Amsterdam and Holland are the strongest brands, and that museums and the coast are the most important attractions. City tourism is growing strongly in The Netherlands. It is obvious that spatial policy and investment should be concentrated on precisely these sectors and the development of clusters within them.

Development strategies

In making development strategies more specific, the distinctions among developmental phases introduced by Buck Consultants, discussed above, can be helpful: start, development and ongoing growth. If we apply them to the culture clusters, we see the following.

REALIZING NEW CULTURE CLUSTERS

At the present time, in the four largest cities there is no indication of the development of completely new clusters. Clusters normally develop from one or more existing facilities. The presently rising clusters often lie on the periphery of the cities. In choosing the location and supply of cultural facilities and events, the tone can be set for the type of cluster that might come into being over the longer term.

In Amsterdam, that concerns the Westergasfabriek, the NDSM Wharf and the ArenA-Boulevard. These do not yet fulfil the quantitative definition of a culture cluster, but are rapidly developing in that direction. The ArenA cluster is explicitly conceived as a 'second' entertainment district for the city, in order to somewhat relieve the pressure on Rembrandtplein and Leidseplein. After the opening of the Ziggo Dome, the new concert hall with a capacity of 15,000 visitors, the cluster will

Impression of the Beatrix Theater, Utrecht
Public space designed by HKB stedenbouwkundigen

undoubtedly fulfil the quantitative definition. The Westergasfabriek and NDSM site clusters, in particular, run largely on events. Such specialized sites reduce the pressure on the city centre.

At present the Scheveningen culture cluster has only two institutions, the Circus Theatre and the Beelden aan Zee Museum, and therefore does not fulfil the quantitative definition. However, the Circus Theatre alone draws 700,000 visitors per year. Moreover, the institutions are part of a complete entertainment district with hotels, shops and beach pavilions along the boulevard, the Kurhausplein and the Palaceplein. The City of The Hague and Joop van de Ende Theatre Productions are working together intensively to broaden the selection and improve the public spaces.

A new culture cluster might also arise from the investment around the Station district and the Beatrix Theatre in Utrecht. Unlike the others, this is not a peripheral location, albeit that the complex in Utrecht itself is difficult to reach and is not embedded in the city in any obvious way. In the regional and national perspective, however, it is one of the most centrally located sites.

Development of existing clusters

During their development phase, the most important factors for clusters are usually the number of institutions, accessibility, the design of their public space and the supporting programme. With regard to the Museumplein, the redesign of the space in the 1990s and the realization of an underground parking garage can be seen in this light. In Amsterdam the Ring Canal cluster, the Waterlooplein cluster, the Wallen/1012, Plantage and Oosterdok clusters are all in this development phase. The same is true in The Hague for the Spuiplein, in Utrecht for Vredenburg, and in Rotterdam for the Binnenrotte cluster and Wilhelmina Pier. The programme and the significance of all these clusters is highly in flux.

For example, countless cultural institutions have located in the Amsterdam Ring Canals in recent years, including the Municipal archives, FOAM photo museum, and the Purse and Handbag Museum. The designation of the Ring Canals as a site on the UNESCO World Heritage list, and the Grachtenfestival have strengthened the cluster. The Waterlooplein cluster was expanded with the addition of the Hermitage. The Plantage cluster will become easier to reach with the parking garage at Artis. The Oosterdok cluster developed with a large parking garage and the addition of the Public

Impression, Ziggo Dome, Amsterdam
Design: Benthem Crouwel Architects

Library. The Wilhelmina Pier added the Luxor Theatre and Las Palmas. The Muziektheater in Vredenburg is being transformed into the Muziek-paleis.

In all these cases the issue is what the clusters have to offer, in the broadest sense. This is not merely a matter of expanding or improving the institutions, but also of having a lively mix of functions on the ground floor, cafés and restaurants, and safe and attractive public space. That can have a whole different character.

In the case of the Wallen, for instance, the emphasis lies on breaking through the extreme specialization in function, dismantling the criminal infrastructure, and realizing a high-quality entry to the city.[55] The centrepiece of the 1012 policy is an active policy on the part of the city with regard to issuing permits and acquiring problematic properties, redesigning the Damrak and the Rokin – rolling out the Red Carpet – and projects such as Red Light Fashion and Red Light design.

In the case of the Rotterdam cluster around the Binnenrotte, the Laurens Quarter, a spectacular market hall with an underground parking garage, designed by MVRDV, is being realized. It is a means of broadening the local visitors' profile of this cluster.

Ongoing growth

The ongoing growth phase begins with a leap forward in the quality of the institutions. Subsequently the accent lies on the accommodation of larger numbers of visitors, improving the quality of the public space, and better relations with the surrounding areas.

As a result of problems in the construction of its large underground parking garage, the development of the Museumpark in Rotterdam appeared to stagnate. After it was finally opened, however, accessibility for the cluster was greatly improved. Furthermore, the NAi has recently been renovated,

and will assume a wider function as a result of its fusion with institutions in the field of design. The expansion of the offerings, and the improvements in relations with the vicinity, can herald continued growth.

The Museumplein and Leidseplein are also clusters in this phase of ongoing growth. The renovation and expansion of the museums can help the Museumplein cluster grow into the greatest attraction in The Netherlands. That in turn will place new demands on the design and furnishing of the public space. Several of the institutions around Leidseplein have also recently been renewed: the new DeLaMar Theatre, the performance space with a flat floor in the Schouwburg, the creation of extra halls in De Melkweg, the renovation of the City cinema, and the Apple Store opening in the Hirsch Building. If a corresponding radical improvement in the quality of the public space does not follow, then the opportunities for continued growth will not be optimally realized, and in fact the opposite is possible: stagnation, or worse, shrinkage.

The shopping district around the Dam is also on the threshold of possible ongoing growth. After the opening of the North/South metro line and the realization of the Red Carpet along the Damrak and Rokin, a great leap forward in quality is possible. In this, it will not be only the quality of the cluster which is at issue, but also its relationship with other clusters.

Developing combinations

Improving the relations between clusters, and the combination of clusters, is at least as important as investment in the development of the individual clusters. What is crucial here is that the way visitors use the city is changing. Day trippers come not just for one part of the day, but for several parts. Visitors who stay over do so not just for one night, but for several.

The visit to a large institution in a specialized museum cluster such as Amsterdam's Museumplein can easily take up a whole day. Many institutions therefore have cafeterias or other provisions for lunch. In mixed clusters, simple combinations can be made during one part of a day: shopping can be combined with a lunch, or a visit to a compact exhibition. Visitors can have cocktails or dine before or after a performance in a mixed culture and entertainment cluster. Now that visitors come more often for several parts of a day, the location of the clusters and the relation among them becomes more important. If various clusters lie within 10 or 15 minutes walk from one another, simple combinations are easy to make.

In this way the Museumplein cluster in Amsterdam can benefit from not only the P.C. Hooftstraat and the Pijp, but also the nearby Leidseplein cluster. An afternoon on the Museumplein can be followed by an evening around the Leidseplein. To realize this, formidable barriers, such as getting across the busy Stadhouderskade, must be reduced. The construction of the East/West metro line announced in the infrastructure vision could also be a driving wheel for the creation of a 'culture district' in this area.[56] A metro station under the Singelgracht with exits to Leidseplein and the Rijksmuseum at either end, a parking garage on the level above it, and re-routing traffic on the Stadhouderskade puts the development of both clusters in an entirely new light. Accessibility to, and as a consequence of that, the reach of this potential culture district would be enormously improved. That would be true not only for the region – an east/west line would of course run through to Almere – but also internationally, with a direct connection to Schiphol.

Similarly, there are enormous opportunities for Rotterdam in the improvement of relations between the Lijnbaan quarter, Museumpark and the Leuve-haven cluster. The interchange on the metro, at

← **Impression, Markthal, Laurens quarter, Rotterdam**
Design: MVRDV (© Provast)

Beurs, is at the heart of this area. In previous years the emphasis lay on the development of the Beursplein and improving the relation between Hoogstraat and the Lijnbaan. The Koopgoot was realized here, and major investment in the real estate around it followed. Relations with the culture clusters on the south side however have been ignored. The Westblaak and the development of office space in this southern section create a barrier to strong continuity. Here too it would appear that an intervention to deal with the automobile traffic is unavoidable, in order to obtain coherence in the functioning of the interaction environments. Particularly the Witte de Withstraat can become an important link.

The combination of clusters permits one to move up to a higher scale. In Amsterdam the Museumplein culture plaza and the Leidseplein culture quarter could develop into a culture district. The same is true for Rotterdam, for the combination of the Museumpark, Lijnbaan quarter and Leuvehaven.

Amsterdam's Marine base – culture garden, wharf, or park?

The east side of the centre of Amsterdam presents a formidable challenge. It is a section of the city full of contrasts. Somewhat in the lee of the cosmopolitan shopping district, the Ring Canals and the culture squares lies a complete urban archipelago of former harbour islands.[57] Over the past century the east of the city centre has been subject to a whole series of interventions, from the slum clearance of the 1920s, through the demolitions after the deportation of its Jewish population, to having new motorways driven through it, and the construction of the Stopera in the 1970s. Since the 1980s however the area has begun to experience a rebirth, under the influence of urban renewal and urban repairs. The Nieuwmarkt has become a favourite entertainment spot and appealing culture clusters have developed in the

Plantage and around the Oosterdok and Waterloo-plein. The potential repurposing of the Marine base – officially the Marine Complex – on Kattenburg could usher in a new phase.

The Marine base lies on an artificial island raised in the 17th century by the Admiraliteit van Amsterdam, and accommodated 's Lands Zeemagazijn (now the Scheepvaart Museum) and a massive shipyard. In 1915 all the Navy's shipbuilding activities were moved to Den Helder, and the shipyards in Amsterdam closed. Since then the site has been used for all sorts of Navy and Marine activities, but there is also discussion about the role of the site in the city.

A number of designers have gotten their teeth into the site over the past three decades. Many of the submissions to the 1983 Oosterdok Competition, won by Alle Hosper and Henk de Boer, involved the site with their perspective for Oosterdok. A couple

of years later, in the final round of the Prix de Rome, Wim van de Bergh and Koen van Velzen proposed a science museum for the site. Marijke Bruinsma competed in the Archiprix 2010 with her 'Hidden City'. The proposed cut-backs for the Ministry of Defence now bring such perspectives within reach.

The Marine base is about 12 hectare in size, is in walking distance of Central Station, and lies within the Oosterdok cluster discussed above. New cultural facilities and their supporting programme could enrich this cluster. The typology of culture clusters can be of aid in focusing the perspective more sharply.

The private development of a new culture garden on the wharf could realize immediate incomes for the shrinking defence budget. The site is almost as big as Artis zoo, and considerably greater than Tivoli. But what would the formula be: a family amusement park

Possible future plan for the Marine base and environs in Amsterdam
DRO

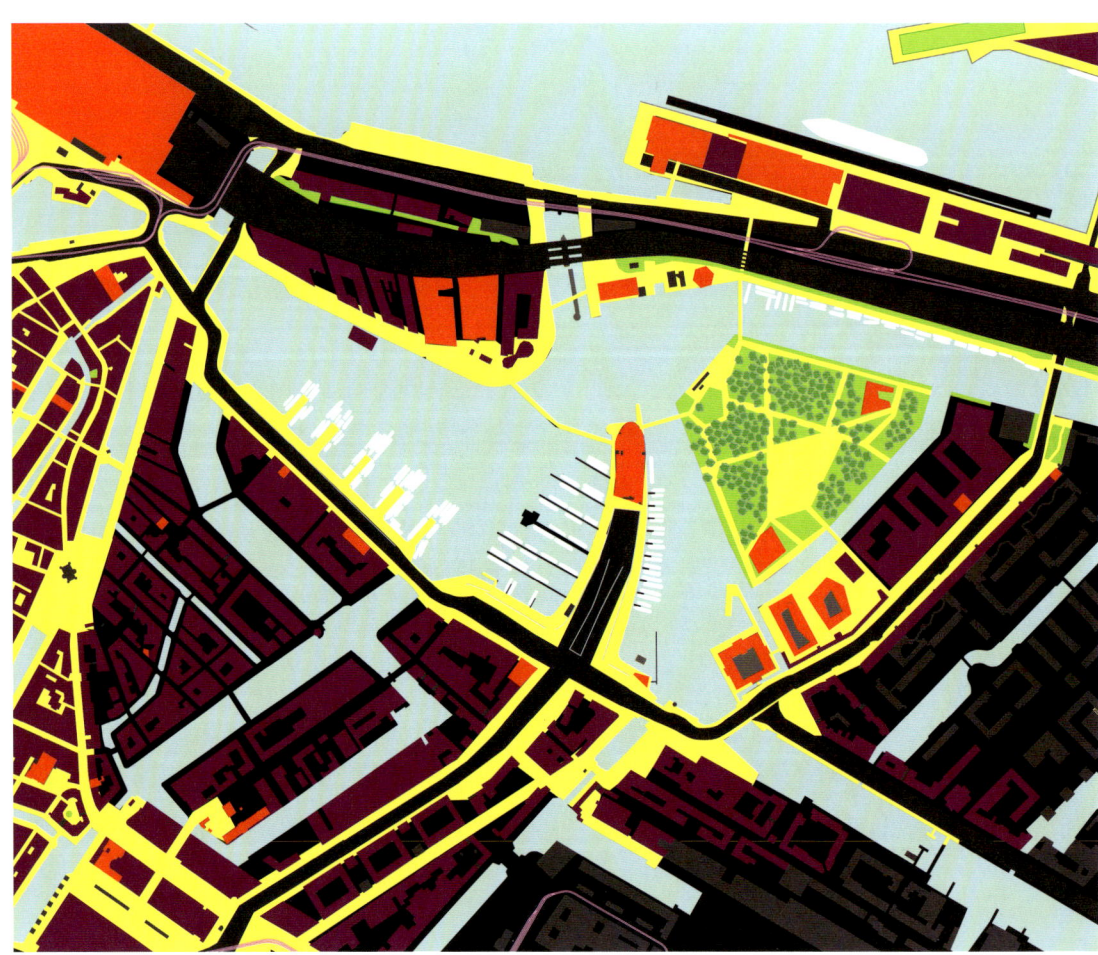

themed around 17th century voyages of discovery, sea battles and pirates, with a fort and lookout tower? It is a question whether – so close to Artis and Nemo – there is room in the tourist market for a new, commercially exploited culture garden in Amsterdam. The contribution of the garden to its surroundings would be limited. After all, anyone exploiting the attraction would want to have as much of the supporting programme on site as possible. Handling a large number of visitors through the existing entrance to the site on the Kattenburgerstraat is also problematic. There are no tram stops in the immediate neighbourhood. Shifting the entrance to the north-west side would improve access from Central Station, the IJtram and the parking garages on Oosterdok Island and by the Muziekgebouw. But then Kattenburgerstraat becomes 'out back'.

It would seem a more obvious solution to make the site public, and develop it as a culture park or culture wharf, in connection with the development of the Oosterdok cluster and the other clusters on the east side of the city. Except for the small Wertheim Park, and a number of 'gardens' such as the Artis, Hortus and Hermitage, the east side of the city has hardly any parks. The Marine base is almost as large as Oosterpark. Existing buildings on the site could be given a new function as cultural facilities in the park.

Such a project could draw its inspiration from a similar development, the Skeppsholmen, in Stockholm. This island was also a former navy base, and was vacated by the military as early as 1969. It is almost 18 hectare in size, and has a special atmosphere thanks to the magnificent trees and historic buildings, warehouses and dwellings. All sorts of cultural facilities are now housed in these monuments, including the museum for modern art and architecture, a theatre, and a hotel in the former barracks. In the 1990s Raphael Moneo designed plans for a new building for the Moderna Museet, and Renzo Piano for the café. In addition, for years the island was the stage for the successful jazz festival, 'Sthlm Jazz Fest'.

The buildings on the Amsterdam Marine base are less historic. Immediately next to the Scheepvaart Museum are some beautiful 17th century buildings which belonged to the shipyard. It would seem natural to use them – with the harbour basin and obviously present remnants of the ways – as an open-air museum, where the history of the site could be seen. The city would also have sports facilities and a conference centre fall into its lap. Other buildings could easily be rebuilt as a hotel. The open space lends itself perfectly for festivals and events.

The most important intervention would be opening up the site for the public. With a couple of bridges it would be easily accessible from Oosterdok Island and the Muziekgebouw, and thus become a part of the circuits around the Oosterdok and to the IJ. These bridges could be built tomorrow, as it were.

The wall along the Kattenburgerstraat could undoubtedly be integrated into the design of the park. The perspective for the street itself is more complicated. A complete make-over of the apartments designed in the late 1960s by the architect Dick Apon is the least that would be

Skeppsholmen Museum Island, Stockholm

needed. The present use and ambiance of the plinth is depressing. Across from the culture park and along the through route to the Eastern Harbour area, non-residential functions must be able to flourish on the ground floor.

The Dutch coast – Scheveningen, Katwijk, Zandvoort

After the coordinated reconstruction of the seaside resorts after the Second World War, the coast played hardly any role in national spatial policy. Only now that its safety is at issue, as a result of climate change, are programmes being developed by cities, provinces, water boards and the national government. At this moment a series of projects which are part of the Strengthening Weak Links programme are being realized along the coast. This is intended to deal with the most problematic points along the coast. These include a number of the resorts, such as Scheveningen, Katwijk and Noordwijk, and more closed sections such as the Delfland coast. In 2008 the national government started the Delta Programme. This is focused on the security of the whole Dutch water system, over a

term of 50 to 100 years. The Delta Programme Coast is a part of this.

In terms of spatial perspectives, it is important to see possible measures for strengthening the coast in relation to other developments, to achieve possible synergy in any solutions. This theme is explored in the graduation studio at the Department of Architecture at the TU Delft, *Delta Interventions*. It is

also a popular theme in other curricula.

The simplest measure for strengthening a coast is sand supplementation, widening the beach by dredging up sand from the ocean. That is occasionally being done here and there, but could become more systematic, possibly even by making the beach along the Dutch coast a kilometre wide. The wider and higher the beach, the easier it is for

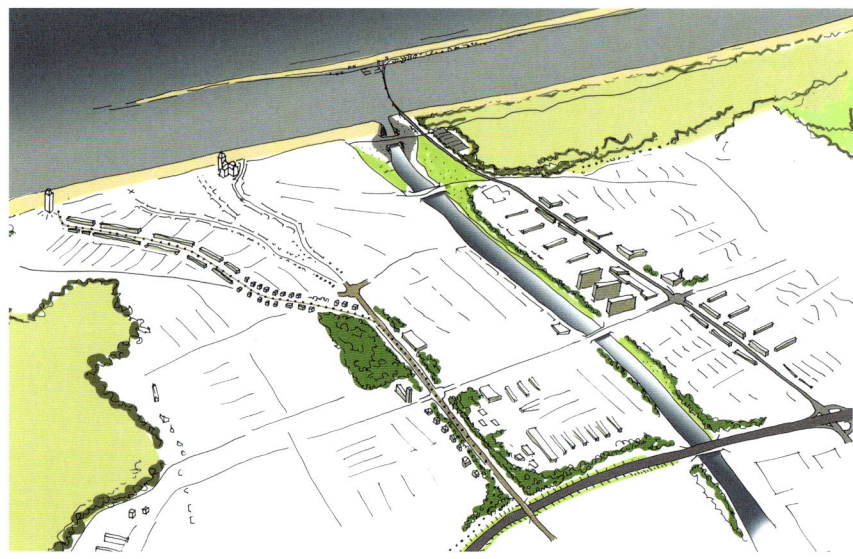

the processes that form dunes to occur. In this way, the dunes are strengthened naturally. In strengthening the Delfland coast, the natural transport of sand along the Dutch coast is also being employed. Over the next decades – and possibly more quickly – the sand in a sandbar, dredged up in 2011, will be deposited along the whole arc of the coast from 's Gravensande to Loosduinen.

Very broad beaches and new dunes have a beneficial effect on the ecological quality and natural values along the coast, but at the same time they fundamentally affect the quality of the seaside resorts with beach boulevards. The boulevards suddenly lie farther from the ocean. New dunes block the view of the sea. It is a question then whether other means of strengthening the coast are conceivable, which leave these qualities intact, or even enhance them.

The three graduation plans by Dorrith Dijkzeul, Maike Warmerdam and Miriam Verrijdt apply different principles. In Dorrith Dijkzeul's plan for Katwijk, an artificial reef is raised off the coast. It is a long, narrow sand bank rising only a couple metres above the sea, enough to break the waves. That would sufficiently protect Katwijk, even in heavy

storms, and with a rising sea level. The existing boulevard and the characteristic family beach can remain intact.

Now and then the reef would flood, and it is therefore not suitable for permanent buildings. It would offer room for temporary structures in the form of hotels, pavilions and vacation homes, and could be used for events and for all kinds of functions which could withstand occasional flooding, such as marinas. For reaching the reef, there is a permanent bridge from the mainland, which connects with the access road to Katwijk from the hinterland around Leiden.

The dunes at Zandvoort are high and wide enough. However, there are no new developments permitted in the safety zone, while these are desirable for improving the quality of the resort. The post-war reconstruction and additions from the 1960s were not very successful. Maike Warmerdam proposes to replace a good deal of the existing seafront. The steep edge of the dunes could then be replaced by a dune which gently slopes away. This would in fact form a coastal defence. Stairs, and a plateau halfway up form the entrance to the beach. This would connect with a new promenade from the

station to the sea. Around it lie all the facilities that are needed to make the resort an attractive destination in the Amsterdam region. A significant residential programme could also be realized on the new seafront. It could even be increased if the present race track were reconstructed. All that would enhance the urban character of the resort. Zandvoort would then become an outpost of the metropolis on the sea.

At present, Scheveningen already functions as such. On busy days the public spaces can hardly deal with the pressure of parking. Miriam Verrijdt combines a solution for this with a new form of coastal defence in the form of 'hooks'. A barrage constructed at an angle to the coast would break the waves and retain the sand. The beach would become larger. Further up, the strip along the sea would erode, creating a dynamic dune landscape. In fact, the barrage is a form of breakwater, similar to what is now used for coastal defence. Parking facilities are built into the barrage, and a promenade laid out on top. The barrage connects with an access road from the hinterland.

Artificial reef off the coast of Katwijk
Design: Dorrith Dijkzeul, plan and Bird's-eye view

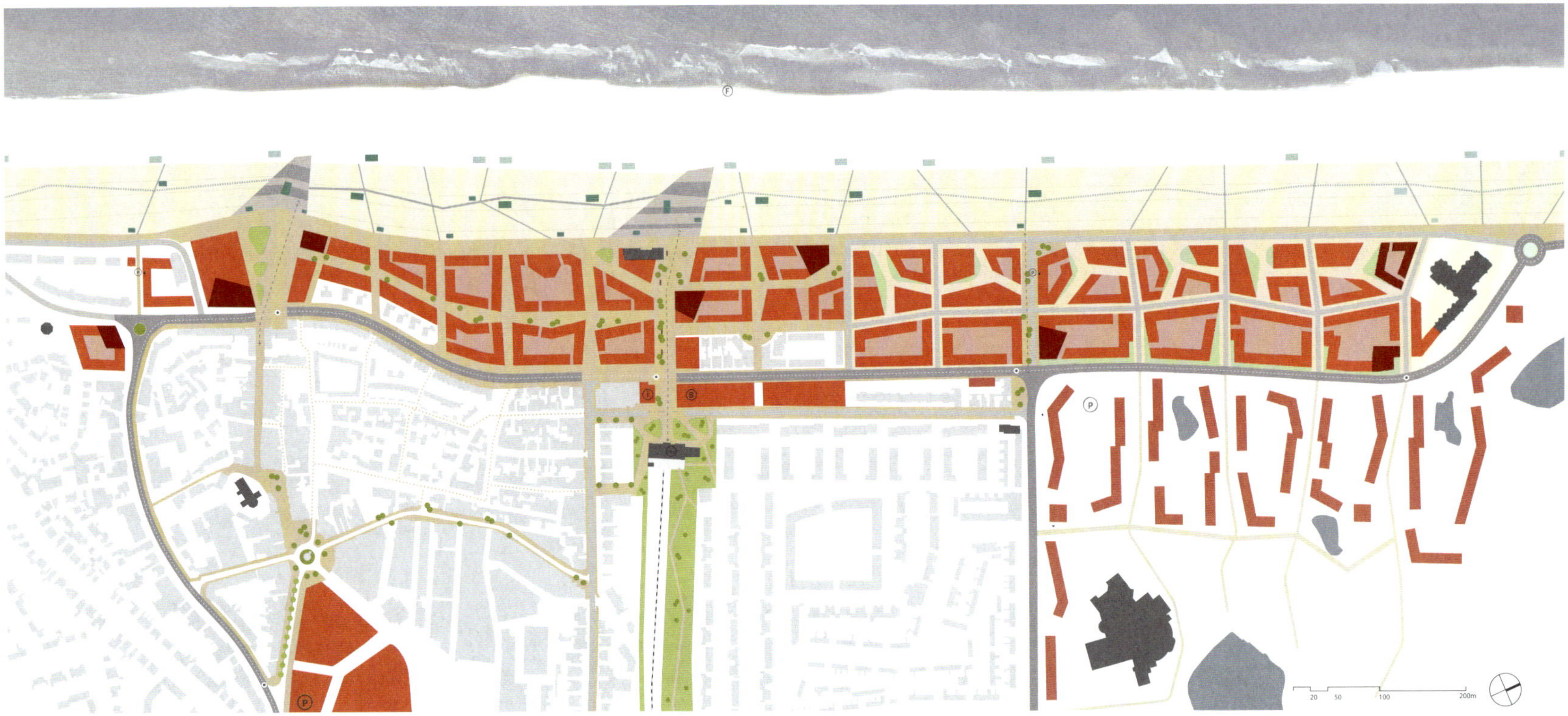

Transformation of the seafront in Zandvoort
Design: Maike Warmerdam, plan and cross section

Barrages on the coast at Scheveningen
Design: Miriam Verrijdt, plan and impression

Convention clusters

On 16 August, 1864, the cast iron and glass Paleis voor Volksvlijt (Palace of Industry) opened its doors on the Frederiksplein. Amsterdam stepped into the modern age.[1] The versatile medical doctor Samuel Sarphati had been responsible for promoting the construction of this exhibition centre, designed by Cornelis Outshoorn, with a nod to the examples of the famed Crystal Palace in London (1851) and the Glaspalast in Munich (1854).[2] Six months later the Maatschappij ter Bevordering van Kruidkunde en Tuinbouw (Society for the promotion of botany and horticulture) organized the first exhibition, with submissions from a number of European countries. Simultaneously, a large international conference was held.

The Paleis voor Volksvlijt burned down in 1929, but the formula is alive and kicking today. In 2011 the HortiFair in the RAI drew 600 exhibitors and 30,000 visitors from over 100 countries. Moreover, the HortiFair in the RAI was combined for the first time with the FloraHolland Trade Fair in Aalsmeer, under the name of Holland Horti Week. The international horticultural community met one another during product presentations, guided tours, networking meetings, workshops and congresses at all sorts of places around the city and region.

Almost 40% of the overnight hotel stays in Amsterdam are related to business trips. Obviously, that is not limited to events like Holland Horti Week, but they do represent an important contribution to the total. Amsterdam is a popular city for conventions.

In this chapter we explore the perspective for the development of trade fairs, congresses and conventions in the Netherlands, for large-scale events where people become acquainted with products, exchange information and meet one another. This will raise various questions, such as: how does this sector develop, what types of facilities can be distinguished, how are they embedded in the cities, and what are the possibilities for new formulas?

AutoRAI, Europahal, RAI complex, Amsterdam

Developments in the trade fair and convention sector in The Netherlands

The RAI – to give it it's full name, the Nederlandse Vereniging Rijwiel- en Automobiel Industrie – traces its roots to the Vereniging Rijwiel Industrie (Bicycle Industry Association) which was established in 1893, and was initially one of the users of the Paleis voor Volksvlijt. In 1928 the RAI moved into a new building on the Ferdinand Bolstraat, in the southern part of the Pijp, on a site that Berlage, in his Plan South, had reserved for a 'building serving the people'.

In this same period a number of European cities, including Geneva, Cologne, Milan, Paris, Vienna, Barcelona and Frankfurt, were building new exhibition complexes. The Jaarbeurs in Utrecht also dates from this same decade. After the Second World War all these complexes were vastly expanded, bit by bit. The overwhelming success of the Hannover Messe, established in 1947 by the British in the zone of Germany they controlled, was an important stimulus for this. In a couple of weeks, almost 750,000 visitors came to the fair, where 1300 businesses were exhibiting their 'Made in Germany' products in a 30,000 m² factory complex which had been rebuilt especially for the occasion.

The site on the Ferdinand Bolstraat offered the RAI little possibility for expansion. The 1934 General Expansion Plan for Amsterdam had already projected a new exhibition site on the Amstel, adjoining the new garden city of Buitenveldert, on the site where Amstel Park is today. This site, however, lay outside the city limits. Thus the choice was made for the present site on the Europaplein. In the late 1940s the General Expansion Plan was revised to reflect this. Alexander Bodon prepared the design for the large Europahal (1951-1961) and for the congress centre realized a few years later (1965). The Amstelhal followed in the 1970s. In addition to trade fairs and congresses, from that date the complex has been used for parties, sports events and theatre and musical performances.

In Utrecht the Jaarbeurs complex was also moved from the Vredenburg to its present location south of Central Station after the War. The Julianahal was designed in 1956 by Gerrit Rietveld. Its expansion was from the hand of Rein Fledderus (1965-1973). The adjoining Jaarbeurs Congress Centre was opened some years later.

Rotterdam and The Hague, on the contrary, realized separate trade fair and convention facilities: the Ahoy complex (Groosman, 1968-1971) and the Doelen (Kraaijvanger, 1966) in Rotterdam, and the Houtrusthallen (renovated 1972) and the Congresgebouw (Oud, 1965-1967) in The Hague.

Most medium-sized cities in The Netherlands reconstructed their livestock markets as multi-functional complexes during these years: Frieslandhal in Leeuwarden (1963), Groenoordhal in Leiden (1969), Brabanthallen in Den Bosch (1969) and the IJsselhallen in Zwolle (1972). In Groningen the new Martinihal was built as an exhibition and event complex in 1969. The construction of the MECC in Maastricht only followed a considerable time later, in 1983.

During the 1980s the importance of events increased. It was then, for instance, that the Sportpaleis Ahoy was revamped along the American model as an 'Arena'. Next, the globalization of the economy, trade, science and management in the 1990s led to a steep growth in the international conference market. The Congresgebouw in The Hague was transformed into the World Forum. Many hotels also began to open convention facilities. These decades also saw the area of the RAI almost doubled by the realization of the Hollandhal (1982) and Parkhal (1993).

By the 1990s the remaining livestock markets were suffering a fatal financial decline, and appeared to be the source of all sorts of animal illnesses. Most were closed during this period, the buildings demolished or radically transformed, like the Brabanthallen in Den Bosch. In 2000 the Houtrusthallen in The Hague were also demolished. On its site

Bird's-eye view, Ahoy complex, Rotterdam

a much smaller sports hall was rebuilt.

In the meantime the renewal of the larger facilities went on unabated. In 2009 the RAI opened the Elicium, connecting existing buildings and containing a ballroom, conference and meeting facilities. A mega-cinema opened adjoining the Jaarbeurs in Utrecht in 2011, and a new casino and hotel are under construction. The redesign of the public space around the World Forum in The Hague is to be completed in late 2012. The Sportpaleis Ahoy is being totally renovated, and will focus more explicitly on concerts and sports events.

In this manner, the variety in the trade fair and convention sector is being increased. Five tendencies play a role in this: increased variations in reach, specialization, integration of fairs and conferences, diversification and network development. Each of

	ICCA	UIA
1	Vienna (154)	Singapore (725)
2	Barcelona (148)	Brussels (486)
3	Paris (147)	Paris (394)
4	Berlin (138)	Vienna (257)
5	Singapore (136)	Seoul (201)
6	Madrid (114)	Barcelona (193)
7	Istanbul (109)	Tokyo (190)
8	Lisbon (106)	Geneva (189)
9	**Amsterdam (104)**	Madrid (175)
10	Sydney (102)	Berlin (165)
11	Taipei (99)	London (164)
12	Beijing (98)	Budapest (144)
13	Buenos Aires (98)	Sydney (137)
14	London (97)	**Amsterdam (131)**
15	Copenhagen (92)	New York (127)

**World rankings of convention cities in 2010
According to UIA and ICCA** [5]

**Top 10 roofed exhibition centres in The Netherlands
in m²**

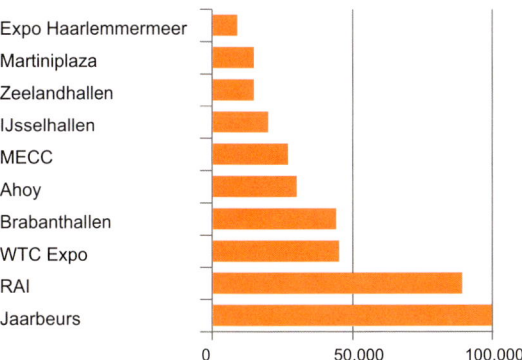

these aspects is discussed separately in the next section.

Increasing differences in reach

First and foremost, the larger venues differentiate themselves in terms of their reach. When the organizers of a conference or trade fair in The Netherlands wish to hold a major event, there are really only two places where that can take place: the Jaarbeurs in Utrecht, with 100,000 m² of space, and the RAI in Amsterdam with 87,000 m². These are far and away the largest exposition facilities in the country. Complexes like the Brabanthallen in Den Bosch (44,000 m²), Ahoy in Rotterdam (30,000 m²) and the MECC in Maastricht (27,000 m²) are considerably smaller. In the market for business visitors, this gives Amsterdam and Utrecht a substantial advantage over the other cities. Moreover, Amsterdam and Utrecht have the advantage of their central location with relation to the Dutch railway and motorway network. The complexes in the two cities have fast and direct connections from all over the country.

All of the major trade fairs in The Netherlands, from the Horecava to the Electrotechniekbeurs, are thus held in the Jaarbeurs or the RAI. These are fairs with a national reach. Although there are international exhibitors at many of the fairs, such as the German, American or Swedish auto manufacturers at the RAI, these trade fairs primarily attract a domestic audience.

Because international events also often require large spaces, once again Amsterdam and Utrecht, enjoying the advantage of accessibility, are the most obvious candidates. In practice, Amsterdam, with its closeness to Schiphol, and the additional advantages of the historic heart of Amsterdam and a wider selection of hotels, is the only city which succeeds in drawing a large number of international events. Four times as many international exhibitors come to

Amsterdam as to Utrecht. In Amsterdam 48% of the exhibitors at fairs come from foreign countries, as opposed to 12% in Utrecht.

With regard to international conventions, the distinction is still clearer. There are two authoritative lists which keep track of international conferences, that of the ICCA and the UIA. Amsterdam is ranked among the top in both lists. According to the UIA, in 2010 Amsterdam was the 14th ranking city for conventions in the world; according to the definitions of the ICCA it was in 9th place. [3] Amsterdam's competitors for attracting fairs and conferences of international stature are therefore New York, Paris, Las Vegas and Milan, rather than Utrecht or The Hague. The city's most important trump card is Schiphol. [4] In addition, its infrastructure permits Amsterdam to occupy a top spot as an international business destination: enough hotel space in the higher four and five star segments, museums, shopping and entertainment venues, cultural heritage and a tolerant and hospitable image. Amsterdam thus has international reach, Utrecht national. Groningen, Zwolle, Rotterdam, Den Bosch and Maastricht are primarily regional in their reach.

Specialization

The market is more open if an event does not require a large space. The World Forum in The Hague is perhaps a more suitable location for international conferences than the RAI – particularly if the event involves the themes of peace and human rights. Because of this specialization, the city has succeeded in attracting important international events such as the 2009 Afghanistan conference. The World Forum is also the stage for annual international conferences such as those sponsored by the International Criminal Court (ICC), the Organization for the Prohibition of Chemical Weapons (OPCW) and The Hague International Model United Nations (THIMUN). At a different level of scale, the Doelen Congrescentrum

in Rotterdam also functions as a specialized convention location.

In the field of entertainment and amusement, the large fair complexes in the Netherlands compete with facilities of an entirely different sort. With their RAI Theatre and the Beatrix Theatre, the RAI and Jaarbeurs, respectively, have realized separate buildings for theatre performances. Their fair facilities can also be used for very large concerts and parties. Ahoy uses the same space for trade fairs, sports events and concerts, and after the expansion in 2012 will provide a location for concerts with 13,000 visitors. In the same year the Ziggo Dome in Amsterdam Zuidoost, with a capacity of 15,000 visitors, expects to open its doors. Its neighbour, the Heineken Music Hall, has also rapidly succeeded in winning a place among the most familiar pop stages in the country.

The new generation of football stadiums however make up the outdoor category for concerts. Inspired by the success of mega-events in Rotterdam's Kuip, the design of a number of the stadiums built in the 1990s took other events besides just sports competitions into account. The Gelredome in Arnhem, with a capacity of 34,000 visitors, is now *the* location in the east of The Netherlands for large events. Its ingenious construction permits half the stadium to be closed off, to create a more intimate atmosphere. The ArenA in Amsterdam can even accommodate double that number of visitors. Selling out the ArenA is a status symbol among Dutch performers.

Specialization has meant that the above facilities have become frontrunners in the niche markets of conventions and entertainment. The trade-off is that they lack the flexibility of the halls in the great exhibition centres. It is precisely this flexibility that provides them with a competitive advantage here. In this, the exhibition centres are aided by another of the important trends in the sector of business

tourism entertainment: integration of various sorts of events.

Integration of fairs and conventions

Trade fairs and conventions are becoming increasingly interconnected. It is difficult to find a fair without an accompanying convention, workshops, lectures and presentations any more. This can particularly be seen at trade fairs which, unlike their more public counterparts, are pitched primarily at professionals. Such integrated trade fairs are called conventions.

To an increasing degree, the economic activities in any particular sector will cover the whole world. This means that colleagues - and competitors – are found at greater distances. When they have a chance to meet each other at fairs, this is an opportunity for contact and exchanging knowledge. Thus there are often lectures by leading scientists or entrepreneurs within the profession organized in parallel with the fair. For these lectures and product presentations different kinds of spaces are needed, convention and meeting halls. Moreover, the presence of so many people from a particular sector is an ideal moment for product promotion. Leading businesses in an industry and suppliers of raw materials and semi-manufactured products often organize receptions and dinners to strengthen ties with their clients. A trade fair is a good moment for this too.

Thus the focus of fairs on trade and expositions is increasingly further integrated with the exchange of information, promotion and networking. These new dimensions have become ever more important as *raisons d'être* for the large fairs. Seeing products and placing orders can also be done outside the fair by internet or telephone; the contacts and confidence that is created during the fair are more important, as they contribute to knowing which product must be looked at and purchased.

Going in the other direction, exhibitors have also entered the convention circuit. In addition to the advantages of integration discussed above, the provision of booths for producers is a source of income for the convention. For instance, manufacturers of pharmaceuticals are often prepared to pay to bring their products to the attention of a medical congress. And this often means a welcome supplement to the budget for the organizers of scientific conferences.

This is not true for all conferences, however. It is important at this point to make a distinction between what are called association conferences and non-association conferences. Association conferences are organized by societies, non-association conferences by individual businesses. Many associations organize gatherings for their members with a specific frequency. These meetings are not sensitive to economic cycles, and have a long preparation time. There is often also a distinction made among scientific, political and non-governmental associations. The medical sector is dominant among the scientific conferences. This sector has a large number of specialities, and is sponsored by the medical industry. As examples of political conferences, one can think of summit conferences among international leaders, or a convention of the Association of Dutch Municipalities. Non-governmental conferences are held by all kinds of NGOs, such as Greenpeace or Friends of the Earth.

Non-association conferences by individual businesses are often organized around product presentations, training or business anniversaries. Sponsoring by means of exhibitors is thus much less important. Often this sort of event is an opportunity for the sponsoring firm to entertain lavishly. Thus non-association conferences are often combined with an extensive social programme: excursions, receptions, dinners and luxury hotels. Because such conferences are often organized for a certain occasion, such as the introduction of a new product or a particularly successful business year, and the lavishness of the event is dependent on the financial situation of the firm, non-association conferences are in general booked shortly before they are held.

Diversification

Traditionally, in addition to large commercial conference centres, cities have always had venues and societies for discussions and debates. In Amsterdam, Felix Meritis received a new breath of life in the 1960s; later it was followed by De Balie in 1982 and De Rode Hoed in 1990. New initiatives such as Pakhuis de Zwijger, and more recently De Nieuwe Liefde, demonstrate that discussion is still a vital social need. Since the 1990s, there have also been more commercial facilities added. Many hotels built meeting, conference and exhibition spaces, or expanded their existing facilities. On Amsterdam's South Axis, in addition to the RAI, there arose two smaller conference and exhibition centres.

It is interesting to note that, in addition to their main purpose, many new initiatives in Amsterdam provide spaces reserved for conference facilities. For instance, from its inception, the transformation of the Westergasfabriek took the possibility of holding fairs and conferences there into account. With the opening of the Passenger Terminal, Amsterdam not only obtained a stronger position in the international cruise market, but the city also got a conference and exhibition space with it. The Theaterfabriek, opened in 2004, can also be rented during the week for business events.

As a result of all this, not only has the total number of square metres in the city for rent expanded strongly, but the diversity of the facilities has also greatly increased. By coupling conference facilities with other activities in the building or in the vicinity, the spaces gain a theme. For instance, that makes the Artis and Tropical Museum in the east of Amsterdam unique for the city. Characteristic Amsterdam buildings like De Bazel and Berlage's Exchange lend a special character to a conference. With increasing frequency it is also possible to rent special places for a gathering. For example, while lobbying for the 2018 World Cup football matches, the representatives of FIFA were wined and dined in the gallery with Rembrandt's Night Watch. In this way the diversification of conference facilities keeps pace with the ever-increasing variety of business gatherings.

Beurs van Berlage, Amsterdam

Network development

Furthermore, the diversification means that many facilities in the city with their own profile are not only competitors, but also complementary. As it happens, they aim at different target groups in terms of size, sort and the aura around the event. In attracting events to Amsterdam, these facilities therefore profit from each other's proximity. A large event at the RAI, for instance, also provides a market for the rental of specialized locations elsewhere in the city. After a day in convention meetings, it is a relief to hold a dinner or closing party in a different space. For this, Amsterdam as a city is able to accommodate a wide diversity of events. An additional advantage is that fairs can 'move up' within the city. After s successful start in 2002 in the PTA, the Millionaire Fair moved up to the RAI for 2003, and Amsterdam was able to retain this event.

The Parisian ViParis goes a step further. It unites ten conference and exposition facilities in the vicinity of the French capital. They offer organizers one address to which they can come for any event in Paris. Together with the organizer, they review which location fits best with their event. These locations vary from the large halls at the Porte de Versailles and Villepinte to business location in La Défense. At the same time, the organization has access to a prestigious gallery in the Louvre. As a result, the Parisian facilities do not compete with one another in terms of prices, but assure that an event ends up in the most suitable spot. If a location is already booked by another event for the dates desired, a solution is sought within ViParis.

In The Netherlands, the RAI and Jaarbeurs made an attempt in the 1990s to combine forces. That was however vetoed by the Netherlands Competition Authority. Within Amsterdam, most facilities also still operate autonomously.

Significance of the sector

Estimating the economic importance of the convention sector is not easy. Among the aspects which play a role are the spending by visitors, employment opportunities and the effect on the image of cities and countries. The NBTC has calculated that over a quarter of the 9.9 million overnight stays in The Netherlands have a business purpose. Together, these business visitors spent 1.27 billion.[6] However, far from all business visitors come for a fair or convention. In 2004 LAgroup calculated the spending of foreign visitors at non-corporate conferences at 116 million Euro. For an accurate picture of the fair and convention sector, however, domestic visitors and visitors to fairs and corporate events must be added to this figure. Therefore it is apparently more interesting to note their finding that visitors spent an average of 344 Euro per day.[7] That is much more than touristic visitors spend.

The RAI has calculated that for each Euro spent at the RAI, there is a spin-off of 5 Euro in the region for hotels, transportation, visits to tourist attractions and eating and drinking. In terms of job opportunities, that means one job in the RAI equals eight jobs in the region in security, exhibition stand construction, transport and the hotel, restaurants and café sector.

The market for tourism and conferences thus has a considerable economic effect. This effect is not only in added value and job opportunities, but also in promotion. More and more governments regard fairs and conferences as outstanding ways to build the image of their city or country. Business visitors often add several days to the conference to enjoy the city. As a result of a positive experience, they will consider coming back for vacation as well.

Fair and convention clusters in the largest cities

In order to obtain insight into the structure and function of the fair and convention sector, an analysis was made of the location of all facilities in the four largest cities. Facilities with one or more halls for more than 100 persons were included in the analysis. Obviously, the large exhibition and convention centres will be included. In addition, clear clusters of conference hotels and more specialized facilities emerged. The clusters in the four cities are of various size.

Location of venues comprising ViParis

Amsterdam

With 39% of the total, the capital attracts far and away the largest share of business visitors to The Netherlands. As is to be expected, then, a large number of conference and meeting locations are to be found there, from the massive RAI to small halls in hotels in the city centre. One finds two clusters in Amsterdam: one in the city centre and one around the RAI. In addition to the two clusters there are a large number of hotels with conference facilities spread across the city: along the A10 Ring Road in the west, near Amstel and Sloterdijk stations, and on the NDSM site. The lounges and galleries of the ArenA can also be rented separately for conventions and product presentations. Finally, several hotels at and around Schiphol offer convention and meeting facilities. It is advantageous for businesses to hire these facilities when foreign colleagues and business partners are being flown in for brief periods.

CITY CENTRE CLUSTER

Within a radius of 750 metres in and around the centre of Amsterdam lie 35 facilities with one or more halls accommodating at least 100 persons. The selection is highly differentiated. The PTA and the Beurs van Berlage offer the largest facilities designed to handle fairs and conventions. In addition there are a large number of conference hotels, with a concentration around Leidseplein. These conference hotels are primarily used for corporate meetings. 79% of the business meetings in Amsterdam take place in four and five star hotels.

The selection is complemented by discussion centres (Rode Hoed, Felix Meritis, De Balie), hall rental facilities (Akantes), and special spaces for rent (Tropical Institute). Facilities such as these, specially focused on meetings and conferences, are more interesting for the non-corporate sector. 82% of such meetings take place in specialized facilities. The facilities are of particular interest for smaller, urban-oriented conferences, and less so for fairs and conventions that need larger areas. These are chiefly to be found outside the city centre and along the IJ.

SOUTH AXIS CLUSTER

The RAI and the South-WTC railway station are the most important supports for the South axis cluster. In the course of time all sorts of complementary facilities have developed, such as the Okura Hotel, Holiday Inn and Novotel. The Olympic stadium, Amstelpark, ExpoWTC and the Vrije Universiteit also offer facilities for meetings and small conventions and conferences.

The cluster is however dominated by the RAI. The total RAI site is 23 hectare in area; the complex itself has a floor area of 87,000 m². For extremely large fairs another 10,000 m² of temporary halls can be added. In addition to the conference centre with the large hall for 2000 visitors, the complex includes 66 permanent and 59 temporary smaller halls[8] and a new ballroom in the Elicium, which can accommodate dinners for up to 750 guests.

Depending on the calendar of events within any one year, the RAI draws 1.5 to 2 million visitors per year.

Floor plan Amsterdam RAI

Legend for pages 107, 109, 111 and 113

hotels

conference locations

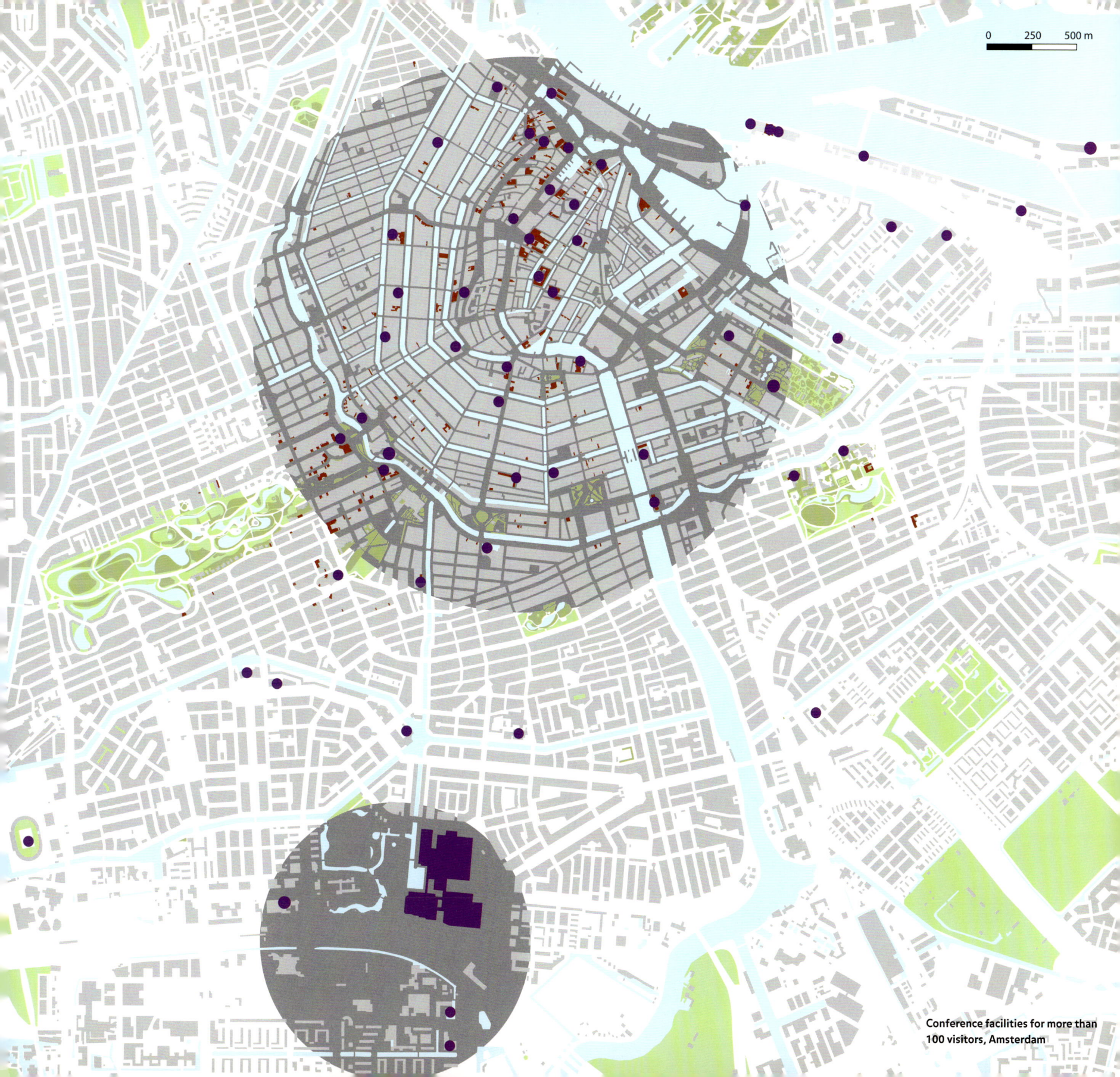

Conference facilities for more than
100 visitors, Amsterdam

Utrecht

CITY CENTRE CLUSTER

Within a radius of 375 metres in the heart of Utrecht there are 18 facilities with one or more halls for 100 or more persons.

JAARBEURS

The Jaarbeurs profiles itself as the Village Square of The Netherlands, and is home to a large number of national fairs. It is strongly oriented to the important public transportation hub surrounding Utrecht Central Station. This is the busiest station in The Netherlands, and lies at the centre of the network. Complementary facilities include the Beatrix Theatre, a large Holiday Inn, a mega-cinema and casino. These also offer conference facilities. The Beatrix Theatre, for instance provides facilities for conferences of up to 1500 persons.

The cluster is dominated by the Jaarbeurs. The site is 30 hectare in size, and the total floor space in the twelve exhibition halls is 100,000 m². The largest of these is almost 14,000 m², and ten metres high. Other components of the complex include fifteen conference halls, running upward in size from 150 persons. The Expozaal in the Beatrixgebouw is 2500 m². The Jaarbeurs attracts over five million visitors a year.

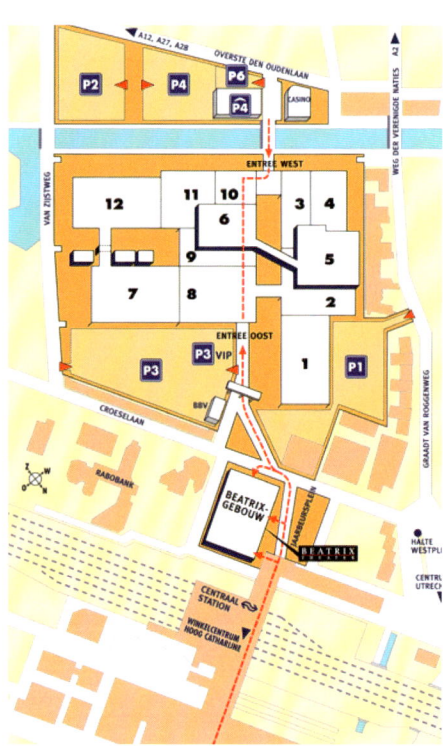

Floor plan, Jaarbeurs, Utrecht

Conference facilities for more than 100 visitors, Utrecht

Rotterdam

There are two clusters in Rotterdam, the city centre cluster and the Ahoy cluster. There are various locations for meetings in hotels and hall rental centres scattered around the city, in the Kop van Zuid and at Feyenoord Stadium, Blijdorp Zoo and the former Van Nelle factory.

City centre cluster

The Rotterdam city centre cluster covers an area with a radius of 375 metres, and accommodates six facilities with large halls. The most important venue is De Doelen, right by Rotterdam Central station. It has three 'hall areas' with separate entrances, accommodating 80 to 465, 250 to 700 and, in the largest hall, 700 to 1755 persons. The maximum capacity is 3000. Dinners for up to 250 are possible. Here too there is an extensive complementary selection of smaller hotels and special venues, such as the Euromast.

Ahoy

Ahoy is the most multifunctional complex in the Randstad. At its heart lies the Sportpaleis, modernized in 2011, for sports events and concerts from 2500 to 15,000 visitors. It is a real 'arena', in the American sense of the word. Additionally, the complex has a conference and meeting centre for up to 650 persons, and six halls for exhibitions, with a total floor area of 30.000 m². In 2010 Ahoy drew 1.7 million visitors. The Ahoy complex lies near the Zuidplein shopping centre, and can be accessed by the Metro. There are no hotels around the complex. The shopping centre does have the Zuidplein Theatre, with two auditoriums for 585 and 166 visitors.

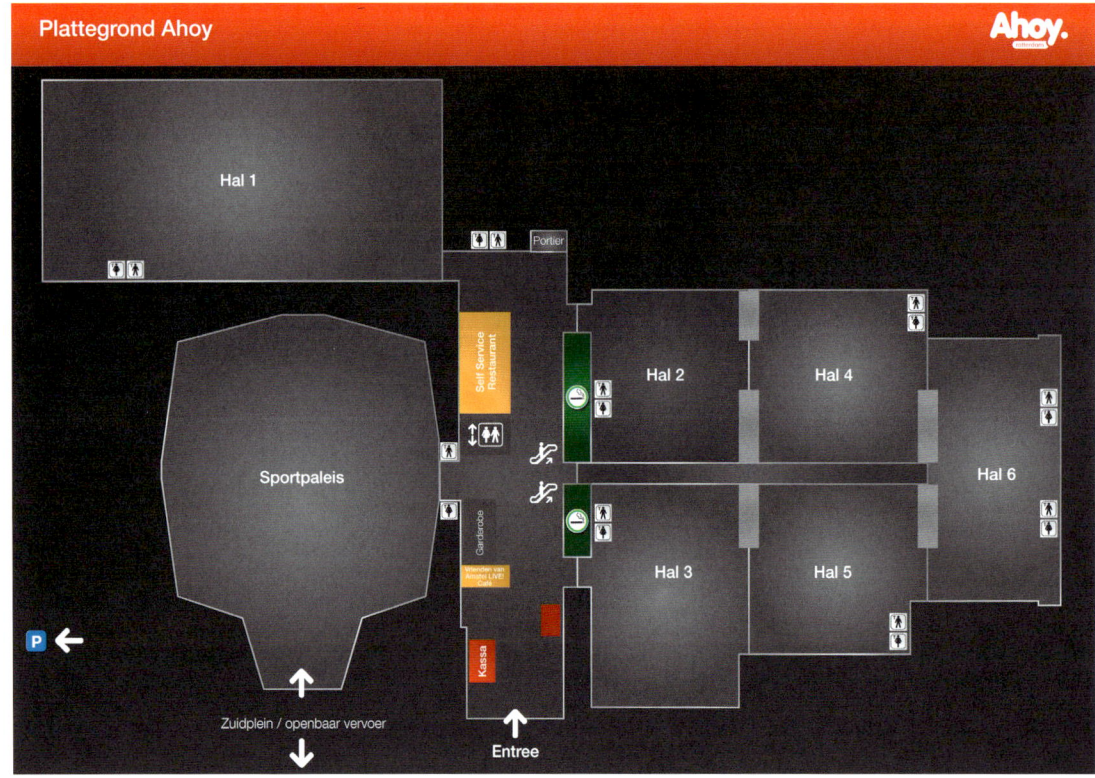

Floor plan, Ahoy, Rotterdam

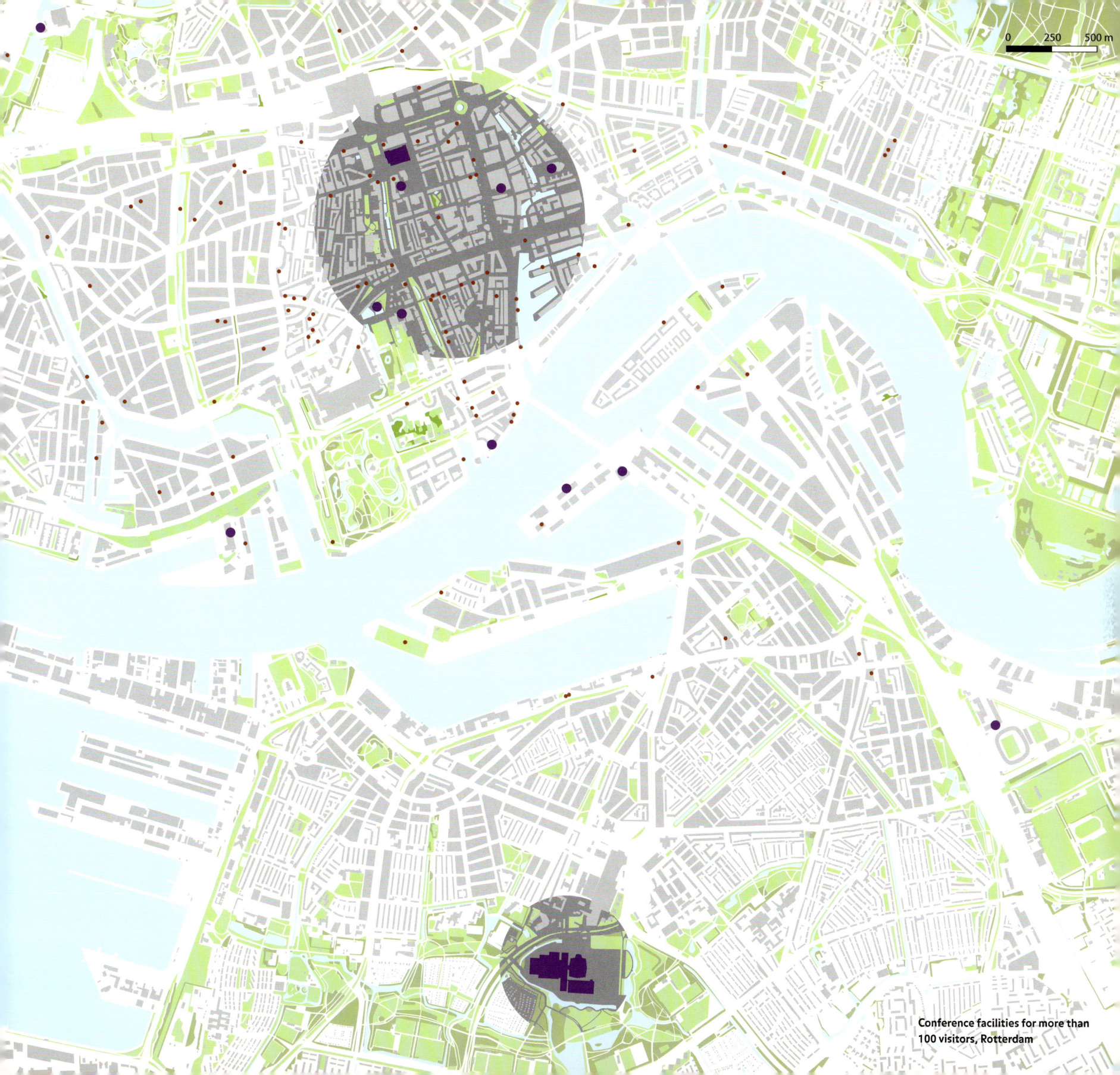

Conference facilities for more than
100 visitors, Rotterdam

The Hague

The Hague has three clusters: the city centre cluster, the World Forum cluster, and the Scheveningen cluster.

CITY CENTRE CLUSTER

A large number of conference facilities are spread around the centre of The Hague. The cluster covers an area with a radius of about 375 metres, and includes 12 facilities with large halls. In addition to many chic and less chic hotels, churches and hall rental facilities, The Hague has a number of clubs and associations, such as the Sociëteit de Witte, Pulchri Studio and the Nieuwspoort press centre. For very special occasions the Ridderzaal and its surrounding smaller halls are available.

WORLD FORUM

In 2006 TCN redeveloped The Hague's Congrescentrum as the present World Forum. The Congrescentrum, designed by the architects J.J.P. and H.E. Oud, opened in 1969. The World Forum has a total of 65,000 m² of space, and a multifunctional auditorium with 1600 seats. At the same time it was renovated, surrounding hotels were also expanded, and an underground parking garage with 590 places was realized. The Statenhal was demolished to make way for the offices of Europol. The World Forum supports an extensive cluster around it. Several hotels, such as Novotel Den Haag, the Crowne Plaza and the Bel Air hotel, are in the immediate vicinity. It is also possible to rent halls in the adjoining culture cluster: Museon, the Municipal Museum and Omniversum. At a somewhat greater distance lies the Peace Palace, seat of international organizations such as the International Court of Justice, but also the backdrop for countless international conferences. Several large hotels, such as The Hague Hilton, lie around the Peace Palace.

SCHEVENINGEN

Several of the large resort hotels in the Scheveningen tourist cluster have discovered the conference market. Beach pavilions and the Circus Theatre can also be rented, in whole or in part. The Kurhaus supports the cluster. From 1979 to 1995 there was also a casino located in the hotel. This moved to a new building on the other side of the street in 1995. In the renovations which followed, the capacity of the Kurhaus was massively expanded. Its large hall measures 1000 m² and when set us as a theatre seats 500. Sixteen smaller halls for meetings and dinners – often with ocean views – surround it.

Conclusions

In all four of the large cities in the Randstad we find mixed city centre clusters with a wide assortment of hall rental centres, discussion centres, conference hotels and several specialized facilities such as de Doelen in Rotterdam, the Ridderzaal in The Hague and the Beurs van Berlage in Amsterdam. The selection in Amsterdam (37) is wider than in Utrecht (18), The Hague (12) and Rotterdam (6). The area of the cluster in Amsterdam is also larger. The city centre clusters in The Hague, Rotterdam and Utrecht cover an area with a radius of about 375 metres. The Amsterdam cluster is much larger; in fact, it covers the whole city centre, with a concentration around the Leidseplein and a part of the Museum quarter. It is twice as big.

The largest facilities all lie outside the city centres, but their surroundings are dissimilar. The RAI in Amsterdam is part of the South Axis, an internationally oriented business district. The Jaarbeurs in Utrecht lies immediately next to Central Station, the central hub of the national railway network. The World Forum in The Hague adjoins the museum cluster around the Municipal Museum.

Only Ahoy lies in a truly peripheral location. It is also the most specialized facility. The arena of the Sportpaleis plays an important role for national events in the fields of sports and music. On the other hand, the fairs and expositions held in the Ahoy complex have a regional and local character.

With regard to its selection and size, Scheveningen is comparable with the city centre clusters of Rotterdam, Utrecht and The Hague. It however has a unique character because of its seaside location.

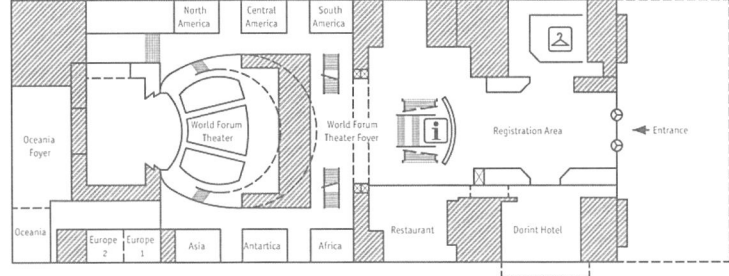

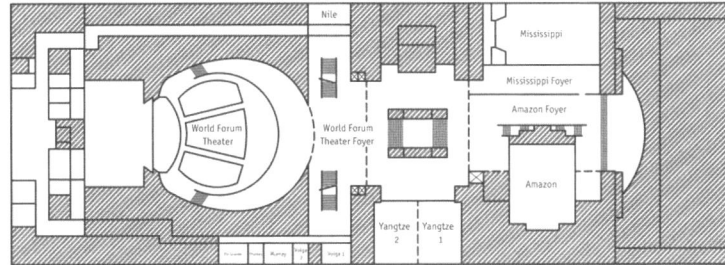

Floor plans for ground floor and first storey, Worldforum, The Hague

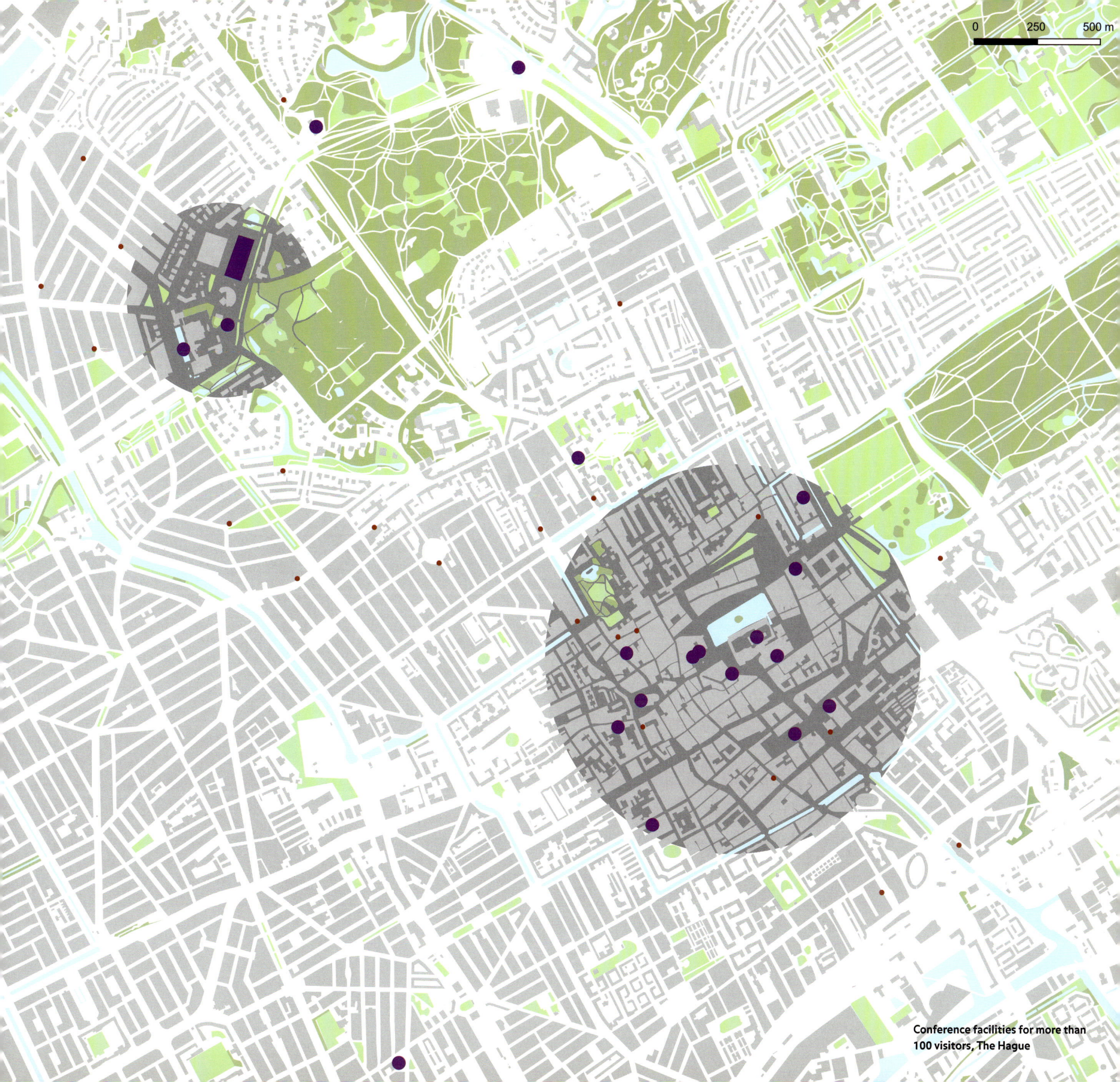

Conference facilities for more than 100 visitors, The Hague

Typology of fair and conference clusters in the largest cities

On the basis of the material collected, we can conclude that the number of types of facilities for fairs and conferences is limited. There are centres, quarters and an occasional district. At the same time, it is clear that the centres differ greatly among themselves. There is a high degree of specialization to be found in facilities of this type. Fair and exhibition centres, conference centres and convention centres differ in sizes, structure and location. These subtypes will therefore be discussed separately. The 'arena' subtype will not be dealt with here. Such specialized centres are generally used for sports and music events – comparable with Madison Square Garden in New York.

In Germany many exhibition sites are denominated as *Gelände*. In addition to the actual buildings in the complex, the surrounding open areas, generally used for parking, can also be used for temporary expositions or outdoor exhibitions. Sometimes these areas are also termed 'parks'. Despite there being a couple of fine examples from the past, sites of this sort are rare in The Netherlands. Only the Floriade sites are related. The *Gelände* type is also discussed separately.

Centres

A *centre* is a complex of one or more interconnected, roofed-over meeting spaces. We will successively discuss fair or exhibition centres, conference centres and convention centres. Trade fairs are organised in exhibition centres, conferences in conference centres. The two activities impose different requirements and must be incorporated in the urban fabric in different ways. The types represent the two extremes in the present market for fairs and conferences. Various intermediate forms are however being built with increasing frequency. Where in the past a complex of meeting rooms might be built to accompany the halls of an exhibition site, or an exposition area developed to go with a conference centre, more and more often now the two activities are being integrated. Here conference and exposition spaces are equal and integral parts of the complex, often being joined by ballrooms, banquet halls, foyers and recreational centres. In the United States, where most such facilities are to be found, these buildings are called convention centres. We will retain that term here.

FAIR AND EXHIBITION CENTRES

Showing products at fairs is a European tradition which has its roots in the annual markets of the Middle Ages. The seven largest fair sites in the world therefore are to be found in Europe. Germany in particular has a number of large exhibition centres, including Hannover, the largest in the world, with almost 500,000 m² of covered exhibition space. Preferably only the ground floor is used as an exhibition hall. Moving goods in and out and channelling visitors are more difficult if one is working with multiple layers. Moreover, exhibitors prefer halls without columns or partitions. This limits the weight that upper floors can carry. Thus multi-storey buildings are more expensive and less practical. It is for this reason that exhibition centres often cover immense areas.

Moreover, exhibition centres often create immense traffic problems in their vicinity. These involve both the installation and removal of exhibits, and visitors' traffic. Before a fair the exhibits have to be set up, and dismantled after it. This involves all sorts of freight traffic, with the stands, products to be shown, catering and delivery of printed materials. All these elements must come together in the exhibition centre in a short time. This is a serious logistic exercise.

During the event the problem becomes how to handle the floods of visitors. The location of the centre with regard to infrastructure will play a major role in this. Facilities in the centre of a city are generally easier to reach by public transit, but on the other hand there is less parking space available in urban centres.

Thus it is not surprising that new exhibition centres are often built outside the urban core. Complexes which in the past were built on the edges of the city, and in the course of time have become surrounded by further urban development, are now reaching the limits of their growth. Moreover, the logistical problems they confront in their locations are becoming insurmountable. Such facilities are therefore being demolished, in whole or in part, or repurposed. A newer, more peripheral complex is then financed with the monies thus generated. With an eye to international access, these new complexes often lie close to airports.

Milan is a characteristic example of this tendency. The original fair complex lay on the edge of the city centre. The transformation of a former oil refinery outside the city into a new fair complex made it possible to repurpose the old location near the centre as a city park with a museum, conference centre, and residential development. This reduced the congestion problems in the city centre. The construction of a new subway line from the city to

Messe, Hannover
(© Deutsche Messe AG)

the new exhibition centre made it easy to reach. Milan now has the second largest exhibition centre in the world, with an area of 345,000 m². Some of the halls on the old site were retained, and the conference centre, designed by Mario Bellini, has developed into one of the largest convention centres in Europe. Milano Congressi has three large halls for 4000, 2000 and 1500 visitors, respectively. Comparable developments have occurred in Munich and Madrid.

CONFERENCE CENTRES

At the other extreme are the pure conference centres. These facilities, built since the 1960s, often have a large number of halls of various sizes. This makes it possible for them to host different conferences at the same time, or hold several sessions of the same conference concurrently. The quality of the amenities and the finish of the halls, in terms of lighting, temperature control, acoustics and materials, is much higher than in exhibition halls. Exhibition halls are much more basic than conference halls.

Because the numbers of participants in conferences are generally much lower than visitor numbers at fairs and there is no necessity for large floor areas for exhibitions, the large halls of the exhibition centres are not needed. Most conference centres have a large auditorium seating 1000 to 2000. Because of their smaller size and the lack of any need for floors to bear great weight, conference centres can easily be multi-storey structures. As a result, they take up less space in the city, and are thus more often found in city centres.

The layout of a conference centre is very important. A large hall for 2000 persons is necessary for large conferences, but a number of other spaces of various sizes around it are even more important. The large hall is generally used for only the opening and closing sessions of the conference. During the event there are sessions with various numbers of participants around different topics or for specific activities, held in the smaller spaces. Many conference centres today thus have halls and auditoriums which are flexible in size, and can be subdivided or opened up. Variation can be

introduced by means of the layout of the chairs, but also by means of moveable partitions and facilities for image projection and sound amplification. Used cleverly, these techniques can create halls of any suitable size.

One of the largest conference centres is the Palais des Congrès in Paris. It was built in 1974 where the Axe Royale intersects with the zone around the Boulevard Périphérique. The centre was designed by Guillaume Gillet, and renovated in 1999 by Christian de Portzamparc. The large hall seats 3,700 visitors, the smaller 650. The Palais des Congrès is part of ViParis, which was mentioned above, the organization which coordinates conferences and fairs in the Paris region.

CONVENTION CENTRES

In recent years the traditional distinction between fair and conference buildings has been disappearing. With increasing frequency fairs and conferences are becoming integrated. Initially this was accomplished primarily by adding conference rooms, or whole conference centres, to exhibition complexes. More problematic, cause of the need to fit into the space available, was the addition of exhibition spaces to conference complexes. Over the years, many conference centres and conference hotels have in fact added small exhibition spaces. These are often spaces which can also double as an extra conference hall, dining room or ballroom.

Many new complexes are less exclusively intended for fairs and conference activities. They have less exhibition space than the traditional German fair complexes, but more than pure conference centres. In the United States this hybrid form is generally termed a convention centre. They generally lie in, or on the edges of, the city centres. They claim less space than the traditional fair complex, certainly if the halls can be stacked up, and parking and logistics are integrated into the building.

CNIT, Paris

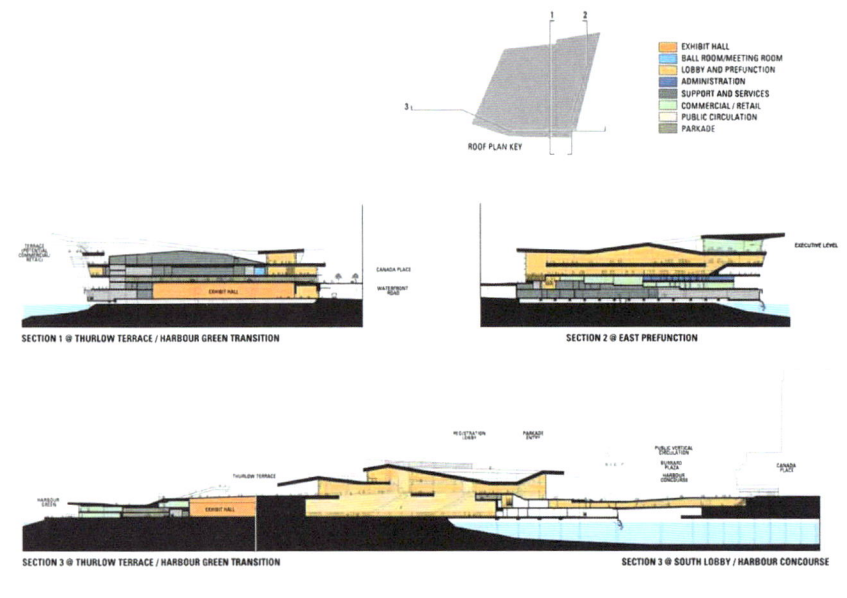

BUILDING SECTIONS

VANCOUVER CONVENTION CENTRE WEST
LMN Architects + MCM/DA

Vancouver Convention Centre, façade, cross sections, and floor plans of ground floor and level 1
Design: LMN Architects, Seattle

Their location in or near the city centre enables these facilities to profile themselves as an urban venue. In addition to the event, participants are also visiting the city. This makes the event more attractive. The qualities of the city can be added to the qualities of the complex. In this way convention centres profit from the quality and selection of restaurants, cafés, hotels, the urban fabric itself, and tourist attractions in the area.

A fine example is the compact, multi-floor Vancouver Convention Centre. It is comprised of two building complexes. The older part was built for the World's Fair in 1986. The expansion with the West Building was realized for the Winter Olympics in 2010. The beautifully designed building accommodates the media and press centre. The West Building is 31,000 m², with 20,000 m² of exhibition space, 6000 m² conference space, and 5000 m² of ballrooms.

An extremely large example is the Hong Kong Convention and Exhibition Centre, on the edge of Hong Kong Island, in the heart of the central business

Hong Kong Convention and Exhibition Centre
Design: Skidmore, Owings & Merrill

Midtown New York

district. It has been expanded several times since it was first constructed in 1988. With the motto 'size matters', it is now more than 90,000 m^2. The halls are stacked up above one another.

Hotel and conference quarters

The city centre clusters of The Hague, Utrecht and Rotterdam and the seaside cluster of Scheveningen are characteristic examples of a hotel and conference quarter. Although this is never its dominant function, in the centre of these cities there is a considerable concentration of conference locations and spaces to rent. The other city centre amenities in the vicinity function as a support programme for the evening hours or free day.

For some specialized facilities, conferences are the main function. For most of the others it is an additional function. That is the case for instance with restaurants, hotels, universities, theatres and museums which also rent out halls. Many universities organize their conferences in their own facilities. They reach out to other locations only for the larger gatherings with a higher budget.

The major competitors for the mono-functional conference centres in the field of international meetings are the large, generally four and five star hotels with conference halls. These sometimes offer halls with places for up to 1000 persons. According to the data from the ICCA, in 2007 there were even more international conferences held in hotels than in mono-functional conference centres.

Entirely different rules apply to the regional conference market. Here the atmosphere of the conference location is very important, particularly, for instance, the popularity of newly opened locations. An experimental formula for organizing conferences is also to use several locations in one city.

Internationally there are few places which sell themselves as conference quarters. However,

internationally concentrations of meeting facilities do tend to coincide with clusters of hotels, culture and entertainment. In Brussels the promotion agency Visit Brussels distinguishes six convention districts.[9] The largest and most versatile is the Kunstberg, where in addition to several large museums there are also a number of conference facilities. Halls can also be rented in BOZAR (Centre for the Fine Arts). The central conference facilities in the city are however the Square Brussels Meeting Centre, the former Palais des Congrès constructed for the 1958 World's Fair. In addition to 4000 m^2 of exhibition space, the large hall provides space for a maximum of 1200 visitors.

Hotel and conference district

The ultimate step up for the quarter is the district. Midtown New York is the most famous example. Here too the district coincides with the Theatre District around Times Square and Broadway in the west, and with the headquarters of the United Nations in the east. NYC Company, the city's tourism and conference agency, counts almost 36,000 hotel rooms in Midtown, and over 75,000 m^2 in rentable spaces.[10] All the large hotel chains are represented with conference halls, ballrooms and banquet halls. The Javits Center, which lies a bit to the south on the Hudson, with a comparable floor area, is the largest convention centre of in the city.

The central district of Amsterdam and the chic International Zone in The Hague are also examples of this type, but have less density. The aura each projects is also considerably different. The next section will deal with the International Zone in greater depth.

Exhibition site – park – *Gelände*

Many German exhibition centres were established as part of a *Vergnügungs- und Ausstellungspark*. After the Second World War these increasingly became more restricted sites with more restricted access. Some sites however remain public, and are characterized by a wide diversity of functions. The Prater in Vienna is an appealing example. It in fact combines the qualities of the culture clusters described in Chapter 2 with an exhibition centre. The Prater is actually one large culture park. There are also extensive outdoor areas around the Messe in Munich. For the BAUMA, the largest trade fair, these are used for demonstrating cranes and excavating

equipment, and at automotive exhibitions test rides can be conducted there.

Another tradition is that of exhibitions where temporary or permanent pavilions are constructed, similar to World Fairs. Recent examples in Europe include the expositions at Seville (1992), Hannover (2000) and Saragossa (2008). World's Fairs are massive events drawing millions of visitors in only a couple of months. The crowds of visitors can only be accommodated by combining the pavilions with large

open spaces between them, to permit the streams of visitors to circulate. Most of these exhibition sites become moribund if no suitable function can be found for them after the event is over. In the case of Hannover, the buildings around the Expo Plaza have been given a new purpose as part of the city's new media centre. This Plaza lies between the Messe-gelände train station and the extensive fair complex. The whole site of the Messe in Hannover is however at least 160 hectare, so that a large portion of the

Biennale Park, Venice

Expo site is hardly ever used. The spectacular pavilion by MVRDV is half-overgrown today.

The formula involving the Biennale park in Venice is more successful. Here the repetition guarantees that the national pavilions will be maintained and updated. The central pavilion in the Giardini was built in 1894. In the course of time 29 national pavilions have joined it. The Dutch pavilion was built by Gerrit Rietveld in 1953. The most recent is the South Korean pavilion, from 1995. Since 1995 exhibitions have also been set up in the Arsenal.

The series of exhibitions which were held in Rotterdam in the 1950s on the site where the Museumpark now lies are at least as inspirational. This series was briefly described in Chapter 2. In the course of the summer hundreds of thousands of people flocked to the city, in 1950 to learn everything about the post-war reconstruction of the city and in 1955 to learn about everything connected with energy. The temporary character made possible experiments of every sort. A large number of architects and artists contributed to the design of AHOY' and E'55. The architects Van den Broek and Bakema supervised the design, and built several pavilions themselves. Aldo van Eyck designed the steel sculpture near the entrance of AHOY'. For E'55 Karel Appel painted an 'energy wall' 80 metres long. These exhibitions still come the closest to the approach of the 19th century world expositions.

Floriade

The third exposition in the Rotterdam series was the 1960 Floriade. A great number of exhibitions of plants and flowers had previously been held in The Netherlands, but every decade since 1960 the Dutch Horticultural Council has organized a summer-long international garden exhibition. These have been, successively, in Rotterdam (1960), Amsterdam (1972, 1982), Zoetermeer (1992) and in the Haarlemmermeer (2002). In the spring of 2012 the next Floriade

opened in Venlo, and Almere, Amsterdam, Boskoop and Groningen are already competing as candidates for 2022. The Euromast in Rotterdam was built for the 1960 Floriade. In Amsterdam, Amstel Park and Gaasperpark were realized. A woods remains from the Floriade in Zoetermeer, and in Haarlemmermeer a park with the high Big Spotters' Hill. In Venlo the current Floriade is the centrepiece of a series of business parks realized as part of Greenport Venlo. In tried and true fashion, the exhibition is comprised of an indoor component with product presentations by the horticultural industry, and a beautiful outdoor section. Often the tents and pavilions are demolished after the event; in Haarlemmermeer the hall still serves as a venue for events.

Organizer Jac Kleiboer with a map of the E-55 festival site in Rotterdam

→ Aerial photo of Floriade site, Venlo, 2012
Beeldwerk-Baarlo

Relations with other interaction environments

The clusters of conference and meeting facilities in the city centres are naturally integrated with their surroundings. They support the mixed assortment of interaction environments in the city centres. The integration of the larger facilities is less self-evident. In this section we will examine some plans which have been made in recent years to achieve this.

Amsterdam

The RAI is part of Amsterdam's South Axis business district, but is less than perfectly integrated with it. The RAI is precisely at one of the more problematic spots in the urban fabric, created as a result of a series of changes in this part of Berlage's Plan Zuid. It stands where Berlage had projected a link between Rooseveltlaan and South Station. This link was never realized. A projected highway to Rotterdam was also never realized. As a result, this area remained undefined. Roads and watercourses end abruptly. The fragmentation was only increased by the expansion of the RAI and Beatrix Park. Traditionally the lunch rooms, ice cream parlours, cafés and restaurants of the nearby Scheldestraat provided a pleasurable supplement to a visit to the RAI. In recent years a station for the North/South metro line has been excavated under the forecourt, and the plaza has been redesigned to also function as a site for events. Together with the new Elicium and a newly revamped route to the RAI railway station, the entry has become a bit better.

In the sub-area identified as the Head of the South Axis, on the other side of the plaza, there is space for high density hotels, offices, apartments and metropolitan amenities. Together with the RAI this would create a cosmopolitan work, dwelling and entertainment quarter. In 2010 a new synagogue for Amsterdam's Liberal Jewish community was built, from the plans of Bjarne Mastenbroek. A new complex for the Regional Community College of Amsterdam is under construction. However, Joop van

Vision for the future RAI
Dienst Zuidas

de Ende has placed his plans for a musical theatre in this area on the back burner. Another major drawing card for this area – in addition to the RAI – has not yet been found. The question is whether it might not be better to focus on creating stronger relationships with the central part of the South Axis, around South Station. Rather than establishing separate quarters, by improving the relations between the clusters the South Axis can grow into one contiguous district. We will return to this in the final section of this chapter.

Utrecht

After years of debate, at the end of 2003 the Utrecht city Council adopted the Masterplan Stationsgebied Utrecht. The intention is to better integrate Hoog Catharijne, Central Station and the Jaarbeurs into the city centre, to become the 'enlarged heart' of the city, as it is termed in Utrecht. Seen on a larger scale, it is to strengthen connections with the western part of the city (Lombok, Kanaleneiland, and the new district of Leidse Rijn. Work is presently under way on realizing crucial components of the plan in and around the station; it is one of the national Key Projects. It is expected that the new public transport terminal will be delivered in 2014. After that will come the make-over of Hoog Catharijne and improved access to the area around the Jaarbeurs. The city is also building its new municipal offices on the new Jaarbeursplein.

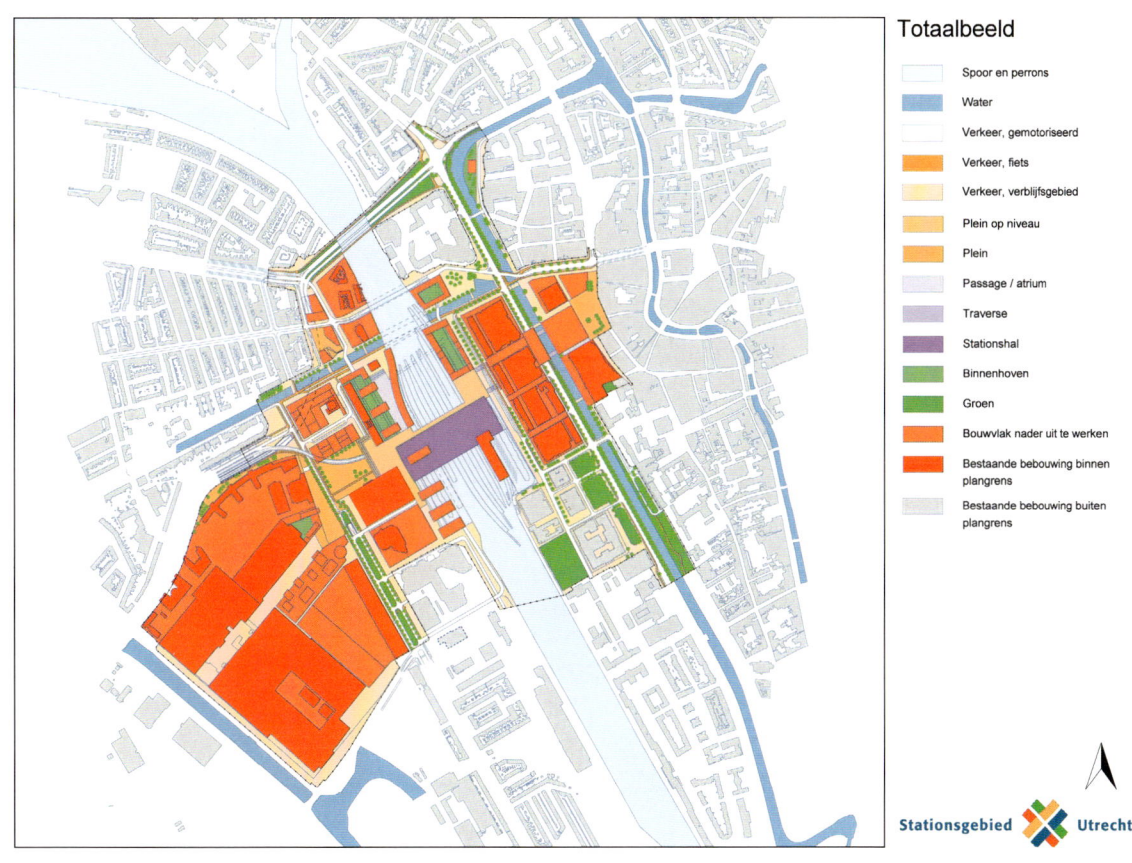

Totaalbeeld

- Spoor en perrons
- Water
- Verkeer, gemotoriseerd
- Verkeer, fiets
- Verkeer, verblijfsgebied
- Plein op niveau
- Plein
- Passage / atrium
- Traverse
- Stationshal
- Binnenhoven
- Groen
- Bouwvlak nader uit te werken
- Bestaande bebouwing binnen plangrens
- Bestaande bebouwing buiten plangrens

Stationsgebied Utrecht

Masterplan Utrecht Station vicinity
CU2030

In connection with this, the Jaarbeurs is reinvigorating its entrance area with new leisure facilities which will broaden out the present provisions for fairs and conferences: a casino, mega-cinema and hotel. These facilities will be realized by the private Jaarbeurs Utrecht. This company, like VNU Exhibitions Europe and Jaarbeurs Catering Services, is part of the Jaarbeurs Holding. The new leisure facilities will be accessible from public space, but also from the new entrance building, with above it the new Galaxy ballroom with a hall for 1500 persons. Unlike the RAI, the Jaarbeurs is thus making efforts to provide an expanded assortment of leisure activities.

Rotterdam

With the Sportpaleis, Ahoy is the most specialized large facility among the fair and conference centres in the Randstad. For Dutch visitors to concerts and sports events the selection of supplementary facilities in the vicinity is less important; accessibility matters much more. This is not, however, optimal. For regional exhibitions and conferences the combination with the nearby Zuidplein shopping centre is a plus point.

In 2011 the course was charted for the renewal of 'The Heart of the South'. The shopping centre, designed so that it turned in on itself, and confusing bus station are to be made more welcoming. A plaza with cafés and restaurants will tempt visitors to see

the space around the buildings as more than just a space to cross on their way in or out, or from one conveyance to another. The construction of a new library and swimming pool will increase daily use. The city is seeking a partner for a public/private partnership, still to be set up.

Within the context of the renewal plans, the idea arose of expanding the Ahoy complex with an International Convention Centre. The city of Rotterdam is investing heavily in the development of the area. Although the feasibility of the Convention Centre was extensively studied, the chances of its realization remain an open question. It is likely that such a venue fits better close to Central Station, with its High Speed Rail service, or by the new junction at Stadionpark.

Several years ago studies were done with regard to the construction of a new metro line in Rotterdam, to improve connections between the South and the rest of the city. The line was to begin in the east Kralingse Zoom on the north bank of the Maas, cross the river to Stadionpark, and then run westward via Zuidplein and Stadshavens before crossing back to the north bank to Marconiplein and Schiedam. This would vastly improve the importance of Zuidplein as a transportation junction. This line was not however included in the planning for the Heart of the South. Local and regional access can of course be considerably improved by tram connections. However, that is insufficient for the success of an international venue.

The Hague

The World Forum cluster abuts the culture cluster around the Municipal Museum, in the super-block bounded by Stadhouderslaan, Eisenhowerlaan, Johan de Wittlaan and Kennedylaan. The buildings of the OPCW and Yugoslavia Tribunal are also there. An integral renewal plan has been drawn up for the whole super-block. After the demolition of the Statenhal and the construction of the building for Europol and a large parking garage, attention is now turning to the redesign of the public space. For the sloping central area, a dune park with a promenade is being laid out. This connects the museums in the south with the Forum, with the triangular Oud Tower and Europol, and finally with the water feature in front of the Yugoslavia Tribunal's buildings and the Churchillplein.

The design was developed by DS Landscape Architects. The natural stone of the promenade contrasts nicely with the dune grasses. After the construction of the promenade the museums will also get entrances and amenities, like the 'Brasserie Berlage' in one of the Municipal Museum's annexes, on what is now the back side. The first phase is now being carried out.

Viewed on a larger scale, this new cluster is part of what the Structural Vision for The Hague terms the 'International Zone'. The Hague promotes itself as the International City of Peace and Justice. After the Peace Palace opened in 1913, all sorts of international organizations concerned with these issues have located in the city. Most of these organizations and institutions lie in the narrow, extended strip between the centre of the city and Scheveningen. During the Second World War, this area was part of the Atlantic Wall, the German defensive line along the coast, and the previous buildings in it were demolished. After the war, on the basis of Dudok's reconstruction plans, the strip was transformed into a green zone between The Hague and Scheveningen, with space for a ring road, parks, urban amenities and institutions, such as the Municipal Museum, which was already standing, and the new Congrescentrum. The Hague has enhanced its position as the City of Peace and Justice over the past decades with the establishment of a series of new institutions, including the Yugoslavia Tribunal (1991), the Organization for the Prohibition of Chemical Weapons (1992) and the International Criminal Court (2002).

The parks, hotels, embassies and monumental buildings in the International Zone make it an attractive place to locate. It is in fact a green district. At the same time the location between the centre of The Hague and the entertainment centre of Scheveningen guarantees the proximity of urban amenities. Several avenues transect the area, which in the course of time will begin to function as the north-western segment of a beltway around The Hague. In order to reduce the dominant visual presence and nuisance created by parts of these roads, the construction of the Hubertus Tunnel was suggested several years ago. A plan to better integrate the road near the Museum cluster and World Forum by creating a tunnel for through traffic has been explored, but appears to have gone on the back burner.

Projects in the International Zone, The Hague
City of The Hague

124

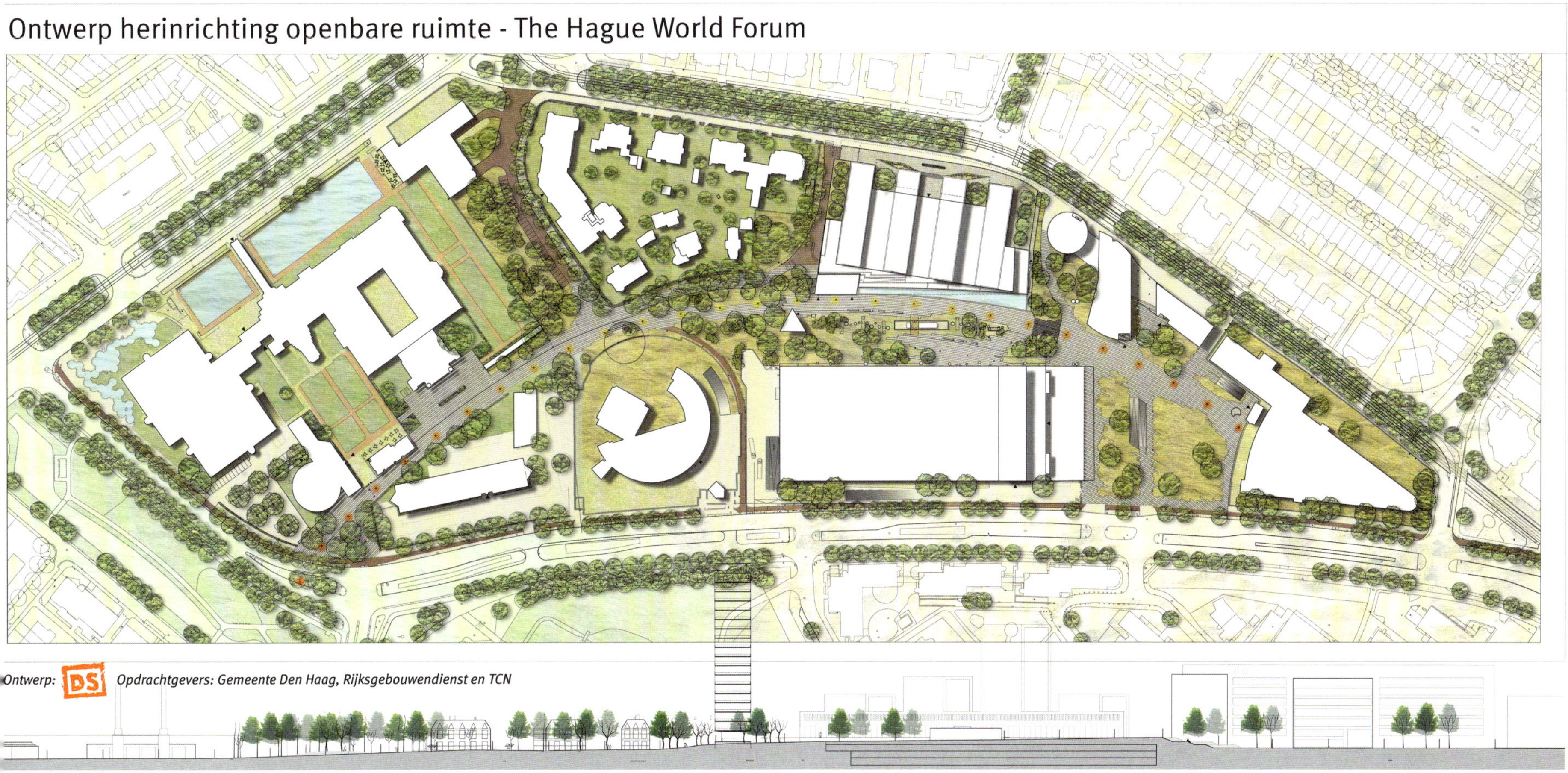

Ontwerp herinrichting openbare ruimte - The Hague World Forum

Ontwerp: **DS** Opdrachtgevers: Gemeente Den Haag, Rijksgebouwendienst en TCN

↑ → **Redesign for public space surrounding the Worldforum, The Hague**
DS landschapsarchitecten

→ → **OPCW Monument for victims of chemical weapons**
Design: Wiebe de Gruyter
Public space designed by
DS landschapsarchitecten

Holland cluster

Within the Randstad there are also a number of other cities, including Amersfoort, Haarlem, Schiedam, Delft and Dordrecht which have all kinds of conference and meeting locations. Outside the Randstad it is principally the MECC in Maastricht (maximum capacity 1650) and Martiniplaza in Groningen (2500) that are significant. The conference centre Papendal, next to the sports facilities of NOC-NSF, can accommodate sizeable numbers (2000). These facilities are chiefly of regional importance.

The most important location outside the four largest cities is Noordwijk. This seaside resort has 13 hotels with conference and meeting accommodations, and thus has a greater assortment than Scheveningen. The most prestigious are the Grand Hotel Huis ter Duin, with 254 rooms and 19 halls, and the Hotels van Oranje, with 288 rooms and 50 halls. The Conference Hotel Leeuwenhorst in Noordwijker-hout is the largest location, with 513 rooms and at least 120 halls. The largest hall, when set up as a theatre, seats 1200 persons. Noordwijk has a central location with respect to the Randstad, but unlike Utrecht, the other centrally sited location for meetings, in Noordwijk one is on the coast and away from the hustle and bustle of the city. Hotels van Oranje are going to realize the 16,000 m² Noordwijk International Convention Centre on the Koningin Wilhelmina Boulevard. The complex is to have 300 hotel rooms, conference and meeting rooms, and underground parking for 500 cars. The boulevard has recently been re-profiled as part of strengthening coastal storm defences. Using the 'dike in dune' principle, a weak point was reinforced by the creation of a high, strong dike in a strip of dunes in front of the boulevard. Unfortunately, this eliminated the open view of the sea from the boulevard – and the terraces along it. Undoubtedly the next following round will be for the conference hotels to construct elevated terraces.

Capacity of largest hall

> 2.000

1.501-2.000

1.001-1.500

501-1.000

500

Conference facilities in the Randstad with a capacity of more than 500 visitors
Source: www.vergaderlocaties.nl, presentation by DRO

Hotels van Oranje, Noordwijk

Stimuli

At first glance the playing field for fairs and conferences in the Randstad appears to have a clear form and be clearly subdivided. The international fairs and conventions take place in the Amsterdam RAI, the domestic ones in the Jaarbeurs. The World Forum in The Hague and Ahoy operate in interesting niche markets. Alongside this, the city centre and coastal clusters provide attractive locations for smaller congresses and for parallel sessions. With the recent additions to the RAI and the forthcoming opening of the North/South metro line, the integration of the Jaarbeurs in the 'expanded heart' of Utrecht, and the development of a mixed cluster of conference facilities and international and cultural institutions around the World Forum, it would appear that promising new directions are being exploited.

The international market is however in flux. All over the world new conference and exhibition centres are springing up like mushrooms. Between 2000 and 2005 the number of square metres of exhibition space available worldwide increased by 40%.[11] In the same period the number of international conferences rose by 30%.[12] As a consequence of the credit crisis, since 2008 there has been a steep reduction in the number and size of fairs, conferences and conventions (including here in The Netherlands). Nevertheless, it may be expected that these forms of meeting and exchange will continue to play a vital role in the development of technology,

the economy and science.

It is striking that despite the crisis, the International Broadcasting Convention (IBC) in the RAI drew 45,000 visitors in 2010, and increased this to 50,000 in 2011. Most of them came to the city for a number of days and in addition to the convention also attended all sorts of workshops, briefings, armchair sessions, training and product presentations. The community of the international media world meets one another here. More than 1300 businesses showed their latest products and technologies at the concurrent exhibition.

If you look at European competitors such as Munich, Milan and Madrid, then Schiphol, with its world-encompassing network of air links, would appear to be the obvious place for a new state-of-the-art exhibition complex in the Amsterdam region. The competition have realized large, new exhibition complexes near their airports, and thus freed up space in the city for new development. Connected with the ambitions that Schiphol has for growth, a new exhibition complex could be built with a new arrival and departure hall on Schiphol North, at Badhoevedorp. And, just as in Milan, a park with a compact convention centre, a museum and towers by Zaha Hadid, Arata Isozaki and Daniel Liebeskind could not be out of place on the site of the old RAI on Amsterdam's South Axis.

↑ → **Maquette photo and ground plan of CityLife Milan: park, residential building, offices, convention centre**
Design: Zaha Hadid, Arata Isozaki and Daniel Libeskind, realization 2009-2017

Moscone Center, San Francisco, seen across Howard Street, looking toward Yerba Buena Gardens

also. A new complex at Schiphol is thus a costly threat rather than a step forward.

The question then becomes what an attractive perspective for a better integration of the large fair, conference and convention complexes in the city itself might be. In any case, it is certain that for – if only for their size alone, at 23 and 30 hectare, respectively, the present complexes of the RAI and Jaarbeurs are aliens of a sort in the fabric of the city. Therefore it is better to look at other examples. For instance to Vancouver and San Francisco, where new venues have been built in the city, or on the other hand to Paris, where a new perspective has been sought primarily in the organization of the sector.

VANCOUVER AND SAN FRANCISCO

For the construction of both the Vancouver Convention Center and the Moscone Center in San Francisco, the cities opted for a compact solution. The programme is partly stacked, and there has even been a park realized on top of the Moscone Center.

The Vancouver Convention Center consists of two building complexes on the bay of Vancouver Harbour, on the site of an old harbour rail emplacement and piers. The East Building was constructed for the 1986 World's Fair and has an 8500 m^2 (185 x 50) exhibition hall which can be divided into three sections. A vast canvas roof is stretched over it. The city's cruise terminal is also located on the pier. The expansion with the West Building was realized in connection with the Winter Olympics in 2010. It was designed by Mark Reddington, of LMN Architects in Seattle. The West Building is 31,000 m^2 in size, with 20,000 m^2 of exhibition space, 6000 m^2 of conference space, and 5000 m^2 for ballrooms, all on a footprint of 4.5 hectare.

The entrance level on Canada Place and the surrounding streets lie on level +1. A large exhibition hall, loading docks and all the technical service areas

That would, however, not be the wisest thing to do. The day of massive trade and public fairs is over. The future lies in mixed, several-day-long conventions. You can still suggest that, through a differentiated selection of larger and smaller halls, outstanding architecture, and particularly its combination with hotels, restaurants, museums and all sorts of other attractions, the new airport complex would provide a unique environment for such conventions. However, that would have to be a better selection than the present one, with the proximity of the city centre as the most important quality and selling point of Amsterdam.

In Milan and Madrid the new venues have a rather one-sided programme, without too many fancy trimmings. With a further extension of the North/South line to the airport, a sober new complex at Schiphol could be supported by the complementary programme of the city centre. In the Dutch situation, however, it is out of the question that such a sober complex would be built. After all, it demands an enormous investment to build, and could only be exploited commercially if an extensive complementary programme were realized with it. In addition to conventions, rather rapidly sports events and concerts would have to become components

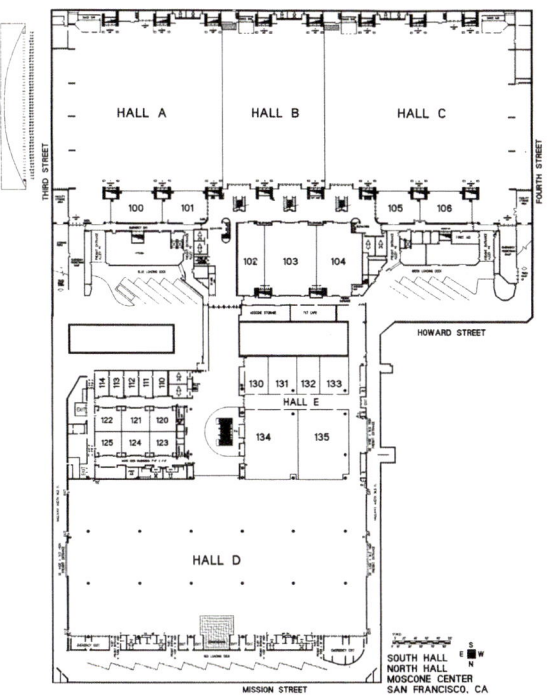

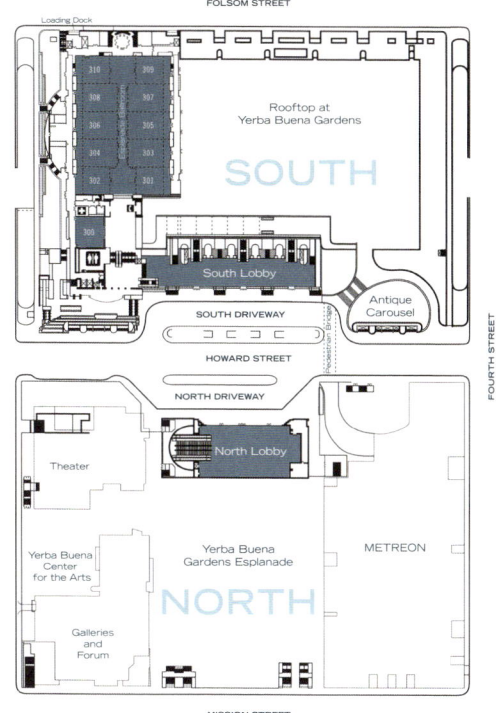

Moscone Center, floor plan hall level and Yerba Buena Gardens level

could therefore be situated at the old ground level of the emplacement. The 20,000 m² exhibition space can also be divided into three halls, and measures 90 x 225 metres. The hall has pillars in a 30 x 30 metre grid, part of which supports the floors above, and part of which supports the structure of Canada Place. The hall is 9 metres high. Four fifteen metre high ballrooms, fifty meeting rooms and a whole series of restaurants and lounges lie on the three upper floors. The floors of the ballrooms have a limited weight capacity. The galleries, with glass façades, afford spectacular views of the harbour and the backdrop of the mountains behind the city, the highest of which is 2600 metres.

The Moscone Center lies in the midst of San Francisco in an area south of Market street which has undergone a metamorphosis since the 1960s and become a part of the city centre. This did not happen without a fight. The original residents resisted the demolition of their neighbourhood and the construction of a large convention centre.[13] Ultimately, in 1981 the convention centre was built recessed below ground level, and an Esplanade and the Yerba Buena Gardens laid out on its roof. The second phase followed several years later, likewise

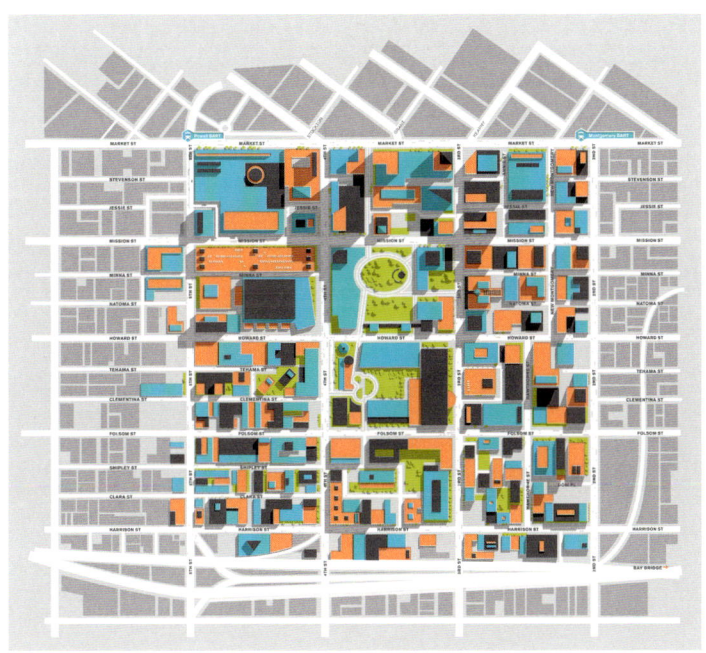

Map of vicinity of Moscone Center

Yerba Buena Lane, San Francisco

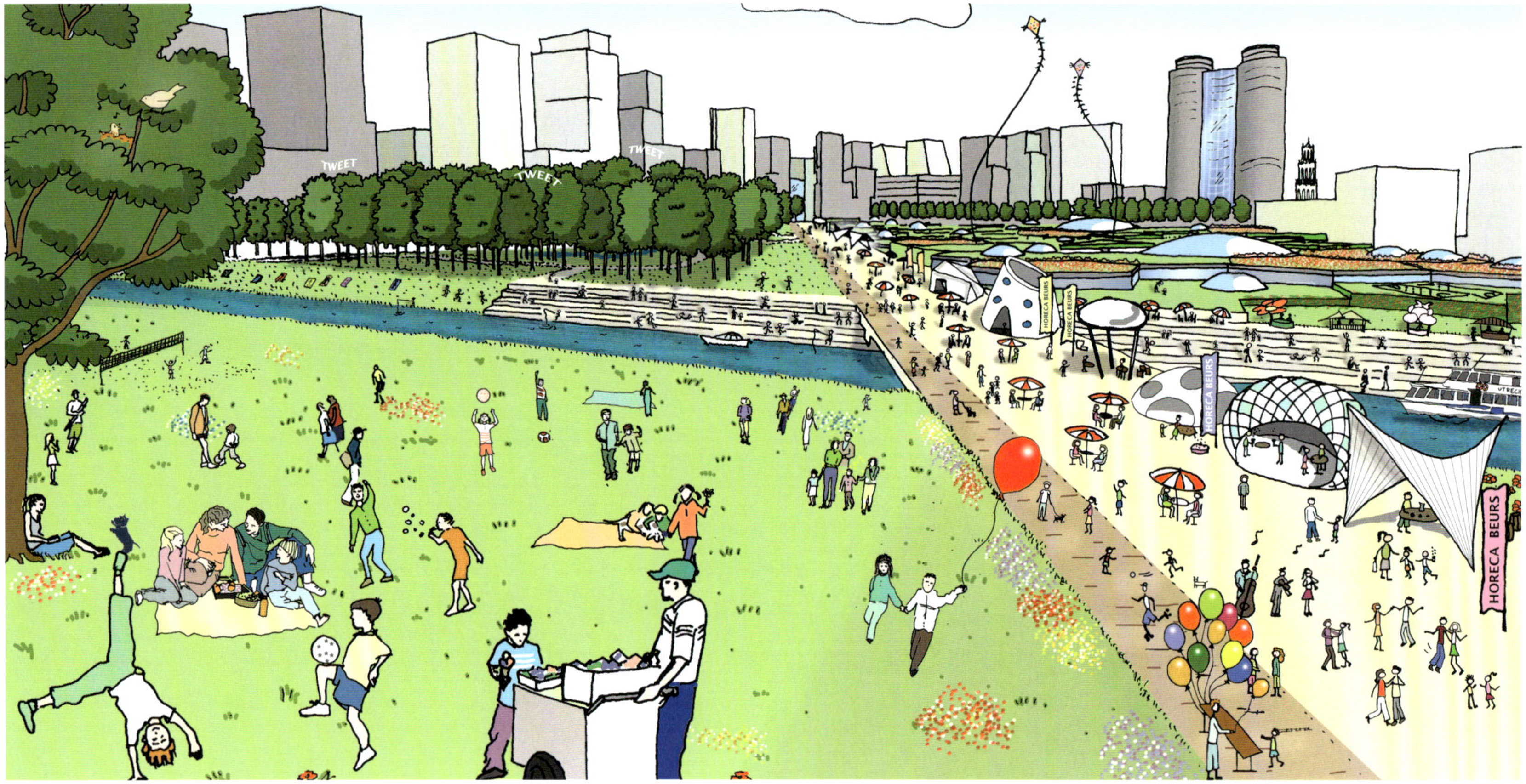

Study for redevelopment of the Jaarbeurs, Utrecht
Design: HKB Stedenbouwkundigen

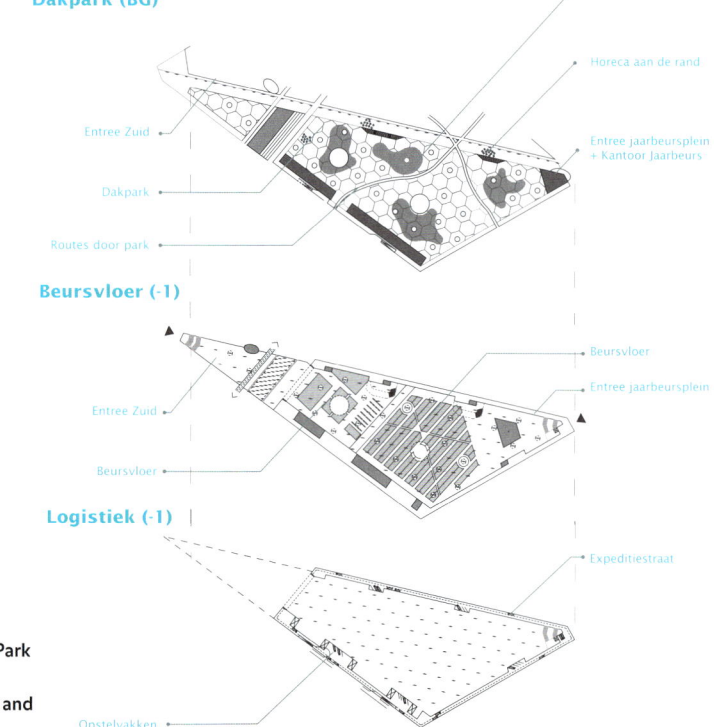

Dakpark (BG)

Bloemenvelden

Horeca aan de rand

Entree Zuid

Entree jaarbeursplein + Kantoor Jaarbeurs

Dakpark

Routes door park

Beursvloer (-1)

Beursvloer

Entree jaarbeursplein

Entree Zuid

Beursvloer

Logistiek (-1)

Expeditiestraat

Opstelvakken

← Perspective and ground plan, Jaarbeurs Park

→ Floor plans of logistics, convention floor and roof landscape, Jaarbeurs

with a public roof with all sorts of facilities. The complex was designed by HOK, Hellmuth, Obata and Kassabaum, now one of the most important architectural agencies in the US.

The five large exhibition halls are sunken at level -1. Their combined area is 41,000 m². The largest hall, 24,000 m², has a ceiling 11 metres high, spanning 84 metres. This hall can be divided into three sections. A smaller hall measures 13,000 m², is less high, and has columns in a 27 metre grid supporting its roof. A subterranean street with loading docks for lorries surrounds the halls. On the roof of the hall on the north side lies the Esplanade. Around it are the Yerba Buena Theatre, the Yerba Buena Center for the Arts, and a shopping mall. The actual open area is 120 x 140 metres, comparable with the large meadow in Amsterdam's Oosterpark or the space in front of the former Film Museum in Vondel Park. In the course of time it has become a popular place for all sorts of events and concerts. The Theatre became world-famous for the presentations of all new Apple products there by Steve Jobs. (Apple is one of the sponsors.) The roof terrace on the south side is less park-like in character. It accommodates a children's museum, ice rink, bowling alley and an old, restored merry-go-round. This part of the Gardens is also intensively used.

In 1995 the San Francisco MOMA was built next to the Esplanade, from designs by Mario Botta. A further, colossal expansion designed by the Norwegian architects Snøhetta is under construction. Just a little further up stands the Jewish Historical Museum, Yerba Buena Lane has recently been built between the Gardens and Market Street, with stores, restaurants and the Museum for Craft & Folk Art. The end result is that the area has become a vital component of the tourist circuit in San Francisco.

A decade ago an adjoining plot of land was acquired for a first major expansion. This is connected with the Moscone Center by an subterra-

nean circuit beneath the street. The same will be done for another new expansion on the other side. There will be no large halls, but chiefly conference and meeting facilities. These buildings fit into the fabric of city blocks.

Despite their substantial size, complex logistics and intensive use, the convention centres in Vancouver and San Francisco have become a natural part of the surrounding city.

JAARBEURS UTRECHT

Over the last few years Henk Bouwman of HKB Stedebouwkundigen has been working on the Masterplan for the area around Utrecht Central Station. With a good deal of persistence the complicated puzzle of traffic flow, phasing and spatial forms has been solved. One of the staff at the agency, Dominic Tegelbeckers, graduated from Technical University in Eindhoven in 2009, with a plan for the Jaarbeursplein as his graduation project, in which the traffic flow is separated still more radically than in the current plan. That makes it possible to reach the Jaarbeurs more easily. For his work, in 2010 he received the Schreuders study prize for underground building.

HKB then made a study plan for a radical intervention in the Jaarbeurs area. It proposed that, just as in San Francisco, a large part of the Jaarbeurs should be taken underground, and a new city park realized over it. On the roof of the exhibition halls themselves the conditions for a park are less ideal, but through efficient planning of the space and access to the exhibition floors, much of the space in the present Jaarbeurs area can be freed up. A part of that could be used for a 'full ground' park, and part for intensive urban development, comparable with the recently realized Rabo Towers. The robust measurements fit beautifully with the large space of the park. The park could be as much as 27 hectare, and run through to the Merwede Canal. Parking

facilities are situated on the other side of the canal. A bridge and an avenue bring visitors to the Jaarbeurs. At the same time this is a more pleasant route for slow traffic from Kanaleneiland to the station than along the busy auto roads to the city.

It will not be easy in these times to find supporters for the development of a whole area with 500,000 m² of office space, but the stimulus for reconsidering the possibilities for use and the quality of this fragmented side of the station district could be enormous. One crucial question which must be answered is a construction issue. Particularly for large exhibition spaces, a column-free, continuous space is extremely important. The Moscone Center, and in a certain sense Vancouver also, are less than perfect from this perspective. A first optimization could be to build only the large exhibition floors underground, as in Vancouver, and the meeting facilities above ground, with a comparable spectacular view of the park and city.

RAI AMSTERDAM

The design task in Amsterdam is comparable with that in Utrecht, albeit that most of the halls are of a more recent date. This is especially true for the newly opened Elicium. Moreover, Bodon's Europahal deserves protection as a monument. Complete demolition is thus out of the question. The same is true for moving to a new location in the South Axis. Then an attractive new function would have to be found for the Europahal: Kunsthal? Swimming pool? Ice rink? That is not so easy. The better approach seems to be to seek a solution for optimizing the existing complex. Various smaller halls can be modernized or replaced in the coming years. That offers the possibility of better integrating the complex with its environment.

The stimulus here should be sought primarily in reinforcing the relations with the central part of the South Axis. Bicyclists and pedestrians could cross the

RAI site, under the aerial walkways that connect the halls with one another on level 1, but this is far from a pleasant or obvious route. The mouth of the South Axis tunnel is also to be placed at Beatrix Park. That will only increase the fragmentation in the area.

The plans for the South Axis now focus strongly on the central section, around Station South and the 'axis' of Minervalaan. This part of the South Axis promises to become one of the most compact development areas in The Netherlands. Close to Schiphol, and adjoining the new public transport junction at Station South, it also offers the best opportunities for realizing an attractive, mixed business quarter. In recent years considerable energy has therefore been devoted to expanding the programme, for instance by creating a stronger relationship with the Vrije Universiteit complex and developing it as the knowledge quarter of the South Axis.

Stronger relations with the RAI would enhance the international image of the South Axis, and at a practical level, the visitors to the RAI could also contribute greatly to the vitality of this new urban area. Moreover, stronger links could also make possible a jump upward in scale for the South Axis, in terms of both its size and significance, as it develops from being separate quarters into a larger and more complete district.

To improve the connections between the RAI and the station, the best plan would be to construct a wide avenue for all sorts of traffic: cars, bicycles, trams, pedestrians, taxis, parades. It could be a fine avenue with wide pavements, beautiful trees, pavilions, terraces and shops: everything that makes a city pleasant. An obvious place for this new avenue is on top of the tunnel on the north side of the station. Extended on to the east, and the avenue ends at Europa Boulevard. In order to build the avenue, a new place would have to be found for the two southern halls of the RAI complex. That could be underground, and stacked, on the sites of halls that must be modernized. Other more unorthodox solutions – such as under the water of the Boeren-wetering – should not be peremptorily excluded, however.

This leads to the important question of how large the renewed complex should be. Presently the RAI has 80,000 m² of exhibition floor, excluding all conference and meeting facilities. During the IBC the whole complex is in use, plus several temporary pavilions in the entrance area. The IBC is one of the largest conventions in the world, and they are not likely to become much larger. With more temporary halls to accommodate peak usage, the new complex could make do with fewer square metres of exhibition space. However, the new spaces would have to be more flexible, and of higher quality, moving from a raw exhibition atmosphere to a more sophisticated convention atmosphere. Roofs spanning large spaces, and several spaces of 70 x 150 metres which could be subdivided are also an absolute must for the future. The new, compact RAI would present itself to the new South Axis avenue. The complex would not lie, as it was once conceived, on the entrance to the city for auto traffic from Rotterdam, but would be a vital component of a lively new urban district.

ViParis – betting on smart organization

Paris is betting on a radically different concept. The city has a highly varied collection of exhibition, conference and convention facilities: large exhibition

← **Amsterdam RAI seen from the air, looking east**

→ **EYE Filmmuseum, Amsterdam**
Photo Rene den Engelsman

centres, such as at Porte de Versailles or at Le Bourget; more compact exhibition facilities like the CNIT in La Défense; large conference centres like the Palais des Congrès; and more compact and representative meeting spaces such as the Louvre and the Grande Arche. They present themselves collectively, and with increasing frequency are also being used in combination.

For a convention spanning several days, it is interesting to have sessions at various places around the city. Visitors make their choice of who they will meet, and where. Exhibitors can choose the place which best suits them. Evening programmes of various kinds can be held in the conference hotels which lie around the venues.

Analogous to ViParis, a different selection is also possible in Amsterdam. In addition to the RAI, the larger facilities in the city centre can also play a role. The halls around the IJ – Muziekgebouw, Passenger Terminal, Beurs van Berlage, Public Library, the new Film Museum, the conference hall under the Shell tower and the Tolhuistuin – could collectively host large conventions. There is also a magnificent space with views of the city lying above the main lobby of Central Station, which is just waiting to be kissed awake. These spaces could become an independent cluster, but could also function in combination with the RAI. The major challenge would appear to be exploring whether an organization such as ViParis is possible on the scale of the Randstad as a whole.

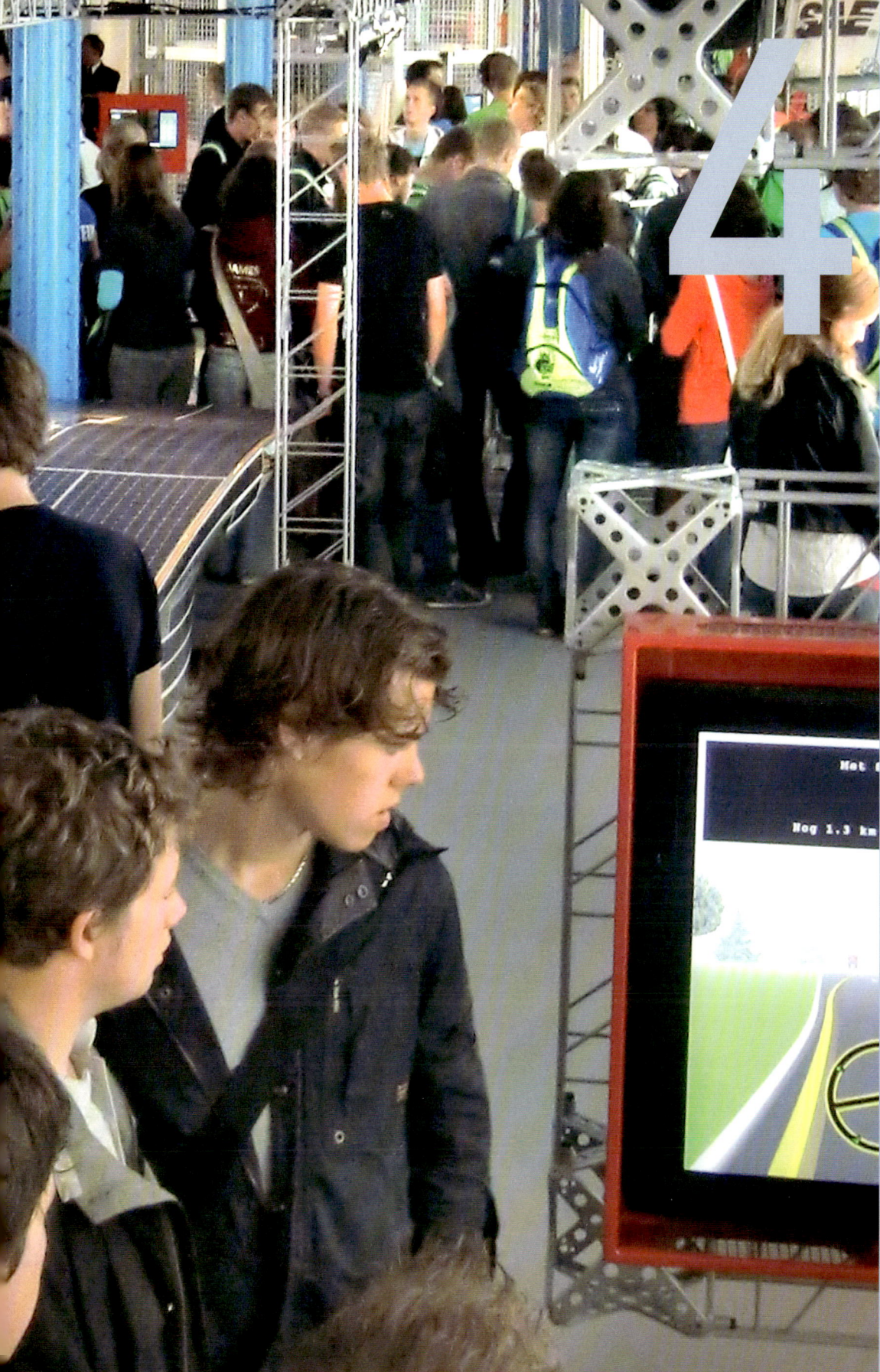

Knowledge clusters

4

The knowledge sector in the Netherlands has undergone rapid development since the 1960s, but in the last few years this motor of the economy has begun to stall. The government has sought to provide a new impulse for development in the sector in their recent Top Sector policy. Although attention has been given to the spatial clustering of knowledge institutions in The Netherlands, very little in an explicit spatial policy has been presented.

Many of the knowledge clusters in and around the cities are presently termed campuses. This term entered the language when, in the early years of the 20th century, the need arose to distinguish university buildings in a green environment (around a 'yard' or 'green') from the traditional complexes around courtyards in the city centres. The term is presently used in a much more general sense. Analogous with the typology of culture clusters, various types of campuses or knowledge clusters can be distinguished: in addition to the urban complexes and the green campuses, there are centres, knowledge quarters, science parks and complete knowledge districts.

In this chapter the structure and possibilities for development of knowledge clusters will be analysed, with a focus on knowledge clusters in the university cities. Recent plans will also be analysed. We will look at how the relation between knowledge clusters and the city can be strengthened. Many of the research institutions and R&D centres associated with corporations are not, however, to be found in the university cities, and often not even in the Randstad. In the Dutch top 60, technology clusters take shape around the three technological universities, and around Wageningen University. In addition, there is a cloud of institutes in the 'broader' North wing, from Petten to Nijmegen. Is this the Dutch Silicon Valley? And how can stronger relations be established between the knowledge development in the Valley and the knowledge application in the cities, in sectors such as ICT, media, advertising and gaming? Finally, in the closing section we will sketch a perspective for a firmer anchoring of the Delft knowledge district in the city, and in the South Wing.

Science Centre, TU-Delft

Development of the knowledge sector in The Netherlands

The earliest institutions in the Netherlands for the transmission of knowledge were the monastic schools.[1] The Dom school in Utrecht dated from as early as the 7th century.[2] It was only under the Republic that universities were established in Leiden (1575), Franeker (1585), Groningen (1614), Utrecht (1636) and Nijmegen (1656). The 'illustrious schools' of Harderwijk (1599) and Amsterdam (1632) were a variant. They lacked the *ius promovendi*.[3] Amsterdam's Atheneaum Illustre was transformed into a university in 1877. Several years later a second university was established in Amsterdam, the Vrije Universiteit, founded on Protestant Christian principles.

Technical education was also reshaped in the 19th century. After the Artillery and Military Engineering School had been established in Delft at the beginning of the century, in 1842 the Royal Academy

Laboratory of the Bataafsche Petroleum Company, predecessor of Shell, in Amsterdam

for Engineers was founded. This was transformed into the Polytechnische School in 1864, and into the Technische Hogeschool in 1905. In 1904 the different curricula at Wageningen were joined to create the National Agricultural, Horticultural and Forestry School, after 1918 known as the national Landbouw Hoogeschool.

In the first decades of the 20th century large businesses in The Netherlands were also establishing their own research laboratories, often in cooperation with professors at universities. This followed a trend which had been visible for some time already, for instance in Germany, where chemical companies such as BASF, Hoechst, Agfa and Bayer had already established independent laboratories around 1880. In The Netherlands the predecessor of Shell, the Bataafsche Petroleum Maatschappij, opened a laboratory in 1906. The Physics Laboratory at Philips, established in 1914, also belongs to this first batch. An important reason for starting laboratories was the passage of the Patent Act of 1912, on the German model, which protected discoveries, allowing them to be marketed.

In addition to this legislation, around the First World War the national government also carried out an active policy of stimulating industry. The establishment of the Dutch Industrial Consulting Service in 1910 was quickly followed by the Netherlands Rubber Research Service (1911) and the Netherlands Fibre Research Service (1917). One of the principle responses to the crisis of the 1930s was investment in the exchange of knowledge between universities and business. A whole series of institutes which still exist today were founded for that purpose: KEMA (1927), MARIN (1929), TNO (1932), WL (1933), RIVM (1934), Geodelft (1934), and NLR (1937). Each province also was given an Economic-

Number of staff in the largest laboratories in The Netherlands in 1940
Source: Homburg, 2003

Laboratory	number of staff
BPM-Laboratory Amsterdam	1350
Natuurkundig Laboratory Philips	516
AKU Research Institute	150
Gist- en Spiritus factory Laboratory	90
Central Laboratory State Mines	80
Vereenigde Oliefabrieken, Zwijndrecht (Unilever)	30 (in 1937)

Technical Institute. All these institutions did both research under contract for businesses, and their own basic research, and had close links with universities. A new generation of business laboratories also followed in this period, including DSM, AKU and Unilever.

In the 1950s and '60s the knowledge sector underwent rapid development. Supported by the Marshall Plan, in the 1950s there were already plans to expand the number of universities and institutions of higher education. A study by the Central Bureau for Statistics in 1956, which predicted a doubling of the number of students between that date and 1970, played a central role in this. In practice, it rapidly proved that the actual growth in the number of students was even higher. In the 1960s, many existing universities were expanded, and new ones founded. The construction activities were characterized by a move to the edges of the cities. In Nijmegen, for instance, As early as 1950 the university had begun rebuilding, with a new complex on the outskirts of the city. Utrecht, Tilburg, Rotterdam and the Vrije Universiteit in Amsterdam followed in the early 1960s.

The top priority in this period however were the polytechnics. Engineers were needed for the reconstruction of the country after the war. Moreover, there were great expectations for the development of the industrial sector. From the middle of the 1950s, work began on a new Technische Hogeschool district in Delft. Responding to the rapid growth of businesses such as Philips and DAF, it was decided to found a Technische Hogeschool in Eindhoven (1956) and in Twente (1965). Many of the new buildings had a severely functional design – and their principle function was to facilitate the leap upward in scale, in terms of student numbers. In both the new construction on the edge of the city, and in the city centres, the choice was often made to combine multiple

Casa Confetti student complex in the Uithof in Utrecht
Design: Architectenbureau Marlies Rohmer

departments in one complex of buildings. For instance, the 15-storey main building of the Vrije Universiteit, from 1973, serves the departments of Humanities, Philosophy, Theology, Economics and Business.

The late 1960s also saw an unprecedented wave in the construction of new academic medical centres: Hoboken (Rotterdam), the Vrije Universiteit, Utrecht and Leiden. Radboud and the UMC Groningen were radically rebuilt on their former sites. These institutions expressly combined education, research and medical care. At the same time too the facilities for the research departments of several large, increasingly international firms such as Philips, Shell, AKZO, Unilever and DSM were considerably expanded. The same was true for institutes such as the TNO and the Hydraulic Laboratory in Delft, which also expanded in this period. Finally, there were new research institutes established, such as the Netherlands Reactor Centre (1956, becoming the Netherlands Energy Research Centre in Petten, 1976) and the European Space Technology Centre, Noordwijk (1975). The first Bio Science Park in the Netherlands was realized in tandem with the University Medical Centre in Leiden in 1984. With

this, the application of medical knowledge in product development took on a more important role in research clusters.

The last decade has once again seen renewed large-scale investment. Almost all the universities have revitalized their campuses, Utrecht's Uithof being a front-runner with its much discussed buildings. New clusters have been created by a wave of mergers in tertiary professional education, and Philips, Shell and Unilever realized new research centres.

Lagging investment – Strengths and weaknesses

Despite this investment in facilities, the knowledge sector in The Netherlands is regarded as being uncompetitive, and many voices argue for its stimulation by still wider investment. All over the world, and particularly in industrialized countries, furious efforts are being made to develop the knowledge economy. These are, after all, the countries where traditional economic sectors such as agriculture and heavy industry are being eclipsed. Therefore everywhere goals are being set with regard to educational levels for the labour force and the size of R&D expenditures.

Development of the knowledge economy has

Central hall, Shell Technology Center, Amsterdam

even become a part of supra-national policy. In 2000 the European Commission launched the Lisbon Strategy, with the aim of making Europe the most competitive knowledge economy in the world. This was chiefly a response to competition from the United States, where research has traditionally been at a high level, and innovations generally also find their way to businesses easily. China too is a rising competitor. There the number of students rose from 3.4 to 21.5 million between 1998 and 2008.

As an extension of the Lisbon Strategy, in 2002 it was announced that the ambition was to see at least 3% of the GNP devoted to R&D. Most European countries have not met this goal. The Netherlands too has fallen short: in 2007 only 1.7% of the GNP was being devoted to R&D. Expenditures would have to nearly double to meet the Lisbon goals. To alter this trend, the National Innovation Platform was established in 2007, chaired by the then Prime Minister, Balkenende. In it, the government and business joined forces. At the European level, in 2010 the EU-2020 Strategy was presented as a successor to the Lisbon Strategy. To date it has not booked much success.

The countless studies produced in the framework of these goals do however offer a good insight into the strengths and weaknesses of the Dutch knowledge sector. The Netherlands is strong in preconditions: it has plenty of students, highly regarded institutions and universities (as measured by articles published and citations), and a well-educated labour force for the science and technological sector.[4] The hardware, such as broadband, is also in place, and it is accessible internationally, and occupies a central location.

The volume of investment however lags far behind that of the European top, and the R&D expenditures as a percentage of the GNP are scarcely growing. Still more problematic are the Dutch scores on what are called output indicators: job opportunities in high-tech sectors, patent applications, the share of high-tech products in its exports, and the share of innovations in business income.[5]

Thus the valorization of scientific knowledge resulting in economically profitable innovations has a high priority in the innovation policy of the new Ministry of Economic Affairs, Agriculture and Innovation. The policy focuses on nine top sectors: creative industries, logistics, horticultures, agrofood, life sciences, energy, chemicals and high tech. These are not only sectors in which The Netherlands is strong, but also sectors which can contribute to solutions to future problems.

The emphasis lies on strengthening the cooperation between businesses, research institutes and the government. Recently working groups from the sectors have made proposals to the Ministry. Although these are sectors which are spread widely across The Netherlands, most of the proposals lack any spatial component. This is strange when you consider that in the last few decades a large number of studies have been done into the spatial clustering of sectors and the advantages of agglomeration. The top sectors are thus not exempt from the question of which spatial conditions would be most beneficial for them, precisely if they are striving for mutual cooperation and interaction.

Innovation regions and knowledge clusters

In the economic-geographic literature there is considerable attention devoted to innovation regions and knowledge clusters. Although researchers are not terribly optimistic about the mutability of clusters, good analysis can contribute to an understanding of how an innovation system develops and functions. Two of the regions which have been studied most intensively are Route 128 in Boston and Silicon Valley in California.[6] Both are regularly cited as international benchmarks for innovative regions.

After the Second World War job opportunities in the industrial and textile sectors in the Boston area shrank rapidly. Various factors assured that high-tech production took over a much greater share of the economy. The first of these was the presence of a number of universities, including the two top institutions of Harvard and MIT. Over the years especially MIT opened a number of strongly technologically-oriented research institutes which produced a constant flow of highly educated researchers. For instance, during the Second World War the group that had worked on the development of radar was brought from Great Britain to MIT, so that if the Nazis had managed to occupy Britain this technology would not fall into their hands. The laboratories produced not only innovations and highly-trained personnel, but also spin-off businesses, of which some, like IBM, grew out into complete multinationals themselves.

Because of the presence of these institutes and businesses, the region could claim a large part of the federal defence budget, particularly for programmes that focused on the application of computer technology. Various businesses developed in the region which specialized in the production of mini-computers, given that name because they were much smaller than the gigantic mainframes that were initially developed for defence, and which were also used by large numbers of corporations.

Silicon Valley, the region south of San Francisco bay, had no industrial past. However, the prestigious Stanford University was located there. Like Harvard and MIT, this university produced a constant flow of highly-trained workers. To an even greater degree than in Boston, there were active efforts to link up with business. Under the leadership of Professor Terman, the Sandford Industrial Park was set up in 1951, with the aim of offering a place for innovative businesses which grew up around the university. Countless innovation parks and high-tech campuses have arisen since, based on this concept. These businesses also focused primarily on electronics. They were so successful in their efforts that Silicon Valley also attracted investment from the Department of Defense, particularly for the aircraft industry. Here too this investment served as a strong stimulus for the continued development of the sector.

Midway through the 1980s both regions had an economy which was strongly centred around electronics, in both cases supported by top research and educational institutions, and by high defence budgets. From that time, Silicon Valley continued to develop, whereas Boston slipped back. Kenny and Von Burg explain this difference in terms of their central products.[7] In Boston, this was the mini-computer, which from the mid-1980s was rapidly replaced by the still smaller and handier personal computer. The large computer firms in the region were not able to make this change-over on time. In Silicon Valley the emphasis lay not so much on the end product, but on an application, the semi-conductor. These were widely used not only in computers, but in other electronic apparatus. This made it advantageous for new businesses in the computer industry to locate in the vicinity of these firms.

Thus, in addition to a certain randomness that is involved with the choices of individuals about locating in a certain spot, the development of a region to a great extent coincides with the dominant industry there, and the capacity of this industry to adjust to new developments.

In the development of an economic sector in a particular region there are all sorts of processes which reinforce one another which play a role. These are often summed up as the term agglomeration factors. In other words, success breeds success. A whole network of suppliers and service providers arises around a dominant sector, which in turn attracts new businesses. For instance, a whole range of businesses that provided services in the field of patent applications developed parallel with the innovations in the Boston region. The ability to attract venture capital from investors is also important here. Not every new idea will succeed, but to find out if it will, start-up capital is necessary. Both Boston and Silicon Valley had large numbers of venture-capitalists, although in the case of Silicon Valley, particularly in the early phases of its development, it was largely entrepreneurs who themselves had become wealthy in the sector who made money available for new initiatives. Furthermore, the success of a region also contributes to the prestige of the laboratories and institutions, attracting talented students and staff from outside the region. In this way a region which is already growing stronger in comparison with other regions further enhances its own development.

Although, as Boston in the 1980s indicates,

MIT, Boston

Hightech business, Silicon Valley

success is not guaranteed, it is in such environments that the rise of new sectors is the greatest. As successors to the hardware electronics, Silicon Valley is now populated by content and software businesses, generally related to the internet 2.0. Businesses like Facebook are the new 'growth industries', which arise from and capitalize on the conditions which were already shaped by previous sectors.

Developments not unlike those in the United States can be seen in the rapid growth of the Eindhoven region over recent decades.

Levels of scale

It is interesting that in the explanation for the development of innovation regions, the levels of scale constantly differ. The level of an urban region is in order when it comes to the innovative environment of universities, institutes, businesses, support services and suppliers. Institutions and businesses do not need to be immediate neighbours, as long as they can make use of one another. Moreover, the infrastructure of a region presents the opportunities for keeping in touch with the rest of the world (airports, convention centres, hotels, high speed rail links, internet hubs). The assortment of attractive housing also plays a role at this level of scale.

For the incubation of new ideas, the level of the campus appears to be the most appropriate. The Stanford Industrial Park offers spin-off from the university the opportunity to develop inexpensively, and in close proximity to the university network and supporting facilities. University campuses and research laboratories benefit from the daily interaction between students and researchers. For students, the city is also of importance, as well as the campus. Although top universities provide the high level of amenities and sufficient housing on their own campuses, in addition to living space and amenities cities also offer space for encounters, in the broadest sense.

The basic idea behind forming campuses is that proximity encourages innovation. Interaction and confidence keep transaction costs low, help in coordinating supply and demand, and encourage competition. Specialized knowledge moves between businesses with the employees. Such theories only hold true however when the production factor is non-codifiable or tacit knowledge. When it comes to the transfer of data or other exchangeable information, the role of the employees, and with it the role of interaction and trust, is much smaller, at the most becoming a matter of keeping one another abreast of the availability of this information. In that case, data can simply be acquired in the traditional manner, and this knowledge can much easily be transmitted over long distances. With this, the necessity of clustering disappears.

Many researchers have racked their brains trying to define the right spatial level of scale for clusters. In practice, they appear to differ quite a bit, from urban campuses to research districts on the periphery of a city, and from purely scientific campuses to more mixed environments. Rather than trusting blindly in the success of the clusters, it would seem more reasonable to delve more deeply into the phenomenon and see what lessons can be drawn from it.

Trends in Academia

Three developments are of great importance for the way in which the Dutch academic world is presently thinking about clusters. First, much more than before, universities were forced to raise money externally. Furthermore, since 1995, universities had to manage and maintain their own real estate. Finally, the role of the library, one of the central functions in knowledge clusters, has changed fundamentally in recent years.

Cooperation among universities, institutes and business is becoming increasingly important. This is a trend which has been under way for some time. The

table on page 142 indicates that the share of secondary and tertiary funds in the financing of universities has risen.[8] The table also shows the incomes for education. This is entirely financed by the government. The share of external financing for research is therefore considerable. This involves project or programme financing and research performed under contract for third parties, which can include governmental authorities, European funds as well as businesses.

By allocating research funding to universities through organizations like the Netherlands Organization for Scientific Research (NWO), research can be more strongly focused on fields of science which are regarded as important. In 2010 the NWO invested 741 million Euro in research. Over 200 million of that was invested in research institutes. Eight institutes in the natural sciences, such as AMOLF in Amsterdam, Astron in Dwingeloo and the Royal Dutch Institute for Sea Research on Texel are accommodated under the NWO itself. Eighteen institutes in the life sciences, social sciences and humanities, such as the IISG in Amsterdam and Rathenau Institute in The Hague, are financed by the Royal Dutch Academy of Arts and Sciences (KNAW).

The integration among science, institutes and business also has its physical expressions. Like foreign models, increasing numbers of campuses in The Netherlands are of a more mixed nature, particularly around technical departments. TIC Delft, the Bio Science Park in Leiden, and the Science Park in Amsterdam are examples. The KNAW is considering the possibility of accommodating some of Amsterdam's institutes in the field of the humanities, such as the NIOD and the Meertens Institute, in the vicinity of the new home of the University of Amsterdam's Humanities Department on the Binnengasthuis site.

Many foreign universities have traditionally owned their own land and buildings. For universities such as Harvard and MIT, that is an important foundation for their solid financial position. In The Netherlands university buildings were traditionally the property of the national government. In 1995 the buildings and land were transferred to the universities, to give them more flexibility in their operational management and make them more aware of the costs of their real estate. Housing costs now had to be weighed against costs for education and research. Everywhere discussions immediately arose about the number of square metres to be devoted to education and research, and about opening hours, cleaning schedules, security, etc.

The transfer of the real estate came precisely at a moment when many university buildings were in need of renovation. After all, the largest part of the Dutch universities' real estate portfolio is comprised of buildings from the 1960s and 1970s. New buildings were also needed for the growing numbers of students. Around the millennium all of the universities therefore presented a vision for the development of their real estate. As an extension of this, all of the university cities are now undergoing a large-scale reshuffle. In many cases, clustering is

regarded as a good means of increasing efficiency an encouraging cooperation.

The third development involves the significance of libraries. Because of the digitization of scientific journals, the function of libraries in loaning and providing reading rooms for them is reduced. Encyclopaedias, newspaper articles and dictionaries are also available in digital form today. Many libraries have moved their stacks to a distant location, from which books can be supplied on request.

While calm and quiet are still hallmarks of libraries, many of them are livelier than ever. The computers which were at first primarily for searching for digitized data now provide access to databases of articles and academic networks, and are favourite places for studying. Moreover, the library is a place for meeting fellow students and like-minded friends. Many universities have built new libraries, with fewer bookshelves and more study places. Spread through various academic departments, there are more study centres, learning centres and flexible work spaces being set up, with wifi and all sorts of coffee right at hand. The study centres are the most central sites on many university campuses.

'New Work' and innovation

The latest trend is much more general. Applying the concepts of the 'New Work', many businesses are introducing radical changes in the location, organization and form of working. The times and places for work are becoming much more flexible. A recent report sketched these developments in the Bay Area, around San Francisco, Oakland and Silicon Valley. The report was put together by SPUR (San Francisco Planning and Urban Research Organization), an NGO which is dedicated to 'good planning and good government in the Bay Area through research, education and advocacy.'[9] The organization has its headquarters in the Yerba Buena culture quarter.

Increasing numbers of businesses are seeing interaction among employees, and between employees and the city, as necessary for innovation. In the creative knowledge economy everything revolves around knowledge – but even more, around its creative application. That is what leads to innovation. A room in an office is not the best place for that. An ever-changing environment, with new contacts, is much more stimulating. That is presently

Development of income at Dutch universities 1985-2000

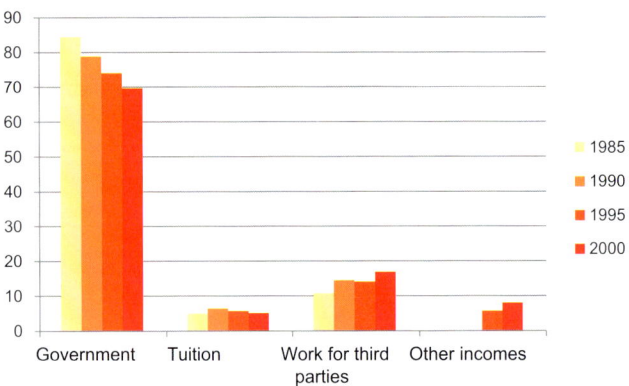

Total square metre per university in the Randstad
Source: Den Heijer, 2011

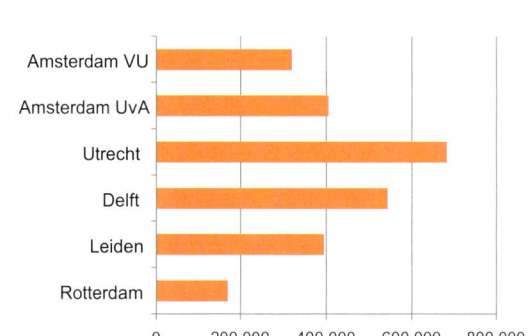

true for traditional innovation too. Tests set up in laboratories still play a role, but only as part of a total process. There too things more frequently revolve around innovative applications, attractive design and good marketing concepts. For instance, among the important new products for Philips in the last few years were Senseo and the Coolskin electric razor. These were only made possible by intensive cooperation with Douwe Egberts and Nivea, and by cast iron product branding.

Innovation of this sort is benefited by an urban environment. The interactions there are more diverse than in traditional working environments in business parks or isolated campuses. In addition, the fact that increasing numbers of business tasks are contracted out plays a role. Legal services, advertising and consultancy are typically urban sectors. Thus ever more businesses are being forced to seek a more diverse environment. In fact, this is a reversal of the trend during the 1960s, when increases in scale and internalization of all support tasks led to the massive medical and research centres.

Such colossal complexes are becoming ever less necessary. Businesses are becoming smaller and smaller. Twitter has only 600 employees, and Facebook 2000, while Google still has 28,000 employees, and Hewlett Packard 300,000. With every new generation of computer and software businesses, the size of the firms appears to be decreasing. The only category of businesses where there is still growth are one-man operations.

The concentration of Web 2.0 firms in the San Francisco Bay Area reveals two strong clusters: in Downtown San Francisco, and around the Stanford Industrial Park.[10] In the city centre it is primarily SOMO (South of Market Street) that is popular, the area around Yerba Buena Gardens, which was described in the previous chapter. The Stanford Industrial Park has however undergone a metamorphosis that is at least as radical. Against all the original principles, the campuses have become more public, and dwellings and restaurants and cafés have been added.

Knowledge clusters in the university cities

There are six universities in the Randstad, spread over five cities. There are eight universities outside the Randstad. Of the total of 210,000 students, however, 60% are registered at the Randstad universities, and a bit more than 27% at the two Amsterdam universities. The share of the staff in the Randstad is about 50%, and in Amsterdam 18%.[11] The Hague is not a university city, but has still been included in this research. The city is home to a large number of institutions, a branch of Leiden University, and a large cluster of institutions offering post-secondary vocational education. Furthermore, in this analysis the government ministries are regarded as a special sort of R&D institutions; they translate knowledge into policy.

Many university buildings are clustered. As our working definition for a culture cluster, in Chapter 2 we used the formula of a collection of at least three cultural institutions (museums, theatres, music venues, discussion centres and libraries) within five minutes walk of one another, which together draw at least 500,000 visitors per year. In a next step, diverse sorts of clusters were distinguished. The spatial form and size of these clusters differed, as did the density of institutions and the supporting programme.

Most university buildings are clustered. Only in the centre of Amsterdam can a diffuse pattern be distinguished. The differences in size among the knowledge clusters are however much larger than in the culture clusters. The actual dimensions of clusters of university departments and institutes (with facilities such as museums, sports centres, libraries, study halls, etc.) is therefore used as the point of departure. In the following section, the types of clusters are described.

Numbers of students and staff per university in the Randstad
Source: Den Heijer, 2011

University	Students	Academic FTE	Support staff FTE	Total FTE	Number of staff	Parttime ratio	Students/ Academic FTE
Rotterdam	19,500	840	650	1,490	1,760	85%	23
Leiden	17,600	1,840	1,470	3,310	3,970	83%	10
Delft	14,400	2,580	1,850	4,430	4,990	89%	6
Utrecht	29,200	2,890	2,350	5,240	6,360	82%	10
Amsterdam UvA	27,100	2,190	1,620	3,810	4,600	83%	12
Amsterdam VU	19,300	1,780	1,450	3,230	3,970	82%	11

Legend for pages 145-159

- universities
- institutes and business
- academic hospital
- cultural institutions
- cafés, restaurants
- retail stores

Amsterdam

Amsterdam has two universities: the University of Amsterdam (UvA) and the Vrije Universiteit (VU). They have 32,750 and 24,500 students and 4000 and 3500 full time staff, respectively. The UvA has seven departments, the VU thirteen. The UvA is carrying out an ambitious housing plan, with the aim of concentrating the departmental buildings on four urban campuses, for the humanities, technical sciences, social sciences and medical sciences, respectively. At present, particularly the departments in the city centre are scattered widely. The VU complex is part of the South Axis; here too preparations are being made for a transformation.

There is one other research cluster in Amsterdam: the Slotervaart cluster, with the Netherlands Cancer Institute, the Antonie van Leeuwenhoek Hospital and the headquarters of the Sanquin Blood Bank. In addition, spread around the city, there are several other research centres of greater or lesser size: the Shell Research Centre in Amsterdam North, the National Aerospace Laboratory of The Netherlands (NLR) Schinkelhaven/Lelystad, and the International Institute for Social History, whose holdings include archives of the labour movement.

Shell's laboratories – long called the Royal Dutch Shell Laboratory Amsterdam, today the Shell Technology Centre Amsterdam – have been located on the north bank of the IJ since 1914. The old, 27 hectare site had 29 buildings housing its activities. A new building of somewhat over 80,000 m² (including the parking garage) was realized in 2009, on a much smaller, 7 hectare site. The complex provides work for 1350 persons, distributed across laboratories, testing facilities, workshops and offices.

The NLR has a complex of 13,500 m² on a 3 hectare site in the Schinkelhaven, and a staff of 700. A plan for the renovation of the 1950s building, designed by Maaskant and Van Tijen, was prepared in 2010. The new building was designed by Inbo, in collaboration with Wessel de Jonge.

Slotervaart Hospital

Binnengasthuis with UvA buildings

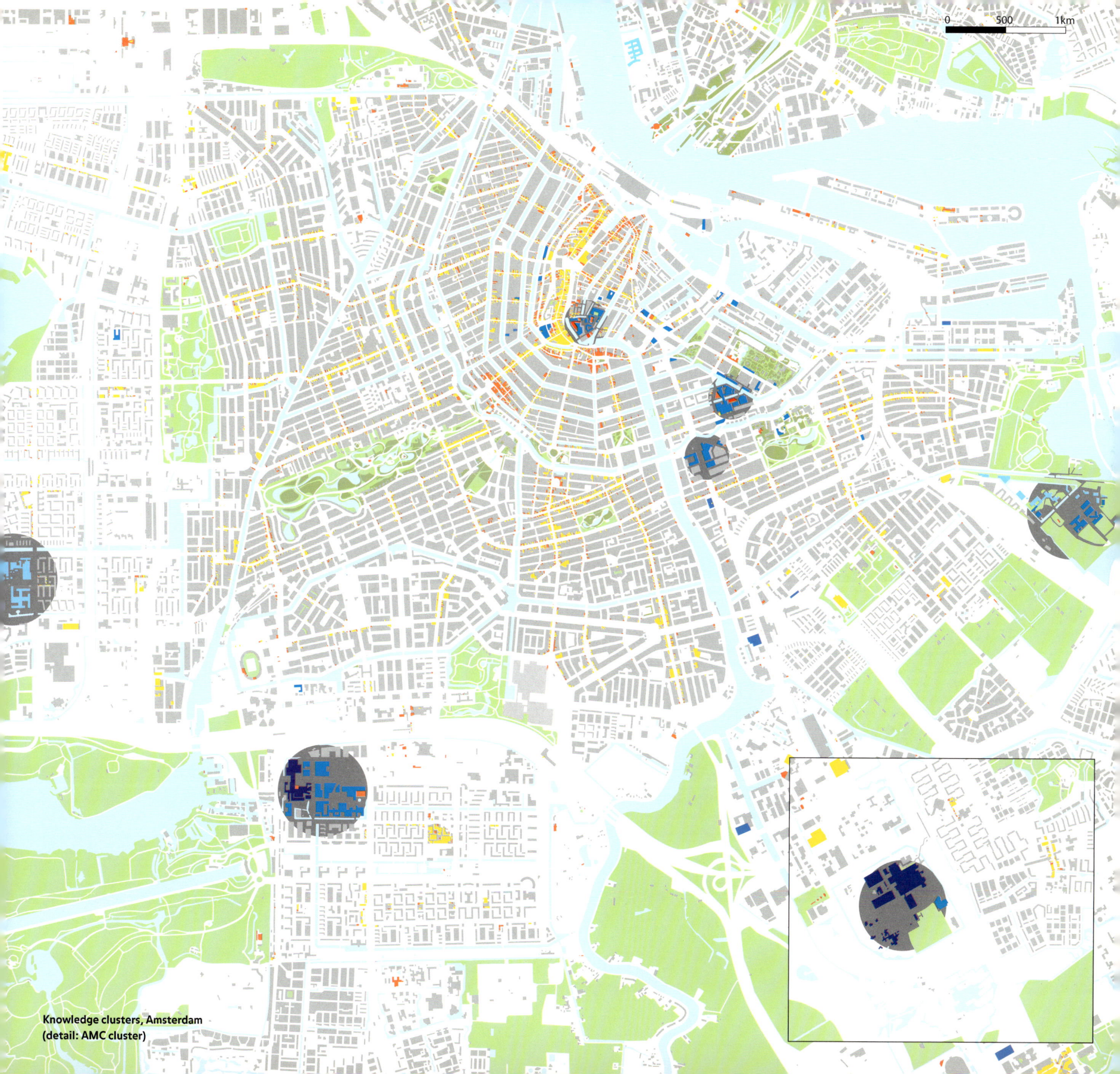

Knowledge clusters, Amsterdam
(detail: AMC cluster)

0   500   1km

Academisch Centrum Tandheelkunde Amsterdam

ACTA and the VU Hospital, looking west

CITY CENTRE – BINNENGASTHUIS CLUSTER

Presently a large number of faculties and departments are housed in buildings spread through the centre of Amsterdam. In the future only the Humanities division, with its 7000 students and 1200 staff, will be housed there, in and around the Binnengasthuis site and the Oudemanhuispoort. Among the departments involved are Dutch, Languages, History and Philosophy.

Another component of this cluster is the Library, with its Special Collections including the Bibliotheca Rosenthaliana, the Allard Pierson Museum, and the University Theatre. The projected new building for the Library and Humanities, designed by the Spanish architects Cruz y Ortiz, will be central to this cluster.

After the departure of the Social Sciences departments for the Roeterseiland complex, consideration is being given to accommodating several of the KNAW institutes, such as the Meertens Institute, the Institute for War, Holocaust and Genocide Studies, and DANS in their former quarters around the Oostindisch Huis, Spinhuis and Bushuis. The cluster is directly accessed by the Rokin stop on the new North-South Metro line.

ROETERSEILAND CLUSTER

As early as the 1930s parts of the UvA were located on Roeterseiland and the Muidergracht, near the Artis and Hortus Botanicus. Several of the buildings in the characteristic architecture of the Amsterdam School remain from that period. In order to cope with the growth of the student body in the 1970s, a large volume of space was added, stretching over a canal. The total complex is now 110,000 m². It is being radically reconstructed to provide an 'open campus' for the departments of Economics and Business, Law, Social and Behavioural Sciences. It is intensively used, with 15,000 students and 2000 staff. Most of the entrances are along the Nieuwe Achtergracht. This is also where restaurants and cafés and other amenities will be found, such as the refectory, Crea, the Student Centre and an indoor sports centre. The complex will also include student housing. The Kriterion cinema lies on the Roetersstraat. The Weesperplein metro stop is a 150 metre walk away.

The Hogeschool van Amsterdam (HvA) is realizing its Amstel Campus in the immediate vicinity, on the Rijnspoorplein. It will be the main location for the HvA, with a floor area of 100.000 m², for about 25,000 students. Part of the plan involves the renovation of the historic buildings that once housed the Amsterdam offices of the Internal Revenue Service and the Labour Council, and a new building on the site of the former Wibauthuis.

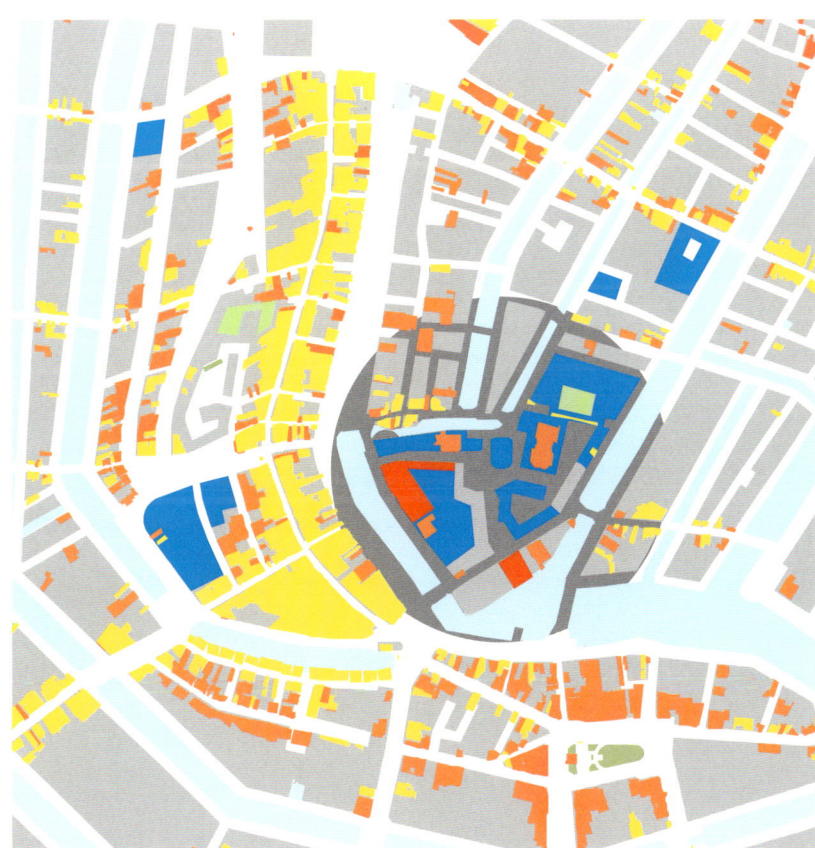

Binnengasthuis cluster

Roeterseiland cluster

SCIENCE PARK

Since the 1950s the university's institute for subatomic physics, Nikhef, has been located in the Watergraafsmeer Polder, later joined by the Centre for Mathematics and Information (CWI), the Institute for Atomic and Molecular Physics (AMOLF), and the SARA Computing Centre. These institutes are now part of a mixed campus of 70 hectare, with the buildings of several departments, the Amsterdam University College, Universum (the student sports centre), 1300 student residences, 500 rental and owner-occupied dwellings, restaurants and cafés, a conference centre and a hotel with more than 200 rooms. The building housing the departments of Natural Sciences, Mathematics and Information measures 55,000 m², accommodating 3,000 students and 1400 staff. The new building, designed by Rudy Uytenhaak and Herman Hertzberger opened in 2010.

Additionally, all kinds of businesses are located on the site. MATRIX Innovation Centre now rents turn-key office space to a hundred businesses in their start-up phase, with all sorts of facilities and laboratory spaces. The direct connections to the AMS-IX, the Huygens Computer, data centres and a 150 kV substation make the area attractive for ICT businesses. The Science Park railway station opened in 2010.

AMC CLUSTER

The Amsterdam Medical Centre (AMC) is a large complex on 64 hectare, with a floor area of about 450,000 m², built since 1980. In addition to the University hospital, it comprises the Emma Children's Hospital, the Department of Medicine and a series of institutes, including the Netherlands Institute for Neurosciences (NIN-KNAW) and the Spinoza Centre

for Neuroimaging. The UvA's nursing programme and the Bascule, an outpatient facility for youth psychiatry, are also on the site. 7000 people work there. In 2010, 370,000 outpatients were treated. The adjoining AMC Medical Business Park provides another 100,000 m² of space for medical businesses, in thirteen buildings. In order to provide support for patent applications, locating partners and establishing spin-off businesses, the Technology Transfer Office (TTO) and a holding company have been set up. The AMC complex is served by the east branch of the metro, and the Holendrecht railway station. It is also directly accessible from the A2 and A9 motorways.

VU CLUSTER

The Vrije Universiteit was the outcome of efforts by Abraham Kuyper to establish a university reflecting

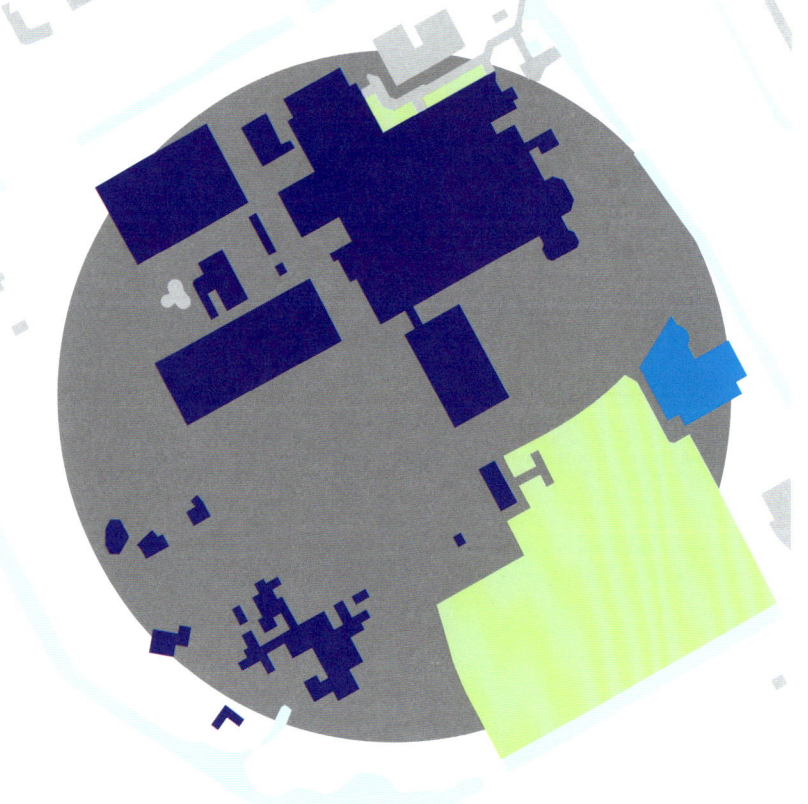

Science Park   AMC cluster

Protestant principles. Its first building was opened in 1884 on the Keizersgracht. In 1933 the Physics Laboratory was built on the Lairessestraat. Since the 1960s the VU has been located on the De Boelelaan in Buitenveldert, close to the A10 ring road and Station South. In actuality, there are two separate complexes, for the university and for its Medical Centre. In total the complex measures about 300,000 m², on 20 hectare, and houses the Hospital, the 15-storey main building of the university, laboratories, institutes such as the Netherlands Institute for the Study of Crime and Law Enforcement (NSCR), ACTA and the Tinbergen Institute, the Duisenberg School of Finance, and the Protestant Theological University.

With the 2005 construction of the Hogeschool Inholland's training centre for Care and Well-being, designed by Jeanne Dekkers, the campus took on a more mixed character. Arising from a new vision for the campus, the VU has now begun to build NU.VU, a 35,000 m² building designed by Meyer and Van Schooten. This complex, to be completed in 2017, will be the first step in the development of a knowledge quarter for the South Axis. The total projected new building programme comprises over a million square metres, a quarter of which will replace existing facilities. One component of the plan is the construction of 95,000 m² dwelling space.

Slotervaart cluster

Next door to the Slotervaart Hospital lies a cluster of research institutions, with the Netherlands Cancer Institute, NKI), the Antonie van Leeuwenhoek Hospital (AVL) and the headquarters of the Sanquin Blood Bank. Since they were founded in 1913 the NKI and the AVL have formed a unit where research into and treatment of cancer take place alongside one another. In 1979 the laboratory on Plesmanlaan was opened, and in 2003 the adjoining hospital followed. In 1976 several hospitals in Amsterdam were concentrated in the newly built Slotervaart Hospital. Sanquin was created in 1998 with the merger of the Central Laboratory of the Dutch Red Cross and various blood banks. After recent new construction of laboratories and production facilities, 3000 people work here in a 8000 m² site. Together with the 56,000 m² of the Slotervaart Hospital and the 72,000 m², of the NKI-AVL, these institutions comprise an extensive medical cluster. 2000 people work in the NKI-AVL, and 1500 in the Slotervaart Hospital. The only public transit connections for the cluster are by tram and bus; it is easily accessible via the A10.

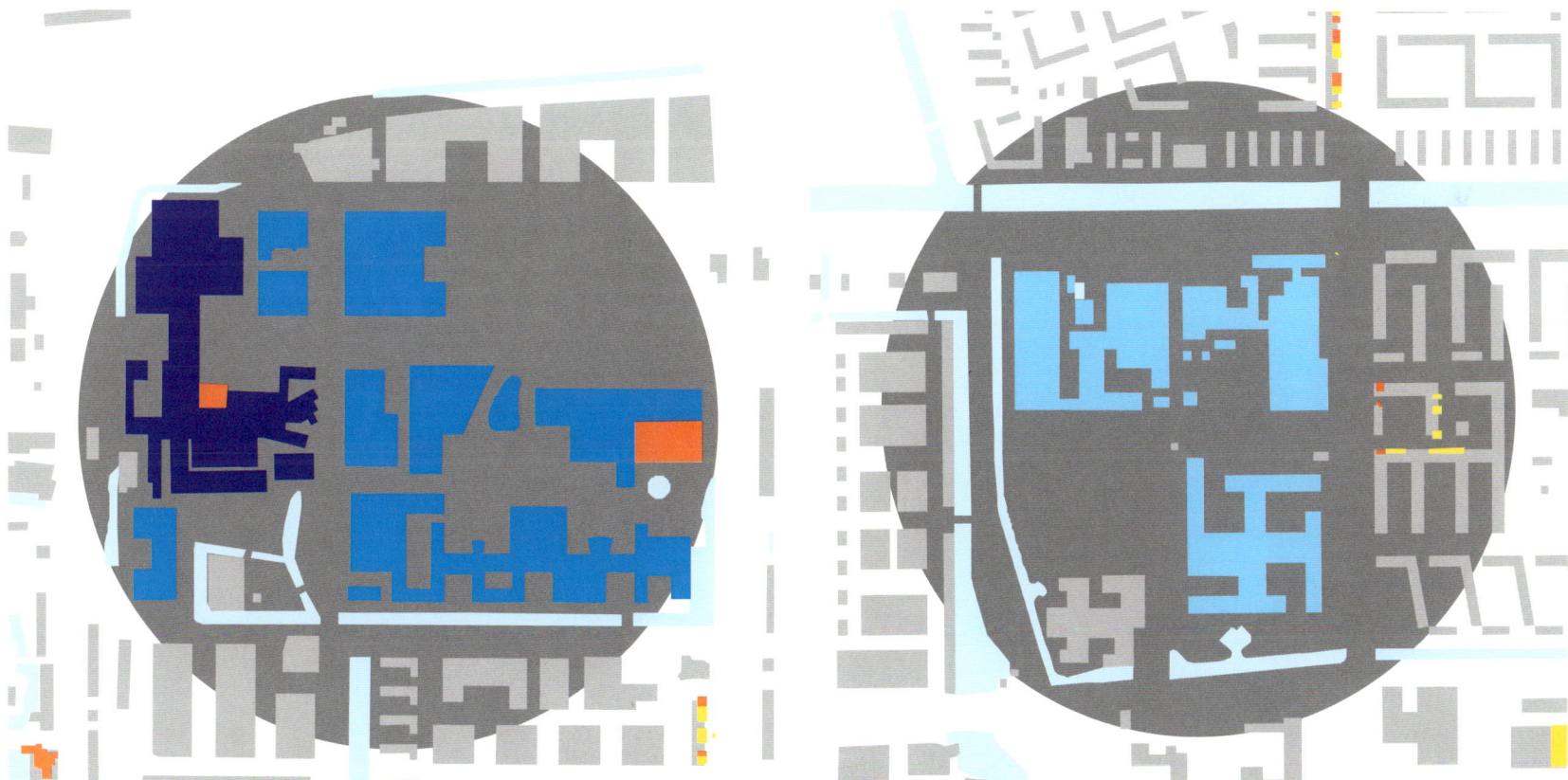

VU cluster

Slotervaart cluster

149

Delft

Delft has an extensive knowledge cluster around the TU Delft. In addition, on the northern end of the city, there is the biotechnology complex of DSM, a successor to the Koninklijke Nederlandsche Gist- en Spiritusfabriek, and the later Gist-Brocades. The site is 36 hectare in size. It contains both production and research facilities, and about 1000 people are employed there. In the future it will be redeveloped as a business park for biotechnology and life sciences companies. On the Westvest, on the edge of the heart of Delft, several institutes are to be found, including UNESCO-IHE, an international educational institute in the field of water resources, and the International Water and Sanitation Centre.

TU DISTRICT

With the founding of the Polytechnische School in 1864, Delft assumed a key role in the training of Dutch engineers. In part as a result of initiatives by Delft engineers, several successful industrial firms were founded there in the second half of the 19th century, including the Nederlandsche Gist- en Spiritusfabriek (1869), the Nederlandse Oliefabriek (1883, later Calvé), the Lijm- en Gelatinefabriek (1885) and the Kabelfabriek (1913).

As early as the 1920s the university had outgrown its city-centre location, and a campus was realized 'across the Schie' to the south of the city centre, with new buildings for the departments of Geodesy, Mining, Roads and Hydraulics, and Chemistry. This was in the period when the national government was investing in establishing all sorts of knowledge and research institutes. Through this the Hydrodynamic Laboratory (1927) and the Laboratory for Soil Mechanics (1934) came to Delft, and the city also was given its own branch of the TNO.

The demand for engineers in the 1960s led to the construction of a whole TU 'district'. Farther to the south of the old campus, in the Wippolder, a new auditorium and a whole series of departmental buildings and institutes were built, designed by Van den Broek and Bakema. Merkelbach and Elling built the sports centre. Following in the wake of the University, numerous businesses and institutions such as the TNO and the Hydrodynamics Laboratory (now part of Deltares) made the move too.

As with many other universities, a new campus vision was formulated at the end of the 1990s. The goals were concentration of the University in the central part of the district, and the blending of allied institutions and student housing. A new university library, designed by Mecanoo, was built next to the auditorium in 1997. Parts of the TNO and Haagse Hogeschool followed. Old departmental buildings were repurposed to accommodate collections of miscellaneous businesses, or housing.

The destruction of the Department of Architecture by fire in 2008 derailed the concentration strategy. The former main building on the 'old' campus was pressed back into service. Presently the TU Delft has 17,300 students and 4500 staff, spread over eight departments. The total size of the TU's sites is 170 hectare.

↑ DSM research Delft North

← Central area TU district

Knowledge clusters, Delft

Leiden

The University of Leiden has 18,600 students and 3150 staff, spread over seven departments. One department is located in The Hague, the rest in and around the centre of Leiden. A new plan for accommodating the university was drawn up in 2005. With this in hand, various buildings have been renovated or disposed of, and programmes and institutes rehoused. There are now three clusters: the humanities around the Library and the Academiegebouw in the Rapenburg cluster in the city centre, the Department of Medicine on the Boerhaave Campus, next to the University Medical Centre, and the natural sciences and the sports centre on the Gorlaeus Campus. The latter two comprise the Leiden Bioscience Park.

RAPENBURG CLUSTER

About 14,000 students are educated in the city centre. In addition to the departments of Archaeology, Humanities, Law and Social Sciences, a large number of central functions are accommodated in this cluster: the Academiegebouw (renovated 2009), Library (renovated 2007) and Administration Building, with the International Office, and institutes such as the Institute for Linguistics, Geography and Ethnology, the National Museum for Antiquities, and the Hortus Botanicus.

BIOSCIENCE PARK

In the 1920s the Academic Hospital moved from the city centre to what was called the Boerhaave Quarter, west of the railway station, with separate buildings for different medical specialities. In 1985 many of these buildings were vacated for the newly built Leiden University Medical Centre (LUMC).

Beginning in the 1960s, a new building for the natural science departments and a sports centre were realized in the area beyond the Hospital, then called the Leeuwenhoek. Since 1984 the whole area has been called the Bioscience Park. Today, including a 36 hectare expansion on the west side of the A44 motorway, it is a 110 hectare cluster in the field of the life sciences. These two campuses have somewhat over 4700 students. The LUMC alone has a staff of 7000. Seventy life sciences businesses are located in the Park, with 3100 staff. An additional 4000 people are employed by institutions such as the Leiden Hogeschool, a branch of the TNO, and Topinstitute Pharma. Among the familiar businesses in the Park are Crucell and Galapagos. Although the number of student residences is limited, the park has a strong mix of functions. Big drawing cards for the public are two attractions oriented to the sciences, Naturalis and Corpus.

Rapenburg cluster

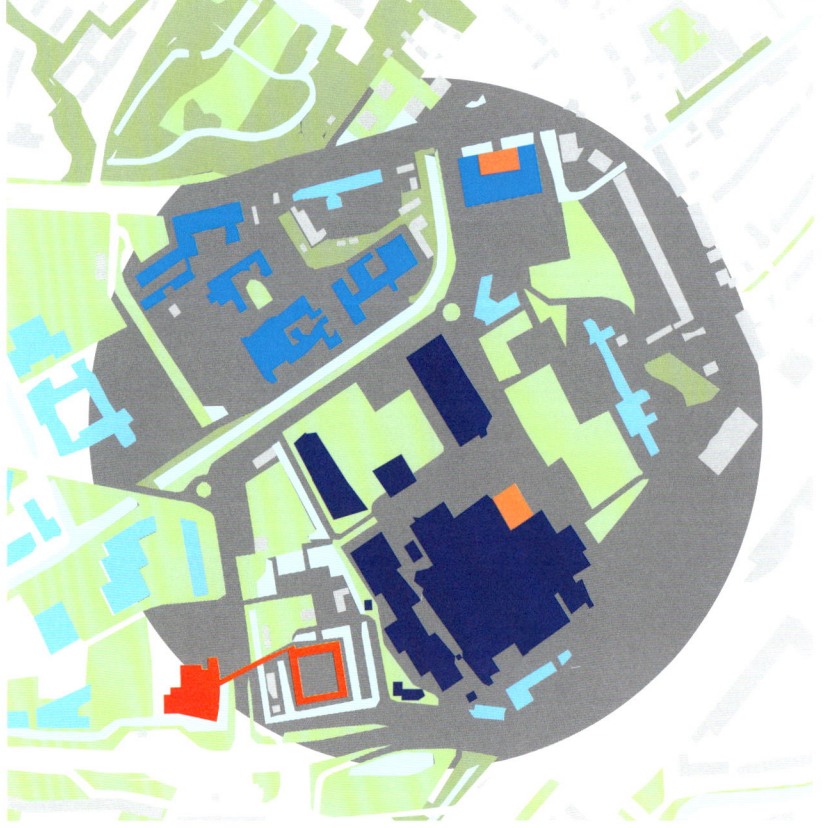

Bio Science Park

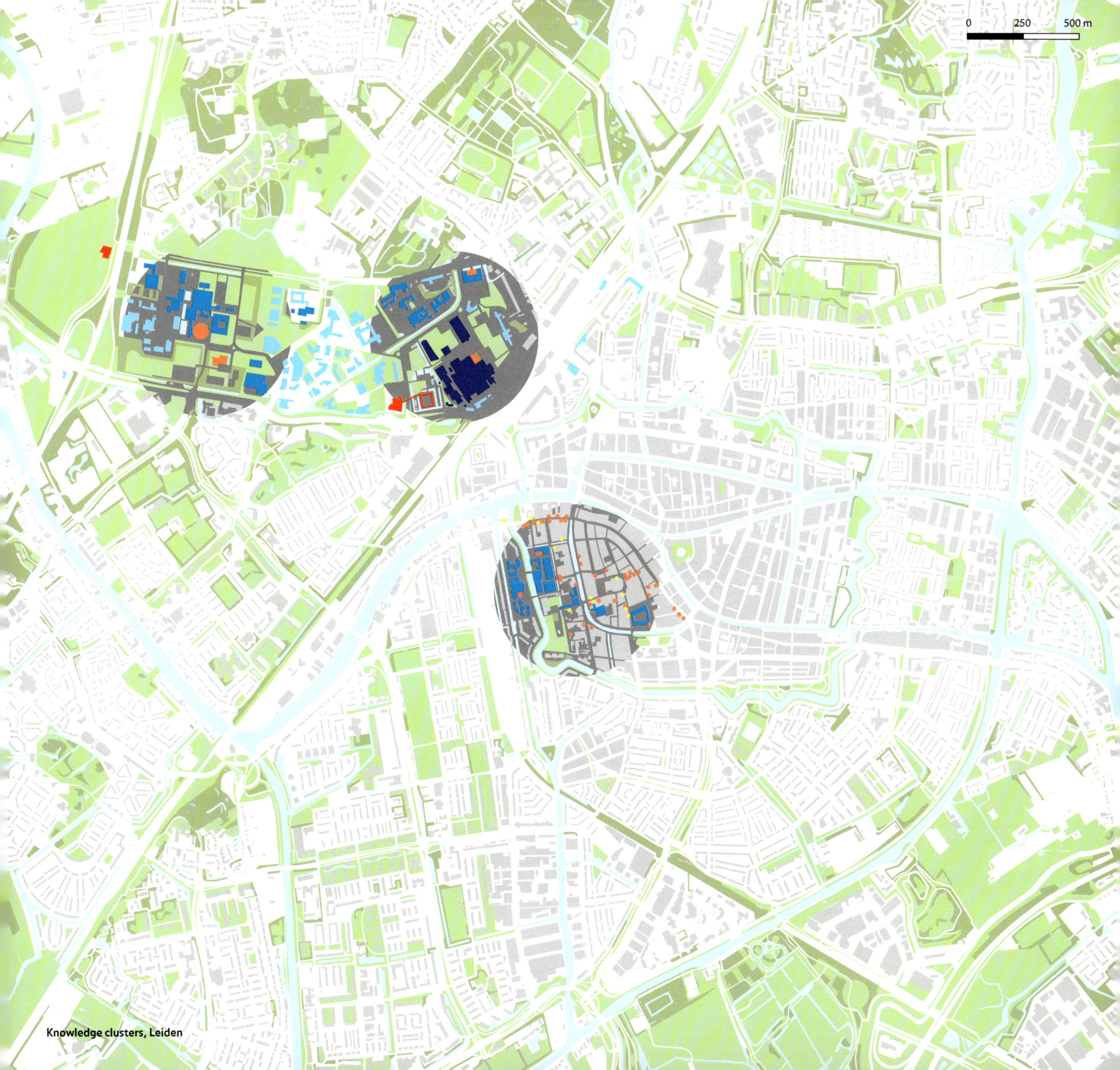

Knowledge clusters, Leiden

0   250   500 m

Rotterdam

Erasmus University has 21,000 students and 1900 staff, in seven academic departments. The departments are concentrated in two clusters: the Hoboken cluster, and Woudestein. The new University College will be located on the Nieuwe Markt, in a building that was formerly the main public library, and then Education Museum. Rotterdam has very few research centres associated with corporations. Unilever's R&D centre is located in nearby Vlaardingen, employing 1000 staff.

HOBOKEN CLUSTER

Next to the Museumpark, on the west side of the former estate of Hoboken, there is an extensive knowledge cluster around the Erasmus Medical Centre (EMC). The Dijkzicht Hospital had already been on this site since the 1960s. The EMC was created in 2002 from a merger of this hospital with the Sophia Children's Hospital, the Daniel Den Hoed Clinic and the Erasmus University Department of Medicine and Health Sciences. Almost 10,000 people are employed there, and over 2700 students are enrolled in its courses. In the coming years the Erasmus Medical Centre will be radically rebuilt, to integrate the Den Hoed Clinic and educational facilities into the complex. After the reconstruction, at 185,000 m² this will be the largest medical centre in The Netherlands. Facilities of the Hogeschool Rotterdam lie to the north and west of the EMC.

WOUDESTEIN

In the early 1960s the Nederlandse Economische School moved to what is now the Woudestein campus. Presently it is home to the departments of Economics, Law, History, Philosophy and Social Sciences, the Rotterdam School of Management, and the Institute of Health Policy and Management. The Hogeschool Rotterdam also has a building in the south-east of this 16 hectare campus. In addition the campus houses important university functions such as the auditorium in the west, the Library, and indoor and outdoor sports facilities, both in the north-east. The campus has a total of 184,000 m² of programming space, and 20,000 students take courses there. Because the central functions do not lie in the middle of the campus, it lacks a central orientation. A recent masterplan for the campus seeks to remedy that by creating two central axes. The new heart of the campus will lie at the intersection of these axes.

In addition to university buildings, the campus is also home to the Erasmus Expo and Conference Center, with conference facilities for up to 930 persons, and 4000 m² of exhibition space.

Hoboken cluster

Woudestein

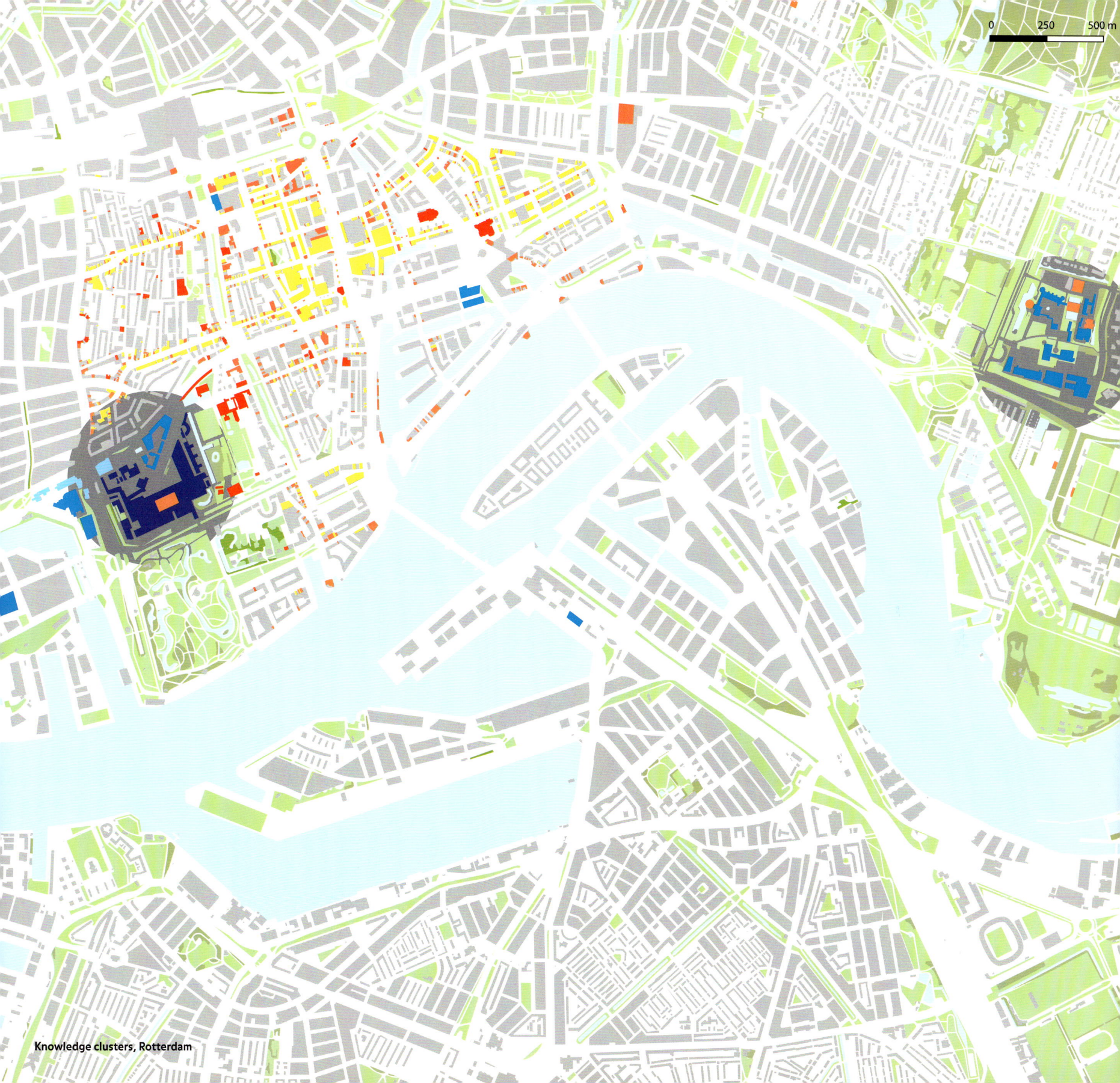

Knowledge clusters, Rotterdam

Utrecht

Until well into the 20th century the whole University of Utrecht was located in the centre of the city. Lack of space however necessitated seeking possibilities for expansion elsewhere. These presented themselves with the passage in the 1960s of the 'Ring Law', decommissioning the defensive works of the Nieuwe Hollandse Waterlinie. In 1967 the Department of Veterinary Medicine was the first to move to the Uithof. Over the course of the years more departments and institutes followed, including the University Medical Centre (UMC) in 1999. A further stimulus was provided the location of the largest part of the Hogeschool Utrecht there in 2005. The University of Utrecht has about 30,000 students, spread across seven departments. The University's buildings are now largely concentrated in the Uithof. Only a few departments remain in the city centre. The University College is located in the former Kromhout Barracks.

DOM CLUSTER

The departments of Humanities and Law, Economics, and Management and Organization are still located in historic buildings around the Dom. A number of the core functions of the University are also located in the city centre. The Library was recently renovated. The Academiegebouw lies behind the Domplein, and the University Museum is further up.

THE UITHOF

The Uithof lies in a relatively isolated location outside the city, in a landscape dominated by the Kromme Rijn and the Hollandse Waterlinie. Its autonomy is further emphasized by the internal grid of north/south and east/west streets. The site comprises 366 hectare, including nature reserves and areas for projected future growth. The University and Hogeschool presently have buildings of 570,000 m² in use. The UMC contributes another 500,000 m². The Wilhelmina Children's Hospital and the Central Military Hospital are both incorporated in the UMC. The cluster also includes the University Sports Centre

and about 4000 dwelling units for students.

The Uithof also provides locations for increasing numbers of businesses and institutes, primarily concentrated in the south-east corner, including the Central Bureau for Fungal Cultures, the Hubrecht Institute for Developmental Biology and Stem Cell Research, and the Netherlands Institute for Space Research. The new Danone research institute is to open in 2013. The National Institute for Public Health and the Environment, now located in Bilthoven, will open its new building in the Uithof in 2018. The new structure is to be 55,000 m², and will house 1450 employees. There has been an emphasis on trend-setting modern architecture. Among other architects represented are Wiel Arets (Library), Rem Koolhaas-Art Zaaijer (Masterplan, 1986, and Educatorium), Rudy Uytenhaak (student complex), and Herman Hertzberger (David de Wied building). The University College Utrecht, based on the model of American colleges, lies between the Uithof and the city in the 1908 Kromhout Barracks. It has 677 students from 68 countries.

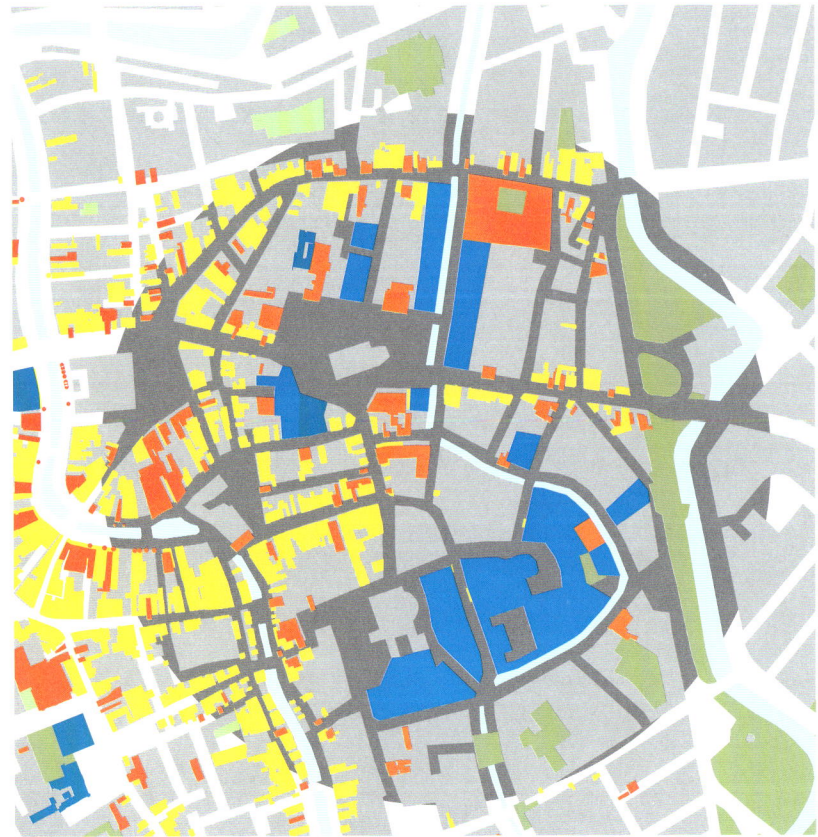

Dom cluster

The Uithof

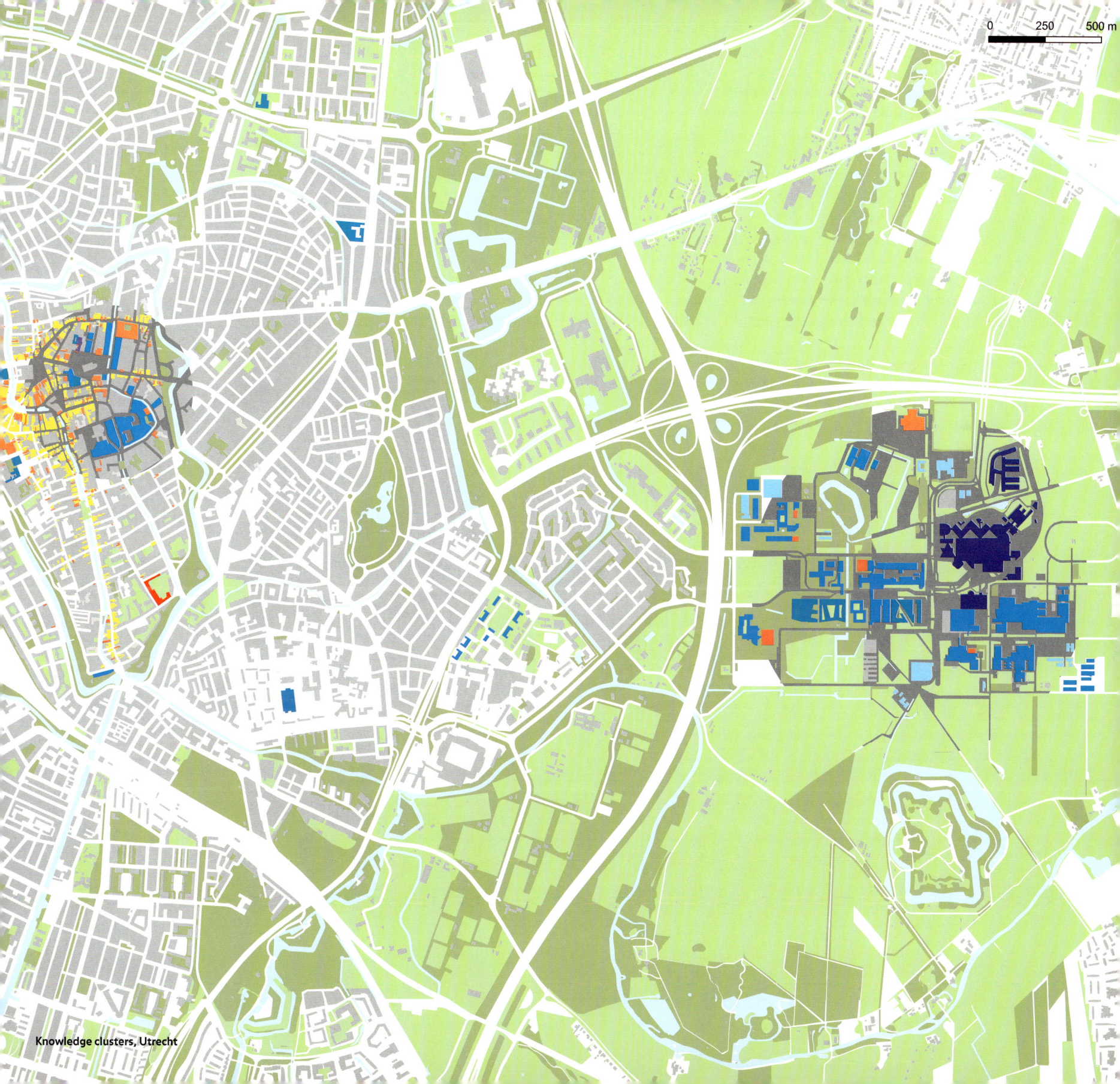

Knowledge clusters, Utrecht

The Hague

The Hague has a large number of scattered research institutes such as the KNAW institutes ING-Huygens, the NIDI and the NIAS. Many other institutes are part of the HAC, the Hague Academic Coalition. This is a cooperative body of academic institutes in the field of international relations, international law and international development.

Members of the HAC include:
- The Carnegie Foundation and the Hague academy of International Law, in the Peace Palace,
- The Hague Institute for the Internationalization of Law (HiiL),
- The International Institute of Social Studies, of Erasmus University (IISS),
- The Netherlands Institute of International Relations, Clingendael,
- The T.M.C. Asser Institute,
- Leiden University, Hague Campus,
- Leiden University College, The Hague,
- The Hague University of Applied Sciences (Haagse Hogeschool).

The HAC works closely with the International Court of Justice and the Permanent Court of Arbitration, both in the Peace Palace, the Yugoslavia Tribunal, in the Aegon building near the World Forum, and the International Criminal Court. The Criminal Court is presently located on the Maanweg, at the Utrechtse Baan, but is going to move to a new building on the Alexanderkazerne site. This site is 72,000 m² in size. The new building, with 46,000 m² in floor space, is designed by the Danish architects Schmidt Hammer Lassen, and will be ready in 2015.

Wijnhaven quarter

A number of government ministries are, or in several years will be located in the Ministry cluster in the southern portion of the Hague city centre, around the Turfmarkt and Oranjebuitensingel. Only the Ministry of General Affairs is located in the Binnenhof. The Ministry of Economic Affairs will remain on the Bezuidenhoutseweg, the Ministry of Defence on the Plein, and the Ministry of Finance in the recently renovated complex on the Korte Voorhout. Since 1975 the Ministry of Internal Affairs and the Ministry of Justice have been housed in the towers on the Schedeldoekshaven, designed by Lucas & Niemeyer. In 2013 they will move to the new building designed by Rapp & Rapp, on the site of the demolished Zwarte Madonna. The move toward concentration began in the 1990s with the construction of the former Ministry of Housing, Regional Development and the Environment on the Rijnstraat, right next to Central Station. This building with its characteristic atria, designed by Hoogstad, will become the home for the Ministry of Infrastructure and the Environment, and for Foreign Affairs. After renovation, the building next to the 1998 Ministry of Public Health, Welfare and Sport, with the towers by Soeters and Graves, will accommodate Social Affairs and Employment. Since 2003 the Ministry of Education, Culture and Science has been in the Hoftoren, designed by Kohn Pedersen Fox Associates.

Wijnhaven quarter

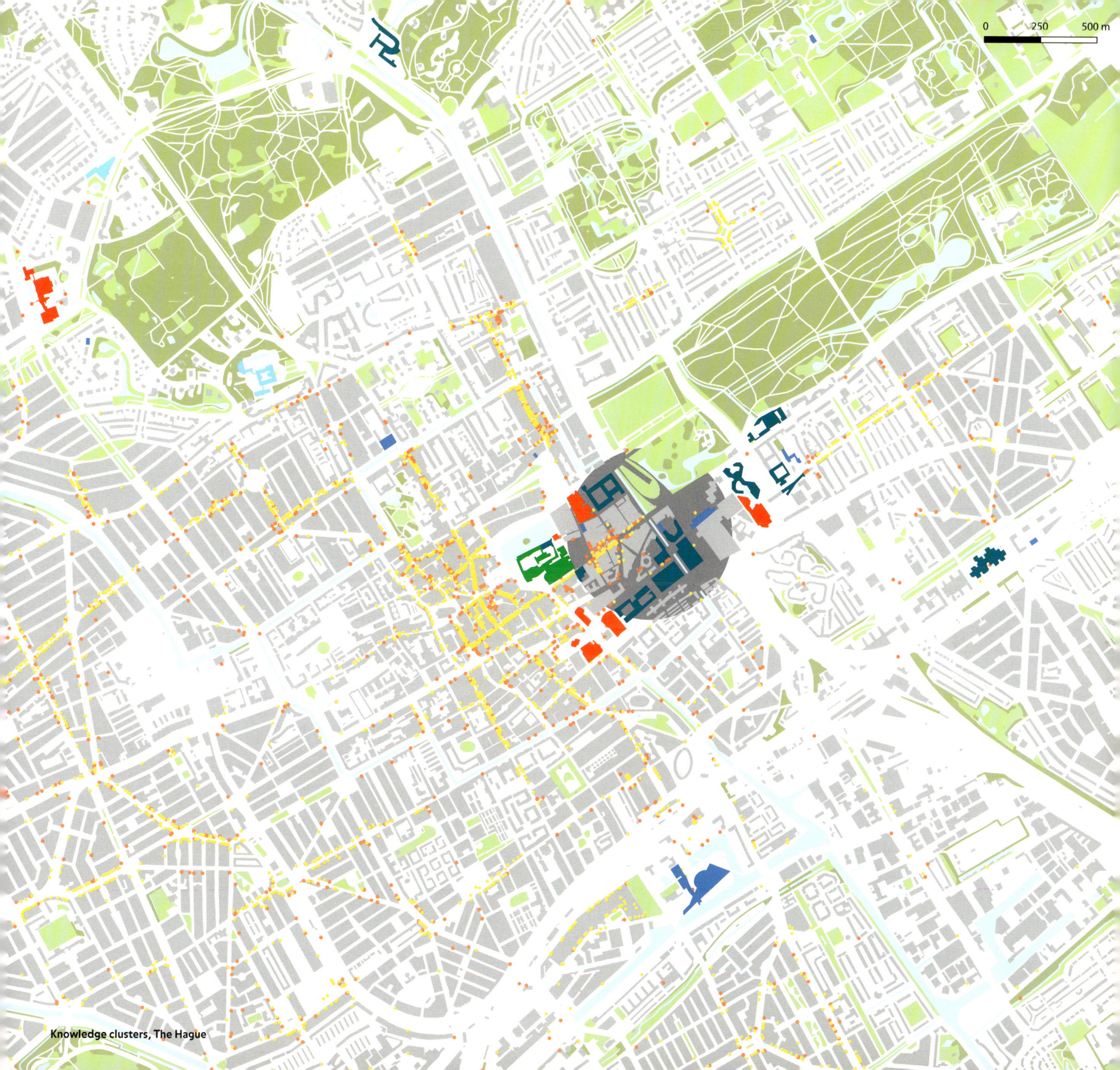

Knowledge clusters, The Hague

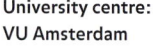

University centre:
Roeterseiland, UvA
Amsterdam

University centre:
VU Amsterdam

Typology of knowledge clusters

The term 'urban campus' is presently often being used for a cluster or concentration of university buildings in an urban setting. The word campus made its appearance in the 19th century when the need arose to distinguish university buildings in a green environment (around a 'yard' or 'green') from the traditional university buildings in city centres. Given this history, the concept of an 'urban campus' is paradoxical, and not very specific. In addition to the traditional 'campus on the green', distinctions can be made among courtyard complexes, centres, quarters, science parks and districts. These types vary greatly in size and in the degree of concentration of academic buildings, and are interwoven with the surrounding city in diverse ways. The types also differ in terms of their programme of facilities.

Courtyard complexes

The oldest European universities lay in the midst of the city, and were organised around a courtyard (Cordoba. Bologna, Coimbra, Oxford, Cambridge). The form was inspired by monasteries and the monastic schools where education was conducted in the early Middle Ages. This form closed the university off from the city and its temptations. Students, and often the staff as well, lived at the university. Therefore a large part of the building was initially intended as a dormitory. The facilities were situated in and around the courtyard, and were entered from it. A building or storey – in the English tradition termed the 'hall' – served as the library and dining hall. In many cases a chapel, sometimes with a high bell tower and an exuberantly decorated façade and choir, dominated the complex. Initially the closed courtyard design assured that there would be limited interaction between the university and the city. Extensions and the addition of new courtyards, as at Oxford and Cambridge, created larger

Courtyard complex: Binnengasthuis,
UvA Amsterdam

complexes, connected by a system of gates and passages. In many cases these were publicly accessible, permitting interaction with the city.

With the concentration of the now scattered buildings of the Humanities Department and the construction of the new library on the Binnengasthuis site, Amsterdam will obtain a university campus of the courtyard type: a collection of university buildings connected with one another by a system of courts and squares. The courtyard campus has a strong identity because of the closed building wall around it and the limited number of entrances.

On the other hand, the gates, passages and short cuts provide for a firm anchoring in the city. The Binnengasthuis site differs from its illustrious forebears, such as the central part of Oxford University, because of its agglomerate character, major architectural contrasts and irregular basic shape. These are the product of a large number of transformations, from the building of the Oude and Nieuwe Nonnenklooster in the 14th century and its renovation as the Binnengasthuis hospital after the Reformation, through the 19th century insertion of the Dutch National Bank along one edge and the renovation to accommodate various medical specialities in their own buildings, to the transformations for residential construction, the University and Theaterschool after the hospital and the Department of Medicine moved to the AMC in 1981. The design of the new library by Cruz and Ortiz, on the site of the Second Surgical Clinic and the Nurses' Residence, will forge the fragmented complex together. It will be a new, centrally situated element, in the middle of the complex, on the central square. The entrance to the site from the Nieuwe Doelenstraat will also receive a new, more inviting treatment. In both its use, and its spatial significance, the Binnengasthuis University Library can become the heart of the cluster. The average walking distance between the departmental buildings and the library is 130 metres. The radius of the whole complex is 150 metres.

Centre – research centre

Centres are large buildings or complexes where the buildings are linked with one another by covered walkways or aerial bridges. This type has its roots in a combination of the rising student populations after the Second World War, and a thoroughgoing separation of functions. For instance, educational facilities and laboratories are often accommodated in different but connected buildings. Facilities such

NYU near Washington Square Park, New York City

Binnengasthuis and the Wilhelminagasthuis in Amsterdam, was abandoned. In its more advanced state, the 'pavilion' type was in fact a green university campus. With the development of business parks around the medical centre, such as the AMC Medical Business Park, planners are once again reaching back to this green quality.

During the 1960s and 1970s many of these centres were also being built in other countries. A unique hybrid form, between the centre and the courtyard complex, is found in the *Rost- und Silberlaube* complex on the Dahlem campus of the Freie Universität in Berlin. This is a connected university centre around a system of internal streets, with a whole series of green courts which are not, however, accessible to the public. The complex was designed in the 1970s by the architects Candilis, Josic and Woods. In 2005 a new library for the humanities, designed by Norman Foster, was built in one of the courtyards.

University quarter

If they wished to remain in the city, over the years urban universities that did not have large, connected

as libraries, study centres, auditoriums and refectories are located at intersections in the centre, accessed from a central hall, atrium or plaza.

In their original state, the Roeterseiland building complex of the UvA and the main building of the VU can be characterized as 'centres'. The radii of the area in which these centres are situated are 185 and 375 metres, respectively. The internalizing of the university functions creates a sharp separation between the university and its surroundings. Both the UvA and the VU are therefore transforming their centres into more open urban campuses. Many recent complexes housing polytechnic schools

(*hogescholen*) have an internal organization that is based on the centre type, but often have architecture that is more open to the city, and public functions in the plinth (Haagse Hogeschool, Ichtus, Amstel Campus). The four medical centres in the university cities also belong to this centre type (AMC, UMC, LUMC and Hoboken). These are the largest buildings in The Netherlands, with enormous floor area and very high density. For the new buildings for the VUMC, the aim is a floor-space index of 7.

When the centres were built, the urban hospital pattern with multiple 'pavilions' around a courtyard or in a complex, as had been found in the

Ministries in the Wijnhaven quarter, The Hague

162

sites were forced to acquire plots of land in the vicinity of their existing buildings for their expansion. This created neighbourhoods which were to a greater or lesser extent dominated by the university: university quarters. NYU, around Washington Square Park in New York City, and the Humboldt Universität Berlin-Mitte are examples of this.

As long as the buildings are of sufficient size, this concept permits the realization of special buildings designed as assembly halls or libraries. Like the 'campus on the green', the distances in university quarters often require providing libraries, study centres, and cafeterias in separate buildings.

Although often the dominant function, the university is rarely the only function in the area. Other city-centre and university-related functions are to be found mixed in with the university's buildings. This provides for a lively mix of students, tourists, local residents and employees. The NYU university quarter is so strongly dominated by university buildings that variety in the area is achieved only through the attraction and programming of Washington Square Park.

The university is less dominant in the centre of Berlin, so that everyday use creates a more natural mixture. A new central library of Humboldt Universität in Berlin Mitte, the Jacob-und-Wilhelm-Grimm-Zentrum, designed by Max Dudler Architects, was built in 2009. It has a total floor area of 36,600 m². The library is extremely multifunctional, with exhibition galleries, reading rooms, spaces for education and research, video conferencing, and a 180 seat auditorium.

The Rapenburg cluster in Leiden, the city centre cluster in Utrecht and the ministry cluster in The Hague are also 'quarters'. Presently the section of Amsterdam bounded by the Rokin, Damstraat-Hoogstraat, Kloveniersburgwal and Binnenamstel in fact functions as a university quarter, with the university buildings on the Binnengasthuis site and

around the Oudemanhuispoort, and the Spinhuis-Bushuis-Oostindisch Huis ensemble occupied by the department of social sciences. The radius of a quarter can vary from 250 to 375 metres. The average distance between the library and the departmental buildings in the Humboldt quarter is 395 metres.

Campus

The Campus on the Green is the characteristic type for the classic American universities (Harvard, Penn State). Well before American independence, British colonists had founded universities, but unlike the urban locations in England, in America, where anti-urban sentiments were greater, they opted for campuses on the edges of, or outside the cities. Although over the course of the years the universities opened themselves up more to the communities around them, the campuses are almost always gated and able to be closed off. The early American campuses often had separate buildings scattered around or through a 'yard' or a 'green'. Later the more erudite term 'campus' came into use. In time, complete cities grew up around these campuses, and the rural setting disappeared. The 'green' has in most cases been preserved, so that there is a still an noble sense of tranquillity. Certainly, if the university owned large, contiguous plots of land, it was easier to expand, add to or replace buildings on a campus than with a courtyard type university. That can be done without affecting the urban structure. Therefore this type affords greater flexibility.

Special campus facilities like libraries are generally housed in separate buildings. Cafeterias or canteens often are found on the ground floor of a central building. The greater distances to central facilities in a cluster of this type implies that there will be study centres, coffee and sandwich shops scattered in various buildings all across the campus. Because all the facilities used by students – including dormitories and sports facilities – are present on the

campus, while the campus is not open for non-university functions, the interaction with the city in this type is more limited than in the other types. The Woudestein campus has a radius of 375 metres, comparable with that of quarters.

The large campuses which have been built outside cities in Europe in recent decades (Berlin Adlershof, Marne-la-Vallée Cité Descartes, University of Twente, Eindhoven) are related to the Campus on the Green. Because of the increase in scale many universities have undergone, the separate buildings are now much larger, and that has changed the size of the campus. The distances which students and staff have to travel are greater. This in turn necessitates the provision of small-scale amenities at the building level.

An interesting example of a new campus for the research department of a corporation is the High Tech Campus in Eindhoven. Developing out of Philips's Natlab, in the late 1990s the site was opened up for other businesses, and underwent a fundamental redesign. Facilities are centrally situated on a promenade along a large water feature. Here the 'green' is blue.

Woudestein is the only example of a campus among the five university cities in Holland. The campus lies just outside the city, past Kralingen and the Woudestein sports park. The site is enclosed by a fence in a hedge, and is not accessible at night or on Sunday. The central complex of buildings was designed by Elfers and Van der Heiden in the 1960s for what was then the Economische Hogeschool. In the 1990s various other buildings were realized from plans by Wim Quist. The landscaped setting suffered as a result. The present masterplan once again calls for a sizeable volume of construction. A pedestrian promenade is the central element, to which the new facilities are oriented. The connection of the promenade with its surroundings – including public transit – is also less than ideal.

Central yard, Harvard campus

The campus type is in fact also the basis for the 19th and early 20th century – but now largely vanished – hospitals in Amsterdam, Leiden and Utrecht, with their separate clinics. Only on the Wilhelminagasthuis site in Amsterdam have any large number of these pavilions been retained and repurposed. The site has been opened up, however, and streets and parked cars now dominate the public space.

Science Park

The Science Park is another variant of the campus, albeit with a couple of crucial differences. The most important is that in addition to academic departments, institutes, student housing and other university functions, business premises are also realized, often in the form of buildings with flexible internal plans for accommodating collections of small firms. Most Science Parks are accessible to the public. For security reasons many laboratories have been surrounded with fences and hedges. That often compromises the natural setting and park-like atmosphere of these clusters. The Bioscience Park in Leiden and the Science Park in Amsterdam are examples of this type. An hotel and dwellings have also been realized around the Science Park. The sports facilities, and in Leiden Naturalis and Corpus, also make the parks attractive for visitors.

Because of their dimensions – Leiden initially 75, and now 110 hectare, Amsterdam 70 hectare – the

164

High Tech Campus, Eindhoven

parks are significantly larger than the previously discussed types, and that applies to the walking distances in them too. It is noteworthy that the Bioscience Park incorporates two 'campuses', for different academic disciplines, each with its own programme of facilities.

As a type, the Science Park is related to the 'office park' and 'business park', which in the 1990s caught on as alternatives for the soporific business sites of the previous decades. In comparison with these parks, the quality of the Science Parks is on the whole much higher. The differentiation in the programme is stronger, the buildings are often larger, and because of their special functions also have a stronger architectonic ambiance. That is much less true for many of the buildings on the parks accommodating random collections of businesses.

District

The district is the superlative step of the park. Just the central part of the MIT university district alone in Cambridge, outside of Boston, measures 69 hectare. 11,000 students study there. The district around the old Yard of Harvard, just a short distance away, is 200 hectare. 21,000 students are registered there. The city promotes itself with the fact that in and around the campuses more than 160 firms in the life sciences and technological sector have their offices. In 2010 five of the ten largest employers in the city

were businesses from the biotechnology sector, together having 8,000 employees.

The Uithof in Utrecht and the 'TU district' in Delft are Dutch examples of the 'district'. The total site of the Uithof is 366 hectare, and it has a radius of about 750 metres. The compactly built up central area is about a third of this total. Although the TU site in the district is 'only' 170 hectare, the total district is much larger. The whole district, including TU North with the botanical garden and science centre, and including the sites of the TNO to the east and Deltares to the south, is almost 500 hectare, and has a radius of at least 1500 metres.

Conclusion

A total of 14 knowledge clusters lie in the six largest cities in the Randstad. Five of these knowledge clusters are centres, relatively turned in on themselves. There are two medical centres, in the Bioscience Park in Leiden and the Uithof in Utrecht.

Types of clusters in Dutch university cities

city	number	types
Amsterdam	6	1 court complex, 4 centres and 1 park
Leiden	2	1 quarter, 1 park
The Hague	1	1 quarter
Delft	1	1 district
Rotterdam	2	1 centre, 1 campus
Utrecht	2	1 quarter, 1 district

That means that centres are to be found in half of the clusters.

Beyond this, there is very major differentiation. One courtyard complex and three quarters lie in city centres. In addition to the Wijnhaven Quarter in The Hague, with the ministries, these are the Humanities Departments in Amsterdam, Utrecht and Leiden. In other words, all of the humanities departments in the Randstad lie in city centres. Other clusters lie more on the periphery of the cities: the only campus-on-the-green is in Rotterdam, the two science parks in Amsterdam and Leiden, and the two districts in Utrecht and Delft.

At first glance it would appear that Amsterdam, with its six clusters, is strongly represented. These are, however, relatively small clusters. The Roeterseiland, Binnengasthuis and Slotervaart clusters are, respectively, 2, 3.7 and 6 hectare. The VU is 20 hectare. It is true the Science Park and the AMC cluster are larger, at 64 and 70 hectare, respectively, but these are smaller than the Bioscience Park in Leiden (100 hectare) and the districts in Utrecht (366 hectare) and Delft (170-500 hectare). Are the Amsterdam clusters better integrated into the city than the clusters in Leiden, Delft and Utrecht?

Entrance to the Science Park, Amsterdam

Position of the knowledge clusters in the cities

In Chapters 2 and 3, in a section comparable to this, we examined the relations of culture and conference clusters with overlapping and adjoining clusters. That will be done in this section also, but from a different angle.

One of the important themes in recent literature dealing with the future of universities is the relation between innovation and the city. At present, quite a few knowledge clusters in the Randstad are only moderately integrated into the cities. Almost all the universities are carrying out radical plans for renewal. A large number of the knowledge centres are becoming better embedded in their surroundings. In order to better integrate the peripheral and scattered institutions into the city, Rotterdam has introduced the concept of the Knowledge Axis. There is a comparable task for Amsterdam around the Weesperplein. With regard to the two districts, Utrecht will always be handicapped by their peripheral location. The district in Delft, on the other hand, offers all sorts of possibilities for better integration into the city. These will be discussed in the closing section.

Integrated knowledge clusters

The courtyard complex in and around the Binnengasthuis site and the three quarters in Utrecht, Leiden and The Hague are well integrated knowledge clusters. With the exception of the Wijnhaven quarter in The Hague, these are clusters where universities have been located for centuries. The functions of buildings changed over the course of time, and other urban functions established themselves around and in between the university buildings, creating an attractive mix.

The move to concentrate university functions around the Binnengasthuis site still remains the most problematic. The construction of a new University Library has run into all sorts of objections. Rather

than opting for a very compact courtyard cluster, it would be worth the effort to investigate whether the application of the knowledge quarter type might offer some comfort. After all, the new library could also be situated in another centrally located building on the site. Space nearby would have to be found for the academic department presently located there, perhaps in the vacant Fortis building on the Rokin, or in one of the present university buildings in the complex around the Oostindisch Huis. That could mean that a more attractive mix could be created with the KNAW institutes that are being relocated. The RIOD and the Meertens Institute, for instance, would fit very well with the UvA's History Department.

Knowledge centres

Knowledge institutions of the 'centre' type are difficult to integrate with their surroundings. They are organized around plazas or atria in the middle of the building complex. Large-scale transformations are being prepared to strengthen the relation of the UvA's Roeterseiland complex, the VU, and Erasmus University's Hoboken complex. The public space in and around the Roeterseiland and Hoboken centres will be made accessible and redesigned. Moreover, new 'public' amenities will be added, which will be accessible from this public space. Parts of the VU complex will be moved, to become fully integrated into the new, strongly mixed South Axis Knowledge Quarter. The centres in the Slotervaart cluster in Amsterdam's New West can also be better integrated into their setting. However, the even greater question is whether the medical research centres in this relatively small cluster could be better integrated into one of the others. That is also the question for the stand-alone centres which are scattered around the cities, such as the Shell Technology Centre and the NLR in Amsterdam, DSM in Delft and the cloud of institutions in The Hague.

The type of knowledge worker using the cluster will also play a role in the consideration of whether or not to integrate the knowledge cluster in the city. In the planning for the UvA clusters a distinction is made between the humanities, technical and natural sciences, the social sciences, and medical sciences. Those in the humanities and social sciences prefer urban settings, those in the hard sciences and medicine prefer suburban environments.[12] This was the reason for accommodating the technical and natural sciences in the relatively peripheral Science Park, and the humanities and social sciences in city-centre locations. The suburban orientation for the natural sciences may hold true for the researchers, but it is an open question whether it does for the students. A university's location in the city would appear to be essential for students in the technical and natural sciences too: inexpensive housing, lots of amenities, and lots of external stimuli.

Rotterdam Knowledge Axis

In Rotterdam's Knowledge Axis concept the connections between the university and the city are dealt with at all possible levels. The Knowledge Axis is defined as the area in which the whole range of knowledge available in Rotterdam, and the housing and support facilities associated with it, are situated. It runs from the Woudestein Campus in the east, through the Oostplein, Blaak and Hoboken Centre, to Coolhaven Island on the west. All the knowledge institutions in the area are accessed via the metro stations of the Caland line.

A relatively large percentage of Rotterdam's students do not live in the city, and use the Caland line. The intention of the Knowledge Axis concept is to link the students more firmly with the city, and, from the other direction, to make the knowledge institutions and the life around them more visible. To that end, it is proposed that the knowledge clusters themselves should be reinvigorated, and that a more

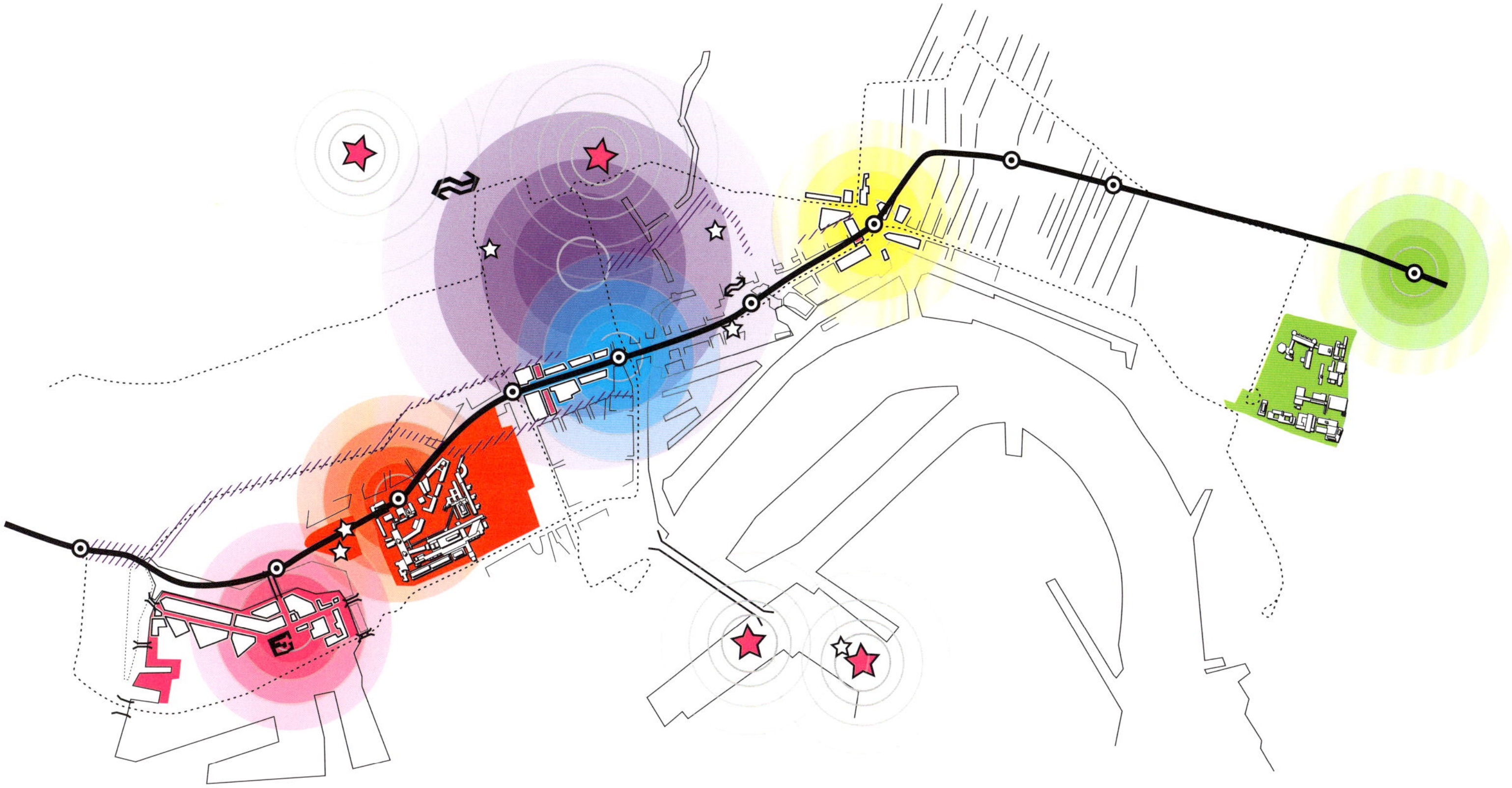

Knowledge Axis, Rotterdam

Vision map, Rotterdam Hoboken
2030

TrouwAmsterdam: culture platform and restaurant in
the former Trouw editorial offices and printing plant on
the Wibautstraat

differentiated programme, specifically oriented to a young audience, be developed around the squares and urban boulevards in the city centre.

The Woudestein Campus would be renewed and made a more vital location, by building new student residences and amenities. The first phase began in 2011, with the construction of a parking garage and temporary college classrooms. The Masterplan was drawn up by the Sputnik agency, in cooperation with Juurlink and Geluk.

Around a reinvigorated Oostplein a stronger accent will be placed on the quality of the square itself and the classic student societies, bars and restaurants surrounding it. Most of the buildings providing facilities for the students already lie in Kralingen. Farther along the Axis, the Erasmus University College would be located in the former Education Museum on the Nieuwe Markt. Erick van Egeraat prepared the plans for its conversion.

A large number of ageing office buildings line the Westblaak. This is an interesting incubation place for businesses starting up or re-starting. Erasmus Medical Centre recently located its Knowledge Transfer department here. The Cinerama is regularly the venue for The Right Movie Night, sponsored by the Erasmus School of Law. A popular skate park lies in the islands in the middle of the boulevard.

Erasmus Medical Centre/Hoboken will be radically renovated and made more public. Various residential projects are being developed around the complex. Direct connections are also being made with the cluster of polytechnic training programmes in the expanding Hogeschool Rotterdam, on the west side of the Maastunnelweg. Various arts schools and programmes are already located on Coolhaven Island. In its totality, the prospective expansion of the programme around Erasmus Medical Centre and the Hogeschool will be about 200,000 m².

Finally, near the Marconiplein stop, under the title Clean Tech Delta the city of Rotterdam and a series of partners from knowledge institutions and businesses are experimenting with the development of the Vierhaven area as a test plot for sustainable development. The ground floor of the recycling office in the Handelskamer has been converted into a café and meeting space by Doepel Strijkers, Architects. The other storeys of this architectural monument are rented out to starting businesses.

The chain of pearls that comprises the Knowledge Axis in Rotterdam can improve the relation between the city and its university at all levels. The relatively small knowledge clusters and all sorts of related functions will begin to form a part of the city in a natural manner.

Utrecht and Amsterdam

In Utrecht the integration of the Uithof will be rather more problematic. The Uithof district essentially lies at the other end of the world, four kilometres from Vredenburg, and has an enormous, but quite one-sided programme. Although it provides housing for 4000 students, only a small fraction of its 53,000 students will live in the Uithof. Moreover, it is expected that in several year's time 30,000 people will work in the Uithof. Every day now 40,000 riders already make the commute to and from the Uithof by public transit. It is expected that this figure will reach 60,000 by 2020. This increase finally was decisive in the decision to construct a new high-quality public transit link, in the form of a tram. This Uithof line must be operational by 2018. After years of discussion, a southerly route was chosen. The tram will soon run from Central Station, skirting the southern part of the city centre, via Galgenwaard Stadium, to the Uithof. It will not run through the city centre or past the Dom cluster. The two clusters will therefore continue to function relatively independently, the one well integrated, the other only moderately so.

All the Amsterdam university clusters lie in the proximity of railway or metro stations, although they in no sense form an axis of any sort. However, paying more attention to the ways in which students and staff reach the clusters, and to the integration and visibility of the clusters in the city could also help here. This will be problematic for the peripheral AMC cluster. The best opportunities exist for the integration of the Roeterseiland cluster. Many students and staff arrive at this cluster from Weesperplein, by bicycle or with the tram or metro. The new Amstel Campus of the Amsterdam Hogeschool is also accessed from Weesperplein. Redesigning the square, and encouraging more public functions in the plinth, would radically increase the attractiveness of this double cluster. The square would also be a highly suitable spot for public functions of the university.

In the longer term, it is to be expected that many of the offices around the adjoining Weesperstraat will become available for repurposing. The extensive civil service apparatus of the city and metropolitan region is still located there. The first building to become available has the highly fitting name of the Metropool. Parts are already used by creative businesses. The other office buildings which will become vacant provide a wonderful opportunity to accommodate knowledge institutions, start-ups and all sorts of creative activities. The success of similar buildings further up on the Wibautstraat indicates that there is sufficient demand. This could create a whole knowledge quarter around the Weesperplein.

0   15   30 km

Cluster NL – Technology clusters and the North Wing cloud

Top 60

In 2009 research was done into the top 30 businesses and top 30 institutes, in terms of personnel and investment in R&D.[13] Among the corporations, a handful of large firms account for the lion's share of the R&D expenditures. The front runners are Philips and ASML. The investment among institutions are, on the average, much lower. However, the Dutch government dispersed a total of over 3.8 billion for knowledge development among universities and research institutes in 2007.

Of the 60 businesses and institutes, it appears that a quarter are located in the six cities of the Randstad. The largest number of these are institutes. If we look more closely at the location of the sixty Dutch businesses and institutions, it appears that they are clustered primarily in the vicinity of the technical universities of Twente, Delft and Eindhoven, and the agricultural university in Wageningen. This is also where the technological giants like Philips, Thales and Getronics, and technical institutes like TNO, Deltares and ITC, are to be found. Of the 60 businesses and institutes, almost half lie in one of these four technology clusters.

Through the presence of the universities the businesses and institutions in these clusters are assured of a constant flow of well-trained workers. Furthermore, their proximity to one another also facilitates complementarity and exchange. Here one sees in practice the advantages that were previously discussed when we described the developments in Boston and Silicon Valley.

As well as the four technology clusters, there is a more diffuse cloud of research institutes and corporate research centres which stretches from the coast, through Amsterdam and Utrecht, to Arnhem and Nijmegen. Only a handful of R&D centres associated with businesses and institutions are to be found outside the clusters and the cloud.

Technology clusters

Of the four technology clusters, only the TU district lies in the Randstad. The other three lie outside it. The Twente Knowledge Park in Enschede, the High Tech Campus in Eindhoven and the campus of Wageningen University form the cores of these technology clusters. According to recent research by Buck Consultants, carried out for the Ministry of Economic Affairs, together with the Science Park in Amsterdam and the DSM-Chemelot campus in Sittard, they make up the five 'campuses of national importance'.[14]

It is striking, however, that only a small percentage of the businesses from the technology clusters are located on these parks and campuses themselves. For instance, of the large R&D firms in and around Eindhoven, only Philips and NXP lie on the High Tech Campus. The other businesses are sited on other business parks in the city or elsewhere in the region (ASML in Veldhoven, CCM in Nuenen, Stork Food in Boxmeer and Océ as far away as Venlo. Even more remarkably, the university's research institutes do not lie on the High Tech Campus either. They are concentrated on the campus of the TU Eindhoven. The High Tech Campus therefore revolves around Philips rather than the University.

Something similar applies for the technology cluster around Wageningen University. It is true that Friesland-Campina has built a new R&D centre on the campus for its 450 staff, but other firms lie in a wide circle around it. Because of the presence of this sector, this area has come to be known as Food Valley, but the Food Valley Foundation itself is located on a nearby Agribusiness Park. At least 115 firms are members of this Foundation. This network of businesses extends all across The Netherlands. In this light, clustering is a relative term. What is crucial is a core-area with a strong supporting institution which gives the cluster a certain aura, has the capacity for major investment in research, buildings and material, and produces spin-off which populate the campus.

Cloud

The North Wing Cloud is a remarkable phenomenon. The businesses and institutions that form this cloud are not all from any particular sector. Factors other than the presence of strong supporting businesses or institutions appear to be of importance for the decision to locate here. The inner side of the coastal dunes, the Gooi, the Utrecht Hill Ridge and the Veluwezoom have traditionally been suburban residential areas. The principle that businesses, in their choice of where to locate, also take into account the residential preferences of their potential staff, appears to have applied here for some time. This is in fact the Dutch Sun Belt.

Two recent developments are interesting in this context. First, in the last few years a substantial number of businesses and institutions in the Cloud have chosen to move their headquarters to the international business district of Amsterdam's South Axis. Production facilities and R&D remain in their old location. This is true not only for AkzoNobel, but recently also for the engineering firm Arcadis. In addition, some businesses are seeking more central locations for specific divisions, or for the whole of their research centre. Sometimes they opt for a place in an existing knowledge cluster, as did RIVM, which is moving from Den Dolder to the Uithof in Utrecht, and sometimes for an urban location, as did ECN, from Petten, which opened a location for policy studies in Amsterdam. Such trends were observed in the research on the future of work in the San Francisco Bay Area which we cited above. Although the activities there were of a different kind, it appears that parts of traditional research institutes are seeking other environments.

These trends have been at work in the media

Research & Development clusters in The Netherlands
DRO Amsterdam, based on the Top-30 Business R&D
and Top-30 knowledge and research institutes
in : *Technisch weekblad*, 17 April 2010

sector for some time. The facilities of the public broadcasters were traditionally located in the Gooi. However, for activities involving audiences, since the 1990s they have sought recording locations in Amsterdam (Desmet, Plantage studios, Westergas-fabriek). Commercial broadcasters such as RTL, SBS, MTV and Discovery Channel have also been locating in Amsterdam since that time. Endemol recently opened a new studio complex in Amsterdam Zuidoost.

With regard to this, the distinction between the two sides of R and D is also relevant. The R of Research stands for the production of knowledge, while the D of Development refers to the application of knowledge in new products, and bringing them onto the market. These sub-sectors need different kinds of facilities and thrive in different environments. A familiar example of a sector that focuses on development, par excellence, is the gaming industry. Businesses from this sector are almost all located in city centre sites in Amsterdam.

Conclusion

In The Netherlands, research and development appears to take place primarily outside of the big cities. Almost half of the businesses and institutes from the top 60 are located in technology clusters around the technical universities and several supporting businesses such as Philips, Stork, DSM and Friesland-Campina. The form of clustering varies. Sometimes businesses clump together on campuses or science parks; sometimes, from around compact campuses, they develop networks that encompass the whole of The Netherlands. The high technology cluster around Eindhoven is the largest in The Netherlands.

Traditionally, many other R&D firms and research institutions have been located in the Dutch Sun Belt, the higher-lying, wooded land of the inner edge of the coastal dunes, the Gooi, the Utrecht Hill Ridge,

TU Delft Campus Vision 2030, maquette 1:500

and the Veluwezoom. In recent years departments of some firms and institutes have been seeking out the city, while others are locating in knowledge clusters such as the Uithof. At present, among businesses and institutions in the knowledge sector there does not appear to be a mass migration to the city, as there has been in the media sector or gaming industry.

Stimuli – TU Delft Campus

In only a couple of hours, the fire at the Department of Architecture in the spring of 2008 reduced not only its building, but the whole wish-list for the future of the TU district in Delft to ruins. Where was the department to be housed now? What was left of the new park, now that the largest department was gone? Or was the fire not only a disaster, but a blessing? An international competition for ideas produced four potential locations for a new Architecture department: to rebuild on the old location on the Berlageweg, to remain in the temporary quarters on the Julianalaan, to construct a new building in a central spot on the campus (or in the Mekel Park), or in a new place outside the TU district (in Delft, Rotterdam, split up around the Randstad, or even totally virtual). A think tank subsequently rendered the advice to prepare a new vision for the university campus as a whole, which had to look beyond the present boundaries of the campus. The TU is a strong brand, but to remain attractive investment is necessary. The district will have to develop into a more mixed urban knowledge cluster, which is easily accessible and strongly embedded in its environment. The future of the campus lies in the city.

Diagnosis

On the regional scale, the campus lies very strategically at the intersection of the Rotterdam-Hague metropolitan development axis and the regional landscape park Midden-Delfland. In the local context however this potential evaporates. The TU district lies isolated between motorways and an outdated business site on the Schie. The bridges over the Schie are a barrier rather than inviting links. Moreover, rather than being a stimulus toward quality, replacing the central avenue with the construction of the new Mekel Park has damaged the district's accessibility and spatial orientation.

In addition to the Department of Architecture, which found temporary accommodations in the former main building of the 'old' campus, there are other departments which threaten to leave the central area of the TU district. TNW, a new department created by the combination of Technical Physics and Chemistry, is making plans for a new building in the southern part of the district, called Technopolis. On the other hand, Civil Engineering has too much space. The threatened desertion of the central area would bleed the campus – if not to death, at least to where it lost its vitality.

Outside of working hours, the TU district was always empty and deserted. There are, it is true, 1200 students housed on the campus, and the sports and culture centre is also open in the evenings and on weekends, but the departmental buildings and laboratories are large, and all have only a couple of entrances. The design of the public space is also definitely not attractive. The new Mekel Park is enormous in scale, measuring 100 x 800 metres, but only a couple of front doors open onto it. That is no guarantee for a lively campus.

Part of the city

The 2010 vision for the development of the campus takes in the whole area between the Rotterdam-Hague rail line and the A13 motorway, and between the heart of Delft and Midden-Delfland, about 500 hectare.[15] In addition to the TU district, a large number of other development locations lie within this area: the railway zone, with the new tunnel for trains through the historic centre, the Technopolis science park to the south of the campus, the site of the TNO, and the old campus, presently deserted by the TU. Moreover, the transformation of the antiquated business sites around the Schie into a creative urban environment is under way. In recent years all these locations have been treated as separate fragments. Not surprisingly, there is little cohesion among the projects. In the short term, there is an enormous overcapacity in dwellings being planned, but in the longer term, Delft and the region have nowhere else to go. Although the number of students and staff at the TU will continue to grow in the coming years, the TU still has room to spare. That is where the opportunities lie.

Framework – better connections

The uncertainties in the real estate market necessitate the creation of a strong framework which can be filled in in various ways over the course of time. It is crucial to have a better infrastructure for transportation. A ring road – an avenue with a double row of trees – has been introduced as an interface between the campus and the city. This links the various parts to one another. Connections run off from the rink to surrounding areas of the city. The existing bridge over the Schie in the direction of the city centre has to be replaced. That being the case, it is better to do so now, so that the city centre and the TU district flow into one another naturally. A new bridge over the Schie to the post-war neighbourhoods to the west of the railway line will also provide stronger anchoring. It is precisely in these neighbourhoods were many of the students and staff live.

A new tram line will run through the middle of the campus, anchoring the district in the region. It would appear obvious to have a Park&Ride facility at the intersection with the Kruithuisweg, the road along the southern edge of Delft, not only to make it easy to reach the centre of Delft, but also to be able to get an electric 'white' bicycle there, with your campus card. A bicycle is obviously the ideal means of transport for getting around in the district. The number of parking places for non-residents can therefore be drastically reduced.

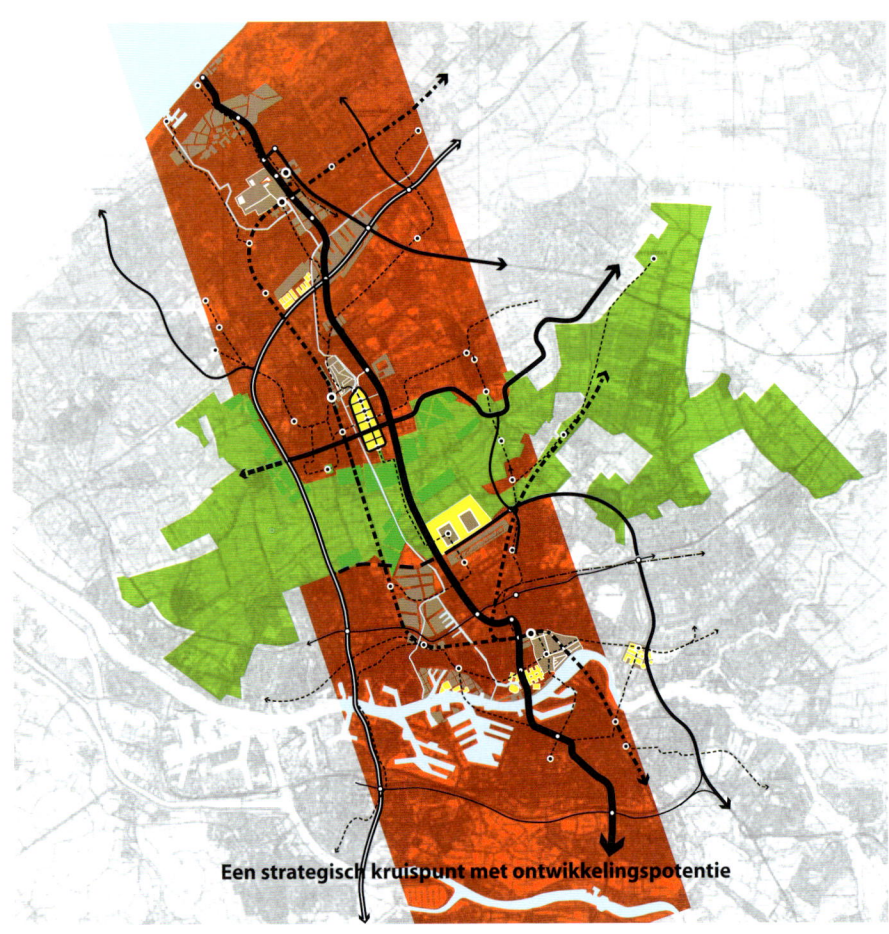

Een strategisch kruispunt met ontwikkelingspotentie

TU Delft Campus Vision 2030, analysis: strategic
crossing point with development potential

TU Delft Campus Vision 2030, concept: an urban
and a green axis

Blending and condensing

The district is so large that sub-communities with their own character can be created around the tram stops. In the north, Architecture can be the nucleus of the design cluster in the courtyard complex of the old campus. The Science Centre and the Botanical Garden are already here, and buildings of all sizes and shapes are being freed up, which would lend themselves well for start-ups, institutes, restaurants and cafés, and cultural experiments.

The central area, around the auditorium and library, can develop into a university quarter, with a strong mixture of functions around a fine-mesh network of streets, small squares, and a more differentiated park. Buildings define the public space, and make it more attractive. That means a conscious programming of the plinths, small-scale functions among the large departmental buildings, broken through or radically transformed here and there, and, especially, more front doors. Urban programming must be imported in the form of dwellings, hotels, a secondary school, amenities such as supermarkets, a swimming pool, restaurants and cafés. New bicycle and walking paths connect the central Mekel Park directly with the new residential areas to the east and west of the campus. In this way, the TU comes to lie on the Schie, and also obtains direct bicycle and pedestrian access to the Delft

South railway station.

The southern park, Technopolis, becomes a science park. There is still a lot of space here. This is an ideal place to accommodate research centres and firms such as DSM among the existing laboratories, when the opportunities arise to do so. The recreational urban axis that connects the centre of Delft with Midden-Delfland runs through the middle of the science park. The real estate crisis is an ally. Buildings can be temporarily repurposed as they come free, unused parking lots planted. The TU district becomes the Nieuwste Plantage.

174

TU Delft Campus Vision 2030,
aspiration for 2030

SCHIEWEG

ROTTERDAMSEWEG

JULIANALAAN

JAFFALAAN

HUYGENSWEG

DREBBELWEG

STIELTJESWEG

SCHOEMAKERSTRAAT

MEKELPARK

BERLAGEWEG

KRUITHUISWEG

WATERMANWEG

HEERTJESLAAN

5 Interaction in the Delta

The Lowlands Festival in Biddinghuizen is a fine metaphor for the Dutch Metropolis. The thousands of small tents stand for the extremely diffuse urbanization pattern; the big tents, at the other extreme, for the strongly concentrated interaction environments. Traditionally, the logistic interaction environments of the seaports, Schiphol and the flower and vegetable auctions have been among the big tents. They form the economic foundation for the Dutch Metropolis. The physical conditions which accompany a Delta City region are utilized to develop a strong and multifaceted logistic complex. The transport sector in the Randstad is the strongest in Europe. In recent years a sizeable number of big tents have been added in other economic sectors. Against the main current of government policies to promote the diffusion of economic activities, it is primarily in the largest cities where all sorts of new interaction environments have been realized. The Dutch Metropolis has become more diverse and raised to a higher level of quality. All across the range of metropolitan functions, in Europe the Randstad even comes in the third place, after London and Paris.

In 1994 Niek de Boer suggested that the Randstad did not exist. To his mind, policies oriented toward the development of highly urbanized, metropolitan functions were grossly inadequate. Almost two decades on, it appears that significant progress has been made. As a daily urban system the Randstad indeed does not exist, but the Dutch Metropolis, as a vital conglomerate of interaction environments, is very much a reality. With improvements in quality and smart combinations, the leap to the next level of quality is within reach.

Lowlands Festival site, Biddinghuizen, 2010
Aerial photograph, Jan Tuijp

Flora Holland auction and surrounding
businesses, Honselersdijk

The Dutch Metropolis

In the BBSR research cited earlier, the Randstad emerges as one of the strongest metropolitan areas in Europe, with widely differentiated metropolitan functions across the categories of politics, economics, science, transport and culture employed by the German researchers. According to the investigators, these metropolitan functions are distributed over seven locations: the four largest cities, the two university cities of Leiden and Delft, and around Schiphol, in the larger Haarlemmermeer.[1]

In Chapter 1 the Randstad was characterized as a Delta City region. Horticulture and transport are the basis of delta economies, and that is true for the Dutch Delta. Dutch sea and airports, along with the interaction environments around the auctions, form an extensive complex. If the transshipment at auctions had been included in the German research, the position of the Randstad would have been even stronger.

The contrast between these logistic interaction environments and the new urban interaction environments in Amsterdam, Leiden, The Hague, Delft, Rotterdam and Utrecht is considerable, in both size and nature. After a brief sketch of the logistic interaction environments, this section will look forward through an analysis of the new 'metropolitan' interaction environments from Chapters 2, 3 and 4.

The four largest cities have a mixed profile. All the metropolitan interaction environments are brought together on one map. Leiden and Delft have a strongly specialized profile. The interaction environments in Leiden and Delft are therefore briefly described, but no collective map has been prepared for these cities.

Logistic interaction environments

How are the logistic interaction environments structured? The seaports and Schiphol occupy vast areas. For instance, the port area of Rotterdam covers 10,570 hectare, 6855 hectare being land.

Block map Second Memorandum on Physical Planning 1965

Imagine that: 68 km²! It is true that the site of Schiphol is smaller – 2787 hectare – but that is almost as large as Amsterdam within the A10 ring road. Even in comparison with other Delta City regions in Europe, the scale of these logistic interaction environments is enormous.

Not only Schiphol's passenger and cargo terminals, but also the business sites on the Schipholring and the areas administered by the Schiphol Area Development Corporation (SADC) are part of the airport's logistic interaction environment. In addition, there are many sites for what can be identified as Schiphol-oriented businesses which lie around the airport. They are not immediately part of the interaction environment linked to the airport, but obviously benefit from it.

In the port areas of Rotterdam, Dordrecht and Moerdijk, and in the Amsterdam-North Sea Canal areas, the same distinction between harbour-linked and harbour-oriented businesses is often made. The boundaries here are however somewhat less easily defined. Many of the harbour-oriented firms are also located on sites that are exploited by the harbour businesses involved.

Within the horticultural clusters the distinction between the logistic interaction environments

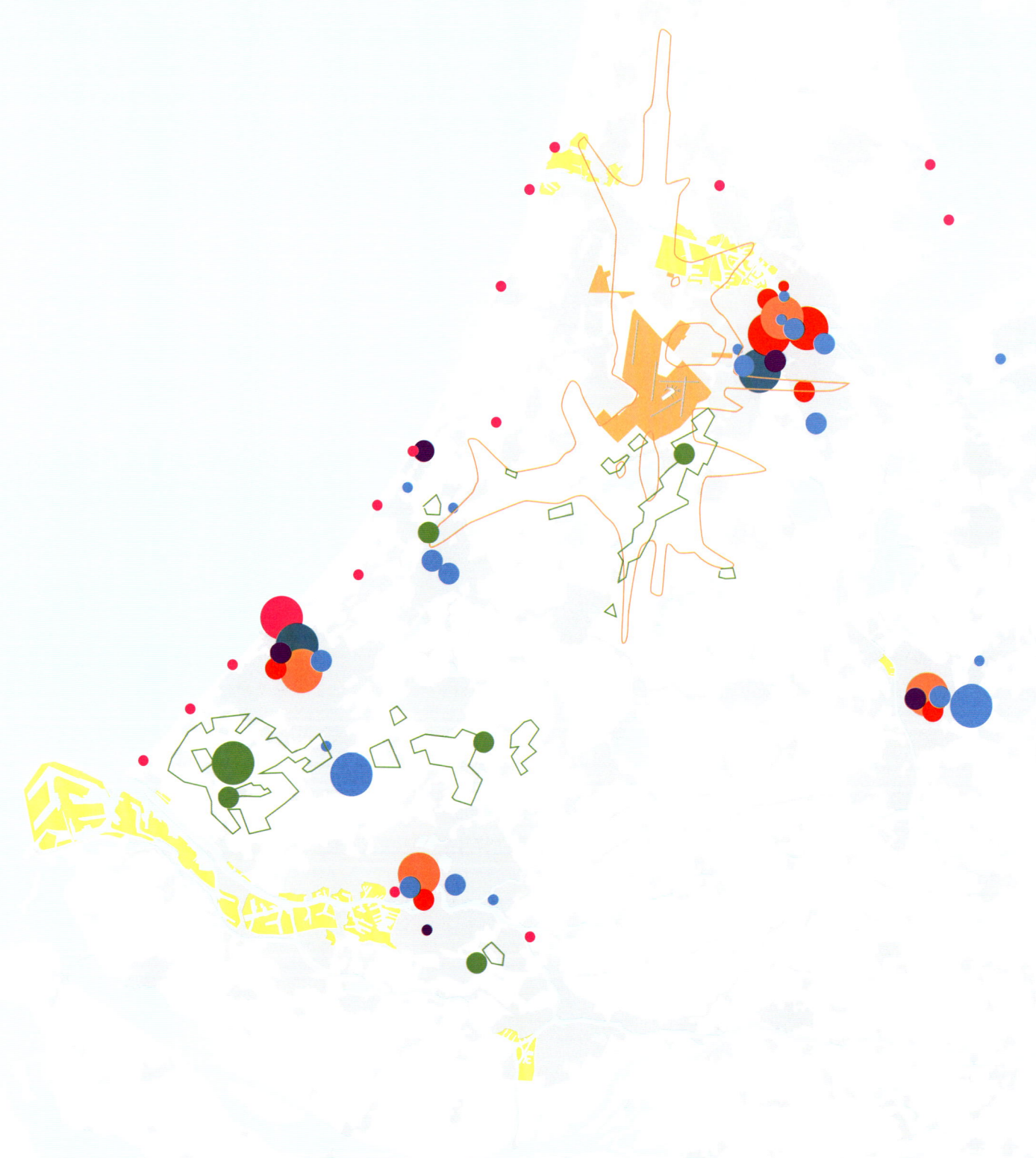

Interaction environments: Dutch Metropolis

around the auctions and the land exploited for agricultural purposes is even becoming ever larger. Forty years ago each self-respecting rural community had an auction which was quickly accessed from the surrounding greenhouses and fields, today the largest facilities are concentrated in Aalsmeer, Honselersdijk, Bleiswijk, Barendrecht and Rijnsburg, and it is becoming clear that still another increase in the scale of concentration will soon be taking place. The agrarian acreage in Aalsmeer and its vicinity, in the Westland, Oostland and Zuidplaspolder, and in the Flower Bulb region and Boskoop is, by analogy with the sea and airports, auction-oriented.

Commercial sites around the auctions are certainly part of their interaction environments. The businesses located there are auction-linked. The cluster of businesses around the Flora Holland auction in Honselersdijk, and around the Westland Trade Park, has an area of a complete district, with a radius of 700 metres.

The logistic interaction environments of the seaports, the airport and auctions in the Randstad together form an increasingly strong logistic complex. Traditionally the flower and bulb production has benefited from the network of Schiphol airport. All sorts of cooled products are transshipped through the Rotterdam fruit pier. These collaborations will become even more intense in the years to come.

Metropolitan interaction environments

In 1965, in the 'block map' in the Second Memorandum on Physical Planning, Eo Wijers sketched a striking perspective for environmental differentiation in The Netherlands. Yellow, orange, red and brown blocks indicate four types of urban environments, A, B, C and D, of varying size and with corresponding density, transport systems and facilities. The Block Map is now part of the canon of Dutch physical planning.

The D environment represented the largest cores, of about 250,000 residents, with, among other things, specialized shops such as furriers and 'pants palaces'. In Wijers's vision, The Netherlands would accommodate at least nine of these D environments, which would include the centres of the four largest cities and Groningen, Eindhoven, Arnhem, Enschede and Dordrecht. The vision was closely connected with the policy of diffusion advocated in the Second Memorandum on Physical Planning.[2]

There is no 'E environment'. Building logically on Wijers's types, that would be an internationally oriented urban environment with, hypothetically, a million residents in a density of 100 dwellings per hectare, a metro network, and a corresponding package of facilities including museums, top institutes, hotels and conference centres.

Despite the policy of diffusion, precisely such a metropolitan E environment has arisen in and around Amsterdam in recent decades. Amsterdam functions as the nucleus of the Dutch Metropolis. That is true particularly for the heart of the city, with urban interaction environments including the shopping district, university clusters and a whole series of entertainment and cultural quarters. In addition, the south flank of the Amsterdam region, in conjunction with the airport, has developed a second set of interaction environments around the business quarter of the South Axis.

Various of these clusters in the city centre and on the south flank of Amsterdam are developing rapidly and are on the brink of a leap forward in quality and size. That is also true for the mixed and more diffuse coastal cluster around The Hague, with its seaside resorts, the R&D clusters in Leiden, and the collection of clusters in and around The Hague itself. This coastal cluster can be characterized as an up-and-coming E environment. More precisely formulated, in the four largest cities, Leiden and Delft, we encounter the following metropolitan interaction environments.

Amsterdam

Of the largest cities, Amsterdam's E environment has a reach from the local to the international level of scale with regard to almost all the metropolitan functions in the series employed by the German BBSR. In the analyses done for this book, we counted seventeen interaction environments in the city – nine cultural clusters, two conference clusters and six knowledge clusters.

Most of the clusters lie in and around the large, historic city centre. The central element is the Dam, a classic culture square. It is in the midst of a mixed district, with cultural facilities, hotels and conference facilities in addition to a large number of non-food stores. It is adjoined by culture and entertainment clusters such as 1012, Leidseplein and Rembrandtplein. Around this central district, but still within easy walking distance, lie a series of other clusters. Museumplein, university centres and various culture quarters. The waterfront along the IJ is also being redeveloped.

The programme and the quality of the interaction environments in the city centre has developed at lightning speed into a situation in which there is now one large and differentiated inner city district and two rising culture districts, Leidseplein-Museumplein and the East City Centre. At some distance lie the much smaller, rising clusters of the NDSM culture wharf and the Westergasfabriek culture park. A second concentration of interaction environments lies around the South Axis, with the RAI fair and conference centre, the VU and its Medical Centre, and the business quarter around Amsterdam's South Station. Together these clusters form a rising, mixed business district. Several other knowledge clusters – the AMC, Science Park, Slotervaart and Shell – and the leisure quarter around the ArenA Boulevard are spread around outside these two concentrations.

181

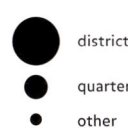
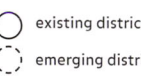

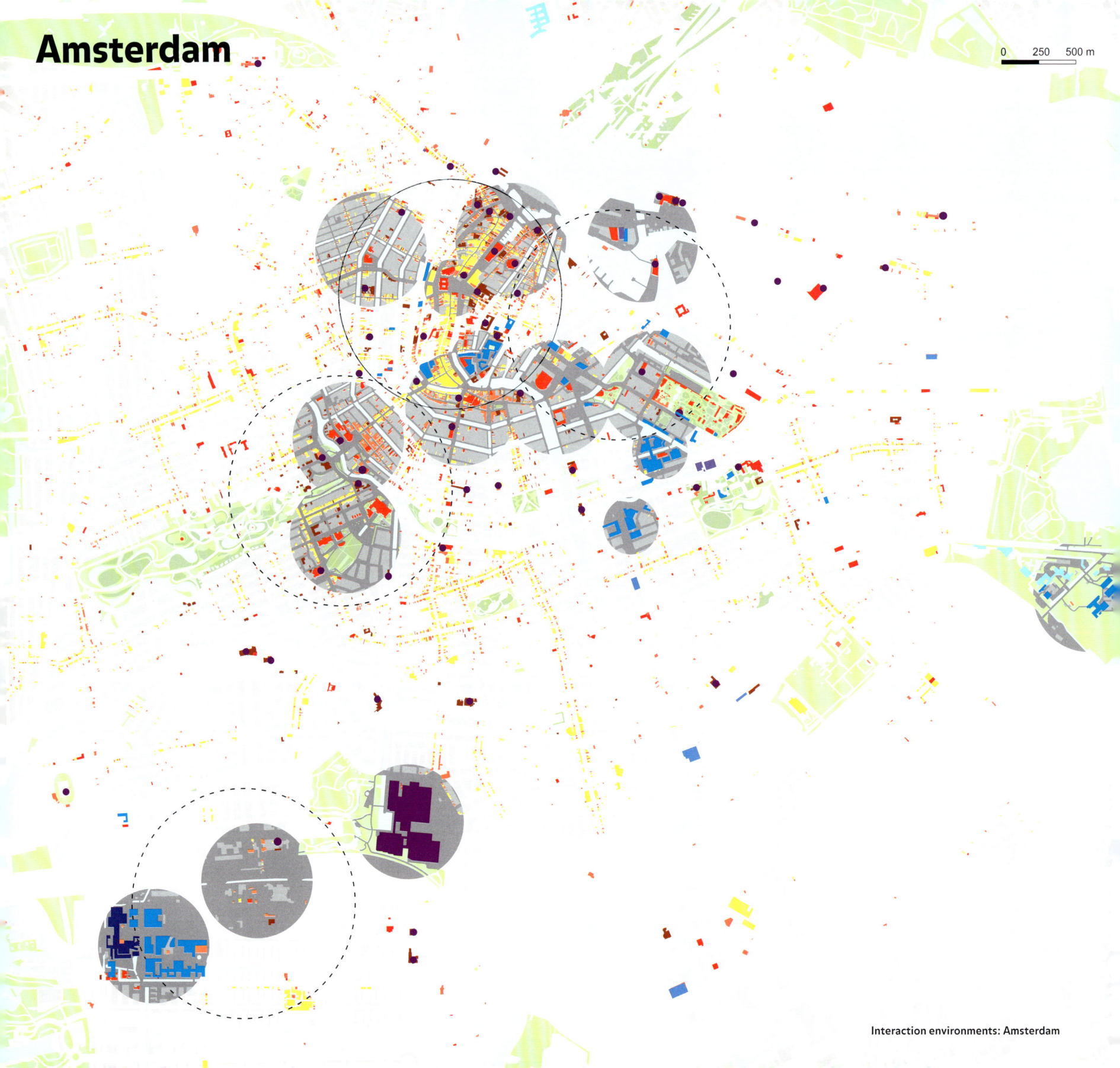

Amsterdam

Interaction environments: Amsterdam

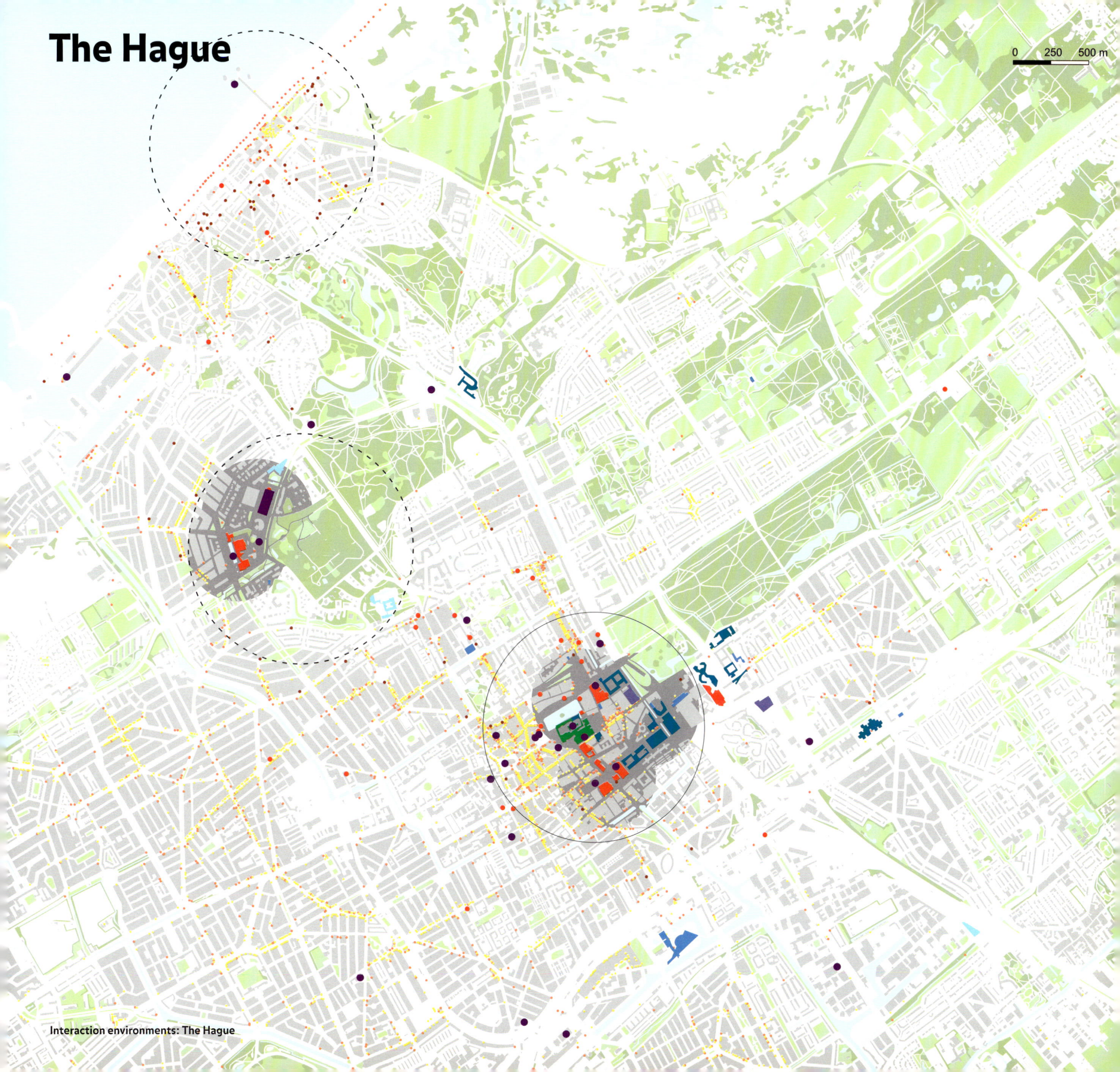

The Hague

0 250 500 m

Interaction environments: The Hague

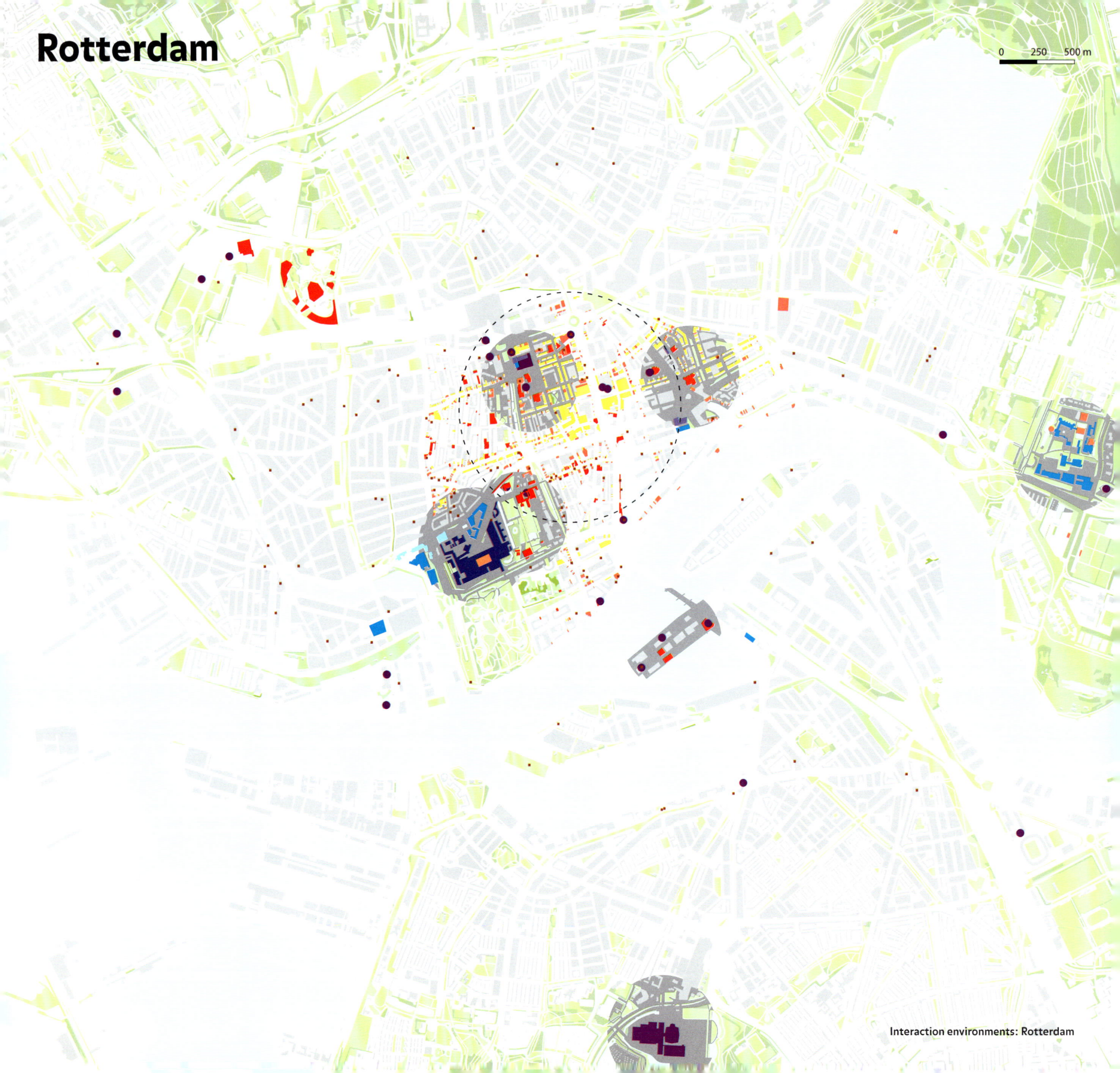

Rotterdam

0   250   500 m

Interaction environments: Rotterdam

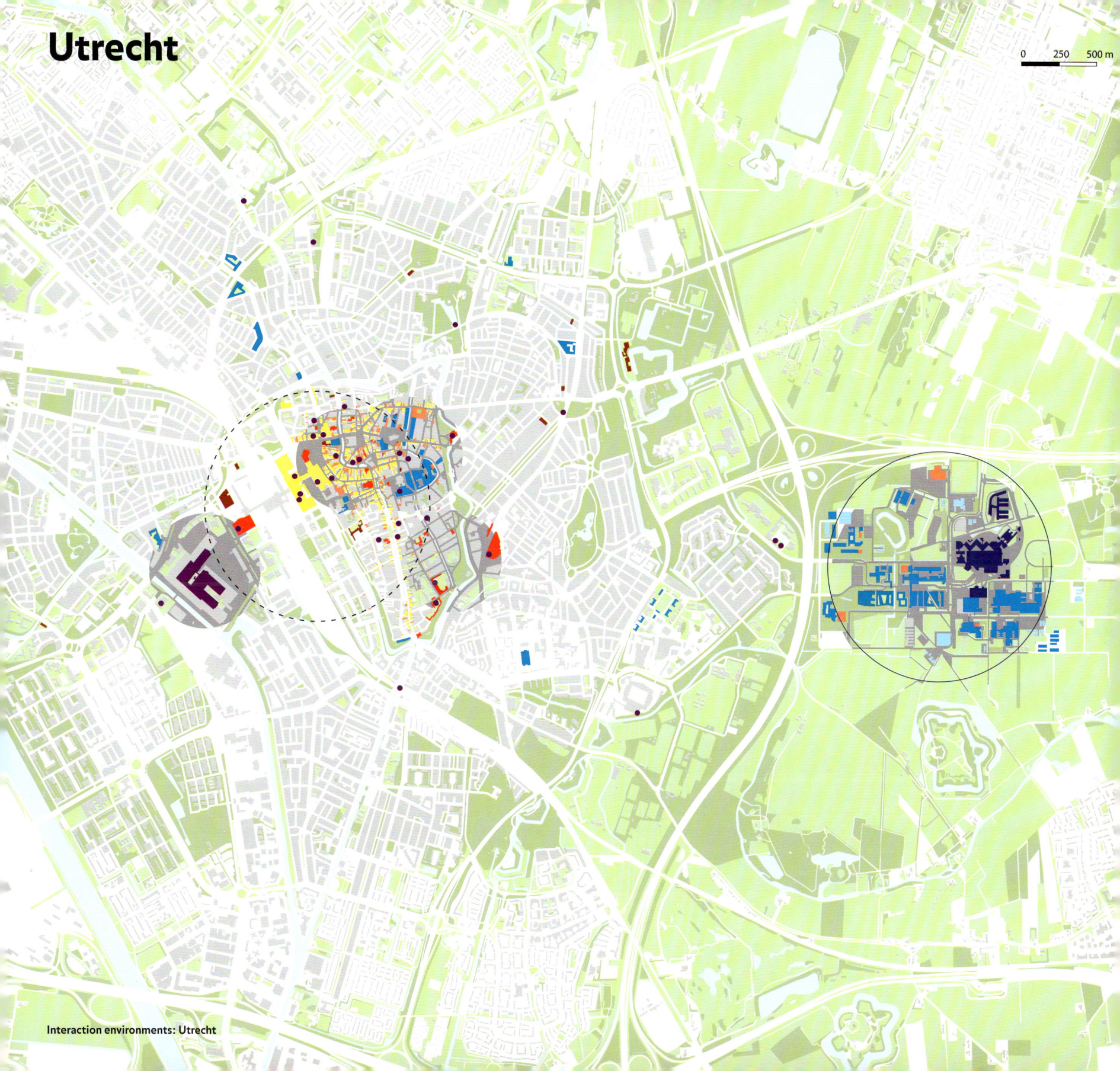

Utrecht

0 250 500 m

Interaction environments: Utrecht

Leiden

Leiden has two knowledge clusters: a mixed university quarter in the city centre and the successful Bio Science Park between the Leiden railway station and the A44 motorway. The conference cluster on the seafront at Noordwijk and the extensive ESA research centre also lie in the region.

The Hague

The Hague excels in the political and administrative niche, counting seven interaction environments, with its three culture clusters, three conference clusters and one knowledge cluster. The clusters are developing rapidly, the offerings are broader, and as a result there is in fact the prospect of a metropolitan E environment here. Some of the interaction environments lie within walking distance of one another in the composite city centre district: the shopping quarter around the Lange Poten and Grote Marktstraat, the cultural clusters around the Binnenhof and the Spuiplein, and the knowledge quarter of the government ministries in the Wijnhaven quarter.

The International Zone is a rising district around the World Forum conference centre and the Municipal Museum cluster. A large number of hotels and a whole series of institutions, such as the Peace Palace and the European Criminal Court (under construction) also lie in this district. A second rising district is taking shape around the Scheveningen beach resort. With the addition of all kinds of cultural and conference facilities this long, narrow entertainment and hotel cluster along the seafront is taking on an increasingly mixed character.

Delft

The extensive but rather thinly built-up TU-Delft knowledge district dominates the city. The DSM R&D centre and several attractions such as the Porceleyne Fles also lie in the city.

Rotterdam

Rotterdam excels in water transport, but also has eight interaction environments, with four culture clusters, two conference clusters and two knowledge clusters. Three of the four culture cluster (Schouwburgplein, Binnenrotte and Museumpark) lie around the central, highly specialized Lijnbaan shopping quarter. In recent years, as a consequence of intensification and blending of the programme and the redesign of public spaces, a more mixed and composite city centre district has emerged. The rising Leuvehaven cluster could also become a part of this district. The waterfront development on the Kop van Zuid and the two knowledge clusters, Hoboken and Woudestein, lie at some distance from the city centre. Blijdorp Zoo, the RDM campus and the Heart of the South, with the Zuidplein shopping centre and the fair and sports centre Ahoy, are still more peripheral.

Utrecht

The six Utrecht interaction environments are distinguished in the areas of science and culture, with two culture clusters, two conference clusters and two knowledge clusters. Most of the clusters lie in and around the relatively small, historic city centre, and are part of a developing, composite city centre district. With the radical reconstruction of the Hoog Catharijne shopping complex, the mixed shopping quarter around Vredenburg, the Museum quarter and the Jaarbeurs fair and entertainment centre will be more strongly integrated. Outside the city lies the extensive and successful Uithof knowledge district.

The Dutch Metropolis

Together, the logistic and metropolitan interaction environments of the Dutch Metropolis yield a different image on a map from the familiar picture of the Randstad. The centres of the four largest cities play an important role, but they are part of a multi-coloured network with a whole series of more peripheral districts, such as the South Axis, the International Zone, the TU district in Delft, the Uithof and Scheveningen, and a cloud of attractions, auctions and R&D centres.

Aside from the logistic interaction environments of the large sea and airport sites, and the auctions, the following eleven districts are the largest and most powerful urban interaction environments in the Dutch Metropolis:

- two city centre districts: the mixed district around the Dam in Amsterdam, and the composite district in the central Hague.
- two specialized knowledge districts in Delft and Utrecht.
- seven rising districts: the Rotterdam central city with its adjoining Museumpark and Leuvehaven clusters, the 'expanded heart of the city' in Utrecht, two rising cultural districts in Amsterdam, the mixed South Axis business district, the International Zone in The Hague, and the seafront at Scheveningen.

A typology of interaction environments

In the analysis of the culture, conference and knowledge clusters, considerable attention was devoted to the diverse types of interaction environments. That permits us to now sharpen the comparison between logistic and metropolitan interaction environments. In point of fact, it appears that there are all sorts of parallel types that can be distinguished in the different sectors. For instance, it appears that there are all sorts of different *centres*: shopping centres, culture centres, conference centres, medical centres and university centres. Comparable examples can be found among squares, quarters and parks.

It is striking that for the description of logistic interaction environments in particular there are no similar precise terms. We have to make do with general terms, such as *sites* and *areas*. At the largest scale we find a parallel between *region* and *valley*.

The various interaction environments can be grouped under four main types: *built*, *urban*, *green* and *neutral* interaction environments.

Built interaction environments:
centres – court complexes – terminals

The Randstad has a large number of *centres*. The criteria which apply to all centres are that they are compact, built facilities with robust programming, and are owned and managed by one organization. The various spaces are not accessed via public spaces, but connected 'indoors' by a system of corridors, passages, interior streets or courts. Often there are set opening hours, and only a couple of entrances. Frequently supporting programmes do not lie around the centre, but are included 'in house'. The *court complex* and the *terminal* are variants of this type.

The most famous centre in The Netherlands is Hoog Catharijne. It contains 160 stores, with a total floor area of 42,000 m². Because of its vast size, Hoog Catharijne could perhaps better be termed a super mall, comparable with examples like the CentrO in Oberhausen, Germany. The discussion which has rumbled on for years about the integration of Hoog Catharijne into the city is indicative of a general problem with centres of this sort. A centre is a city turned in on itself. That is also true for many trade fair and conference centres, and for university centres, as discussed in Chapters 3 and 4. The sites of the RAI and Jaarbeurs are even somewhat larger than Hoog Catharijne. They are major barriers in the urban fabric. Efforts are sometimes made to make the centre more permeable by connecting the separate sections of the buildings not on ground level, but at the first or second level. The larger the centre, however, the more difficult successful integration will be.

The University of Amsterdam centre on Roeterseiland occupies a relatively small area, and can therefore be easily integrated into the city. Cultural centres such as the Muziekgebouw in Amsterdam and the new Muziekpaleis in Utrecht are even more compact. These centres fit easily into their surroundings.

The R&D centres of businesses and institutions like Shell, ESA, ECN and RIVM also cover several hectares, and in terms of built volume are comparable with university centres. However, they often are on large sites outside the city, so that integration into their surroundings is not an issue. The new Shell Research Centre in Amsterdam is relatively compact. With the move of RIVM to the Uithof, the institute will fit into the public nature of the knowledge district.

The court type also looks like a centre. It is compact, and the various parts are often connected internally, but unlike the centre the courts are open to the public. Despite this quality, it is a type of interaction environment rarely found in The Netherlands. For instance, one does not find a self-standing series of public courtyards with shops, like the Häckische Höfe in Berlin, in Dutch city centres.

There are a couple of examples of other sorts. The most beautiful is the ensemble of the Buitenhof, Binnenhof, Hofvijver and Plein in The Hague, with the parliament buildings and the Ridderzaal and their supporting programme of cafés, restaurants and meeting facilities around them. The Binnenhof complex itself has a radius of 100 metres. The court complex with university functions on the Binnen-gasthuis site is the only example of this type in the knowledge sector. It has a radius of 175 metres. There are other smaller – and usually historic – examples of court complexes spread around the cities, such as the Oostindisch Huis in Amsterdam. They are often remnants of monasteries.

Large built facilities for logistic interaction environments are often called terminals. The terminal at Schiphol is comprised of a whole series of spatial elements: arrival and departure halls, parking garages, check-in windows, offices, shops and restaurants, and a whole circuit of piers, baggage belts, gates and platforms. Compared with centres, these complexes have a more composite form, the elements are linked in a series, and are often accessible without leaving the building. Efficient management of the logistical process is the central concern.

Stations are also increasingly often called terminals. Various public transit modalities intersect with one another there, in one building complex, in which all the accompanying facilities are included. You also encounter terminals in sea ports. A cruise terminal is oriented to passengers, but sometimes cargo piers and loading and unloading facilities are also called terminals, as in the case of container terminals. There, however, one rarely encounters buildings.

Urban interaction environments:
Squares – streets – fronts – quarters – districts

Urban interaction environments are characterized by their combination of public spaces and buildings, which are owned and managed by multiple persons, organizations or institutions. The buildings are oriented to, and accessible from, public spaces. There is often a repetition of built units of comparable size: stores, cafés, theatres, departmental buildings and museums in more or less mixed form.

Considered in terms of the area they occupy, the types found here arrange themselves into a series. In European cities squares have traditionally been the most concentrated public spaces for people encountering one another and exchanges of all sorts. It was there that markets were held, and townsmen built their churches, city halls and financial exchanges around them. Presently they come in all shapes and sizes: shopping squares, entertainment squares, classic and modern culture squares. Most squares in The Netherlands are relatively small. The radius of most entertainment and culture squares, including the built facilities around them, does not exceed 175 metres. Only the Museumplein and ArenA Boulevard are larger. The Museumplein stands apart for the extreme dimensions of its open space, the ArenA Boulevard for the massive size of the venues around it – the ArenA itself, but also the Pathé ArenA cinema, the Heineken Music Hall, Villa ArenA and the Ziggo Dome.

Many streets are mixed interaction environments par excellence. Only in a limited number of cases are they dominated by one specific function. Shopping streets are distinguished by the predominant presence of stores. In recent decades most shopping streets with non-food stores in city centres have been redesigned as pedestrian areas, modelled on the successful concept of Rotterdam's Lijnbaan, from the 1950s. Another specialized case is the entertainment street. Amsterdam's Reguliersdwarsstraat hosts 20 cafés and discos, the Zeedijk 12. The Nes, in Amsterdam, is the only culture street in The Netherlands, with three major theatres: Frascati, the Brakke Grond and the Comedy Theater.

The river or seafront with its characteristic public space of a promenade is a mixed form of square and street. The promenade, in the form of a beach boulevard or quay, is built up on only one side, giving it a strong orientation.

Most quarters have a radius of 350 to 400 metres. The relatively strong specialization of quarters in the Holland Cluster is striking – for instance, the shopping quarters in the city centres of The Hague and Rotterdam, the culture and entertainment quarters in Amsterdam, the knowledge quarter in Leiden and the business quarter of the South Axis.

Nieuwendijk, Kalverstraat and Leidsestraat, together with the 9 Straatjes, the Haarlemmerstraat and the Jordaan, form a complete shopping district with 1000 stores and a radius of almost 750 metres. It is a relatively mixed district, including the classic culture square of the Dam in the middle, and a whole series of culture and entertainment squares and quarters around it.

In addition to this city centre district, there are two other specialized districts in the Holland Cluster, the Uithof and the TU district. Amsterdam's cultural districts are presently emerging. With the integration of the various quarters of the South Axis, this area will also grow to the size of a district. The TU district is an extremely large knowledge district. It has a radius of 1500 metres, and it is therefore perhaps better to term this interaction environment a super-district.

Green interaction environments:
Gardens – wharves – parks – campuses

In the interaction environments of the Holland Cluster, the term 'park' is to be found with various meanings. In addition to public culture and science parks, such as the Museumpark, the Westergasfabriek and the Bio Science Park in Leiden, there are countless amusement parks and attractions such as Madurodam and zoos spread through the Holland Cluster, and the more closed R&D campuses that are also termed research parks. The culture wharf is a more unpolished version of the culture park.

It is striking that businesses and institutions also play an important role in the development, ownership and management of the publicly accessible culture and science parks. The Westergasfabriek was developed by MAB Project Developers, and is managed by Westergasfabriek Ltd., and the NDSM wharf by Kinetisch Noord. Universities play a central role in many science parks, and in the commercial exploitation of the sites for non-university functions as well. Rotterdam's Museumpark is an exception, being managed by the city.

Enclosed green space is the characteristic for all these interaction environments. Garden and park are thus – just as was the case for urban interaction environments like quarters and districts – indications of their size. They can lie both in, and outside, cities. The classic botanical and zoological gardens, and playgrounds, are the smallest. Amsterdam's Hortus measures 1.2 hectare. The largest attraction park in the Holland Cluster is Walibi Biddinghuizen, with an area of 120 hectare (40 hectare of theme park, 20 hectare of vacation bungalow park, and a 60 hectare event site), and is comparable with Leiden's Bio Science Park in extent.

Neutral interaction environments:
Site – field – area – region

In everyday speech, various neutral terms such as site, field, area and region are used for a number of interaction environments. They can lie in cities, or outside them. A region transcends the scale of the city.

A site, such as an airport or produce auction site, is a sizeable piece of land. The word is also used for event sites, and sports fields reflect a similar usage. Compared with the other interaction environments which were discussed above, a site has a less distinct form. It is suitable for various uses, and there is often just a simple fence around it. A field is distinguished by the presence of grass, such as on a landing field or sports field. The term area indicates the whole of the sites used for a specific function, such as a greenhouse or harbour area.

The term *region* indicates a large area with common topographic characteristics, such as a coastal region or the flower bulb region. As a knock-off from Silicon Valley, in recent years the term *valley* has been used for a region associated with specific products or facilities, as in the case of Food Valley or Health Valley.

The core of interaction environments: the *hal* or *zaal*

All interaction environments have a central space where the actual interaction takes place. In English this space would generally be designated as a *hall,* as in the case of a departure hall or concert hall. Dutch introduces a distinction by the use of two terms, *hal* and *zaal*. A *hal* designates a transition space, such as is found at airports and railway stations; a *zaal* is designed for longer stays, often with fixed seats, more akin to the English *auditorium,* and would be applied to a university lecture hall, concert hall, cinema or auction room, but also a banqueting hall. A *hal* may well have benches, but they are only intended for brief waits.

Maarten-Jan Hoekstra has linked the terms *hal* and *zaal* with the earliest domestic structures in the Low Countries, the *hallenhuis* and the *zaalhuis*.[3] Both *hal* and *zaal* originally had the meaning of 'a large, roofed space'. In the case of the *hallenhuis* that roof was supported by separate, free-standing uprights; while in the *zaalhuis* the supporting construction was included in the walls. A *hal* is therefore often large, open and flexible, while a *zaal* is more closed and suited for a specific function. This latter distinction is more precise. Sports halls and exhibition halls are not transition spaces, but are large and flexible in their use.

Delving deeper into the differences, we note that the form of interaction which takes place in a *zaal* is chiefly the exchange of information. In the foyer outside a *zaal*, or perhaps in cafés or on the street of interaction environments which include *zalen*, people meet and talk about the lecture they have heard or

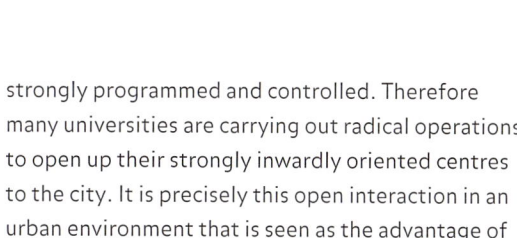

↑ → **Auction hall and auction room, Flora Holland, Honselersdijk**

the play or performance they have seen. The form of interaction in *hallen* is less regimented. You wander through a trade fair or market hall, looking at whatever catches your fancy, meeting old acquaintances or making new ones.

Series

Interaction environments fall into series based on their size. Most centres, courtyard complexes, squares and gardens have a radius of 175-200 metres and an area of 10-12 hectare. Quarters, campuses and parks have a radius of 350-400 metres and an area of 40-50 hectare; districts have a radius of 700-800 metres, and an area of 150-200 hectare: always a doubling of the radius, and a quadrupling of the area. At this small scale, Boeke's and Eames's The Powers of Ten appear to be rather imprecise. De Jong's logarithmic series comes closest to reflecting reality. On the other hand, it remains difficult to formulate a generally valid principle. There are too many exceptions.

Specialized, composite, mixed, integrated

Urban interaction environments are, by definition, more mixed than others, if only as a result of the combination of public space and private objects. In many other interaction environments the public space is limited, or at least there are limits on access to it. That is also the snag; the limited access makes encounters and exchanges less open and more

strongly programmed and controlled. Therefore many universities are carrying out radical operations to open up their strongly inwardly oriented centres to the city. It is precisely this open interaction in an urban environment that is seen as the advantage of being located in the city.

Nevertheless, it is striking to note how little mixture there is in most urban interaction environments. In most cases, a mixed environment is to be understood as one with several other functions in addition to public space and dwellings. Many shopping and entertainment clusters – be they streets, squares or complete quarters – are pretty much limited to that one function. Here and there projects like 'homes over shops', or adjusted night open hours, are being used to encourage mixing. The 1012 entertainment quarter in Amsterdam is probably the most extreme example of a specialized urban interaction environment.

On the other hand, a certain degree of specialization is precisely the strong point of many urban interaction environments. Combination with other similar functions, sectors or even atmospheres, draws specific target audiences and therefore encourages multiplexity. Between 'extremely specialized' and 'fully integrated' there are 'composite' and 'mixed' – two interesting categories deserving further study.

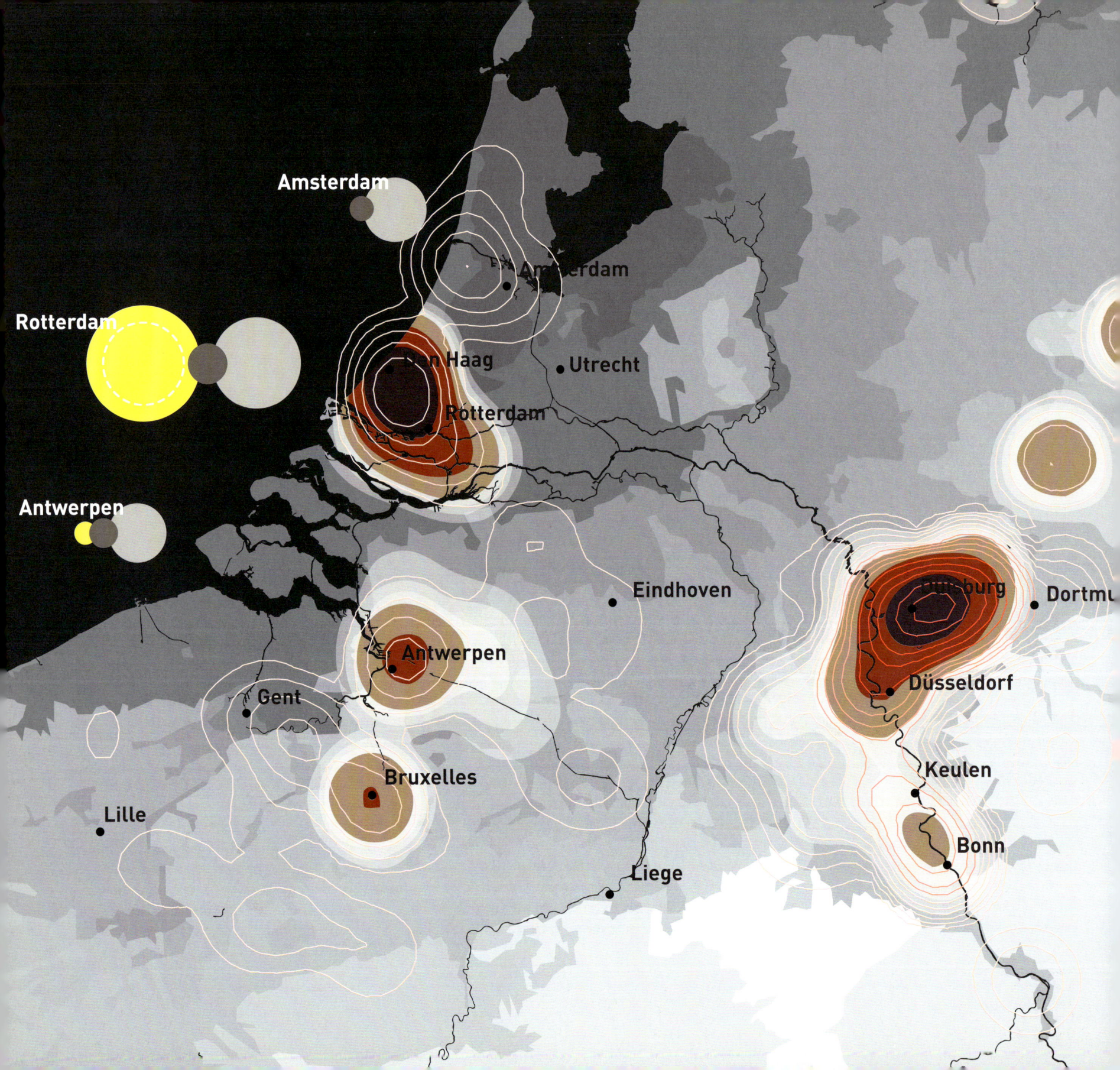

Amsterdam

Rotterdam

Antwerpen

Amsterdam

Den Haag

Utrecht

Rotterdam

Eindhoven

Antwerpen

Duisburg

Dortmu

Gent

Düsseldorf

Lille

Bruxelles

Keulen

Liege

Bonn

The international position of the Dutch Metropolis

To an important degree, the strength of the Dutch Metropolis is determined by its location in the vicinity of other metropolitan regions in Northern Europe. Together with Flanders and the Rhine-Ruhr, the provinces of North and South Holland form the ABC mega-region. Together the three metropolitan regions have a population of 28.8 million, and the total mega-region has 45 million residents. It is one of the most densely populated areas in Europe. Moreover, London, Paris, Berlin and Frankfurt are only a short distance away.

To an ever increasing extent the ABC mega-region is functioning as a coherent spatial-economic system. For years now the federal state of North Rhine-Westphalia has been the most important commercial partner for The Netherlands and – at least as important – that is also true the other way around. In 2010 the total volume of import and export was at least 45.2 billion Euro.

Traditional trading routes ran through the region, but since the rise of mining and industry in the Ruhr and Wallonia there has been a particularly strong fabric of connections and mutual dependence, particularly when it came to the transport of natural resources and goods. Those connections are only becoming stronger. For instance, since the closure of its mines, the generating stations in the Ruhr have

Dutch import and export 2010, by means of transport

Means of transport	Total export	Total import	exp BE	imp BE	exp Ger	imp Ger
Sea	148,193	412,166	949	1,159	5,277	3,507
Air*	740	883				
Inland navigation	167,073	65,829	66,171	29,098	88,495	30,664
Road	88,096	80,074	29,130	24,569	35,427	38,092
Rail	23,926	9,051				
Pipe line**	49,085		26,478			22,607

* totaal EU export 29,000, EU import 20,000 tones
** petroleum and petroleum products figures 2011

run entirely on coal supplied through the harbours of Amsterdam, Rotterdam and Antwerp.

These international connections are also clearly exhibited in international road haulage. International road shipments from The Netherlands appear to be primarily directed toward areas just over the border. In 2009 over 80% of the tonnage that Dutch road transporters carried internationally was picked up or delivered in Germany or Belgium, and about half of that in areas immediately on the Dutch border. More than 27 million tons were carried to and from North Rhine-Westphalia alone; 25 million tons to and from Flanders. About 30% of this flow of goods was food-related: livestock, agricultural and processed food products, and animal feed. Chemical products were another important category. Almost 40% of the cargo carried to The Netherlands from Germany involved minerals and building materials.

Of course, transport is not just by road, but also by water, rail and pipeline. Of the raw oil unloaded from tankers in the harbour at Rotterdam, half is pumped through a system of pipelines to five refineries within the harbour area itself, and the other half to refineries in Vlissingen, Antwerp and North Rhine-Westphalia. There the raw oil is processed into oil products such as petrol, diesel, LPG, kerosene, heating oil, ethylene and naphtha. Many of these products and semi-products are themselves transported by the pipeline system.[4]

Investment

With regard to financial collaborations and investment in other countries, however, The Netherlands is oriented more strongly to Great Britain. Unilever, Reed Elsevier and Shell are well-known examples of British-Dutch businesses. In 2010 the total value of direct Dutch investment in Great Britain was almost 95 billion Euro.[5] After the United Kingdom, Belgium is the second destination for direct investment from The Netherlands. In 2010 the value of Dutch investment in Belgium was over 70 billion Euro, and in Germany 58 billion. Going in the opposite direction, the British have 60 billion invested in The Netherlands, the Belgians 31 billion, and the Germans 37 billion. Nor is the value of investment from Luxembourg anything to be sneezed at: 54 billion Euro. These sums increased enormously since the Schengen Treaty went into effect in 1995. Added together, Belgian and Luxembourg investment in The Netherlands in 1994 was less than 9 billion Euro (converted from pre-Euro currency).

A comparable pattern can be seen in business investment. Dutch businesses have 8722 daughter firms in Germany, 3750 of which are located in North Rhine-Westphalia. Düsseldorf is the most popular location. Going in the other direction, almost 3400 German firms have branches in the Netherlands, chiefly in Amsterdam and Rotterdam.[6] Over 6500 Dutch firms have a branch in Belgium, the majority in Flanders and Brussels.

The most noteworthy new collaborations are taking place in the energy sector. After the privatization of Dutch energy companies at the end of the 1980s, almost all of them have become components in strong multinational enterprises. Various energy firms in Zeeland and South Holland have become part of Electrabel, originally Belgian. It is the largest electricity producer in Belgium and The Netherlands. Essent was swallowed up by the German RWE, with its headquarters in Essen. E.on, from Düsseldorf, is one of the largest energy producers in the world, but has only a limited market share in The Netherlands and Belgium. In 2009 Nuon was taken over by the Swedish Vattenfall, which is also a market leader in northern Germany.

The connections are also expressed by the number of visitors. In 2010 a total of 11 million foreign visitors came to The Netherlands, including almost 2 million Belgians and 2.9 million Germans. More than half of the Germans came from North Rhine-Westphalia. 4.1 million Dutch visitors went to Germany. Among them North Rhine-Westphalia scored low; Berlin, the Saarland and the Mosel region were much more popular. Ruhr 2010 was heavily visited by Netherlanders, who formed the

Import, storage and transit of oil; concentration of employees in the (petro)chemical industry in ABC
Sources: European Environmental Agency (EEA) (2011), Corine land cover 2000, versie 15; Alterra (2007), LANMAP-2; Eurostat (2007) Manufacture of chemicals and chemical products, other non-metallic mineral products and rubber and plastic products at NUTS level 3, Number of persons employed; Eurostat (2007); Manufacture of coke, refined petroleum products and nuclear fuel at NUTS level 3, Number of persons employed

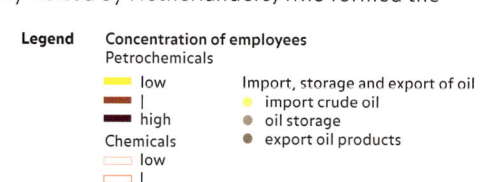

Legend
Concentration of employees
Petrochemicals
- low
- |
- high

Chemicals
- low
- |
- high

Import, storage and export of oil
- import crude oil
- oil storage
- export oil products

largest group of foreign visitors. About 2 million Netherlanders visited Belgium in 2010.

Networks

The oldest trade routes from Cologne to the coast and onward to London ran across Belgium, through Bruges, among other cities. Other routes in ABC included what are called the Hessenwegen, named for the merchants from Hesse, who in the Middle Ages crossed North West Europe in their lumbering wagons on their way from one annual market to another. The water network of the rivers and coastal lagoons was at least as important. A vast area, stretching from Flanders to Denmark, could be reached in relative safety by sailing behind the barrier islands along the coast.

In today's situation many more kinds of networks are important. The Rhine however still plays a structuring role. A system of *Links- und Rechts-rheinische* railways and motorways characterize the networks around the Rhine from Basel to Cologne. To the north of the Ruhr region the river and the associated lines bend off to the west.

The *Rechtsrheinische* lines run in the direction of Rotterdam and The Hague, via Arnhem and Utrecht. Of the various branches of the Rhine, over the course of time the Waal became the most important, both in terms of water volume and in terms of transport of goods. With the development of the Rotterdam harbour, first on the south bank of the Maas and later in the direction of Botlek, Europoort and the Maasvlaktes, a shift took place in the land network. After connections are completed to the existing networks in Germany and around Zevenaar, the Waal, the A15 motorway and the Betuwe rail line will be the central 'multimodal' transport cluster to the hinterland.

To the north of Cologne the *Linksrheinische* system is more diffuse. An extensive network of roads, canals and rail connections stretch from the coast to the industrial cores in the hinterland, running both east-west and north-south. In addition to the Flemish ports, Brussels and Rotterdam are also tied into this network. Motorway, rail and pipeline connections with the Ruhr region run via Eindhoven and Venlo.

In the new European High Speed Rail network it is Brussels that is central. This city has direct connections with Paris and London and, via Luik, with Cologne and further into Germany. In comparison with Brussels, Amsterdam is peripheral. It lies at the end of a long – and still not smoothly functioning – high speed line from the south. The planning for a high speed link from there to the Ruhr region and Cologne has also gone on the back burner. Amsterdam does have connections with Hannover and Berlin, via the A1 motorway and the rail lines through Amersfoort and Twente. There is also a direct link with the Waal, via the Amsterdam-Rhine Canal, but there is no branch running north from the Betuwe rail line. In the infrastructural realm, Amsterdam must be satisfied with Schiphol and the Amsterdam Internet Exchange.

In the middle

A whole series of other cities and urban regions lie in the area between Holland, Flanders-Brussels and the Rhine-Ruhr. Two of them also are to be found in the BBSR research: Maas-Rhine and Eindhoven. Maas-Rhine (37) has three locations with metropolitan functions: Maastricht, Aachen and Luik; it is a Type 2 region with moderate differentiation and is relatively strong in science, transport and culture. Luik is a stop on the HSL between Brussels and Cologne.

Eindhoven (43) has one location with metropolitan functions, is a Type 3 region, with limited differentiation, and is chiefly strong in science. The city lies at the junction of routes from Holland to the south of The Netherlands, and from Antwerp to the Ruhr region.

In addition to these urban regions, in The Netherlands Apeldoorn, Deventer, Almelo, Hengelo, Enschede, Ede, Arnhem, Nijmegen, Breda, Tilburg, Den Bosch, Venlo, Sittard/Geleen and Heerlen each have a population of over 100,000. In Belgium Leuven, Hasselt, Turnhout and Genk are all just a bit smaller, but Charleroi, Namur and Mons on the slopes of Wallonia are of comparable size. The border-straddling group of cities including Lille, Roubaix, Tourcoing and Kortrijk even counts 1.9 million residents.

We previously noted that the ABC mega-region has a population of 45 million. The metropolitan regions of Holland, Flanders-Brussels and Rhine-Ruhr together account for almost 30 million residents. That means that the area in the middle accounts for about 15 million residents, and is thus also a strongly urbanized area. What it lacks is the concentration of metropolitan functions that are present in Holland, Flanders-Brussels and Rhine-Ruhr.

Network development and logistic interaction environments

The harbour of Rotterdam and the auction complexes of Honselersdijk, Bleiswijk, Barendrecht and Venlo have a rock-solid position in the ABC mega-region and north-west Europe through their favourable position in the networks to the hinterland. The Amsterdam harbour, Schiphol and the auctions in Aalsmeer and Rijnsburg are somewhat less favourably located in the networks, but nevertheless have outstanding connections with the hinterland. The construction of Maasvlakte II and the completion of the Betuwe route and the A15 motorway anchor the logistic complex still more firmly in ABC and north-west Europe. Recently there have also been studies done on the construction of a direct rail line from Antwerp to the Ruhr region via Eindhoven, along the A67. This could further reinforce the central position of Eindhoven, and of Venlo.[7]

Rotterdam's vision for its harbour in 2030 forecasts major transitions in energy usage, and with that the use of space in the harbour. These must now be anticipated, in part in relation to the industrial profile of the harbour. In any case, it is remarkable to see that most of the added value produced in the Ruhr region involves raw materials and goods which pass through Rotterdam. An important development in this regard is the construction of generating plants by German firms on harbour sites in The Netherlands. These plants lie close to the sea. That is handy for the delivery of fuel, but it also makes these firms less dependent on the rapidly warming rivers in the hinterland for the discharge of the cooling water. With experiments with biofuels and with wind energy generated at sea, there is also an interesting future for energy ports.

Further, all prognoses point to a further growth in the volume of goods moving through harbours and around the auctions. Despite the possibilities to move a larger percentage of them to the hinterland along rail lines, internal waterways or, possibly, pipelines, pressure on the motorway network will increase further. Transporting cargo via the High Speed rail network could be combined with a further concentration of auctions, and the construction of a Food Centre Holland, à la the Rungis, in Paris. Several years ago H+N+S and DRO already explored the possibilities of a new Holland Food Centre at the rail centre in the Haarlemmermeer, close to Schiphol. The HSL also runs right past Bleiswijk, Barendrecht and Breda.

Goods transport 2008 to and from foreign countries, Belgium and Germany x 1000 tons
Source: CBS Statline

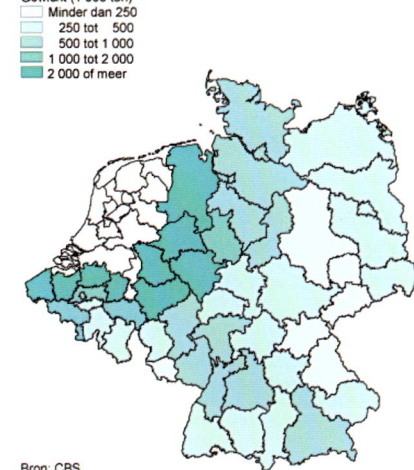

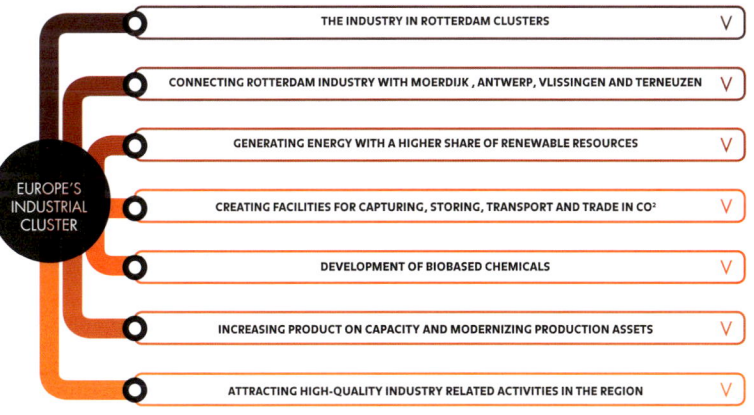

Expansion of the industry cluster in Rotterdam's harbour
Uitvoeringsagenda Havenvisie 2030, Rotterdam

Aerial photo of the central market in Rungis, Paris region

Network development and metropolitan interaction environments

The strong development of the E environment in and around Amsterdam in recent decades kept right in step with the expansion of Schiphol on the successive waves of open EU borders, the rise of price-choppers like Ryan Air and Easyjet, and the Open Skies Treaty with the US. The fusion of KLM with Air France in 2003 appears to have further strengthened the position of the airport.

In addition to the airport, the rapid development of the Internet Exchange was an important condition for businesses and institutions locating in Amsterdam. Road and water connections are less important for the development of metropolitan interaction environments – but unlike them, rail connections are.

Amsterdam lies in a relatively peripheral spot in the network of high speed rail connections in ABC and north-west Europe in general. That applies even more so to the emerging metropolitan environment in and around The Hague. Brussels has a much more central position, with its direct links to Paris, London, Cologne, and, further away, Frankfurt and Berlin. At these distances, travel by rail is appreciably

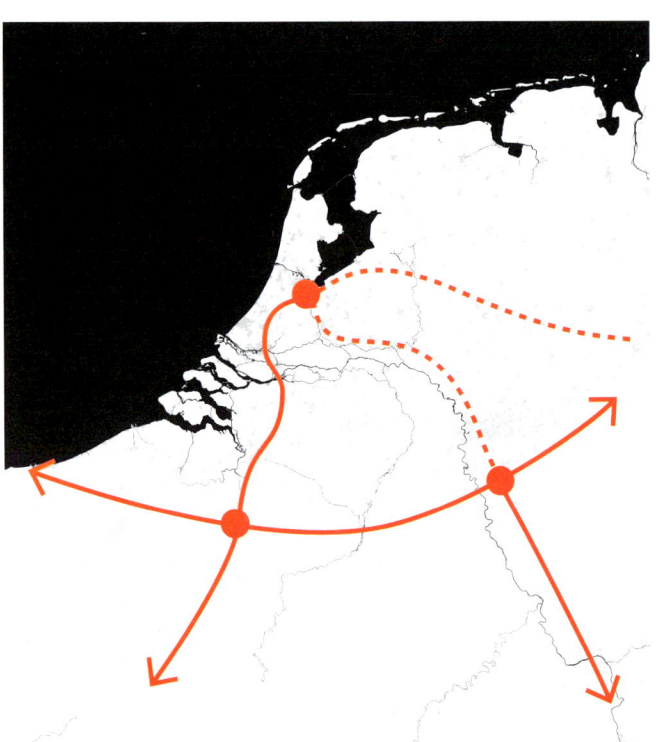

faster than by air. Unlike aeroplanes, trains bring their passengers right to the heart of a city.

It was previously noted that plans for an eastern branch of the HSL, from Schiphol to Cologne, via Amsterdam South, Utrecht and Arnhem, have been put on the back burner. This line would make the connections between these cities a bit faster, and could lead to a further intensification of relations. It is incomprehensible that vigorous efforts are not being made to push this forward, including a branch to The Hague. The same is true for having Eurostar service run direct to Amsterdam. The branch of this line from London to Brussels could easily continue north to Amsterdam.

An eastern branch of the HSL would also benefit Schiphol. Presently its catchment area is limited, and the airport must therefore be satisfied with transfer passengers. Expanding the catchment area to include the Ruhr region could strengthen the airport's position. Schiphol has a much better intercontinental network than the airports in Cologne and Düsseldorf. However, in 2002 a fast rail link was already opened between Cologne and Frankfurt, the hub of Lufthansa. From Cologne one can reach the airport in Frankfurt in under an hour.

Extending the HSL South beyond Schiphol and Amsterdam South would also make Amsterdam less of an end destination. One option for this was to extend the line through the IJsselmeer polders to Groningen, and perhaps farther, to Hamburg. This would have included North Germany in Schiphol's catchment area. However, the detour through Groningen would have added time and kilometres to the trip. For years Amsterdam has had international train service to Hannover and Berlin, via Amersfoort and Twente. It could be interesting to upgrade this route to make it faster. That could be done by improving the existing trackage, but in view of the experience with the HSL, the better option would seem to be constructing a new route generally parallel to the present route, perhaps also calling in at Almere and the Lelystad airport.

Expansion of the HSL network in the direction of Cologne and Hannover

Perspectives for development

The power of attraction exerted by the Dutch Metropolis is defined by a multiplicity of factors. In addition to its accessible location, many studies also cite the accessibility of its residential market, the level of prices and taxes, its hospitality, facilities for overnight stays and international orientation. Nor should promotion and marketing be underestimated; compare Vi Paris in its coordination of the offering of conference facilities in Paris. It is certain, however, that the quality of interaction environments is another strong factor.

Over the last few decades substantial investment has taken place, and all kinds of new interaction environments have been introduced into The Netherlands: culture parks, waterfronts, arenas, convention centres, science parks, leisure boulevards, etc. These have expanded the offerings greatly. Further development of existing interaction environments, and improvements in their quality, is therefore now the much better option than developing more new ones.

The most effective development strategy would seem to be the combination of various smaller interaction environments into larger ones. For instance, the central shopping area in Amsterdam, along the Nieuwendijk, Dam and Kalverstraat, was connected better with the shopping area around the Haarlemmerstraat and the *9 Straatjes*, creating a whole district.

There are seven emerging districts spread across the Dutch Metropolis: the Rotterdam city centre district, the 'expanded heart' of Utrecht, the two rising culture districts in Amsterdam, the mixed business district of the South Axis, the International Zone in The Hague, and the seafront in Scheveningen.

That does not mean that there should not be further investment in districts that already exist. A good example of this is the construction of the 'Red Carpet' in Amsterdam: the redesign of the Stationsplein, Damrak, Rokin and Munt, in connection with the realization of the North/South Metro line. The previously fragmentary public space is once again becoming a whole, barriers are being removed, and auto traffic is being minimized. The effect of the redesign should be that the adjoining 1012 entertainment quarter and the university quarter around the Binnengasthuis will connect with the shopping district around the Nieuwendijk, Dam and Kalverstraat in a natural manner, and become more easily accessible for various groups of pedestrians. That encourages mixing.

Strolling city

The cores of interaction environments are halls, in buildings. There people watch and listen to performances, speeches or competitions, or wander around looking at new products or unusual objects. Impressions and experiences get shared, deepened and interpreted in conversations around the halls, in corridors, foyers and cafeterias in the buildings, but also on the streets, in the cafés, lunchrooms, coffee shops and restaurants along them. This 'supporting programme' in the immediate vicinity plays an important role. The greater anonymity of the public places, as compared with university cafeterias or theatre foyers, guarantees a greater intensity of contacts, and can facilitate unexpected stimuli and encounters. That is one reason that many universities seek to break open their centres and campuses and better integrate them into the city.

Interaction and the city are however natural allies to one another at many more points. Markets and concentrated forms of interaction such as events and festivals thrive in cities. Increasing numbers of visitors combine an afternoon of shopping with an evening out, or stay overnight and make a Sunday morning stroll. Many tourists succumb to the temptation to wander around a city and let it surprise them. In many cases the culture, shopping and cuisine will be decisive factors in the choice of a host city for a convention.

Aldo van Eyck summed up the magic of the city in his design for the pavilion for the Sonsbeek exhibition in the summer of 1966. The pavilion was built as an exhibition space for sculptures. They do not stand in a large space, or in a park, but in a structure with six tall, parallel walls, with niches and apertures. You can only experience the sculptures by wandering through this small city: 'Bump! - sorry. What's this? Oh hello!'[8] That is, in essence, the quality of the city.

Sonsbeek pavilion by Aldo van Eyck, 1966, acquired and reconstructed in the sculpture garden of the Kröller-Müller Museum, in consultation with Hannie van Eyck.
Photo: Kröller-Müller Museum, Otterlo

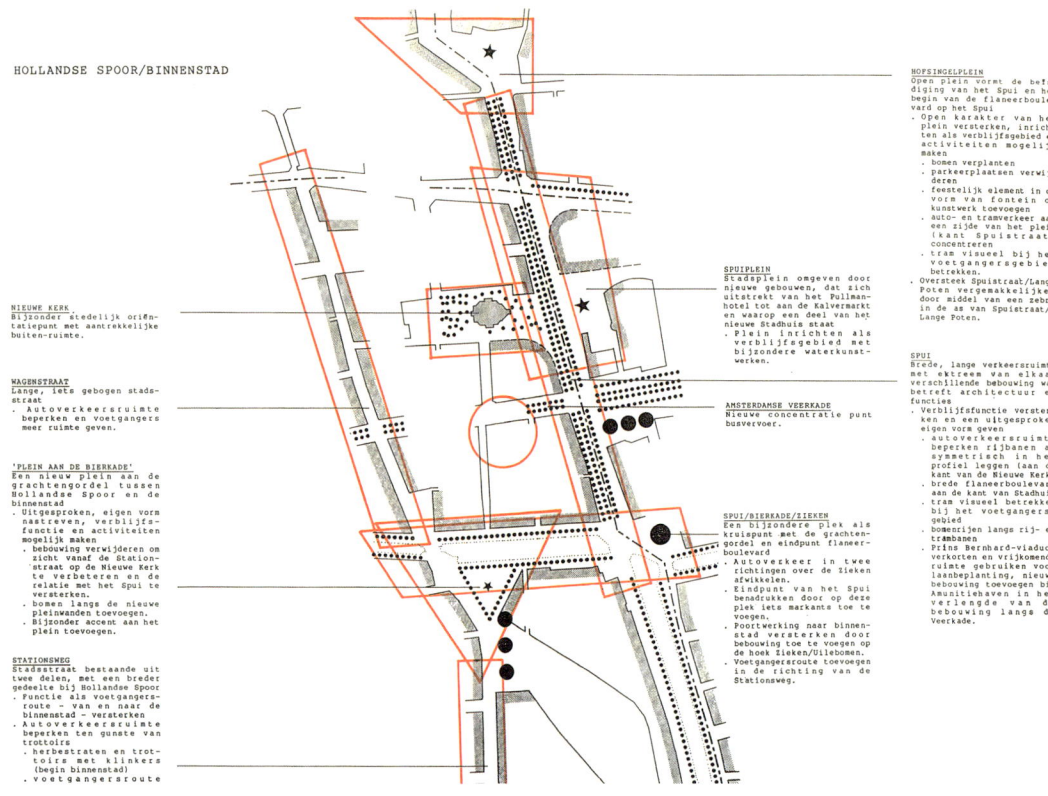

Design of public space

The design of its public space – the floor of the city – is of paramount importance for a city made for strolling. The Dutch norm for this was set in 1988 with the plans for a complete make-over for the centre of The Hague, *De Kern Gezond* (The healthy core). The plan – or better, the programme – was commissioned by the municipal authorities in The Hague, and drawn up by Alle Hosper, at that time working for Bakker and Bleeker.

It is characterized by the choice to use only one type of paving brick and kerb, and for a family of lighting fixtures, sewer grates and street furniture. These create a restful street scene and provide continuity. Within this there are five areas distinguished, each with its own atmosphere and spatial identity, such as wide and narrow shopping streets, and the series of urban and green squares.[9] It is typical of The Hague that these areas are all organized around parallel 'lines'. These supporting lines, and the 'heart line' which crosses them and ties them together, are carefully detailed.

In the course of the 1990s almost all the streets and squares of the central Hague were re-profiled. It has been an unusually successful project. The various shopping and culture clusters have come to form a single district, in a natural manner. In part because of all the construction along it, only the supporting line from the Spuiplein to Central Station has not lived up to its promise, and the integration of the culture clusters around the Spuiplein and the Wijnhaven quarter, with the government ministries, has remained problematic.

The design of public space is crucial for the success of almost all emerging districts. Many of the combinations we have discussed will stand or fall with better integration of auto traffic into the urban fabric. In the case of Amsterdam, for instance, the success of the Museumplein-Leidseplein combination depends on better integration of the busy Stadhouderskade, the success of the eastern city centre on the IJ Tunnel route and Prins Hendrikkade, and the South Axis on a natural connection of the central business quarter, the knowledge quarter and the RAI. For the International Zone in The Hague the central factor is the ability to cross the western ring road conveniently, and in Rotterdam it is the success in making the area around the Westblaak a continuous urban fabric. For the 'expanded heart' of Utrecht the redesign of Hoog Catharijne, the Catharijnesingel and the Stationsplein will be the proof of the pudding.

Focus and acceleration

These important projects for making the Dutch Metropolis more attractive will cost a lot of time, are all too susceptible to compromises, can encounter all sorts of community opposition, and above all often fall prey to the urge for economizing during the final phases of their realization. In many foreign cities an effort has been made to maintain the focus in such projects by coupling them with large-scale events, such as World's Fairs, World Championship football, or Olympic Games. Such events also act as accelerators, because they come with hard and fast deadlines attached.

Barcelona and Sydney both improved the quality of their interaction environments by their bid for, and later actually organizing, Olympic Games. France and Germany organized World Cup football. The new *Hauptbahnhof* in Berlin was opened in 2006, just before the World Cup. London hopes to achieve both new infrastructure, and provide a wide-ranging stimulus for the east end of the city and the region,

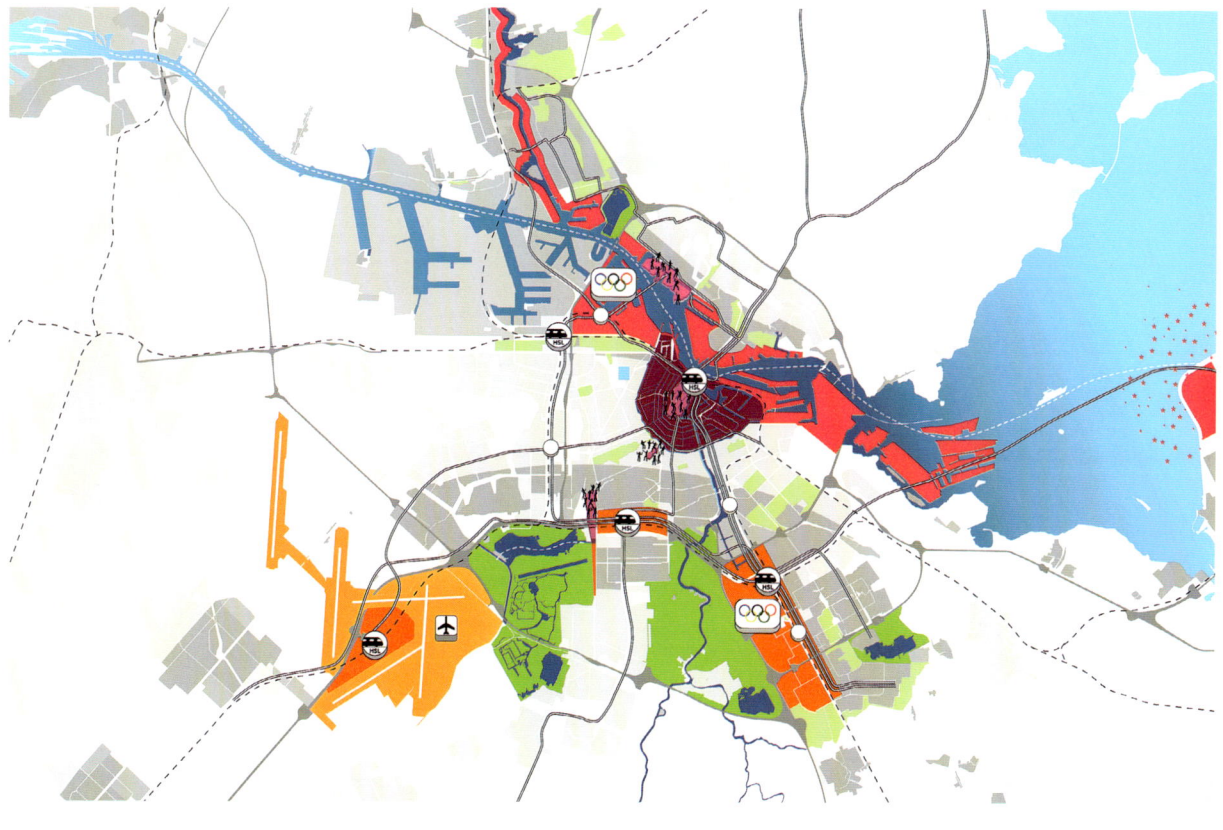

↑ **Possible locations for the Olympic Games in Amsterdam**
Source: DRO

With an eye to a possible Dutch bid for the Olympic Games in 2028, the national government, together with the large cities, has explored spatial concepts and sketched out the main lines of a physical structure for hosting the Olympics. In Amsterdam – the strongest brand – the harbour area within the ring and the vicinity of the ArenA are possible locations for an Olympic Park. The latter is the most obvious location. Along with Schiphol, it could be the motor for the development of the South Axis district with the underground infrastructure, a new station and well integrated RAI and VU complexes, and outstanding links with the city. The aging office parks in the South-east would be a challenging location for an Olympic Village.
An alternative would be locating the Olympic Park in The Hague or Rotterdam. The Games could be the mainspring for accelerating the integration of these two urban regions into a coherent metropolitan region.

← **Public viewing World Cup football, 2006, Stuttgart**

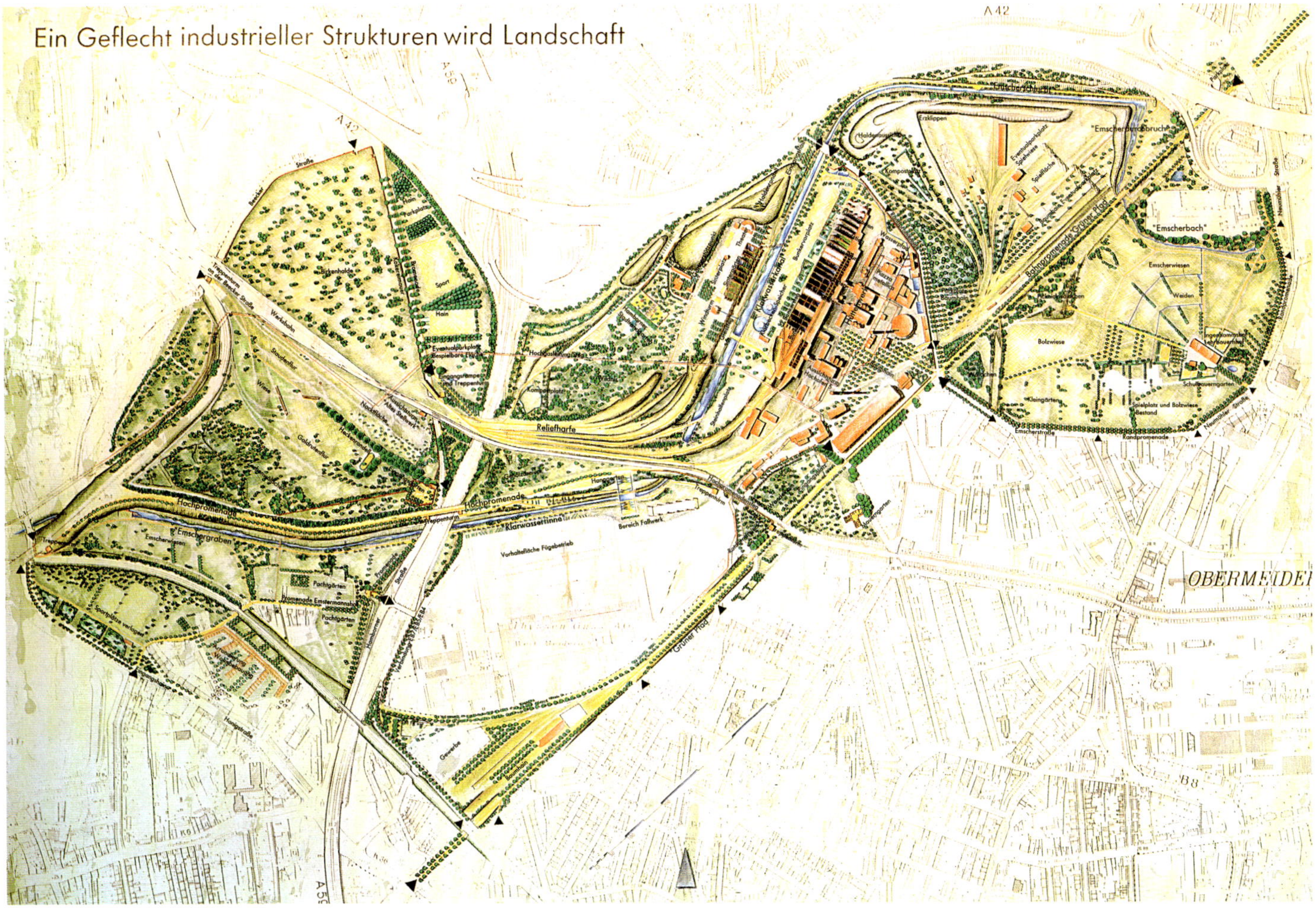

Ein Geflecht industrieller Strukturen wird Landschaft

Map of the Landschaftspark Duisburg Nord
Design: Latz+Partner, © Latz + Partners

**Impression of Landschaftspark
Duisburg Nord**

in the long-running Thames Gateway project.

Massive events of this sort draw large numbers of visitors. It is for that reason that they could also be a good mainspring in The Netherlands for improvements in the infrastructure, such as the expansion of Schiphol and the HSL, or broadband networks. Moreover, visitors often come for a couple of days. Robust expansion of hotel capacity is therefore necessary. All the large cities, and also the seaside resorts, could benefit from this, including from any accompanying programme of investment in interaction environments.

However, in the course of the debate about whether The Netherlands should make a bid for the 2028 Olympics, the Netherlands Olympic Committee/Netherlands Sports Federation has been identifying the legacy of the Games primarily in the broad stimulus they would give to the practice of sports: The Netherlands must be raised to an 'Olympic level' by investing in amateur sports and developing talent. That still doesn't sound very ambitious.

A Universal World Expo is presently held every five years. After the successful Expo in Shanghai in 2010, it is Milan's turn next, in 2015. Smaller versions are held between times. The last of these was in Saragossa, Spain, in 2008, and in Yeosu, South Korea, in 2012. The biggest differences from the Olympic Games are the length of the event, a whole summer long, and the focus on the exchange of knowledge. That makes a World Expo much less transitory.

Although at the time this is being written 78 countries have signed up to build a pavilion at the World Expo in Milan in 2015, it is striking that once again the choice has been made for a site outside the city. The Expos in Seville and Hannover have had a difficult afterlife. In the Dutch situation, integration into the city would be far and away the better choice, for instance utilizing city centre restructuring locations like the Binckhorst in The Hague or the

Stadshavens in Rotterdam, or in the middle of Amsterdam's South Axis, as a motor for mixed development. The various national pavilions could give the up-and-coming South Axis business district colour, and after the event could play a role for business presentations and exhibitions, or as satellites of the RAI.

The Dutch Metropolis

Much more interesting than such large-scale but relatively short-lived events would be for us to orientate ourselves to the German tradition of the IBAs, the Internationale Bauausstellungen. In the 1980s the renewal of Berlin was the central theme, an overture to the great urban regeneration operation after the *Wende*. The Emscherpark IBA took place in the 1990s. Many of the abandoned industrial sites around the Emscher River were transformed into attractive landscape parks. In this way the quality of the living situation was radically improved, and the events became the basis for a whole series of projects which were proudly shown

during Ruhr 2010. The IBA in Hamburg (2006-2013) connects with the debate about the transformation of the harbour area and how to deal with climate change in the Leap over the Elbe.

Events like the IBA permit all sorts of experimentation with crucial themes for the development of cities and regions. On-going projects are evaluated, new projects initiated, a range of parties involved are mobilized, and the results sold to the public in an inventive manner.

In the coming years dozens of buildings and building complexes will be delivered in the eleven metropolitan districts in the largest cities in The Netherlands, tunnels, stations and bridges constructed, streets and squares re-profiled, and parks laid out. The simplest formula for focus and speed is therefore to embrace these projects now and begin preparations for an event every ten years, with exhibitions and debates, directed first and foremost at exchanging and deepening knowledge, and subsequently on defining a new generation of projects for the expansion of the Dutch Metropolis.

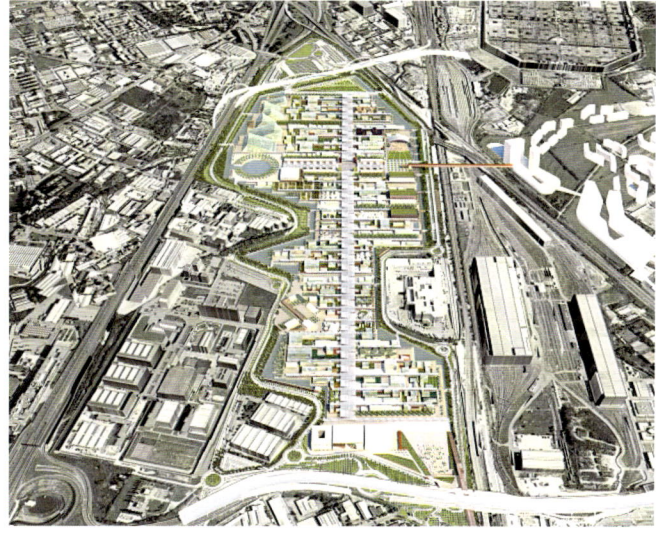

Collage of the plan for Expo 2015 in Milan. Expo 2015, with the title 'Feeding the Planet, Energy for Life', will be held on the Fiera Milano site, north-west of the city. The exhibition site is 110 hectare in size, and is accessed by the new HSL station Rho-Pero.
The coordinating architect for the Masterplan is Stefano Boeri.

↑ → **Winning designs in the contest for the new International Criminal Court in The Hague**
Schmidt Hammer Lassen Architects

New *compagnieën*

The definition of the metropolis used here, with its strong emphasis on metropolitan functions, is related to the manner in which Niek de Boer, professor of City and Region at the TU Delft from 1969 to 1989, looked at environments in big cities. In 1994, in *De Randstad bestaat niet*, he dissected the spatial policy that The Netherlands had maintained since the Second Memorandum on Physical Planning in 1966.[10] He noted that not only the national government, but also the large cities, fell shamefully short in their vision of the development of metropolitan qualities and an attractive, large-scale urban environment, focused exclusively on visitors. In De Boer's view, that was a serious denial of metropolitan quality. De Boer also noted that The Netherlands had no attractive metropolitan environment that counted internationally. Amsterdam scored the best, and The Hague trailed at a distance; Rotterdam and Utrecht did not count at all, according to Niek de Boer in 1994. What is the state of affairs 20 years later? According to the German BBSR, the Randstad stands high in the rankings, but when examined more closely, the picture is more mixed.

After thirty years of debate, Utrecht has finally reached agreement about the redesign of Hoog Catharijne. The realization has, however, not yet begun. The new Muziekpaleis promises much. A great success has already been achieved with the coming of RIVM and Danone to the Uithof, but the new tram to the Uithof goes by way of a remarkable route. The TU district in Delft could very much use the stimulus of such businesses and institutions, and good tram service. For the foreseeable future, the tram route will remain unused.

The development of the Kop van Zuid in Rotterdam is still largely a governmental affair; market parties are hesitant about committing themselves. Moving the Luxor Theater and Lantaren/Venster to the Wilhelminapier was controversial, and subtracted from the quality of the city centre. The new market hall and the University College will be stimuli for the old heart of the city around the Binnenrotte. Will the Museumpark benefit from the new parking garage, and will plans for the better integration of Hoboken succeed?

The Hague appears well on its way. The return of the government ministries to the centre of The Hague has been handled successfully, public space has undergone a metamorphosis, and moreover efforts to bring a number of important institutions dealing with peace and justice to the International Zone have succeeded. The cluster in Scheveningen is under development, and the last obstacles to development around the Spuiplein are being resolved.

To date, only Amsterdam has fully profited from the internationalization of the economy and the boom in the tourism and conference sector. The number of Dutch and international visitors has risen spectacularly. Schiphol is running well, and the calendar at the RAI is fully booked. Yet it is still a mixed picture in Amsterdam too. On the plus side are attractive new destinations such as the Hermitage, the Westergasfabriek and Scheepvaart Museum, the start of the make-over for the humanities and social sciences departments at the University of Amsterdam, and exciting new developments in the advertising and media sectors; on the minus side are the shuttered museums, permanent delays and

limited financial resources. The redesign of Leidseplein has been postponed yet again. The new home for the University Library in the Binnengasthuis has been relinquished in favour of a still unclear future in an existing building. After fifteen years of discussion about placing a part of the infrastructure in the South Axis underground, the national government and Amsterdam finally reached agreement in the spring of 2012, but the replacement of the Cabinet at subsequent elections has thrown the realization of these plans into question.

In other words, the Dutch Metropolis exists, but we are still in the starting blocks for any serious policy, and for serious projects focused on its development. In a Delta City Region things work differently than in a Capital City Region. Successes come only if many parties put their shoulders to the wheel: museum directors, academics, marketing experts, designers, publishers and public administrators.

The final conclusions of the series of lectures and discussions organized by the Deltametropolis Association, *The International Perspectives*, also focused precisely on this theme: urban development is increasingly a task of collaborating parties.[11] Just as the Dutch of the Golden Age formed their *compagnieën*, partnerships of the governing regents, entrepreneurs and technical experts, to discover new worlds and recover their homeland from the encroaching sea, to meet the challenges today we need new 'companies'.

Notes

Chapter 1

1   W. Zonneveld, *Conceptvorming in de ruimtelijke planning. Patronen en processen.* (Planologische Studies, part 9a), Amsterdam 1991.

2   W. Zonneveld en F. Verwest , *Tussen droom en retoriek. De conceptualisering van ruimte in de Nederlandse planning,* Rotterdam 2005.

3   The definition of a FUR is a 'core' with > 20,000 jobs and > 7 jobs per hectare, with a 'ring' of contiguous NUTS-5 areas, from which > 10% of the population work in the 'core'. A FUR is a metropolis when it has > 1 million residents [Group for European Metropolitan Areas Comparative Analysis (GEMACA)]. Several research programmes comparing urban systems in Europe have been carried out in recent years on the basis of this definition and statistical material which has been made comparable to it. All sorts of research groups from universities and regions have made contributions, including research groups at the University of Amsterdam around Robert Kloosterman. The Globalization and World Cities Research Network under the leadership of Peter Taylor, at Loughborough University in Leicestershire, plays a prominent role in this discussion.

4   P. Hall, *The World Cities*, London, 1966. Translated in the Dutch under the title *Zeven Wereldsteden – problemen van groei en leefbaarheid,* Bussum 1978[2].

5   Daan Zandbelt, 'Het Veld. Een wereldstad van acht miljoen', in *Stedebouw en Ruimtelijke Ordening*, vol. 88 (2007), pp. 42-46. Merijn van der Werff, Bart Lambregts, Loek Kapoen, Robert Kloosterman, *The Randstad, Commuting & the Definition of Functional Urban Areas*, Polynet Action 1.1. Institute of Community Studies/Young Foundation and Polynet Partners 2005.

6   Jan Ritsema van Eck, Frank van Oort, Otto Raspe, Femke Daalhuizen, Judith van Brussel, *Vele steden maken nog geen Randstad,* Rotterdam/Den Haag 2006.

7   B. Lambregts, R. Roling, M. van der Werff, L. Kapoen, R. Kloosterman & A. Korteweg, *The Randstad, Qualitative Analysis of Service Business Connections,* Polynet Action 2.1. Institute of Community Studies/Young Foundation and Polynet Partners 2005.

8   Taeke M. de Jong, *Environmental differentiation 1977-2012*, Zoetermeer 2012.

9   Hans-Heinrich Blotevogel (2002), 'Deutsche Metropolregionen in der Vernetzung', in *Informationen zur Raumentwicklung*, 2002, Heft 6/7, pp. 345ff. See also the informative site of the IKM (Initiativkreis Europaischer Metropolregionen in Deutschland): http://www.deutsche-metropolregionen.org/

10   Bundesinstitut für Bau-, Stadt- und Raumforschung (BBSR) im Bundesamt für Bauwesen und Raumordnung (BBR), *Regionales Monitoring 2010*, Bonn-Mannheim 2010.

11   *Metropolräume in Europa*, in: BBSR (Hrsg.): Analysen Bau. Stadt.Raum, Bd.1, Bonn 2010.

12   P.G. Hall and K. Pain,*The polycentric metropolis: learning from mega-city regions in Europe*, London 2006. P.J. Taylor and M. Hoyler, 'The spatial order of European cities under conditions of contemporary globalization', in *Tijdschrift voor economische en sociale geografie*, vol. 91 (2000), pp. 176-89.

13   Catherine L. Ross, *Megaregions: Literature Review of the Implications for Infrastructure Investment and Transportation Planning,* Centre for quality growth and regional development at the Georgia Institute of Technology Atlanta, 2008.

14   Petra Todorovic, *Megaregions, the Building Blocks of a National Infrastructure Plan* (Regional Plan Association, New York 2008). Cf. also: Robert E. Lang, Dawn Dhavale, Beyond Megalopolis: Exploring America's New Megapolitan Geography, Virginia Tech's Metropolitan Institute, Census Report 05:01 (May 2005).

15   Richard Florida, Tim Gulden, Charlotta Mellander, 'The Rise of the Megaregion', in *Contemporary Economic Policy*, 2008, pp. 459-77.

16   Fernand Braudel, 'Kanttekeningen bij 'Civilisation matérielle et capitalisme'' (translated by Jos van Beeck) in *Te elfder ure*, Vol 9 (1982), p. 264.

17   Luuk Boelens, *Rijn-Schelde-delta in internationaal perspectief*, introduction Deltadag 13 December 2006. Luuk Boelens, 'De associatie stad, bottom-up of outside-in', in *Stedebouw en Ruimtelijke Ordening*, vol. 91 (2010), pp. 16-24.

18   The data for protected natural areas is derived from the the European Environment Agency: www.eea.europa.eu

19   Regione Veneto - Direzione Sistema Statistico Regionale.

20   Bouches-du-Rhône Tourisme, Marseille.

21   Toerisme in cijfers 2010 (data for multi-day tourism), Toerisme Vlaanderen. www.toerismevlaanderen.be

22   Cf.: Avignon (89,600), Nîmes (140,700), Montpellier (260,000), Arles (52,400), Aix (143,000), Verona (243,000), Venetië (270,000, waarvan 60,000 in de oude stad), Ferrara (135,300), Vicenza (116,000), Padova (214,000), Ravenna (159,000), Brugge (116,700), Gent (243,000), Leuven (95,000) en Mechelen (81,800).

23   NBTC figures.

24   *Achtergronddocument beleidsinformatie Mainport Schiphol*, Ministry of Transport and Communication, project Mainport Schiphol, The Hague 2005.

25   *Groeicijfers Schiphol,* Rapport Algemene Rekenkamer, included in: Tweede Kamer, vergaderjaar 1998-1999, 26 265, nrs. 1-2, Sdu Uitgevers, 's-Gravenhage 1998.

26   See among others: Strategische agenda mainport 2010-2013, Denken en Doen!, Greenport Nederland, Honselersdijk 2010, and Vitaal tuinbouwcluster 2040, een toekomststrategie voor Greenport Holland, Rapport Adviesgroep Tuinbouwcluster Greenport.NL, commissioned by the Ministry of Agriculture, The Hague 2010.

27   *Nederland verandert – Brainport Eindhoven/A2-zone (Brainport Avenue)*, Ministry of Housing, Regional Development and the Environment, 2010.

28   R. van der Wouden, *Evaluatie sleutelprojecten*, Bureau Stedelijke Planning, Gouda 2005.

29   Buck Consultants International, *Uitvoeringsstrategie duurzame internationale concurrentiepositie Randstad 2040*, Nijmegen 2008 (research carried out for the Ministry of Housing, Regional Development and the Environment).

30   *Naar de top: de hoofdlijnen van het nieuwe bedrijfslevenbeleid*, Letter to the Lower House, Ministry of Economic Affairs, Agriculture and Innovation, The Hague 2011.

31   *Nederlandse clusters in kaart gebracht*, Ministry of Economic Affairs in cooperation with Dialogic, The Hague 2011. See also: Dialogic: *Toelichting & methodologische disclaimers bij de clusterkaarten*, Utrecht 2010.

32   M.E. Porter, *The Competitive Advantage of Nations*, New York 1998[2] (1990[1]).

33   In addition to residential and work environments, on the basis of land use, density and degree of mixing, the Planbureau voor de Leefomgeving distinguishes five centre levels: highly urban, urban, sub-urban and rural centre environments, and peripheral retail environments. See: Jan Ritsema van Eck, Hans van Amsterdam, Johan van der Schuit: *Ruimtelijke ontwikkelingen in het stedelijk gebied, Dynamiek stedelijke milieus 2000-2006,* Planbureau voor de Leefomgeving, Den Haag/Bilthoven 2009.

34   Chuihua Judy Chung, Jeffrey Inaba, Rem Koolhaas, Sze Tsung Leong, *Harvard Design School Guide to Shopping,* Harvard Design School Project on the City 2, Cologne 2001.

35 This spatial typology differs from the frequently employed functional typology in scale and numbers of stores: from dispersed stores and the neighbourhood shopping centre with less than 25 stores, through the district shopping centre of 25 to 100 stores, to the core shopping area with more than 100 stores.

36 S. Sassen, *The Global City: New York, London, Tokyo*, Princeton 2001[2] (1991[1]).

37 Cf also: *Global City Power Index 2008 en 2009*, Mori Memorial Foundation, Tokyo.

Chapter 2

1 Deived from SER-advies 1975-04 Wijziging Vakantiewetgeving, Bijlage 4. The appendix was based on A. Hessels, *Vakantie en vakantiebesteding sinds de eeuwwisseling; een sociologische verkenning ten behoeve van sociale en ruimtelijke planning in Nederland*, thesis Technische Hogeschool Delft, Assen 1973.

2 NBTC figures.

3 Factsheet no. 5 September 2010 - Toerisme 2009, dienst Onderzoek en Statistiek, City of Amsterdam. Part of the increase can be attributed to a change in methods of calculation in the early 1990s. That visitor numbers also increased sharply however in the years before and after that underscores the growth in the sector.

4 Toerisme in cijfers 2009, CBS/NBTC, Voorburg/Heerlen 2009.

5 Christopher M. Law, 'Urban tourism and its contribution to economic regeneration', in *Urban Studies*, Vol. 29 (1992), pp. 599-618.

6 Tracy Metz, *Pret! Leisure en landschap,* Rotterdam 2002. According ot Metz, the number of new attractions and events increased by 800% between 1986 and 1997; in the same period visitor numbers rose by 900%.

7 WTO Figures.

8 *Groeten uit Holland*, Advies VROM-raad no. 035, The Hague 2006.

9 Hotelnota Amsterdam, City of Amsterdam 2008.

10 *Mastercard Index of Global Destination Cities*: Cross-Border Travel and Expanditures 2Q 2011.

11 Jaarboek 2010, dienst Onderzoek & Statistiek City of Amsterdam, table 19.5.7 page 579, based on figures from Tourmis.

12 Global Power City Index 2010 (GPCI), Institute for Urban Strategies at the Mori Memorial Foundation in Tokyo.

13 Jaarboek 2010 O+S, City of Amsterdam 2010.

14 See also: OPERA, Ontwikkelingsplan Economie Regio Amsterdam, ROA 2004, en Economische Agenda Metropoolregio Amsterdam, MRA 2009.

15 The Cultural Council employs the following division of sectors (http://www.cultuur.nl/sectoren): amateur art and cultural education, archives, visual art and design, libraries, cultural heritage, e-culture, film, international and intercultural policy, landscape architecture, architecture and urban planning, letters, media, monuments and archaeology, museums, performing arts.

16 CBS website, figures 2007.

17 From the top 55 museums in terms of annual passes. The Kunsthal in Rotterdam does not appear here. With 165,000 visitors it is one of the larger museums, but is not in the top 10. Also, the list of the largest events begins at 50,000 visitors. Such events have a cosmopolitan atmosphere. It is nevertheless difficult to establish the number of visitors to such events. Totals are always estimates. Furthermore, the number of visitors to the same event can fluctuate from year to year. Bad weather is famously a cause of falling visitor numbers. If Netherlanders have to economize in hard times and take their vacations close to home, that will cause visitor totals to rise. All this makes a survey of the largest events in The Netherlands such as is presented here both random for a given moment and an estimate.

18 Hans Mommaas, 'Cultural Clusters and the Postindustrial City: Towards the Remapping of Urban Cultural Policy', in *Urban Studies*, Vol. 41 (2004), pp. 507-32.

19 Vera Cerutti, *Creatieve fabrieken, Waardecreatie met herbestemming van industrieel erfgoed*, Utrecht 2011.

20 Visitor totals 2010: 130,000 at the Maritiem museum + 105,000 at the Havenmuseum. The Imax theater closed its doors in 2001.

21 In recent decades the Boijmans Van Beuningen Museum has been renovated and expanded several times by various architects: Bodon in 1970, Henket in 1991 and Robberecht and Daem in 2003.

22 Jacques Nycolaas (ed.), *Rotterdam, stedebouwkundig ontwerpen*, Delft 1988. See also: Hans Mommaas: 'Cultural Clusters and the Postindustrial City: Towards the Remapping of Urban Cultural Policy', in *Urban Studies*, Vol. 41 (2004), pp. 507-32.

23 Noor Mens, *W.G. Witteveen en Rotterdam*, Rotterdam 2007. See also: Urban Fabric-Steenhuis stedebouw en landschap, *Hoboken, cultuurhistorische analyse*, Schiedam 2008.

24 Nenijto: Nederlandse Nijverheidstentoonstelling (Netherlands Industrial Exhibition), Rotterdam 1928.

25 CBS: *Dagrecreatie 1995-1996*, Heerlen 1997. CBS: *Onderzoek Dagrecreatie*, Heerlen 2007.

26 Andries van den Broek, 'Mode of Modus', in *Tijdverschijnselen – Impressies van de vrije tijd*, Sociaal en Cultureel Planbureau, Den Haag 2003, pp. 56-8.

27 F. Huls, K. Hoenderkamp, W. Hoffmans, *Recreatiecijfers bij de hand,* Kenniscentrum Recreatie, The Hague 2008.

28 On the basis of Top-100 evenementen 2006, Respons, supplemented by my own research for the years 2008-2009.

29 From: Verslag Discussiebijeenkomst Tempels van Cultuur d.d. 11 March 2008, Stichting Babel.

30 Lynne Sagalyn, *Times Square Roulette: Remaking the City Icon*, Cambridge 2001.

31 Alistair Barr, *SoHo New York, Mixed Use, Density and the Power of the Myth*, University at Greenwich Publication, Urban Design Studies 2002. http://www.barrgazetas.com/papers/SoHo.pdf

32 *SoHo Market Trends*, Trulia Real Estate NY juli 2011. See also: *WOZ-waarde Amsterdamse woningen gestegen*, O+S Amsterdam, 10-3-2010. Dienst Belastingen City of Amsterdam, Makelaarsvereniging Amsterdam, Amsterdamse Federatie van Woningcorporaties: *Woon Amsterdam 2010*.

33 For a description of the redevelopment of waterfronts in American cities see: B.J. Frieden en L.B. Sagalyn, *Downtown, Inc. How America Rebuilds Cities*, Cambridge (Mass.) 1989. Rouse's strategy and the the copies of the successful developments in cities like Baltimore and Boston are analysed sharply in chapter 11 by Peter Hall, *Cities of Tomorrow*, Oxford 1988.

34 Han Meyer, *De stad en de haven, Stedebouw als culturele opgave, Londen, Barcelona, New York, Rotterdam*, Utrecht 1996.

35 Rudi Kegel, Frans Schokkenbroek, Clemens M. Steenbergen, *Parc de la Villette : concours international Parc de la Vilette, Paris 1982: overzicht Nederlandse inzendingen*, Delft 1983.

36 Evert Verhagen, Susanne Piët, *Een park voor de 21ste eeuw. Vijf visies voor de Westergasfabriek in Amsterdam*, Bussum 1998.

37 See note 19.

38 Esther Gramsbergen, ''Tot gerief van dezes stads ingezetenen'. De Amsterdamse Plantage, een publiek project', in *Overholland* 10/11, p. 199 ev. For the history of the 19th century panoramas, see: Cyrille Offermans, *De mensen zijn mooier dan ze denken*, Amsterdam 1985.

39 The newest Amsterdam culture cluster, Overhoeks, shares a comparable ambiguity. Construction of new facilities for the Shell laboratories freed up a site of more than 20 hectare in the middle of the city for redevelopment. Part of it was the historic Tolhuistuin, close to the ferry dock, with Shell's business restaurant, built by Arthur Staal. As with the NDSM wharf, after a competition Cultuur aan het IJ was selected to operate the site for a period of five years. They ran the Tolhuis garden and took on a whole series of partners, including Paradiso, to build for a mix of activities. Although the serious error was made in the redevelopment of the site, in the demolition of almost all the buildings, the Tolhuistuin, the remaining Great Laboratory and the new Film Museum could form an interesting new cluster. The question is however whether the cluster in this form will be able to draw more than 500,000 visitors. For that it will be necessary to develop other cultural functions in the vicinity, on and around Overhoeks.

40 TNS-NIPO commissioned by the het NBTC, *Continu Vrijetijds Onderzoek*, Key figures 2008-2009.

41 This is the number of businesses registered with the Centrum Utrecht, the business association for the historic city centre. See: http://www.centrumutrecht.nl/

42 The ICSC – International Council for Shopping Centres – distinguishes among shopping centres, regional malls and super-regional malls. The latter have an area of over 74,000 m².

43 Rob van Engelsdorp Gastelaars, David Hamers, *De nieuwe stad, stedelijke centra als brandpunten van interactie*, Rotterdam/The Hague 2006.

44 TNS-NIPO commissioned by the NBTC, *Continu Vrijetijds Onderzoek*, Kerncijfers 2011.

45 J. Berndsen, P. Saal, F. Spangenberg, T. van Dijk en K. Ronday, *Met zicht op zee. Tweehonderd jaar bouwen aan badplaatsen in Nederland, België en Duitsland,* The Hague 1985.

46 AMER advisors in cooperation with Van Meijel advisors in culture-history, *Concept-Beeldkwaliteitplan Boulevard Katwijk,* commissioned by the municipality of Katwijk, Amersfoort 2008.

47 Rijksdienst voor het Nationale Plan (S.E. Kouwe, G.H.L. Zeegers e.a.), *Beschouwingen betreffende de wederopbouw der Noordzeebadplaatsen*, The Hague (Staatsdrukkerij) 1947.

48 *Advies over het vraagstuk van de vakantiespreiding*, Uitgave van de Sociaal-Economische Raad 9-1964.

49 M. Smeenge, *Kusttoerisme, een tour de horizon*, Breda 2008.

50 Goudappel Coffeng en Transumo: *De Nationale Bereikbaarheidskaart* (www.bereikbaarheidskaart.nl). Accessibility by auto is calculated outside rush hours.

51 'Ondanks economische crisis goed jaar voor strandpaviljoens', in *Nightlife Magazine*, May/June 2010, no. 3.

52 Sprongen & Partners Horeca-advies, *Het Strandpaviljoen in Beeld*, Profiel van de Strandpaviljoens, jaargang 2009.

53 *Toekomstagenda Vrije Tijd en Toerisme* - Innovatieprogramma voor Gastvrijheid van Wereldklasse, november 2011. De Stichting Innovatie Recreatie en Ruimte (STIRR) acts as coordinator for the programme.

54 In determining the 20 most important logistic hot spots in The Netherland *Logistiek Magazine* compared various regions on the basis of six criteria: (1) availability of land and premises, (2) presence of good infrastructure, (3) accessibility of logistic interchanges, (4) cooperation of governmental authorities/ local communities, (5) availability of staff and training, and (6) flexibility/ motivation of staff. A panel of logistic experts voted for their three preferred regions in each criterion. Counting the preferences produced the list of the 20 logistic hot spots.

55 *Toekomstvisie Hart van Amsterdam*, City of Amsterdam 2009.

56 *Economisch sterk en duurzaam, Structuurvisie Amsterdam 2040*, City of Amsterdam 2011. http://www.dro. amsterdam.nl/publish/pages/357618/plan-01-2011-structuurvisie_amsterdam_2040.pdf

57 Maurits de Hoog, *4 x Amsterdam, ontwerpen aan de stad*, Bussum 2004.

Chapter 3

1   http://www.paleisvoorvolksvlijt.nl/

2   The Crystal Palace was built by Joseph Paxton in Hyde Park in London for the first World Exhibition in 1851. In 1854 it was dismantled and rebuilt in Sydenham – at that time just outside the city – and destroyed by a fire in December, 1936. http://www.crystalpalacecampaign.org/

3   Source: websites of the various organizations: www. iccaworld.com, www.uia.org

4   *De Bosatlas van Nederland*, Wolters Noordhoff Atlasproducties. Groningen 2007, p. 476C.

5   Data obtained from: Amsterdam Tourist and Convention Bureau, *Kerncijfers Amsterdam als Congresbestemming*, Amsterdam 2011. Both the UIA and ICCA take only non-commercial gatherings into consideration.

6   Nederlands Bureau voor Toerisme en Congressen, *M&C Scan 2010*.

7   LAGroup, *Bestedingsonderzoek buitenlandse deelnemers internationale non-corporate congressen in Nederland*, Amsterdam 2004.

8   In the newly built Elicium the RAI has a number of offices that can be temporarily converted into meeting halls.

9   Visit Brussels, *Let's Meet*, 2012.

10 NYC & Company, *Official New York City Event Planner 2012*.

11 Cliff Wallace, *The Global Exhibition Venue Industry: Is there an over-supply in space?*, 5th International CEO Forum, Barcelona 2007.

12 The International Congress and Convention Association, *Statistics Report, The International Association Meetings Market 2000-2009*.

13 Chester Hartman, *City for Sale - The Transformation of San Francisco*, Berkeley 2002.

Chapter 4

1. In writing this section reference was made to: Ernst Homburg, *Speuren op de tast, Een historische kijk op industriële en universitaire research*, Inaugural lecture, University of Maastricht, 2003. Alexandra den Heijer, *Managing the university campus,* Delft 2010.

2. The Brothers of the Common Life established the competing Hieronymusschool in 1474, also in Utrecht, which later became the basis for the Stedelijk Gymnasium.

3. The University of Franeker and the Athenaeum at Harderwijk were disbanded in the early 19th century.

4. This conclusion can be reached on the basis of an analysis of Research and Development a European perspective by Eurostat: *Science, technology and innovation in Europe*, 2010 Edition. Other interesting material contains an analysis focused on The Netherlands by the Nederlands Observatorium van Wetenschap en Technologie: *Wetenschaps- en Technologie Indicatoren 2005*.

5. Eurostat, *Science, technology and innovation in Europe*, 2010 Edition. In this report see particularly the graph on page 43, comparing the size and growth of EU countries.

6. Joel Garreau, *Edge City: life on the new frontier*, New York 1991. Manuel Castells and Peter Hall, *Technopoles of the world, The making of twenty-first-century industrial complexes*, London 1994.

7. M. Kenny and U. von Burg, 'Technology, entrepreneurship and path dependence: industrial clustering in Silicon Valley and Route 128', in *Industrial and Corporate Change*, Vol. 8 (1999), pp. 67-104.

8. Source: http://doc.utwente.nl/47099/1/bekostiging.pdf

9. *The Urban Future of Work*, *How denser, more urban workplaces will strengthen the Bay Area's economic competitiveness*, SPUR Report 1/2012, San Francisco 2012.

10. Web 2.0 Innovation Map: http://www.ryan-williams.net/web20map/

11. Website VSNU, figures per 31 December 2010.

12. Rob van Engelsdorp Gastelaars, David Hamers, *De nieuwe stad, stedelijke centra als brandpunten van interactie*, Rotterdam/The Hague 2006.

13. *Special R&D in cijfers*, *Technisch Weekblad*, 17 april 2010.

14. Buck Consultants, *Fysieke investeringsopgaven voor campussen van nationaal belang*, The Hague 2009 (research carried out for the Ministry of Economic Affairs).

15. Faculteit Bouwkunde TU Delft, Departments of Real Estate & Housing, Urbanism, *TU Delft Campus Visie 2030,* Delft 2010.

Chapter 5

1. The locations are formed by LAU-2 units. Local Administrative Units are the basis for what are termed NUTs regions, employed in many EU research projects; cf. Dutch COROP units (COROP = **Coö**rdinatie Commissie **R**egionaal **O**nderzoeks **P**rogramma 1971). The LAU 2-units are in Dutch communities. That means that greater precision is possible than in much other research that focuses on larger entities.

2. As early as In 1970 the Province of South Holland argued for such metropolitan environments. See: Schets Ruimtelijke Structuur Zuid-Holland, 1970, cited in: W. Zonneveld, *Conceptvorming in de ruimtelijke planning. Encyclopedie van planconcepten* (Planologische Studies, deel 9b), Amsterdam 1991. Max van de Berg and Dienke van der Werf also suggested such an environment in the study report *Het ruimtegebruik in stedelijke milieueenheden* by the Rijksplanologische Dienst (The Hague 1975) in the run-up to the *Third Memorandum*. Their idea was not accepted, however. National policymakers opted for the 'compact city' and for diffusion.

3. M.J. Hoekstra, *Huis, tuin en keuken. Wonen in woorden door de eeuwen heen*, Amsterdam/Antwerp 2009.

4. *Nederland als één logistiek netwerk in 2015*, NEA, Zoetermeer 2010.

5. Agentschap NL, on the basis of data from the Economist Intelligence Unit and De Nederlandse Bank, 2011.

6. Data from Duits-Nederlandse Handelskamer (DNHK), 2011.

7. Buck Consultants International, *Actualisatie haalbaarheidsstudie A-67 spoorlijn*, Nijmegen 2007 (research carried out for the Ministry of Transport and Communication).

8. Aldo van Eyck, 'Pavilion Arnhem - A place for sculpture and people', in *World Architecture* 4, London, and in *Domus* no 461 (1967). Reproduced in: *niet om het even...wel evenwaardig, van en over Aldo van Eyck,* on the occasion of the presentation of the Rotterdam-Maaskantprijs 1982, Amsterdam.

9. Frank de Josselin de Jong, 'Integrale ontwerpopgaven in historische binnensteden – Den Haag: De Kern Gezond', in Han Meyer, Frank de Josselin de Jong, Maarten Jan Hoekstra, *Het ontwerp van de openbare ruimte*, deel 2 van de reeks *De kern van de stedebouw in het perspectief van de eenentwintigste eeuw*, Amsterdam 2006.

10. Niek de Boer, *De Randstad bestaat niet, de onmacht tot grootstedelijk beleid,* Rotterdam 1996.

11. Vereniging Deltametropool, *The International Perspectives*, Reports of lectures and discussions around the programme of the metropolis, Rotterdam March 2012.

Illustration credits

Ahoy Rotterdam 100, 110

Amsterdam City Archive, Collection 136

Amsterdam RAI 98/99, 106, 132

Andrew Havis, www.flickr.com 72

Architectuurstudio HH/UBIKmh 51

Beeldwerk Baarlo, with thanks to Floriade 2012 Venlo 121

Benthem Crouwel Architects 89B

Buck Consultants International 32

Bundesinstitut für Bau-,Stadt- und Raumforschung 14,18, 20L, 22RB, 24R, 26R, 28L

Bureau B+B stedebouw en landschapsarchitectuur 196

Caro Bonink 61, portrait photos

Centraal Bureau voor de Statistiek, www.cbs.nl 193 LA

City of Rotterdam, Projectmanagementbureau Rotterdam, with thanks to Communicatie Stadsontwikkeling 167B

City of The Hague Haag, Dienst Stedelijke Ontwikkeling 124

City of Utrecht, www.CU2030.nl 123

Clarissa Strömer, www.flickr.com 26L

DavidDje, www.flickr.com 28R

Den Haag Marketing, The Hague Online Media Center 54R

Deutsche Messe AG, www.messe.de 114

Dienst Ruimtelijke Ordening City of Amsterdam (Anje Koop, Bart de Vries, Eric Claassen, Joris Vos, Laura Hakvoort, Maurits de Hoog, Miriam Verrijdt, Rick Vermeulen, Ronald Rijntjes) 8/9, 24L, 38B, 42, 46, 50L, 50R, 52, 54L, 55R, 55L, 56, 58L, 58R, 59L,59R, 60, 62L, 62R, 63L, 63R, 64L, 64R, 65L, 65R, 66, 73L, 74, 75L, 77R, 80LA, 80LB, 80RA, 80RB, 82L, 82R, 84, 86, 92, 107, 109, 111, 113, 126A, 140L, 144B, 145, 147L, 147R, 148L, 148R, 149L, 149R, 150L, 151, 152L, 152R, 153, 154L, 154R, 155, 156L, 156R, 157, 158, 159, 164A, 170, 180, 182, 183, 184, 185, 194, 197A

Dienst Zuidas/ Amsterdam RAI 122

Dorrith Dijkzeul 94, 94/95

DS Landscape Architects 125A, 125LB, 125 RB

Duinrell 134/135, 162R

Duinrell, with thanks to Den Haag Marketing, The Hague Online Media Center 85

Eden pictures, www.flickr.com 162L

Edwin van Eis, Fotobank Amsterdam 36/37, 67, 71, 73R, 76, 77L, 104, 138, 146, 160A, 160B, 161, 165

Euromediterrannee, www.euromediterranee.fr 22L, 22RA

Expo 2015, www.expo2015.org 199

Fiera di Milano, www.fieramilano.it 127L, 127R

FloraHolland 178, 189L, 189R

Flying Camera, with thanks to DSM 150R

Foster + Partners 70

Gary Soup, www.flickr.com 129RB

Gemeentearchief Rotterdam Collection, catalogue number PBK 1993-895, 44LA and catalogue number P 005760-1 120

Guillaume Cattiaux, www.flickr.com 115

Harry van Veenendaal, Fotobank Amsterdam 168

High Tech Campus Eindhoven, the Strip, www.hightechcampus.com 35, 164B

HKB stedenbouwkundigen 89A, 130A, 130LB, 130RB

Hong Kong Convention and Exhibition Centre 117

Hotels van Oranje 126B

Institute for Urban Strategies at the Mori Memorial Foundation in Tokyo, *Global Power City Index 2010* (GPCI) 40

Jaarbeurs Utrecht 108R

Jan Boeve, with thanks to De Balie 103

Jan Tuijp 6, 176/177

Jeffery Kuiper, Beeldbank Utrecht 137

John Bösensell 144A

Kees Boeke, with thanks to Celadon Publishers 12

Kröller-Müller Museum, pavilion acquired and rebuilt with support from the BankGiroloterij and members of the Bond Nederlandse Architecten 195

La Biennale, www.labiennale.org 119

Latz + Partners 198A

Maike Warmerdam 96A, 960

Matt Drobnik, www.flickr.com 197B

Michael Toner 38A

Ministry of Infrastructure and Environment, Rob Poelenjee 49, 53, 57, 61

Miriam Verrijdt 97A, 97B

Moscone Center www.moscone.com 128, 129LA, 129RA

Ola Ericson 93

Olgite, www.flickr.com 20R

Port of Rotterdam, *Uitvoeringsagenda Havenvisie 2030* 193LB

Provast, with thanks to MVRDV 90

Qinyi Zhang 172

Ra'ike 198B

Regional Plan Association, *America 2050* 15

Rene den Engelsman, with thanks to Amsterdam Tourism & Convention Board 133

Rotterdam Imagebank, photography: www.totenmetontwerpen.nl 44LB, Daarzijn 75R, en Fred Ernst 102

Ruimtelijk Planbureau, *Vele steden maken nog geen Randstad* 11

Rungis, www.rungisinternational.com 193R

Schmidt Hammer Lassen Architects 200A, 200B

Sean Taylor 118

Stiftung Preußischer Kulturbesitz / Imaging, with thanks to David Chipperfield Architects 68

TU-Delft, Verena Balz cover, 16, 21, 23, 25, 27, 29, 190

Tweede Nota over de Ruimtelijke Ordening in Nederland 179

Vancouver Convention Centre www.vancouverconventioncentre.com 116A, 116LB, 116RB

Vera van der Vesse 108LA, 108LB

VIParis, www.viparis.com 105

World Forum 112A, 112B

Yerba Buena Gardens, www.yerbabuenagardens.com 129LB

Zandbelt&vandenBerg 140R, 167A, 174L, 174R, 175

The publisher has made every effort to trace all copyright holders. Anyone who believes their rights have not been acknowledged should contact the publisher.

About the author

Maurits de Hoog (1955) is an urban planner, and since 1996 has worked for the Department of Physical Planning of the City of Amsterdam. From 2008 to 2012 he was professor of practice in Regional and Metropolitan Design at the TU Delft.

His speciality is the design and supervision of large-scale transformation processes: IJ Banks Amsterdam, IJmeeratelier, Haven-Stad, Zuidplaspolder, Kwaliteitsteam Drechtoevers (1999-2004), Quality Team Ruimte voor de Rivier (2006-present), Atelier Kustkwaliteit (2010-2012).

From 2009 to 2012 he was chairman of the Department of Urbanism and member of the Management Team of the Faculty of Architecture. Since 2011 he has been chairman of the EFL Foundation.

He has been an editor of *Blauwe Kamer* (1991-1995) and is author of *4 x Amsterdam, ontwerpen aan de stad* (2005, THOTH Bussum), *Lange lijnen in Nieuw West* (2007, De Driehoek Amsterdam) en *New Rhythms of the City: Moulding the metropolis in Amsterdam* (2009, THOTH Bussum), and other studies.

Credits

This publication was realized with the financial support of:

the Netherlands Architecture Fund
TU-Delft
City of Amsterdam
City of The Hague
Van Eesteren-Fluck & Van Lohuizen Stichting

The urban anthropological field research was performed by
the Stipo Team for Urban Development and made possible
by the Ministry of Infrastructure and the Environment

Text
Maurits de Hoog
Other contributions to the text
Verena Balz, Rick Vermeulen, Miriam Verrijdt, Daan Zandbelt
English translation
Donald Mader
Urban anthropological field research
Stipo, Ester Heiman; with thanks to Mattijs van 't Hoff, Matthijs Jaspers and all participants
in the teams
Design research, seaside resorts
Dorrith Dijkzeul, Maike Warmerdam, Miriam Verrijdt
Design research, campus vision TU-Delft
Daan Zandbelt (Zandbelt&vandenBerg), Monique Arkenstein, Alexandra den Heijer, Maurits de Hoog
Image editor
Miriam Verrijdt
Maps for cover, Delta City Regions and ABC
Verena Balz
Maps of clusters
Anje Koop, Miriam Verrijdt, based on data from the Cities of Amsterdam, The Hague,
Rotterdam and Utrecht

Graphic design
Ronald Boiten and Irene Mesu, Amersfoort
Printing
Bema-Graphics, Wommelgem
Binding
Boekbinderij Van Waarden, Zaandam

ISBN 978 90 6868 599 2